An Introduction to Trading in the Financial Markets

**Technology—
Systems, Data,
and Networks**

R. "Tee" Williams

AMSTERDAM • BOSTON • HEIDELBERG • LONDON
NEW YORK • OXFORD • PARIS • SAN DIEGO
SAN FRANCISCO • SINGAPORE • SYDNEY • TOKYO
Academic Press is an imprint of Elsevier

Academic Press is an imprint of Elsevier
225 Wyman Street, Waltham, MA 02451, USA
525 B Street, Suite 1900, San Diego, California 92101, USA
The Boulevard, Langford Lane, Kidlington, Oxford OX5 1GB, UK

Notices
Knowledge and best practice in this field are constantly changing. As new research and experience broaden our understanding, changes in research methods, professional practices, or medical treatment may become necessary.

   Practitioners and researchers must always rely on their own experience and knowledge in evaluating and using any information, methods, compounds, or experiments described herein. In using such information or methods they should be mindful of their own safety and the safety of others, including parties for whom they have a professional responsibility.

   To the fullest extent of the law, neither the Publisher nor the authors, contributors, or editors, assume any liability for any injury and/or damage to persons or property as a matter of products liability, negligence or otherwise, or from any use or operation of any methods, products, instructions, or ideas contained in the material herein.

Library of Congress Cataloging-in-Publication Data
Williams, R. Tee.
   An introduction to trading in the financial markets : technology—systems,
data, and networks / R. "Tee" Williams.
       p.   cm.
Includes bibliographical references and index.
ISBN 978-0-12-374840-9
1. Capital market. 2. Stock exchange. 3. Financial instruments.   I. Title.

Set ISBN: 978-0-12-384972-4

British Library Cataloguing-in-Publication Data
A catalogue record for this book is available from the British Library.

For information on all Academic Press publications
visit our Web site at *www.elsevierdirect.com*

Printed in China
11   12   13   14   15   10 9 8 7 6 5 4 3 2 1

Contents

Preface for the Set

The four books in the set are an exercise in reportage. Throughout my career, I have been primarily a consultant blessed with a wide array of projects for many different kinds of entities in Africa, Asia, Europe, and North America. I have not been a practitioner but rather a close observer synthesizing the views of many practitioners. Although these books describe trading and the technology that supports trading, I have never written an order ticket or line of computer code in anger.

The purpose of these books is to describe *what* individuals and entities in the trading markets do. Bob Simon of *60 Minutes* once famously asked two founders of the dot-com consulting firm Razorfish to describe what they did when they got to work each day and took off their coats. That is the purpose of these books: to examine what participants in the trading markets do each day when they take off their coats. These books do not attempt to prescribe what should occur or proscribe what should not.

The nature of the source material for these books is broad observation. In teaching professional development courses over nearly two decades, I have found that both those new to the markets and even those who have been market participants for years become experts in their specific area of activity; however, they lack the context to understand how their tasks fit into the overall industry. The goal of this set of books is to provide that context.

Most consulting projects in which I have participated have required interviews with people working in all phases of the trading markets about what they do and their views on how the markets work. Those views and opinions helped frame my understanding of the structure of the markets and the roles of its participants. I draw on those views, but I cannot begin to document all the exact sources.

I have isolated fun stories I have heard along the way, which I cannot attribute to a specific source, into boxes within the text. These boxes also include asides that are related to the subjects being discussed but that do not specifically fit into the flow.

The structure of the books presents information in a hierarchical form that puts entities, instruments, functions, technology, and processes into a framework. Categorizing information into hierarchies helps us understand the subject matter better and gives us a framework in which to view and understand new information. The frameworks also help us understand how parts relate to the whole. However, my experience as a consultant convinces me that while well-chosen frameworks can be helpful and appealing to those first coming to understand new subject matter, they also carry the risk that their perspective may mask other important information about the subjects being categorized. So for those who read these books and want to believe that the trading markets fit neatly into the frameworks presented here: "Yes," I said. "Isn't it pretty to think so."[1]

---

1   Ernest Hemingway. *The Sun Also Rises*, 1926, New York: Charles Scribner's Sons (Scribner).

FEATURES OF THE BOOKS

Figure FM.1 shows the books in this set with tabs on the side for each of the major sections in the book. The graphic is presented at the end of each major part of the books with enlarged tabs for the section just covered, with arrows pointing to the parts of other books and within the same book where other attributes of the same topic are addressed. I call this the "Moses Approach."[2]

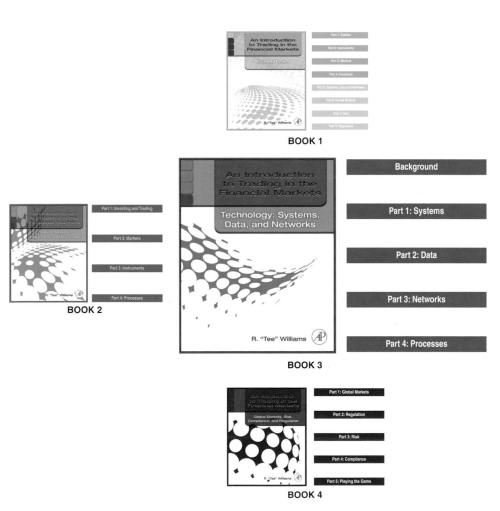

Figure FM.1   The ***books of this set*** are organized as a whole and concepts are distributed so that they build from book to book.

---

2   You may remember from the Bible that God took Moses up on the mountain and, in addition to giving him the Ten Commandments, showed Moses the Promised Land. This seems to be a good approach to organizing information. If you expect people to wander in the wilderness of your prose, you at least owe them a glimpse of where they are going.

In addition to words and graphics, the four books use color to present information, as shown in Figure FM.2. Throughout, the following color scheme represents the entities as well as functions, processes, systems, data, and networks associated with them.

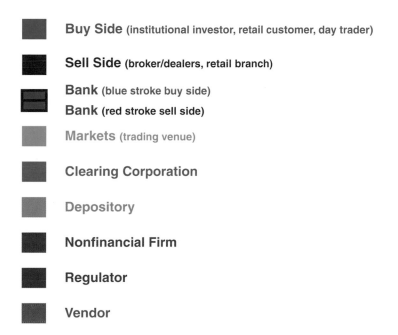

Buy Side (institutional investor, retail customer, day trader)

Sell Side (broker/dealers, retail branch)

Bank (blue stroke buy side)
Bank (red stroke sell side)

Markets (trading venue)

Clearing Corporation

Depository

Nonfinancial Firm

Regulator

Vendor

Figure FM.2   *Color in these books* identifies entities that are central to the trading markets, and also identifies the functions and processes that are associated with those entities.

A frustration of writing about the trading markets is the wealth of colorful and descriptive terms that permeate the markets. These terms are helpful in describing what happens in markets or where people work, but there is no accepted source that defines terms in everyday usage with precision. Good examples of this problem are the meaning and spellings of the terms "front office," "middle office," and "backoffice."[3] Similarly I use "indices" to mean a collection of individual instances of a single index. (For example closing *indices*—that is, values—of the Dow Jones Industrial Average on January 2, 3, and 4.) I use "indexes" to mean a collection of different copyrighted information products measuring market performance (e.g., the Dow Jones, FTSE, and DAX *indexes*).

I have elected to define the terms, as I understand them, within the books. The first instance of words appear in **bold italics**, which relate to definitions in the Glossary at the end of each one. The books use more hyphenated adjectives than

---

3   I separate "front" and "middle" from "office" and combine "backoffice." I believe that "backoffice" is a widely used term throughout the economy, whereas "front office" and more particularly "middle office" are nonce terms that may not migrate into common usage beyond the trading markets.

normal usage would require. I believe it is important to remove all doubt that the term "market-data systems" refers to systems for handling market data, not data systems used by a market.

The books in this set contain a large number of graphics. The goal of them is to provide more than decoration. For many people, graphics help them understand the concepts described in the text. Most of them illustrate process flows, relationships, or characteristics of market behavior. There is neither tabular data nor URLs from websites here. Both are likely to be too dated by the time the books are shipped from the publisher to you to provide any real value.

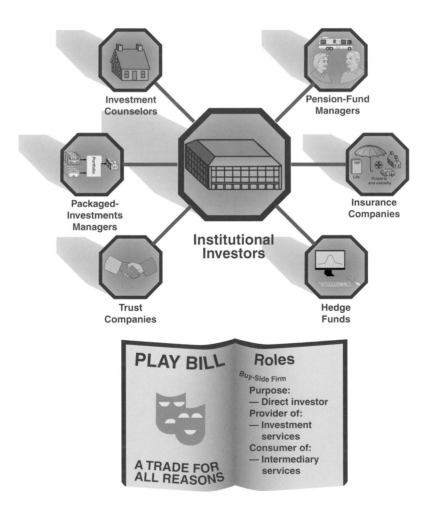

Figure FM.3   *Institutional investors* are introduced as important buy-side entities in Figure 1.1.3[4] of Book 1.

---

4   The figure numbers indicate that this is the third figure of the first category (buy side) of the first part (entities). All figure numbers follow this pattern.

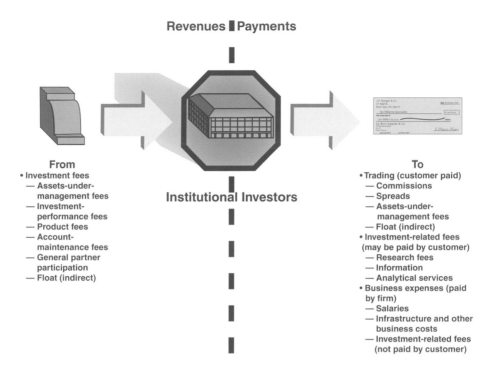

Revenues ▮ Payments

Institutional Investors

From
- Investment fees
  — Assets-under-management fees
  — Investment-performance fees
  — Product fees
  — Account-maintenance fees
  — General partner participation
  — Float (indirect)

To
- Trading (customer paid)
  — Commissions
  — Spreads
  — Assets-under-management fees
  — Float (indirect)
- Investment-related fees (may be paid by customer)
  — Research fees
  — Information
  — Analytical services
- Business expenses (paid by firm)
  — Salaries
  — Infrastructure and other business costs
  — Investment-related fees (not paid by customer)

Figure FM.4 *Institutional investor business models*—revenues and expenses—are illustrated in Book 1, Figure 1.1.3.7.

The graphics (and text) build from book to book. For example, in Part 1 of Book 1 the graphic in Figure FM.3 describing institutional investors appears. It shows the customers, the suppliers, and the products and services for institutional investors. (Subsequent sections describe types of institutional investors based on how they are regulated or the service they perform.)

At the end of each entity subsection, the entity's core business model and what services it purchases from vendors and other providers are explained (see Figure FM.4).

Part 4 of Book 1 describes the functions performed by buy-side traders who work in institutional-investor firms (see Figure FM.5). The figure illustrates which tasks the buy-side trader performs (i.e., which functions), who the buy-side trader serves, which external entities interact with the buy-side trader, and which other functions provide services to the buy-side trader.

Book 2, Part 4, describes the secondary market trading process. The second step in the trading process describes the initial role that the buy-side trader plays in trading.

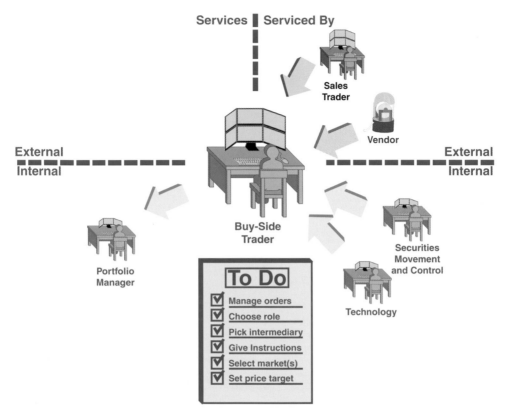

Figure FM.5   ***Buy-side traders*** manage trade execution within institutional investors and their functions are detailed in Figure 4.2.2.1.2 of Book 1.

Figure FM.6 presents the inputs to and outputs from the buy-side trading process as well as the primary focus of the buy-side trader and the decisions that the person must confront. Subsequent graphics in that section examine some of the decisions and alternatives in more detail.

Book 3 returns to the buy-side trader to understand the role of technology in the process. Figure 4.2.2 in Book 3 (Figure FM.7, see page xii) shows the systems and data support buy-side trading. (Networks tend to link functions and are not assigned to any specific function. Therefore networks are considered based on the functions they link.)

The text identifies applications supplied by both internal and external sources that support order management. The buy-side trader generates information that is input directly to internal systems and indirectly to external systems. Finally, networks both within the firm and from markets and vendors provide linkages that facilitate the entire process. Subsidiary figures highlight the specific types of systems, data, and networks that are input to and output from buy-side trading.

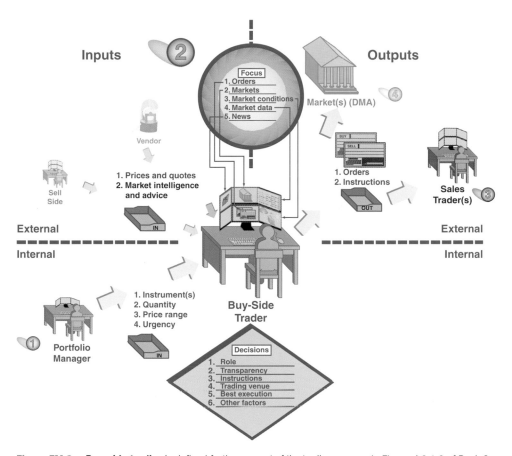

Figure FM.6 ***Buy-side trading*** is defined further as part of the trading process in Figure 4.2.1.2 of Book 2.

Finally, Book 4, Part 5, presents a hypothetical example that describes how a fictitious British investment management firm with a global presence manages an order across multiple markets with time, customer, and market pressures.

Here, David Anderson,[5] a London-based buy-side trader for Trafalgar Asset Management Ltd., is tasked with coordinating the sale of a very large order (500,000 shares) of In-the-Ether Networks (ticker symbol: ITEN) B.V., a Dutch network company with equities that are actively traded globally on the exchanges, ECNs, and MTFs in Amsterdam, Frankfurt, Hong Kong, London, New York, and Singapore.

---

5   All the names in the "Playing the Game" part are fictitious. However, I do know three different David Andersons, all of whom are Brits and work in some portion of the trading markets. These three gentlemen are the inspiration for the name. However, none of the David Andersons that I know are buy-side traders.

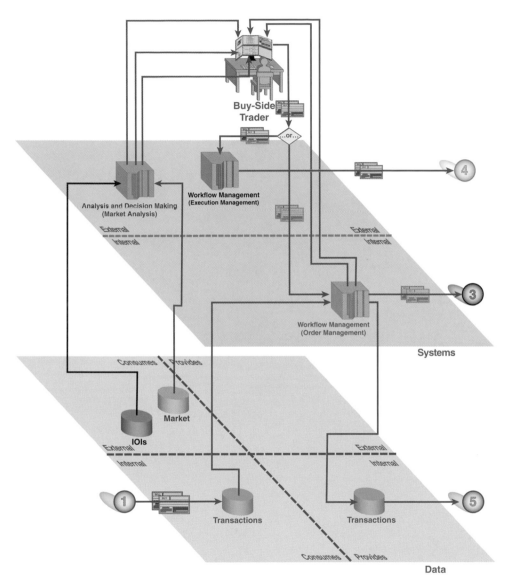

Figure FM.7 *Buy-side trading* requires systems, data, and networks and produces data as shown in this book's Figure 4.2.2.[6]

The graphic in Figure FM.8 shows how the order is received along with instructions for its execution. As the process proceeds, the text describes how the

---

6   In earlier books in this set, we used forecasts of the exact graphic and figure numbers. Since these have changed with the publication of successive books, the later books present the actual figure and figure numbers.

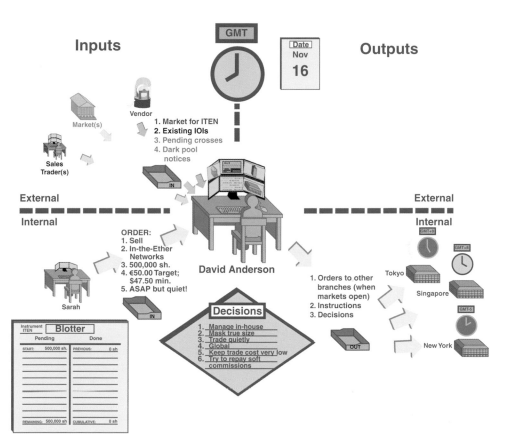

Figure FM.8 *Buy-side trading* is finally illustrated through a hypothetical example bringing together the decision process, technology, and interactions in Figure 5.2 of Book 4.

order is then divided among global offices, electronic systems, and intermediaries to be executed through a continuing global process over two elapsed London days. The text also describes the settlement process following the trade. A large trade in multiple markets strains systems data and communications that were created when national markets were insular and did not interact. Subsequent graphics show how the process described in the narrative unfolds.

Similar linkages among the graphics in this set of books occur in describing instruments and markets.

As noted previously, a Glossary is included at the end of each book in the set. For convenience, there is a Visual Glossary of the graphical metaphors and elements used in the images for each of the books.

ACKNOWLEDGMENTS

This project began as an attempt to write a history of the markets beginning in the 1960s. There are a number of individuals who held important positions in the trading markets during and after the "backoffice crisis" in the late 1960s who helped me understand the markets early in my career. I thought that a book about them and the work they did to hold the markets together and then reshape those markets would be interesting.

There are several good books describing how Felix Rohatyn, Sandy Weill, and many others worked to bail out firms that were in trouble, but they do not describe the activities that occurred in the backoffice in the midst of the crisis. That book on history did not happen, but these books are my attempt to "pay forward" all the help I received from many different people. The descriptions of the markets in these books are built on the foundation of the knowledge that these people unselfishly imparted. I hope these books will in turn help those entering the markets.

In a real sense, these people and many more than I can list are the true footnotes and references for these books. My earliest teachers included

- Junius "Jay" Peake, University of Northern Colorado, R. Shriver Associates, Pershing and Company, and Shields and Company. (Jay was my first and is still my most influential teacher.)

- Morris Mendelson, The Wharton School of the University of Pennsylvania. (Morris offered Jay and me entre into the academic community, and Jay chose to stay. He and Jay wrote many papers together on market structure and automation, and they allowed me to help with some. Jay and I miss Morris very much.)

- Ray Holland, Triad Securities, A.G. Becker. (For more than 30 years, Ray has been a continuing source of information and advice about the mechanics of the backoffice processes required by the markets.)

- Dick Shriver, R. Shriver Associates. (Dick, my first boss, introduced me to consulting and many in the financial community including Jay. Dick remains a lifelong friend and mentor.)

- Don and Jack Weeden, Weeden & Company, and Fred Siesel, Weeden & Company and the NYSE. (Jay introduced me to Don, Jack, and Fred in the mid-1970s, and for a time we tried to foment a revolution in trading mechanics. Over the period since, they have been a source of information and insight that has helped me understand the way the markets operate.)

More recently, a number of others have provided important views on the workings of the trading process and supporting technology. Most of these people worked with me, or I worked for them on projects that form the basis for the books. These people include the following:

- Mike Atkin, Electronic Data Management (EDM) Council and Financial Information Services Division (FISD). (I have worked with Mike over the past 20 years first at the FISD and later at the EDM Council. Together, we have come to understand the processes required to manage data.)

- Dick Cowles, Telerate and Chicago Board Options Exchange (CBOE). (I met Dick at the CBOE, interviewed him at Telerate, and worked with him for USAID as we tried to establish an over-the-counter market in Poland. Along the way, we became friends.)

- Andrew Delaney, A-Team Group. (Andrew taught classes with Craig Shumate and me. Parts of these books related to infrastructure technology, news, and research rely on Andrew's insights.)
- Tom Demchak, Brian Faughnan, SIAC and NYSE Euronext. (Tom, Brian, and their staffs were liaisons on a project to establish a capacity planning methodology for the equity and options markets in the United States and then to understand the impact of the conversion from fractional units of trading to decimals. They explained the issues of managing huge volumes of data message traffic, functions of the technologies that underpin trading markets, and methods for mitigating message volumes in excess of economically manageable capacity.)
- Deb Greenberger, Skyler Technologies and Dow Jones Markets. (In an attempt to resuscitate the Dow Jones Telerate subsidiary, Deb and I visited and interviewed customers in Asia, Europe, and North America to understand how they use data to manage their trading and related businesses.)
- Thomas Haley, NYSE (Tom was a coauthor of *The Creation and Distribution of Securities-Related Information in North America*, a description of the market-data industry that we worked on in 1984. That book presented an explanation of the processes in the market-data industry and was written by Tom with several other industry experts at the time on behalf of the FISD of the Information Industry Association [now known as the Software and Information Industry Association]. I met Tom and the others in the FISD when I served as editor for the book. Tom has been a friend and a constant source of information and advice on the market-data industry ever since.)
- Dan Gray, U.S. Securities and Exchange Commission; Lee Greenhouse, Greenhouse Associates and Citibank; Frank Hathaway, Nasdaq; Ron Jordan, NYSE; and George McCord, McCord Associates. (Dan, Lee, Frank, Ron, George, and I worked with their associates and people from SIAC to define and then specify a methodology for allocating market-data revenues for the different markets that trade NYSE- and Nasdaq-listed securities in the United States. The project caused us to examine the quoting behavior in the markets in great detail and to wrestle with issues such as locked and crossed markets.)
- Sarah Hayes and Kirsti Suutari, Thomson Reuters. (Sarah and Kirsti managed a project in which we visited many major financial centers globally to understand how people trade and the impact of those trading practices on information needs.)
- Alan Kay and Charlie Pyne, On Line Markets. (Alan and Charlie invited me to join them in a project to evaluate the meaning of the information business and how to use information as an entre to create trading venues.)
- Tom Knorring, CBOE; Joe Corrigan, Options Price Reporting Authority; and Tom Bendixen, Mark Grinbaum, and Jeff Soule, The International Securities Exchange. (Projects with and for these gentlemen formed the basis of my understanding of the mechanics and economics of the options markets.)
- Don Kittell, SIFMA, NYSE. (Don was the Securities Industry Association [now SIFMA] manager of a series of projects to forecast the impact of the conversion to decimal trading on message volumes. I was fortunate enough to work as a consultant with Don on those projects, where I learned much.)

- Brian McElligott, Kendall Vroman, and Brian's staff, CME Group. (The people at the CME took me to interview important constituencies in the futures markets to understand how they trade and use information.)
- Peter Moss, Thomson Reuters, and John White, State Street Global Advisors. (Peter and John were forceful advocates for these books. They have also been sources of understanding about the issues facing vendors and market-data users.)
- Leonard Mayer, Mayer & Schweitzer. (Lenny attended one of the classes Craig Shumate and I taught on new trading systems. [He should have been teaching me.] He cofounded one of the premier Nasdaq wholesale firms and was gracious enough to help me understand the business of being a dealer.)
- Lance Riley, SRI Consulting. (Lance was my first boss at SRI Consulting, and together we worked on many projects and interviewed countless people over 20 years. I miss Lance greatly.)
- Richard Rosenblatt and Joe Gawronski, Rosenblatt Securities. (Dick and Joe have been kind enough to take me along as they were trading on the floor of the NYSE. They have also shared their insights on the workings of the markets that they write in an ongoing series of white papers for their customers.)
- Craig Shumate, The Morris Group. (I met and worked with Craig at my first job at R. Shriver Associates, and we have worked together constantly since. He brought me into the business of professional training. It is Craig who pioneered the concept of the eight steps in the trading process and "Playing the Game" as a way to draw together all the aspects of trading in a single process description.)
- Herbie Skeete, Mondovisione and Thomson Reuters. (I met Herbie in London at least 20 years ago, and I try to see him every time I am in London or when he comes to the States. He is a wealth of information on market data and knows a huge number of people. Herbie introduced me to Elsevier and is responsible for my writing these books.)
- Al Thomson, Instinet; Lynch, Jones and Ryan; and AutEx. (Al and I have been collaborators and friends from my earliest work in the trading markets. He set up a great many of the interviews and provided insights that underlie the knowledge presented in these books.)
- Wayne Wagner, The Plexus Group (JPMorgan). (Wayne invited me into a project for the Department of Labor on the meaning of "best execution" in the early 1990s. He patiently explained how many different buy-side motivations resulted in very different expectations from trades.)

I am not able to remember and therefore thank all those that I have interviewed and the many others who worked at the firms for which I consulted for more than 35 years. (By my best estimate, I have averaged several hundred interviews each year since 1974. Therefore, the total number of interviews and thus people to whom I am indebted numbers in the thousands.) Rather than name a few and forget many, I would simply like to thank them all. This book is dedicated to them and most particularly to Jay Peake and Ray Holland.

This book is the third in a set of books that address the **trading markets**. We use the term "trading markets" because that is the most general term we can find for the portion of the financial markets sometimes imprecisely referred to as the **securities markets**. (We explained these distinctions in Book 1, *An Introduction to Trading in the Financial Markets: Market Basics,* and Book 2, *An Introduction to Trading in the Financial Markets: Trading, Markets, Instruments, and Processes,* when we described **instruments**, but basically securities are a subset of instruments. Thus, the term "securities markets" excludes a number of instruments that trade in liquid marketplaces. Here, we examine the broader group of all traded instruments.) In this book, we focus on the technology—systems, data, and networks—that makes the markets and the processes supporting the markets work.

The purpose of this book is not to describe how technologies work, but rather to describe what technology does. We look at the activities in the trading markets that have become automated. We explore some of the types of applications that are central to the markets, but we only begin to describe the breadth and depth of the use of technology in the trading markets. Few industries are as automated as the trading markets, and the scope and speed of financial automation are growing at a staggering pace.

If you are involved in technology, our approach in this book may seem strange. We do not focus on specific technologies at all. Instead, we examine what tasks technology is required to perform in support of the trading markets.

In this book, we focus only on technology used by the **buy side** and **sell side**. If you read Book 1, you understand that there are a number of other functional entities such as **trading venues**, **banks**, **clearing corporations**, and **depositories**. Books of comparable breadth and depth to this book could be written about the technology for those entities, but we do not consider them here except to the extent they interact with the buy and sell sides.

We begin our investigation by examining how technology has evolved in order to understand the impediments complicating technological change. When you think that in the late 1960s most firms in the trading markets were only beginning to implement technology, it is startling to realize how very complex the technology in the trading markets has become and the many layers of technology that employ designs from different generations of technological development. Most every technology project must at some point reconcile legacy systems, data, and networks with the innovation the project intends.

With this as a background, we explore the fundamental tasks required of technology. We believe at the core the things that must be done are both simple and straightforward. The factors that make the application of technology in the trading markets complicated are the number of possible variations for straightforward tasks, not the complexity of the tasks themselves. For example, recording **income** from a bond is a simple procedure until you think of all the different ways the income can be paid.

The bond can pay interest quarterly, semiannually, or on other cycles if the issuer chooses. The bond can also be sold at discount. Further, if the portfolio or owner of the bond must pay taxes, recording income requires an understanding of the tax laws and may require special recording procedures. However, under the layers of complexity, a simple process is at work.

Understanding the purposes of technology and how it has evolved, we examine some of the major systems that support the trading markets. At this point, we focus on their purpose and not on how they are implemented. We define specific tasks that applications perform and then examine how market functions introduced in Part 4 of Book 1 employ applications to accomplish their required tasks.

Next, we look at the data critical to the trading markets. Data on the markets helps traders and investors evaluate investment decisions and price orders in the markets. Data on customers, portfolios, and trading partners supports the trading process, keeps its customers informed about their investments, and satisfies the requirements of regulators.

Our focus in looking at data is to understand the types, characteristics, and purposes of the data. The sale of data from vendors to other market participants is an important activity in the markets. Substantially all data used in the trading markets is not sold but licensed for use under strict requirements that limit how the data may be used and require that data usage be entitled and reported as the basis of invoicing. The investigation of data therefore must consider the economics of the business of data production and marketing.

We describe the different types of networks that join the global financial markets in a single interrelated environment where **transactions** can happen in real time across continents, oceans, and time zones. Activities within a single financial entity are linked both geographically and functionally. Different economic entities are linked into a single functioning process.

One of the most dramatic transformations of the global financial markets in the past half-century is the degree to which individual entities have become interconnected. This interconnection has reduced dependence on physical movements of securities and other documentation and has made huge volumes of transactions possible.

Our final section returns to the processes described in Book 2 to understand how systems, data, and networks support the trading process. Each step in the trading process employs systems, uses and produces data, and is linked by networks. Here, we investigate the technological infrastructure supporting the markets.

This book presents an overview of the technology employed in the trading markets. However, this content integrates with information presented in the other three books in the set. Figure FM.9 highlights the content of this book in comparison with information in the other books. We return to this map at the end of each of the sections to relate the content just presented to major sections throughout the other books in the set.

Before we begin our examination of technology, we present a very high-level overview of the concepts presented throughout this set. The goal of the overview is to provide someone new to the trading markets and those who have not read the other books in the set with enough background to follow the discussion in the remainder of this book. If you are familiar with the basics of the markets, you might want to skip to the Background section.

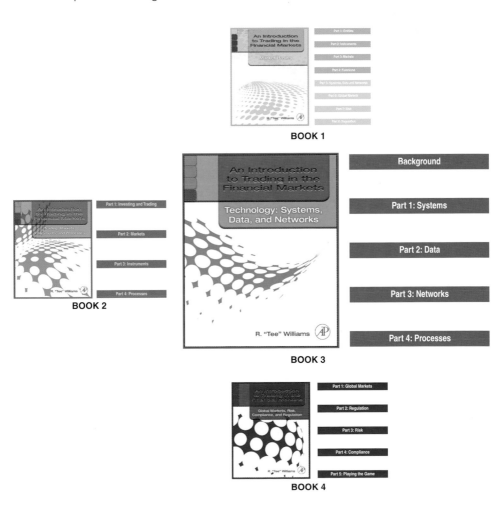

Figure FM.9   The topics in this book and other books in the set.

Overview

The unique feature of the subject matter in this book, as well as the other books in this set, is that we are describing the activities related to and in support of trading in instruments: **stocks**, **bonds**, **options**, **futures**, **currencies**, and **commodities**. We divide instruments in further ways.

Securities (stocks and bonds) are instruments used to raise money for entities. We categorize securities as an important subdivision of a larger category of **cash markets**. In addition to securities, cash markets include trading in currencies and commodities. In effect, we mean by cash markets that we are actually buying a thing—a stock, a bond, and so on. We contrast cash markets with **derivatives**.[1]

Derivatives are instruments that *derive* their value from other instruments or things. Derivatives are primarily used for managing **risk** or to make a limited gamble on expected future market activity without expending the full investment commitment required in the cash market. Derivatives represent a **contingent claim** created by a contract in which one party agrees to perform a service or deliver an instrument in the future if certain conditions are met as defined in the agreement. The traded instruments described in these books are exact or near substitutes for each other.

The term **fungible** is a characteristic of instruments that are "exact or near substitutes" for one another. For example, one share of Siemens is identical to any other, or one futures contract on a U.S. Treasury bond is indistinguishable from another contract on the same instrument. Trading fungible instruments separates the markets we are considering from markets that are not fungible, such as real estate. Although both types of markets share some similarity, real estate is not fungible because no two pieces of real estate are exactly similar, and this dissimilarity affects the value of the land, house, or building.

In the remainder of this section, we provide a brief overview of the elements of trading markets covered in the other books in this set before exploring technology in more detail. If you want more information about the topics covered briefly here, we invite you to explore the other books (see Figure O.1).

---

1   In the United States, the concept of a "security" has become somewhat muddled. Options, which we do not classify as securities, are treated as securities because the Securities and Exchange Commission governs them. You will find this kind of confusion or lack of precision common in the trading markets.

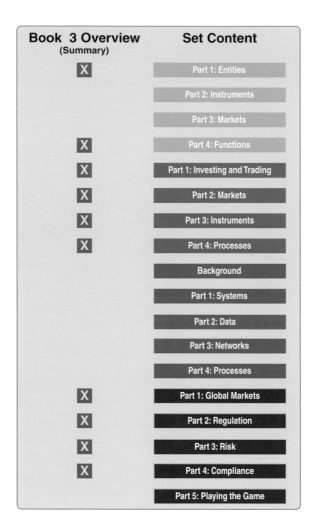

Figure 0.1 Major topics in the overview.

TAXONOMY OF MARKETS

We want to make an important distinction between markets and marketplaces. As we use the term, **market** means all the activities related to buying and selling a specific type of financial asset or instrument such as a stock or bond. A **marketplace** is a physical location such as the New York Stock Exchange building in lower New York city, or a logical location such as the Xetra computerized trading system of Deutsche Börse where trading actually happens.

As we will see, markets include the trading activity, but also many more activities. We also use the general term trading venue to indicate any type of entity or location where executions occur. We have adopted the generalized term "trading venue" to encompass both marketplaces organized as exchanges, marketplaces organized as **dealers** or **dealer associations**, and marketplaces organized as

brokers such as **electronic communications networks** (ECNs in the United States) and **multilateral trading facilities** (MTFs in Europe).

Within the general term "market," there are two components for those instruments that are securities (see Figure O.2). The first component, referred to as the **primary market**, involves the process of creating the security and raising money for entities such as commercial companies, governmental bodies, or **nongovernmental organizations** (NGOs) that issue securities. Instruments that are not securities are not generally said to have a primary market.

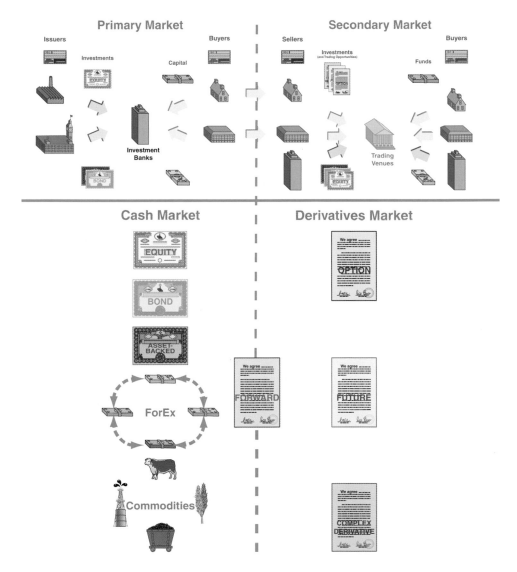

Figure 0.2   ***Markets*** segment into primary versus secondary and cash versus derivative to highlight different aspects of their purpose.

The **secondary market** is the place where trading in instruments takes place after the instruments have been created. When a security, stock, or bond for a company such as AstraZeneca, Microsoft, or Sony is created in the primary market, the revenue produced when the security is first sold goes to the company that issued the security.

After a security is issued and is trading in the secondary market, the revenue generated from a sale goes to the seller of the security, not to the entity that initially issued the security. In fact, the reason for secondary markets is to permit those who buy **new issues** of a security to end or reduce their ownership of a bond before it matures, or a stock so long as the company continues to be in business.

ENTITIES

In most countries, the entities in the traded-instrument markets are highly regulated commercial organizations subject to rules that govern both activities that must be performed (e.g., treat a customer fairly) and other activities in which firms may not engage (e.g., trading on information that is not publicly available to others in the market). In the past 20 years, the unique characteristics of entities in specific countries have been diluted as large numbers of firms have merged across national borders or firms have won the right to be registered in other countries. In Europe in particular, the European Union has worked diligently to ensure that firms operating in the member states are subject to regulations that are consistent from country to country.

Figure O.3 provides a representation of some terms and distinctions for the different entities involved in the trading markets. We use the metaphor of the Street to represent entities. Entities were covered in Book 1, *An Introduction to Trading in the Financial Markets: Market Basics*.

Trading markets' entities are grouped into individuals and organizations that invest money, commonly called the buy side, and organizations that provide **intermediary** services, referred to as the sell side. A third group includes marketplaces and entities providing supporting services.

The terms "buy side" and "sell side" do not mean that one group is buying securities and the other side is selling. Rather, the terms refer to the fact that one group (the buy side) is buying or consuming the trading services while the other group is providing or selling those services. We are not sure of the exact origin of these terms, but they are either in common usage or at least understood in most of the world.

The buy side is divided into **retail investors** and **institutional investors**. The term "retail investors" refers to individuals participating in the markets directly. By contrast, the term "institutional" refers to an organization that operates in the markets professionally. An institution may represent the money for a group

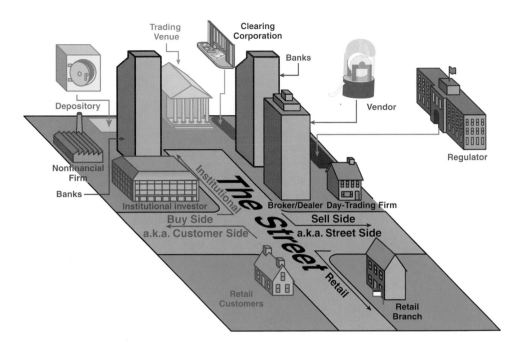

Figure 0.3 *Market entities* include individuals and institutions that invest, intermediaries, and supporting organizations that together comprise the activities of the Street.

of individuals, as in the case of a mutual fund or unit trust, but a professional is making investment and trading decisions on behalf of the individuals that have entrusted their money to the institution. **Broker/dealers** (the sell side) often split their operations into retail and institutional departments, each supporting the corresponding portion of the buy side.

Exchanges and other trading venues are entities that provide a facility for executing trades. Finally, there are a number of supporting entities such as banks, clearing corporations, and depositories that facilitate the trading process.

If you need a better understanding of the entities in the trading markets, you are invited to review Part 1 of Book 1.

INSTRUMENTS

In Part 3 of Book 2, we expanded on our description of instruments presented in Book 1 of this set by explaining some of the major attributes and variations found in different types of instruments. We also described the characteristics of the markets in which different instruments trade.

FUNCTIONS

Within the entities introduced previously, many roles or functions are performed by individuals and departments within the firms. As with entities, these can be grouped into buy-side and sell-side functions as well as support functions. Almost every one of these functions has unique, dedicated technology support described later. Figure O.4 depicts these functions. Many large financial firms have individuals, groups, or departments that perform most of these functions.

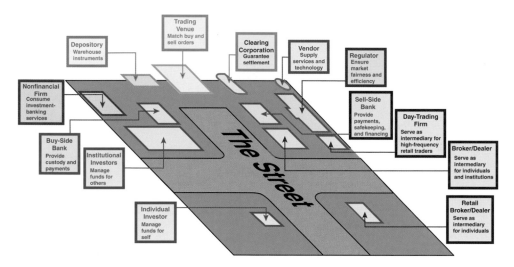

Figure O.4   ***The trading markets*** are composed of the functions of the buy side, sell side, trading venues, and supporting entities that interact to permit the exchange of traded instruments.

Buy-Side Functions

The primary buy-side functions include ***portfolio management***, ***research***, and ***trading***. These functions are often referred to as the ***front office***. An additional front office activity is ***sales*** of the investment service to customers. In the financial markets, the term "front office" is not always used consistently but generally refers to "customer-facing" activities.

The emerging term ***middle office*** is not always used consistently either, but we define it as support for customers, such as ***customer accounting*** and reporting and ***compliance***. ***Backoffice*** functions represent the activities required to support the front office and any reporting that may be required to satisfy regulatory obligations. (The separation of functions among the front, middle, and backoffice is shown in Figure O.4.1.)

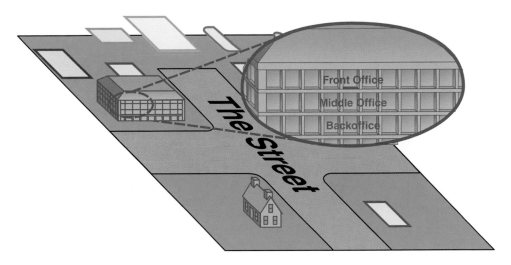

Figure O.4.1 *Buy-side functions* facilitate profiting from owning and sometimes trading instruments that change in market price and may generate income for the individual and/or a firm and its customers.

Among the backoffice functions are activities related to holdings not directly belonging to customers and interactions with the markets. Individual investors perform most of these functions themselves on a rudimentary level supported by their agents.

Sell-Side Functions

The main purpose of the sell side is to act as an intermediary. An intermediary stands between the customer and the markets, and serves to introduce the customer. The intermediary has two fundamental, subsidiary tasks: **customer activities** and **market activities**.

As shown in Figure O.4.2, we define front, middle, and backoffice functions for the sell side as we did for the buy side, although the front-office functions further divide into those of a broker, a dealer, and an **investment banker**. Customer activities can be further divided into retail services and services for institutional investors. In turn, institutional activities include **investment research**, **institutional sales**, and **sales trading**.

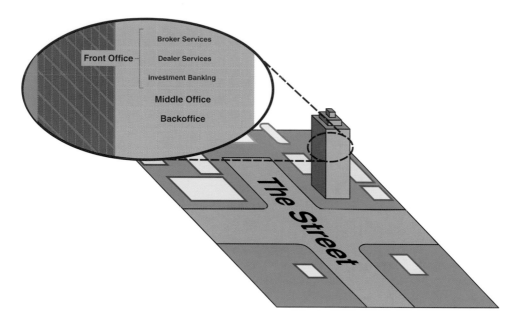

Figure 0.4.2 *Sell-side functions* generate revenues from acting as an intermediary for buy-side customers.

An important sell-side functional distinction within the trading markets is between the role of broker and dealer. A broker, also known as an *agent*, stands as a representative of a *principal*, usually a customer. The broker is expected to act on behalf of his or her principal and in the principal's best interest.

By contrast, a dealer as a principal is expected to look out only for him- or herself. Dealers act for themselves in the markets, attempting to profit from their actions. The term broker/dealer indicates a firm that is permitted to act both as a broker and dealer. In most markets, firms are not permitted to act as broker and dealer in the same transaction.

Customer-side accounting supports front-office customer activities, and we define them as middle-office functions. We also include compliance—the governance activity that ensures a firm complies with both regulatory requirements as well as the specific wishes of customers—as a middle-office function as well.

Market-related activities are also known as *Street-side functions* (e.g., "Street-side" as in facing the Street) and relate to a firm's interaction with the markets and with other firms. *Position management* refers to the firm's management of investments on its own and customers' accounts in specific securities.

Proprietary trading, *arbitrage*, and *treasury* are activities in which the firm manages its own capital for risk management, for profit, and to keep in conformity with capital obligations. The support activities on the Street side include **purchases and sales** (resolving completed trades), the **cashier** (managing the funds involved in trades), and the **cage** (managing securities and other instruments). An important function of the cage is **segregation** of securities—keeping track of both ownership and any **liens** on instrument **positions**.

The sell side has a compliance department that ensures customers are treated fairly and in accordance both with market and national regulations, and with customer wishes. On the Street side, the compliance department makes certain that all trading rules and regulations are observed and the firm maintains all **required minimum capital** positions.

Market Functions

Markets are economic entities with a staff supporting a physical trading floor or an electronic facility that causes the markets to function. These functions within trading venues serve to support the trading process; collect, distribute, and generate revenues from the information produced by the market; regulate the market and its members or participants; promote and sell the services of the market; and solicit and manage listings of companies that elect to have their instruments traded on the market. Not all markets provide all these services, and some markets provide other specialized functions.

Figure O.4.3 presents a representative summary of these functions. We do not focus on the functions of markets in this book except to the extent that marketplaces often engage in selling the data they produce. We do, however, discuss the economics of data from the markets in Part 2 of this book.

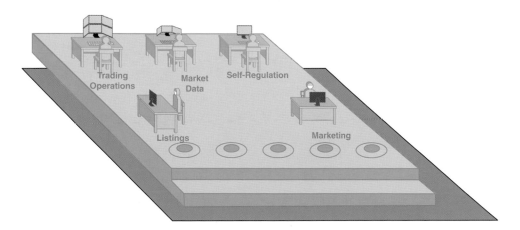

Figure O.4.3   *Market functions* permit trading venues to match orders to buy instruments with orders to sell for traders seeking to exchange instrument and cash positions.

Support Functions

A number of functions are required in support of the trading markets. In many markets, these functions require the entity be registered as a special-purpose organization such as a broker/dealer, an exchange, or a bank. Registration provides the right to conduct certain activities and prohibits engaging in other activities. Figure O.4.4 shows the supporting entities in the markets.

A **correspondent** broker/dealer is a specialized intermediary that provides support functions to other broker/dealers that choose not to perform those activities for themselves. An **interdealer broker** (IDB) operates between two dealers on large trades. Firms providing the services of a correspondent and/or an IDB are also termed **brokers' brokers**.

Other support activities involve banks serving as **custodians**, holding securities on a customer's behalf. Banks also serve as **transfer agents**, recording security ownership, and as **paying agents**, making dividend and interest payments.

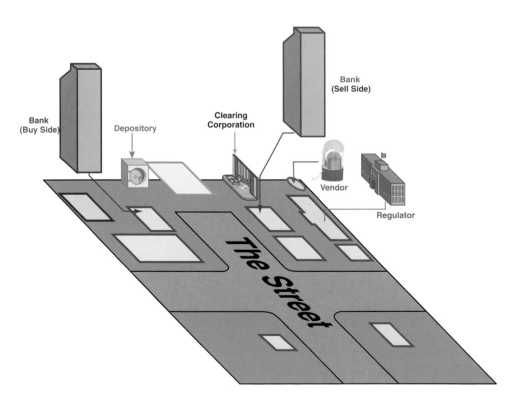

Figure 0.4.4 **Support functions** enable the exchange of instruments for cash among direct market participants.

Clearing corporations are independent entities or extensions of exchanges that resolve any issues between buyer and seller or their intermediaries to ensure the instruments purchased and the money to be paid are delivered at the time and place as the market custom dictates or as agreed by the parties. Depositories warehouse certificates or act as registries of instrument ownership. When trades occur in markets with depositories, the transfer of ownership usually takes place by electronic bookkeeping transfers within the depository. **Vendors** provide data and systems in support of the trading process.

The discussion to this point in the Overview is a recap of the content of Book 1. A brief summary of the content of Books 2 and 4 follows. This book describes technology, which is not summarized here.

INVESTING AND TRADING

Historically, the primary impetus to trade has been the need for investors to alter portfolios—to acquire or add to portfolios instruments that are believed to be attractive and invest funds that are received and to liquidate positions that are no longer attractive to generate cash when needed. When investment is the primary motivation for trading, we must understand the nature of investment strategy to understand how orders are generated, where they are routed, and the urgency of execution. Strategies include value investing, technical investing, **Modern Portfolio Theory**, and many other strategies.

Beyond investing, there are also trading strategies in which trading is its own motivation and the goal is to profit from trades. Examples include day trading and market making, but there are other strategies as well.

Book 2 covers markets with a focus on the mechanics of trading and the tools that facilitate execution. There is also an extension of instruments looking at the features and measures that apply to each instrument category, a discussion of the participants that actively engage in investing and trading in each instrument category, and an exploration of the structure and linkages for trading each instrument group.

PROCESSES

There are two important process streams considered in this set. First, the primary market permits entities to raise capital. Second, we evaluate the secondary market to understand the trading process, which is illustrated in a representational graphic in Figure O.5.

In addition to the basic primary and secondary market processes, a number of supporting processes are required to map instruments created (primary market) and traded (secondary market) to the settlement processes with other entities on the Street and to customer holdings. At the end of this book, we return to the trading process and observe the role of systems, data, and networks in the process.[2]

---

2   Although these books introduce the primary market, trading is the major focus. Therefore, after Book 2, we do not explore the primary market in any additional detail.

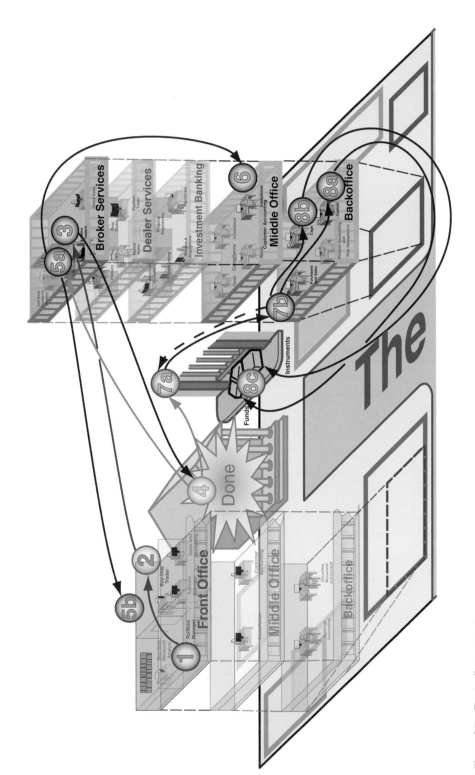

Figure 0.5 The trading process.

GLOBAL MARKETS

Since the 1960s, there have been three major international financial centers, and most of the rest of the world's trading markets have revolved around those centers (see Figure O.6). Tokyo was the major financial center in Asia for most of the past 40 years; however, restrictive financial regulation in Tokyo and high local communications costs in Japan caused Hong Kong and Singapore to become coequal centers for firms seeking an Asian headquarters location.

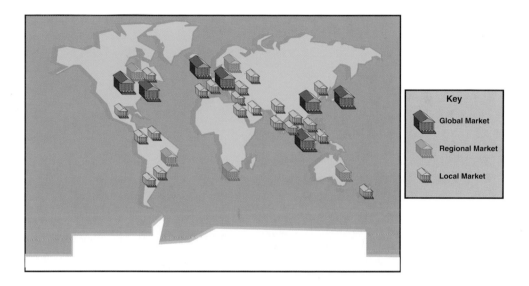

Figure O.6   *Global markets* interact with regional and local markets to permit both local and international trading for market participants.

In Europe, London was a primary financial center for more than two centuries, but other European centers became rivals prior to ***Big Bang*** in 1986. More liberal policies following Big Bang permitted London to resume its dominance. Eurex has made Germany a critical market in futures. New York has been the dominant market in the Americas with the exception of futures markets that center in Chicago.

Beyond the dominant global market centers, there are a number of important regional markets. In Asia, Jakarta, Manila, Seoul, and Sydney are important regional markets, and smaller centers are growing in Bangkok, Kuala Lumpur, Mumbai, and Shanghai. Amsterdam, Frankfurt, Paris, and Milan are important centers in Europe, while Copenhagen, Helsinki, Oslo, and Stockholm represent a coordinated regional submarket known as the "Scandinavian markets."

For the Americas, in addition to New York and Chicago, Boston and Philadelphia have become important U.S. centers, and Mexico City, Montréal, São Paulo, and Toronto are important non-U.S. regional centers. In Africa, Cairo and Johannesburg are important markets. Dubai and Tel Aviv are markets rapidly gaining importance in the Middle East.

In addition to the centers of trading, Basel, Boston, Edinburgh, Geneva, and Zurich have large concentrations of investment management activities.

An important factor in the global markets is the way firms and departments within interact with markets and other entities outside their local market. The way firms trade in a global marketplace is an important discussion in Book 4, *An Introduction to Trading in the Financial Markets: Global Markets, Risk, Compliance, and Regulation*.

Before we begin to describe systems, data, and networks, we need to understand something about how the infrastructure of the trading markets has evolved. Here, we also examine several concepts that will permeate later discussions of systems, data, and networks. By presenting these concepts before we enter more detailed discussion, we can reduce redundancy.

HISTORY

Our goal in this section is not to provide a history of technology per se, but rather to understand how the evolution of technology has created the current environment and structure. In Book 1, *An Introduction to Trading in the Financial Markets: Market Basics,* we provided a brief history of the trading markets that dates back more than 400 years, but the history of technology is much more recent. Indeed, many of those who first brought computer processing to the trading markets are still alive, and several are still working.

Prior to any form of what would now be considered technology, people met in physical places where markets were conducted. Going to a single place to trade—a tavern or later an exchange—was a type of technological innovation. More importantly, physical trading places came to be dominated by individuals who were skilled in interpersonal interactions, and they became wealthy by their skill. The wealth and power of physical traders were employed to fight the encroachment of technology, adding more than two decades to the time from the first application of technology to trading to the point when the full impact was realized.

The first application of what we would consider modern technology dates from the creation of securities ticker-tape machines that were first developed in several different formats in the mid-1850s. Ticker machines were an extension of the telegraph technology that allowed stock prices to be printed on paper tape at locations remote from the exchanges.

At the end of the 1960s, computer technology had not entered the trading markets to any significant extent. There are several reasons for this. First, investment and trading generate relatively complex transactions, and there were comparatively few such transactions in the late 1960s. By contrast, bank demand deposit accounting was relatively simple and obvious to automate because checking transactions are easily automated and the volumes are huge. There were several orders of magnitude fewer portfolio management and trading transactions.

Second, most trading firms were partnerships, and investment in computer technology represented a direct investment (or reduced income) for the partners. Many partners for firms that had developed and thrived in a manual, paper-based environment failed to grasp the need to automate. For many, the realization of the need for automation came too late.

Finally, many attempts at automation failed because of the complex problems of the transition from human to computer accounting systems. In effect, for the period of time from the completion of the accounting software until all accounts were converted and all problems with the software were resolved, both an automated and a manual system had to run in parallel.

Many firms successfully programmed applications that never went into production because the transition from the manual system to the automated system was unsuccessful. Conversion problems were amplified during the backoffice crisis described in Book 1 when the difficulty of converting from a manual to automated system was compounded by the stresses caused by problems settling trades.

Early automated systems tended to replicate manual processes in computer code. This process structure, which had worked perfectly well in a manual system, often failed to take advantage of the strengths of computerized systems. Several generations of applications later, newer applications employ much more efficient designs for computer systems that are optimized to take advantage of the computer's power.

EARL AND JANE AND MARY

In working with a large trust department in Philadelphia in the mid-1970s, we had a chance to observe the bank's first accounting system as it moved to a second generation. As we observed the programs in the "job stream," each program corresponded to individuals and applications from the old manual system. Records passed between jobs corresponded neatly to pieces of paper that moved from outbox to inbox through the manual system. In a very real sense, the individuals in the manual system at the time of the conversion had been enshrined in COBOL, and the programs could have been named for those individuals.

At about the same time, a monograph for the Solomon Brothers Institute at the New York University Graduate School of Business proposed automating the New York Stock Exchange and described an "electronic specialist" and an "electronic two-dollar broker."

A second problem with early systems is that applications often had to be programmed to compensate for the limitations of computer hardware. A modest-sized rack of servers today could easily have more processing power than existed in a whole financial center up through the early 1970s.

Just prior to January 1, 2000, a distinguished panel of computer scientists who had developed systems during the 1960s were asked why they used programming techniques for dates that resulted in the programming problems that had to be corrected in what was known as **Y2K** (the date-change problems that might have occurred on January 1, 2000). They all commented on the severe limitations in computer memory and storage. These limitations resulted in computer applications designed for what was possible, not what was needed. Saving two bytes from a date seemed a useful trade-off.

SPLITTING RECORDS

The same bank trust department mentioned in the previous sidebar elected to use one of the early database systems to build its second-generation trust-accounting system. The staff used the best database design strategies recommended by the computer manufacturer that sold the computers and database software. Unfortunately, the new system took about 48 hours to process a day's work. The entire design staff was laid off.

A market-data vendor during the same period used a storage drum to hold information on market-data prices from exchanges. The records were hard-wired on the drum and had fixed lengths. When data on individual instruments became too large to fit within the storage available on the records, information on instruments had to be split among multiple records, and in some cases creating all the information for an instrument required combining information from different noncontiguous locations.

Real creativity and ingenuity were required to create functioning systems under these limitations. Unfortunately, design decisions made with these constraints have affected future design efforts and in some cases still reside in remote parts of current systems.

Early network technology was very primitive. Transfer rates of just over 100 characters per second meant that only the most critical information—securities prices for the most part—was transmitted electronically. Most information was passed in printed reports and magnetic tape that were physically moved. All networks were closed. This means that each vendor or company that managed a network created its own communications protocols, and message structures were unique to the specific network. To move information from one network to another required a computer program that would convert the message formats.

Data used in applications was initially entered manually or generated by the applications themselves. Pricing data for securities required significant processing before it was available to be used to price securities or for trading. Typically, active equity trading floors had dedicated reporters who would stand in the locations where securities traded and mark down the prices on computer cards that had to be punched or read by a marked-card reader.

Activities on futures exchanges were so intense that it was impossible to track every trade using the prevailing technologies even as late as the mid-1990s. Instead, futures exchanges typically reported only *changes* in price rather than every trade. Data required by regulators, such as corporate financial reports, was delivered to the regulators in paper reports. Reference-data vendors made copies of these reports and entered them on punch cards to produce the data they sold to their customers.

LATENCY IN 1967

An example of true latency for market data occurred during the late 1960s in the Over-the-Counter (OTC) market, which has slowly evolved into the Nasdaq Exchange. A company known as the National Quotation Bureau (predecessor of the Pink Sheets) distributed computer punch cards at the end of the trading day to major OTC dealers. Dealers would write their bids and offers on the cards, which were then collected and processed overnight. The collected quotes were then printed for OTC issues and were circulated the next morning.

By our reckoning, this amounts to a latency of 17 hours, 30 minutes *at best,* because the quotes did not update again until the following day. The OTC quote reporting process during the late 1960s can be seen in this figure.

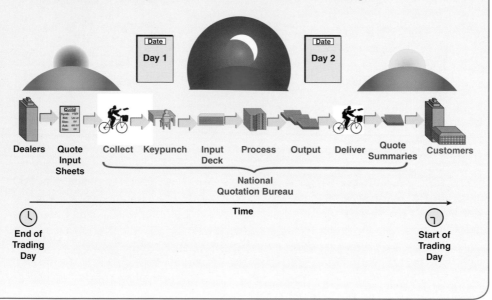

The significance of this background is that deep in the technology infrastructure of the trading markets today are huge chunks of this early technology still in use. We discovered during the massive efforts to convert old date formats in the run-up to Y2K that significant portions of the financial software from the late 1960s and 1970s were still in production and threatened problems. The fixes that occurred prior to Y2K in many cases, however, simply prevented the specific problems of dates rather than reengineering the software using current techniques.

Likewise, when the mandate loomed at about the same time to move to next-day settlement from three-day settlement,[1] the buy-side rebelled because it

---

1   We described the timing of settlement in Book 2, *An Introduction to Trading in the Financial Markets: Trading, Markets, Instruments, and Processes.*

would have forced the redesign of many of these antiquated core systems. Outdated applications running on modern hardware continue to be a significant problem for the markets and create many of the challenges that result in slower change and seemingly unnecessary costs.

CONCEPTS

Several concepts related to the operations of the trading markets form the basis on which technology—systems, data, and networks—depends and are central to understanding the purposes of the technology discussions that follow. To our knowledge, many of the category labels are terms coined in this set of books and do not correspond to any standard categories of which we are aware.

Therefore, we expect that some may argue that the categories are unnecessary, but we have consistently attempted to provide frameworks for all the descriptions we have made. That is the reason for defining these concept categories. However, the concepts within each category are well known. The concept categories are illustrated in Figure B.1.

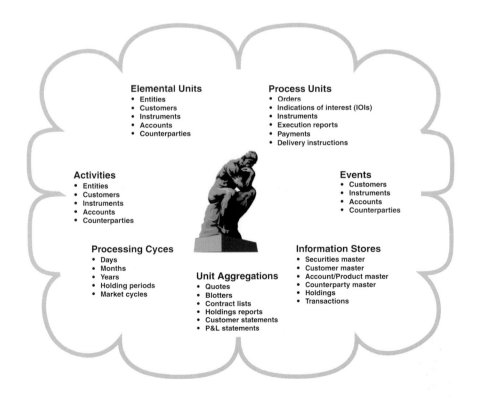

Figure B.1 *Concepts* that are the basis of the technology of the Street include basic factors, activities, events, information, and reporting that support the primary business.

One final note: From this point forward, our discussion of technology centers on the trading process and therefore centers on the buy and sell sides. We mention systems belonging to other entities to the extent they are directly involved in the trading process.

Elemental Units

We define an **elemental unit** as a basic component needed to describe technology, a foundation upon which technology is built, and/or the purpose for technology's existence. Figure B.1.1 shows what we define as elemental units.

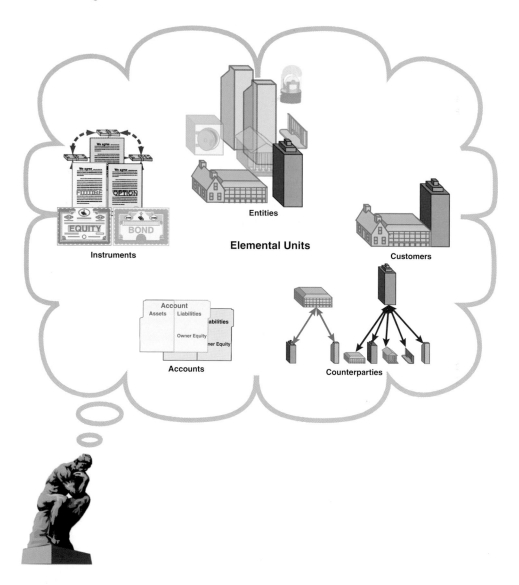

Figure B.1.1 **Elemental units** are the factors that form the foundation of technology on the Street.

As we see in the systems section in Part 1, except for entities, all the elemental units that we list here are the basis for one of the major **master files** that define technology in the trading markets. In fact, we expect that as global, **industry-wide systems** evolve, the need for entity master files that keep the static information defining the attributes for entities and their regulatory requirements on a country-by-country basis will emerge.

Data related to elemental units is maintained by systems. Systems in turn process the data as a part of transactions and as input to **reports** or, as we refer to them, **unit aggregations**.

ENTITIES

Entities are the functional units that form the core of the trading markets. In Book 1, *An Introduction to Trading in the Financial Markets: Market Basics,* we spent all of Part 1 defining entities and summarized that description in the Overview of this book. Remember that we use an entity to define functions rather than corporate units. Therefore, many large firms in the global markets include divisions that are banks as well as buy-side and sell-side units. From the perspective of technology, it is the functional units, not the corporate holding company, that are important.

Until the early 1990s, most technology in the trading markets was internal to entities. The development of the **Financial Information eXchange** (FIX) standard messages represents perhaps the first example of the creation of industry-wide systems that were not the result of a vendor connecting entities (e.g., **market-data vendors** introduced in Book 1, and **matching vendors** described in the affirmation discussion in Book 2) or **mutualized entities** such as **SWIFT**, clearing corporations, and depositories.[2]

Even when we consider emerging industry-wide systems, the entity is the focus of attention when we consider the elements of technology in the next three parts and when we return to consider technology in the trading process in Part 4.

CUSTOMERS

Customers are the basis for substantially all activities in the trading markets, and although we listed two common categories of customer—retail and institutional—in the Entities section of Book 1, our meaning here is somewhat different. Our meaning for the purpose of a discussion of technology is any individual for whom or entity for which a firm performs services (see Figure B.1.1.1).

---

2   Although "mutualized" or "mutualize" is not a recognized standard verb, we use it freely in the books of this set, and we believe it is both commonly used in the industry and fills a contextual need that is not easily serviced by constructions that could replace it. The specific uses of "mutualized" are defined in the Glossary, but generally we mean that an entity or an activity is shared among the participants within the industry. The goal usually is to share a task that offers no competitive advantage and that is expensive to perform. A clearing is a classic example of a **mutualized activity** performed by a mutualized entity.

Figure B.1.1.1 *Customers* are not only the individuals and institutions that use the markets, as intermediaries are themselves customers for supporting institutions. (However, we focus on buy- and sell-side firms.)

Technology uses the concept of a customer to collect the information necessary to provide services. The customer may represent individuals and institutions, but also other firms that are serviced by the entity maintaining the technology. For supporting entities, a customer may be called a *member* or *participant*, but for our purposes all these terms require similar or analogous information for technological purposes.

INSTRUMENTS

Instruments are the focus of trading and the primary reason the markets exist, so naturally they represent an elemental unit. More importantly, however, instruments as initially described in Book 1, Part 2, and again in Book 2, Part 3, have an array of different attributes (instrument to instrument) that create much of the complexity that affects technology, and the features of instruments described in Book 2 account for a major portion of the events considered here. Technology stores information about instruments that permits processing of both transactions and **holdings**.

ACCOUNTS

An account is the mechanism through which owners and their agents control their instrument holdings and the cash balances associated with instruments. We define an account broadly to include not only an account belonging to a customer, but also as most "products" provided by entities in the trading markets, portfolios, trading positions, and the like.

Therefore, an account is the hub at which holdings are aggregated, but it is more basic than a unit aggregation defined later that corresponds generally to the idea of a report or display. Substantially all ownership in the trading markets is channeled through the device of an account. Thus, an account performs an important unifying role in the processing performed by technology. Different meanings of account and different names that can be applied to an account require definition to understand how we use the term.

First, accounts have both owners and purposes. Owners can include individuals, entities, departments within entities, and other accounts. Individuals can have accounts as customers of entities in the financial markets. As portfolio managers, traders, and dealers, individuals control positions or portfolios that technically belong to their employers.

Entities own internal accounts for employees, for departments, and for products they offer. Entities also maintain accounts owned by customers and by counterparties. Finally, an account such as a portfolio may own accounts such as shares in a money market fund to hold cash balances.

The general purpose of all accounts is to provide the basis for holding assets (see Figure B.1.1.2). However, most accounts have more specific purposes. The account may be a portfolio, a trading position, or an investment or trading product. Accounts that are created as products such as mutual funds are divided into shares or units and sold as instruments to investors and traders. (We defined these assets as **packaged instruments** in Book 1.)

An account can have the general structure of a corporate **balance sheet**. Indeed, some accounts as we define them, notably mutual funds, are in fact

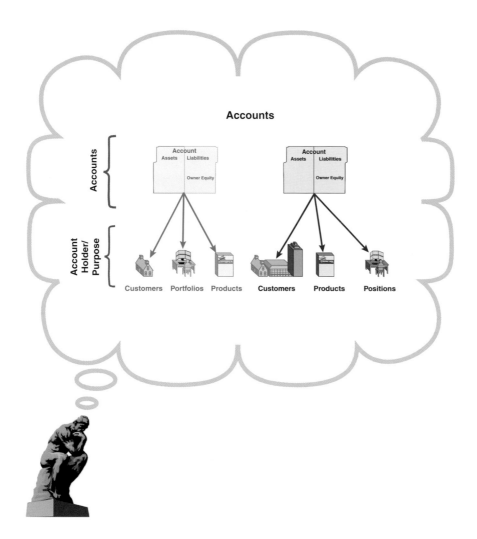

Figure B.1.1.2   ***Accounts*** are the mechanism through which customers and products control holdings in traded instruments.

incorporated. An account's major components include assets, often in the form of holdings; liabilities if the account has borrowed against its assets; and the ownership interest or owner's equity.

Almost every account also generates an ***income statement*** although the format is often different from that of corporate income statements. In the case of dealers' accounts or trading positions, the profit and loss statement corresponds almost directly to other corporate income statements.

The reason we combine different types of asset-control devices under the common label "account" is that each is subject to the same types of activities and events (see discussion later), and therefore, all require the same types of processing.

Technology creates all the information about an account/position/portfolio's holdings of assets and the activities associated with accounts, reporting the information back to customers, entities, and counterparties as needed.

COUNTERPARTY

In many respects, the concept of a **counterparty** is similar to that of a customer, and in transactions in which a customer is dealing with an entity as principal to principal, a customer is a counterparty (see Figure B.1.1.3). However, for the most part financial entities may have regulatory obligations to their customers, but only standard business obligations to a counterparty. The notion of counterparty tends to carry the notion of peer-to-peer interactions, whereas customer relationships imply a service provider to a recipient of services.

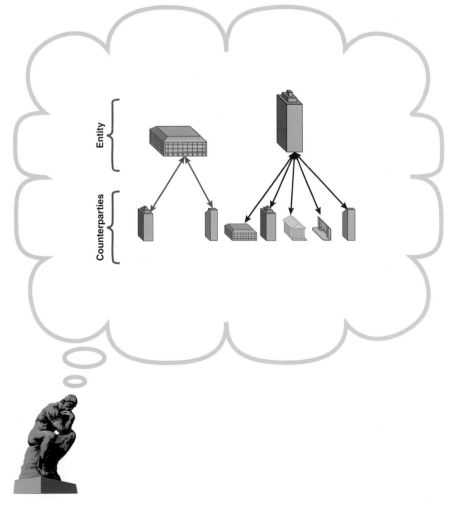

Figure B.1.1.3 **Counterparties** are the other entities that interact with buy- and sell-side firms to complete transactions in the trading markets.

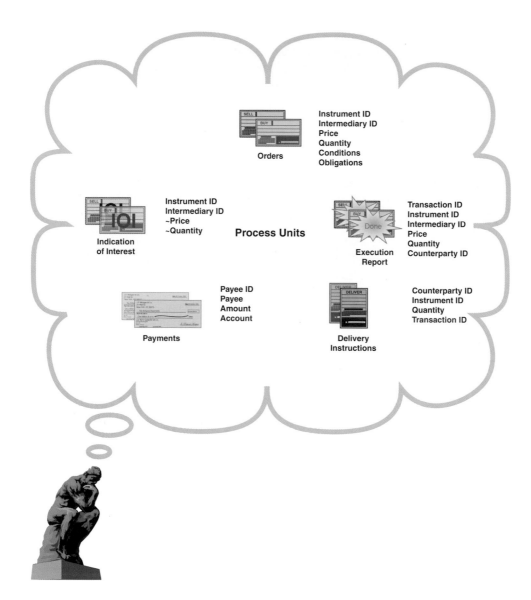

Figure B.1.2   ***Process units***–messages–are the vehicles through which transactions are completed.

Process Units

Process units are basic components that are the focus of a product or process. An order is the focus of the trading process to the point at which an execution occurs, and a trade report is the focus thereafter. Figure B.1.2 illustrates process units.

ORDERS

An **order** may be the most obvious example of a process unit. As we saw in Book 2, *An Introduction to Trading in the Financial Markets: Trading, Markets, Instruments,* *and Processes,* an order usually originates with a portfolio manager and moves to a buy-side trader, where it may be split into more, smaller orders or combined with other smaller orders to create a larger order.

From the buy-side trader, the order moves either through a sales trader or directly (using ***direct market access***) to the market where it is executed. Technology moves the order, handles the alternative routes it may take, and reports on its progress.

INDICATIONS OF INTEREST

We can think of an ***indication of interest*** (IOI) as an immature order. It is a message from an intermediary to a buy-side customer indicating the existence of a ***natural order*** in which the customer may be interested. Technology routes the IOI from the intermediary to the customer, helps the customer evaluate the IOI's value, and permits the customer to ***flip*** the IOI as an order back to the intermediary.

EXECUTION REPORTS

An ***execution report***, not a trade, is a process unit. A trade is an event, whereas the execution report is a notification of the event. The execution report is a technological message from a market to all parties to the execution and to the entities in the settlement process that a trade has occurred.

PAYMENTS

Payments are the basic message units that facilitate the exchange of ownership for monetary value. Payments must be processed and balance the acquisition or sale of instruments. Technology facilitates this by processing both trade reports and payments to account for changes in holdings.

OTHER UNITS

Many other important types of messages are generated and flow throughout the trading markets. For example, exchanges send critical administrative messages that may affect trading and alter behaviors. Similarly, clearing corporations send out margin calls when changes in the price of instruments awaiting settlement cause one or another participant in a trade to have an incentive not to settle.

Activities

Activities are processes that take place within entities, which are initiated by the entity, and can be controlled (see Figure B.1.3). Normal daily processes such as portfolio management and customer reporting are examples of activities. Some activities (e.g., those of the buy-side trader) precipitate ***events*** such as executions. We can think of activities as actions affecting the trading markets that can be planned for and controlled within an entity, whereas events cannot be fully predicted and controlled.

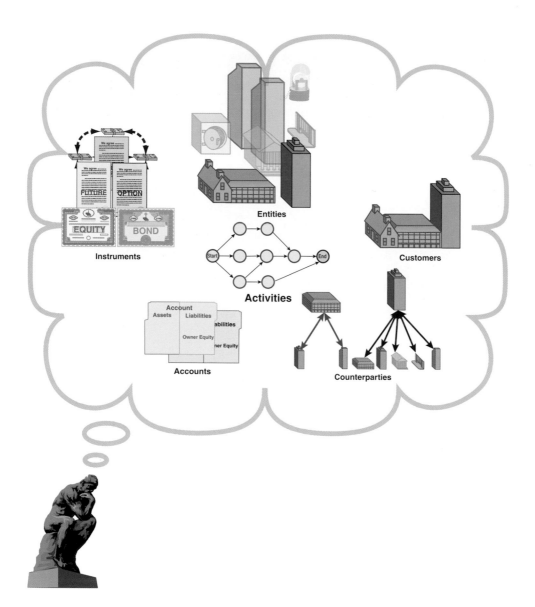

Figure B.1.3 *Activities* are components of workflows controlled by entities on the Street to conduct trading and its supporting tasks.

Each activity we describe here is typically controlled by or supported by systems, which use and produce data and which are interconnected by networks. We describe events in the following section. Because of the breadth and complexity of the types of possible activities, systems are required to monitor the entities to which they are dedicated and anticipate activities that must be undertaken. The nature of systems makes them ideal replacements for the myriad card files and calendar notes that provided the basis for monitoring activities before automation became effective.

ENTITIES

Entities are typically organized around kinds of activities that the entities must perform. In Book 1, we introduced the concept of front, middle, and backoffice, which are terms commonly used to describe the functional areas within the buy and sell side. Figure B.1.3.1 illustrates the functions identified in Book 1. Each of these functions performs or participates in the performance of activities supporting the entity.

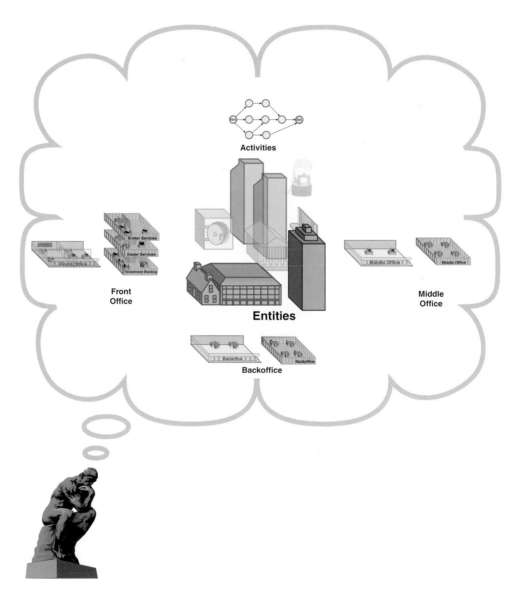

Figure B.1.3.1   ***Entities*** are organized around the activities needed to support customers and conduct trading.

Front Office

Among the front-office activities that we do not consider in this section are all the functions surrounding investment banking and the primary market process. The remaining activities include sales and trading (see Figure B.1.3.1.1).

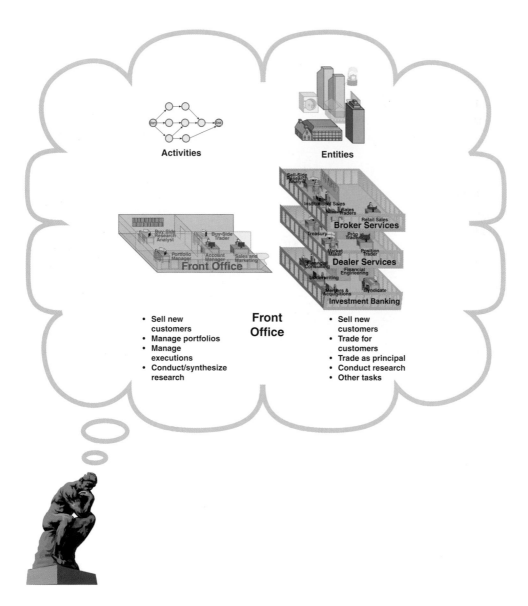

Figure B.1.3.1.1 The *front office* serves to attract new customers, entice them to transact in the markets, and execute the orders they generate.

Sales

Selling activities involve contacting new customers, convincing existing customers to use new or additional services provided by the entity, providing direct customer support, and performing other activities associated with generating new revenues or protecting existing revenues.

Systems supporting sales involve providing information on customer goals and expectations as well as details about customer accounts. The sales process is supplemented by investment research, which suggests new products to be sold and can suggest how new and existing services can benefit the customer.

Trading

Trading activities involve executing orders coming from portfolio managers on the buy side, handling customer orders on the sell side, and managing trading positions for sell-side firms.

Trading systems help agents and dealers manage orders through the execution process and may provide electronic access to alternative trading venues.

Middle Office

Middle-office activities involve supporting customers and in particular providing information that customers need to manage their positions and make ongoing investment decisions (see Figure B.1.3.1.2). As we noted in Book 1, middle-office activities support customers and the front office, but typically do not interact with the customer directly. Therefore, the middle office is engaged in activities that are provided to customers through front-office personnel.

Middle-office personnel may work on the same systems used by the front office or may employ specialty technologies such as systems supporting compliance.

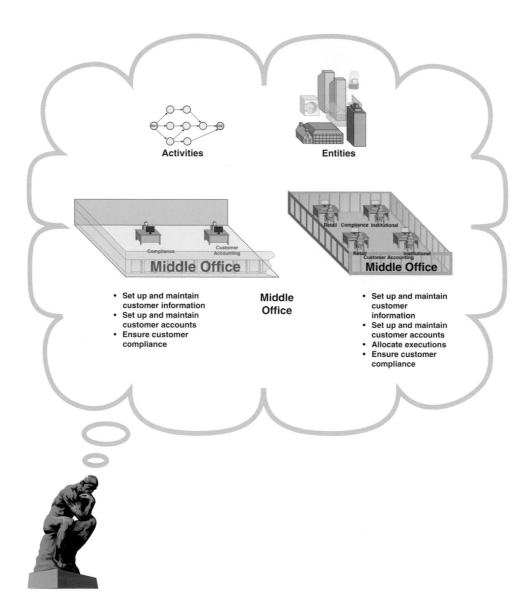

Figure B.1.3.1.2   The *middle office* supports customers by producing reports and helping to map customer holdings to aggregate firm positions.

Backoffice

Backoffice activities involve interactions with other entities on the Street (see Figure B.1.3.1.3). They include managing the settlement process for trades, handling interactions with supporting entities, and sometimes handling interactions with regulators.

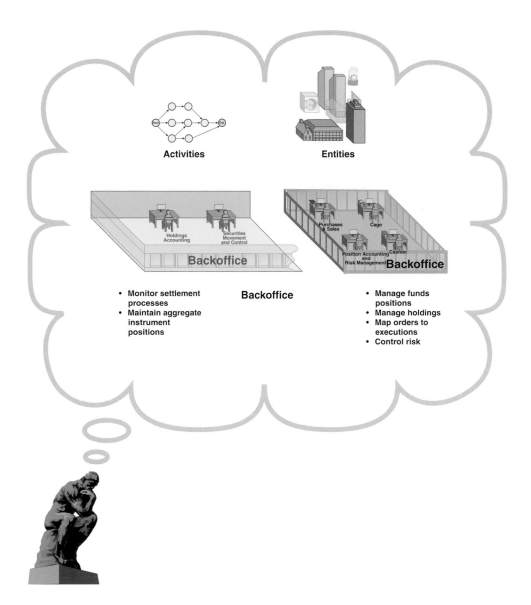

Figure B.1.3.1.3   The **backoffice** links buy- and sell-side firms to the markets and other supporting entities that facilitate the trading and settlement processes.

Backoffice systems involve matching transactions from the markets with orders from portfolio managers and customers, handling the receipt and delivery of cash and instrument positions, and managing interactions with custodians and others.

CUSTOMER ACTIVITIES

We have noted several ways in which customers are supported by functions within entities. However, several specific tasks are required to manage and support customers (see Figure B.1.3.2).

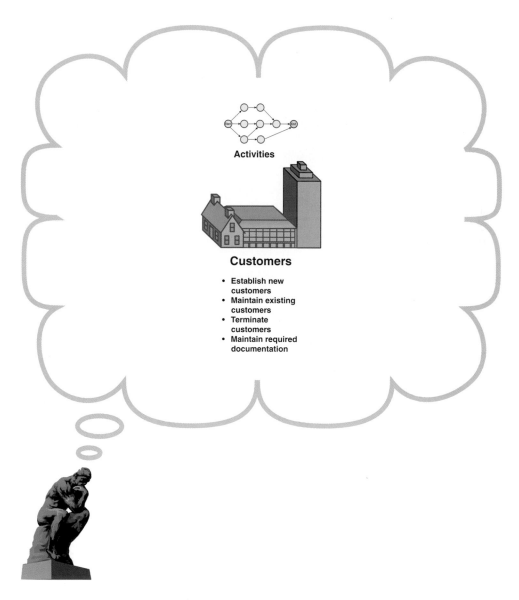

Activities

Customers

- Establish new customers
- Maintain existing customers
- Terminate customers
- Maintain required documentation

Figure B.1.3.2 *Customer activities* are undertaken to fulfill their needs, increase their returns, and keep them up to date on the status of their holdings.

Establish Customers

When a new customer is attracted to an entity, the information about the customer must be recorded and stored. Details such as name, address, personal or work details, account information and the customer's banking relationship, and other information must be recorded and stored for use in servicing the customer.

In addition, for retail customers and some institutional customers, it may be necessary to file documentation required by regulators. This documentation may be submitted to the regulator but most often must be stored by the entity for review if the regulator chooses.

New customer documentation systems facilitate the entry of information from customers and the maintenance and filing of the required documents. Increasingly, the systems permit customers to input information directly into electronic documents rather than paper.

Maintain Customers

For existing customers, data must be updated periodically to ensure that the information maintained by the entity accurately reflects the details of the customers. Moreover, as part of the ongoing business of operating the firm, customers are frequently required to provide formal approval for actions taken on their behalf and/or to provide additional information to complete activities.

Customer maintenance applications facilitate keeping customer details up to date and recently involve the customer in the maintenance process.

Terminate Customers

Although most financial entities do not like to think about the end of a customer relationship (unless the customer is not profitable), customers terminate their relationship with organizations, so actions must be taken when the termination event becomes known. The termination may be as simple as closing accounts and providing any remaining holdings to the customers but may be much more complicated. There is a business service known as **transition management** in which accounts such as corporate **pension plans** are moved from one investment management firm to another using processes designed to minimize the loss in value.

Systems supporting the termination of accounts control the activities required and may provide extended reporting and record maintenance for years after the termination.

INSTRUMENTS

Entities engage in a number of activities associated with the acquisition, maintenance, and sales of instruments (see Figure B.1.3.3). These activities fall into two main categories. Instrument positions must be created through direct actions in the primary and secondary markets and liquidated in the secondary markets. Moreover, entities undertake actions to maintain instrument positions.

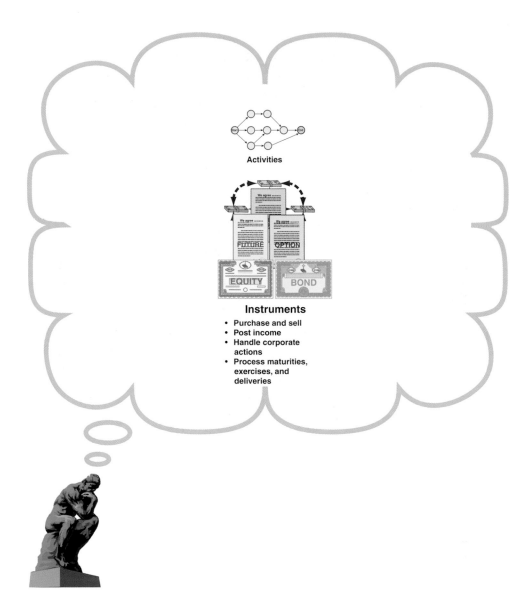

Activities

Instruments
- Purchase and sell
- Post income
- Handle corporate actions
- Process maturities, exercises, and deliveries

Figure B.1.3.3   *Instrument activities* include their purchase and sale to generate returns, the collection of income they generate, and their maintenance as holdings subject to events defined by their issuers.

Purchases and Sales

Instrument positions are generated through the purchase process and liquidated by a sale. The culmination of a purchase transaction is an increase in the holdings in the instrument. For accounts that have tax implications, such as trust accounts and proprietary investment accounts, each purchase results in a separate lot where the purchase price establishes the cost basis for the lot. A sale reduces the holdings and may result in a **gain** or a **loss** as defined by tax rules. Corporate or regulatory accounting policies determine which lot or lots are used to establish the cost basis to compute the gain or loss resulting from the sale.

During the time between when a transaction is initiated and when it is completed, systems within the affected entities manage the transaction. Statuses may change, quantities may be increased or decreased, and new entities may become involved in the completion of the transaction. When the transaction has settled, the new holding or reduction in holdings flows through the firm's clearing accounts and into the portfolio or position that initiated the transaction.

Income

Many instruments generate income as part of their inducements to attract investors. Income is a known (fixed-income) event or anticipated (equities) event, and entities prepare to handle income as it occurs. In the case of equities and some variable-rate instruments, the exact amount may not be known.

Investment accounting systems are designed to post income when it is anticipated. For fixed-income instruments, the system anticipates payment and initiates action in the event the payment is not received. If the amount of a payment is unknown, as is the case with equities, the system can still anticipate a payment, and the quantity can be updated when the announcement event occurs.

Corporate Actions (First Part)

Corporate actions suggest activities undertaken by entities issuing instruments. (The term "corporate" is used even though a governmental body or a nongovernmental organization (NGO), may be the actual issuer.) For the most part, corporate actions, as we use the term, are events to which other entities must react. However, many corporate actions can be anticipated (e.g., a dividend payment) even though the amount and the exact timing may be unknown. (Sometimes the term **capital changes** is used in place of corporate actions to mean the same thing. We believe that capital change is more restrictive because not all corporate actions result in a change to capital structure.)

Systems supporting the trading markets play an important role in helping to anticipate expected events and initiating corrective actions when the events do not occur.

Maturity, Exercise, and Delivery

Many instruments mature or expire as part of their structure, and normal activities are employed at the end of each instrument's life. Instruments mature, and options and futures have a finite life. In the case of some instruments, **elective action** may be required to determine how the instrument terminates.

Systems supporting instrument activities must be aware of the set of actions that may be required and prompt the appropriate action.

ACCOUNTS

In many ways, a customer and an account are similar; for many customers, there is only one account with an entity in the trading markets, and the customer and account are largely interchangeable. However, an account is an accounting device, and a customer is a person or entity, so the differences are real. Another fact about an account is its somewhat **recursive** nature—that is, accounts can own other accounts or an interest in another account. These relationships are shown in Figure B.1.3.4.

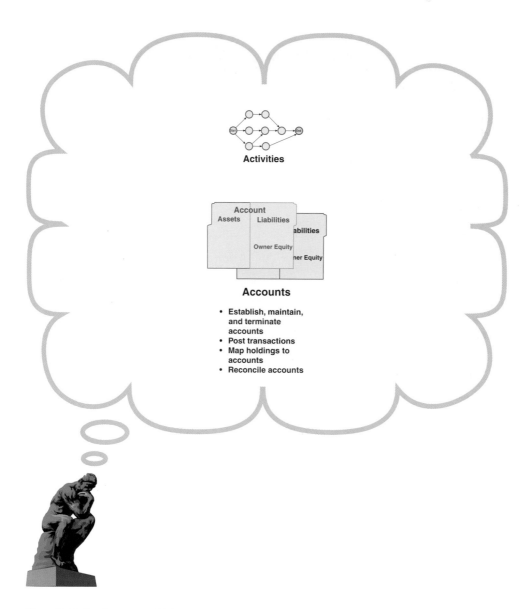

Figure B.1.3.4 *Account activities* support the business account, a mechanism that is the focus of instrument ownership, and the collection and distribution of funds generated through investment and trading.

Establish, Maintain, and Terminate Accounts

Accounts, like customers, require activities at their creation, periodic activities to maintain the accounts, and finally special actions that may be required when or if accounts are terminated. Because accounts are the mechanism that most entities use to offer special investment approaches such as interest-bearing alternatives to checking, educational savings, and retirement, there are many different requirements for investment, historical retention of information, and reporting.

Mapping Accounts

Accounts at the majority of investment and trading entities do not hold instruments directly. Therefore, holdings for the accounts are actually mappings to portions of larger **comingled funds** and investment or trading products. Even in situations where a customer or counterparty owns an instrument directly, the actual holding or holdings record is maintained in an entity-based account that may in turn relate to holdings at a custodian, agent bank, or depository. Therefore, the activity of mapping the holdings of parent accounts or external accounts into customer, position, and product accounts constitute an important activity that relates **Street activities** to **customer activities**.

Account Transactions

We have used the term "transactions" previously, but it is useful to understand exactly what we mean by the term. Transaction is the general term for activities that cause changes in an account as a result of the ongoing investment and trading operations of a financial entity. Trades, payments, the receipt and delivery of instruments, and many other activities constitute transactions. As the roots of the term seem to imply, transactions are frequently actions between or among accounts. For us, transaction implies the handling of the process units and other events that modify or transform accounts.

During the time between when a transaction is initiated and when it is completed, systems within the affected entities manage the transaction. The process of managing transactions may result in changes in quantities, updates to prices, and/or tracking the workflow.

When a transaction is complete, the transaction must be recorded or **posted** for the account or accounts affected.

Reconciling Accounts

Because of the complexity of the mapping process among accounts and the number of transactions that occur in the trading markets, it is necessary to periodically ensure that in the process of modifying accounts there is no break in the relationships and the mappings remain intact. The process of testing the validity of the mappings among accounts is known as **reconciling**.

Reporting Accounts

Reporting from accounts involves a variety of different presentations of information. Reporting is among the dominant activities as a means to manage accounts and their holdings and to satisfy the demands of customers and regulators. Later, we address but a few of all the reports associated with the trading process in the section on unit aggregations.

COUNTERPARTIES

Counterparties represent business relationships among the entities that operate on the Street. Counterparties require many of the same activities (such as initiating, maintaining, and ending relationships) as customers, and most counterparties are represented by an account or accounts (see Figure B.1.3.5).

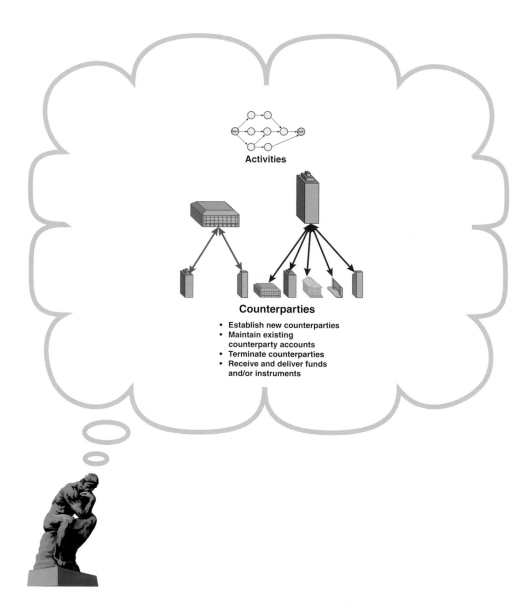

Figure B.1.3.5 *Counterparty activities* involve the interaction with other entities on the Street as required by the investment and trading processes.

Moreover, because counterparties correspond to active, frequent business relationships, entities maintain extensive details on counterparties, their offices, departments, and accounts. This information permits transactions to be completed without having to repetitively enter specific details about counterparties, which do not change often.

Delivery and Payment

Entities on the street must periodically interact with counterparties to complete processes involved with trading and related activities. A buy-side firm manages orders and issues orders to sell-side agents and dealers to initiate trades. A sell-side firm notifies institutional and retail customers of the successful completion of transactions as part of the confirmation process.

For example, in anticipation of settlement, a buy-side firm may require its custodian bank to prepare for settlement with the intermediary that executed the trades to be settled. (These processes were described in Book 2.) A clearing corporation may require specific information from clearing members in anticipation of settlement.

Delivery and payment have very special meaning in the completion of instrument purchase or sale transactions. If one of the parties to a trade **fails** to deliver or pay, not only may the transaction itself be incomplete, but there can also be "knock-on effects." Frequently, traders and sometimes investors sell instruments purchased or purchase new assets planning to use the funds from previous sales. If the first transaction fails to settle properly, subsequent trades may also be threatened.

The problems caused by trade fails are a primary reason for the creation of a central counterparty such as a clearing corporation. However, in markets without a central counterparty, fails sometimes result in chaotic situations known as **daisy-chain fails** that can threaten the market and the survival of participating entities.

OTHER ACTIVITIES

Firms manage their risk by periodically undertaking an analysis of their trading activities and also of their overall capital position. We discuss more about the process of risk management in Book 4, *An Introduction to Trading in the Financial Markets: Global Markets, Risk, Compliance, and Regulation.*

Events

Events are happenings that are beyond the total control of an entity, where the entity must react as a result of the events (see Figure B.1.4). Some events can be controlled or predicted to a large extent. For example, although an entity does not know the exact amount of a dividend, it knows at least the day when it is likely to be announced. An entity that seeks an execution cannot control an execution, but by choosing the price and trading venue, it can assure the execution will occur to a high degree of certainty.

Other events such as extreme market events that result in trading under **duress**, which was described in Book 2, cannot be predicted at all and are often not anticipated.

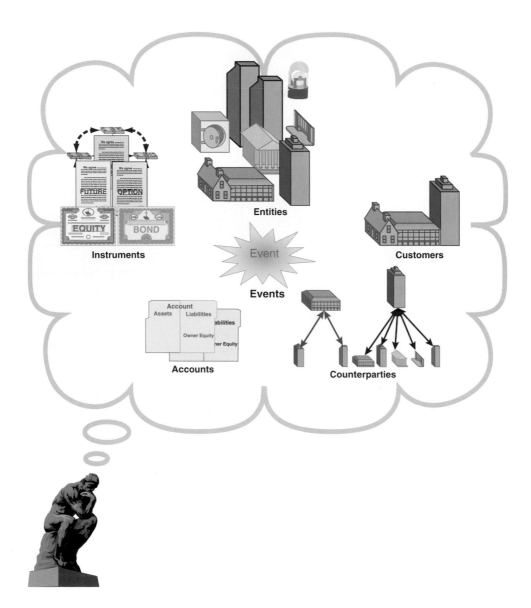

Figure B.1.4 *Events* lie beyond the control of entities on the Street but must be accommodated in the business of investment and trading.

ENTITIES

Although a number of events impact entities, we are not considering entities from the perspective of processing events.

CUSTOMER

A number of events can happen in which a customer takes action to which an entity must respond. For example, the customer may provide new funds that must be invested, the customer may require funds be withdrawn to satisfy customer needs, and the customer may open or close accounts. Each of these events may be unanticipated. The technology of the entity must be able to process these events.

INSTRUMENT

Instruments also have events that cannot generally be anticipated by an entity processing for the instrument. For example, an instrument may have a capital change such as a stock split or may receive income payments. Although the income payments are anticipated, the exact amount may be unknown.

Income Amounts

We noted in the Activities section earlier that income payments from instrument holdings can often be anticipated based on historical precedence or contractual obligation in the definition of an instrument. However, the amount of each payment is often unknown until it is announced by the issuer. The services that provide market data usually provide updated income payment amounts as well as other corporate actions described next.

Corporate Actions (Second Part)

We introduced the concept of corporate actions earlier in the Activities section. As noted, most corporate actions are events for the other entities on the Street.

As we noted earlier, capital change, is often used interchangeably with "corporate action," although capital change implies an instrument's transformation. Therefore, as we use it, capital change is the collective term for a series of transformations that occur in the structure or quantity of an instrument.

Most capital changes are initiated by the entity issuing the instrument, and therefore, using our definition, many capital changes are events. Examples include stock splits and dividends, bond calls, and other transformations. For the most part, capital changes alter quantities but not value, at least as measured by the percentage ownership (of an equity) or the face amount of a bond.

A final element of corporate-action events is that there may be different implications for the owner of an instrument and therefore for the systems that manage holdings. Some corporate actions are purely voluntary. Warrants, tender offers, and similar events are at the discretion of the instrument owner, who may choose to act or not. Other actions are mandatory.

Dividends and instrument payments, stock splits, mergers, and name changes are made by the issuing entity, and the instrument holder has no choice but to accept the effects. Finally, a few events require action but leave the holder a choice among alternatives. For example, a company might provide the choice of a dividend paid in cash or in shares.

Market Prices

Changes in market prices are among the most frequent events affecting instruments and instrument holdings. Investment and trading systems depend on the input in real time of prices from the markets. In Part 3 of this book, we describe the services of vendors that provide most of the information, including prices, required to control the investment and trading processes.

One of the complex events affecting market prices occurs when a capital change occurs to an instrument that is part of a portfolio or where the prices are needed for analysis. When an event such as a stock split or dividend occurs for an instrument, it is necessary to adjust the market prices retroactively to reflect the capital change. In principle, a capital change does not affect the value of holdings. If a stock splits 2 for 1 (i.e., an owner of 100 shares before the split has 200 after the split), the value of the holdings should not be affected.

After the split, each share should be worth 50% of the value before. However, for reporting and analysis purposes, the split creates a discontinuity, and for reports and analysis spanning the split, complex decisions are required to determine how to handle the event. Logic to handle the effect of capital changes on historical pricing and reporting is typically built into accounting, portfolio management, and analytical systems.

Announcements

Beyond corporate actions issuing entities, the markets and regulators frequently make pronouncements that entities in the trading markets must monitor and may require a reaction. These announcements may result in a change in the view of an instrument's worth, resulting in a purchase or sale. Trading venues can change transaction pricing, alter hours, or halt trading temporarily or permanently in specific issues.

Finally regulators may change reporting rules; take actions related to specific instruments, markets, or rules; or change the way standard processes are conducted. Firms must have systems or procedures that monitor these announcements because the changes can have a dramatic impact on the entity's operation. Fortunately, many of these announcements are described in advance, and firms are often invited to comment either directly or through industry associations.

Calls, Exercise, and Delivery

Although most instrument termination results from a planned activity such as the maturity of a bond, sometimes the end of an instrument occurs at the election of another party. If an issuing company chooses to "call" a bond before it matures, the holder of the bond has no say.

In fact, when a bond is called, the reason is that yields have fallen and the bond is expensive to the issuer but attractive to the holder. If an entity or its customer writes an option or a futures contract, there is the potential for the holder of the contract to exercise (an option) or elect delivery (a futures contract), which is an event for the writer. Finally, commercial entities sometimes become insolvent, and this event can have a profound impact on holders of any instrument issued by the insolvent entity.

Systems supporting entities on the Street must be able to handle all the events that can occur for traded instruments.

ACCOUNTS

We have considered a number of activities that surround accounts, but accounts can also be affected by events. In accounts where the customer has direct investment control or shared control, purchases and sales are events from the perspective of the entity managing the account.

Payments and Withdrawals

For most accounts, the receipt of new funds for investment and the withdrawal of funds on demand are events for the firm managing the account.

COUNTERPARTIES

Substantial portions of the events that occur among entities on the Street take place under the control of another entity. Every counterparty action results in at least one event for the entities that are the counterparty(ies) of the initiating entity.

Processing Cycles

We next consider different processing cycles (see Figure B.1.5). Substantially every process in the trading markets requires a cycle during which events and activities are completed or measured. At the end of most cycles, reports are produced or unit aggregations are generated that permit participants in the markets to analyze the actions that have taken place.

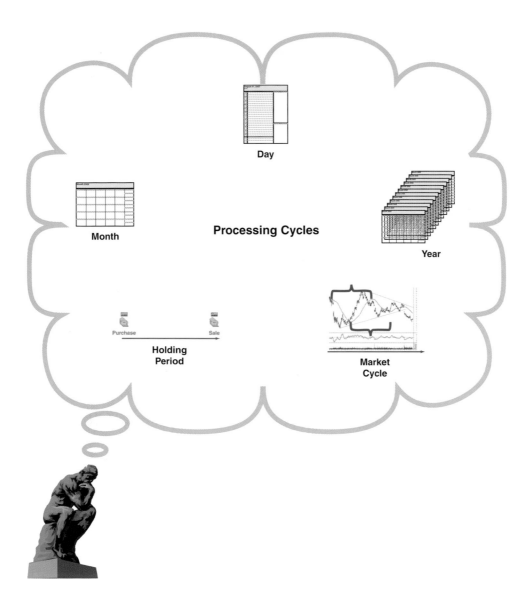

Day

Month

Processing Cycles

Year

Purchase   Sale

**Holding
Period**

**Market
Cycle**

Figure B.1.5   ***Processing cycles*** serve as measurement periods over which the investment and trading processes are managed and assessed.

CALENDAR PERIODS

The most common types of processing cycles center around calendar periods. For example, at the end of each trading day, mutual funds must produce **net asset values** to be reported in the business press, and traders may produce position statements that are input to risk management. Weekly, and certainly monthly, reports are often produced for a wide variety of consumers, including customers, management, and regulators.

The difficulty with processing cycles that cover fixed calendar periods is that many processes that take place in the trading markets, such as investment holding periods, do not conform to calendar periods. Moreover, reporting activities sometimes result in actions that destroy valuable information.

As an example, many portfolio accounting systems use the technique of a simulated purchase and sale as a means to move assets from one account to another. Although this action works perfectly well from an accounting perspective and accurately reflects account holdings, it causes important information to be lost for portfolio analysis.

HOLDING PERIODS

The term "holding periods," which we defined in Book 2, refers to the length of time an asset is filled in the portfolio. For portfolios that have tax implications, holding periods are important. Because portfolios represent a wide array of assets that may be purchased at many different times, accounting for holding periods on an asset-by-asset basis may be complicated.

MARKET CYCLES

Portfolio managers also wish to see how their portfolios change over market cycles and portions of market cycles. Markets seem to follow long-term cyclical patterns. In many cases and for many different reasons, portfolio managers and research analysts track the performance of specific instruments or entire portfolios over these market cycles.

Information Stores

Entities on the Street store information in a series of files that are common in intent for most entities but may differ greatly in specific details (see Figure B.1.6). Through experimentation and a kind of technological Darwinism, most entities on the Street have a set of master files that maintain static or infrequently changing information about customers, accounts, instruments, and counterparties.

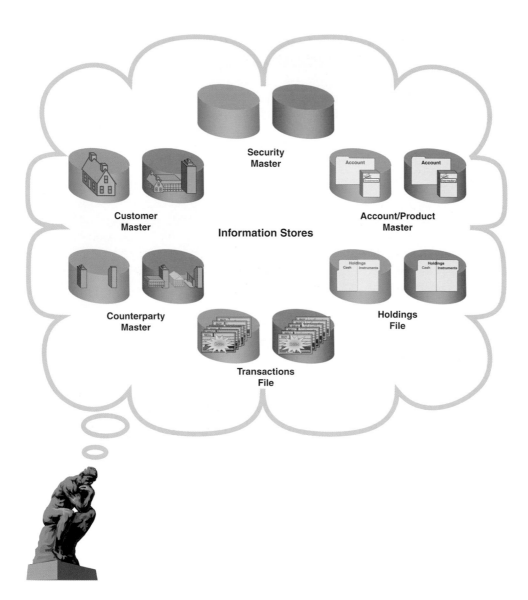

Figure B.1.6 *Information stores* are the database structures used to collect and store information on the investment and trading processes.

For entities with instrument holdings, a holdings file records positions usually down to individual purchase lots. Finally, there is some form of a transaction file that records and maintains transactions from their initiation until settlement or any other terminating event.

Our focus in describing these files is not related to the methods of storage or processing involved, but on the purposes each file serves.

SECURITY MASTER

The **security master file**, as it is commonly called (even for instruments that are not technically securities), holds static details for each different instrument an entity owns or maintains. The file contains some form of widely accepted security identifier; a name for the instrument; information about issues such as pricing cycles, pricing amounts (if known), and maturity or expiration dates (for fixed income and derivatives); and many associated details. Information from corporate actions may be recorded on the security master file. Subsidiary files may be employed to record static information that is unique to specific markets or countries.

CUSTOMER MASTER

The **customer master file** records important information about each customer, such as name and address, branch offices for corporations, tax identification numbers (that may serve as a customer ID number), bank accounts, payment instructions, investment and trading instructions, and many other types of information.

ACCOUNT/PRODUCT MASTER

Details for each account or product are retained in an **account master file**. The variety of different account types can make the account master extremely complicated. In addition to the identifying details such as an ID number that is unique to the entity that owns or manages the account, there may also be details such as tax ID numbers that are similar to a customer. Accounts that are defined as **trusts** are treated as individuals under the law and are able to bring lawsuits to defend the account's property rights.

COUNTERPARTY MASTER

A **counterparty master file** contains information that is similar in scope to a customer master file when the customer is an institution. Some customers may also be counterparties, and the way these entities are handled depends on the specific recordkeeping rules of each entity. Of particular concern with counterparties is tracking the functional offices, departments, or groups within the counterparty that have business with the entity. For each of these groups, the entity needs to track office addresses, banking and/or depository accounts, and other details that facilitate business interactions.

HOLDINGS

Holdings files record individual trades most often as individual lots. The lot includes the effective price, which is often an average price computed by the **allocation process**. (Allocations were described in Book 2 and are described in Part 4 in this book.)

Cross-Reference

Holdings are represented as an aggregate holding for an entire firm or division and for accounts. A mechanism that provides a cross-reference or mapping from individual account holdings to aggregate holdings is necessary. The structure of the cross-reference may be determined by regulatory requirements or by the accounting strategy of the entity.

TRANSACTIONS

Entities need a mechanism to track transactions from initiation until completion. The major mechanism that provides this capability for trades, the major focus of technology in this book, is a group of workflow products tailored for the buy and sell sides. We describe these systems in the next section.

Unit Aggregations

Although unit aggregations may seem like a forced term—20 years ago we would have used "report" for substantially every concept here—we want to emphasize the fact that we are focused on combining process units into usable presentations of information.

Moreover, presentations are increasingly delivered electronically and not in printed form. Only mandated regulatory reports are commonly produced on fixed time frames, and even regulatory reports are commonly delivered as **Adobe Acrobat** (.pdf) electronic documents provided regulators and customers agree.

A second important change represented by the term "unit aggregation" is the idea that information is increasingly delivered in continuously changing presentations rather than period summations. Again, except where required in the form of fixed reports, most units are displayed and processed in continuously evolving form to monitor activities and events in real time.

We examine some of these aggregations in the rough sequence of the trading process. Indeed, Figure B.1.7 shows the trading process developed in Book 2 with important aggregations as they occur. We return to a more complex representation of the trading process in Part 4 and explore the aggregations in more detail.

Although we represent these aggregations with icons that resemble reports, they are frequently in electronic form. Also, remember that an underlying concept in the term "unit aggregation" is the idea that more than one elemental unit is being brought together to represent information in a more useful or actionable form.

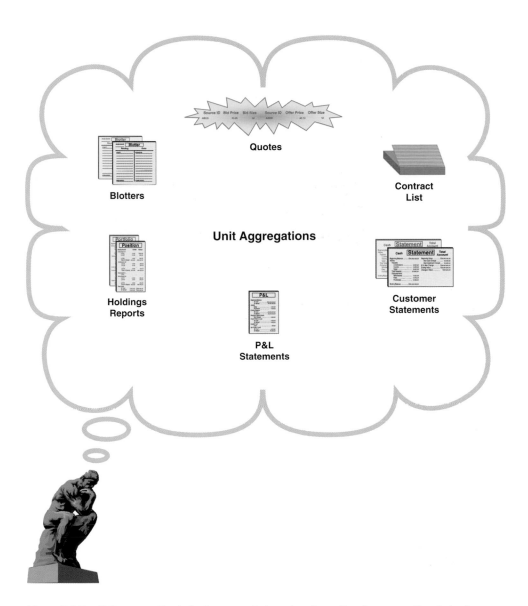

Figure B.1.7 ***Unit aggregation*** is the term we coin to replace "report" as the aggregating device to permit participants to monitor the trading process.

QUOTES

It may seem odd to consider a ***quote*** as a unit aggregation (i.e., a report) rather than as a process unit (i.e., a message) because quotes are disseminated electronic messages. However, at its core, a quote is an aggregation of two components: an order to buy and an order to sell, whether the components come from two principals, as occurs in an electronic system, or from a single market maker.

Quotes were explored in depth in Book 2, where we examined their firmness and the information they convey. Here, quotes are of interest in that they are processed as part of execution events, and they are an important component of real-time, market-data content (see Figure B.1.7.1).

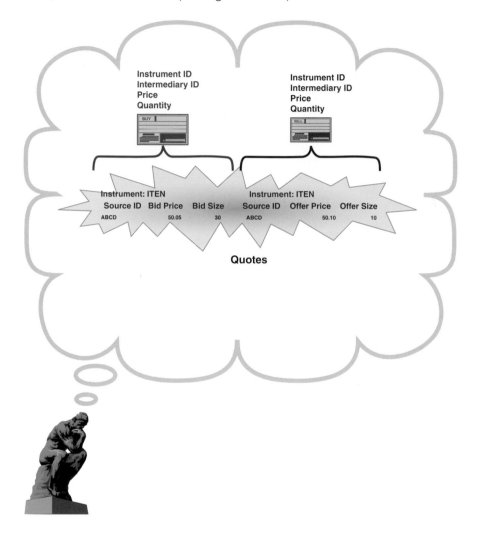

Figure B.1.7.1 ***Quotes*** are aggregations in that they reflect the combination of an order to buy and an order to sell in a single presentation on the momentary state of the potential to trade in the market.

BLOTTERS

A ***blotter*** is a workflow tool that permits a trader to see the orders pending execution and to manage those orders through the execution process. The term "blotter" comes from the early practice of traders to write the orders they were managing on desk blotters. These early blotters were collected at the end of the trading day for processing, often in a manual process.

Blotters are usually formatted spreadsheets with rows corresponding to individual orders and columns representing the components of the order (instrument identifier, quantity, price, and account or position) as well as status indicators such as where the order is (with an intermediary or at an execution venue) or how much of the order is complete. Blotters can be subdivided to represent different categories of orders (e.g., separating bids and offers) or different levels of urgency. The way blotters are organized represents the trading style of the individual trader.

Finally, we need to distinguish the blotter that is a representation of pending orders from the technology that produces it. Blotters are the output of **order-management systems** discussed in Part 1 (see Figure B.1.7.2). For this discussion, we can think of a report as an immediate representation of all pending and the most recently completed orders.

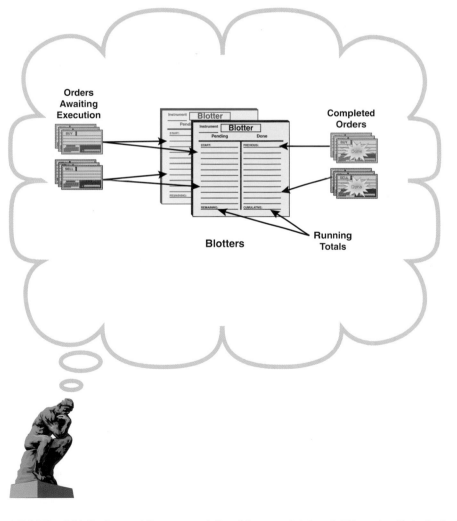

Figure B.1.7.2 A **blotter** is a workflow representation of the current status of all the orders that a trader is supposed to work in the market at any instant.

CONTRACT LISTS

A **contract list** is produced most often by a physical exchange to verify the details of trades and to permit traders to correct problems prior to settlement (see Figure B.1.7.3). In an electronic market, a contract list should not be necessary. In principle, electronic markets do not allow for errors. When a trader creates an order to buy or sell and sends it to the markets, the market processes the order as sent even if the elements of the order were not what the trader intended. Therefore, there should be no need for a contract list.

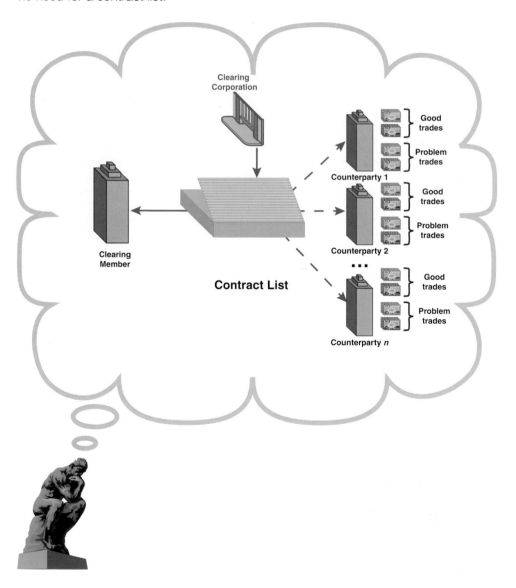

Figure B.1.7.3 A **contract list** is a representation of all transactions for a trading day sorted by trading counterparty that is used to identify trade breaks in markets where trade-recording errors can occur.

In some situations, however, even electronic markets need to unwind trades or to correct them because the effect of the error threatens the market. In a famous error in 2005, a trader in Tokyo entered an order for 610,000 shares at ¥1 rather than one share at ¥610,000. The error created extreme problems because the trader's firm could not pay for all the trades created, and the order exceeded the total shares outstanding in the stock. The equivalent of a contract list was needed to unwind the trades.

HOLDINGS REPORTS

Holdings reports, which might also be called **portfolio reports** or **position reports**, are working documents aimed at portfolio managers and traders managing instrument or cash positions (see Figure B.1.7.4). The reports provide a valued list of all the instruments contained in a portfolio (typically buy side), a product (buy or sell side),

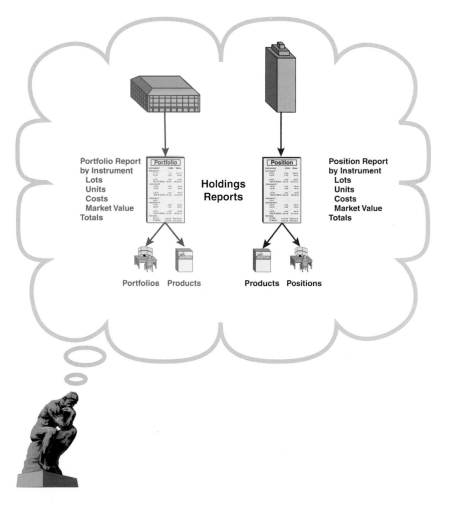

Figure B.1.7.4 **Holdings reports** are working documents that permit portfolio managers and dealers to know their current positions as they manage the instruments and capital given to their care.

or a position (sell side). Moreover, a variation of a holdings report may also serve as backup detail for a customer statement, as described in the next section.

The valuation typically employs either the **official price** or the market price for each component instrument. The official price is typically used for **statutory reporting**, whereas the market price is used to assess positions for trading and risk management. Valuation is computed by multiplying the total units for each holding by the appropriate price. All units in a holding are lumped together unless taxes are involved.

For reports that involve taxes, so-called **tax lots** are maintained. A tax lot represents the total number of units purchased at a single price. When taxes are computed on the change between the price of the holdings when purchased and the price when sold, it becomes important to record the number of units purchased at each different price.[3]

CUSTOMER STATEMENTS

Almost all customers require some form of reporting, although **customer statements** for retail customers are frequently more tightly controlled than those for professional customers (see Figure B.1.7.5).

P&L STATEMENTS

Profit and loss (P&L) statements are reports that provide management and control information to trading groups that are **risking capital** such as dealers, **prop trading units**, and other principal trading units (see Figure B.1.7.6). P&L statements are of huge interest to traders because they are the basis for determining bonuses, which are a huge component of the income traders receive.

---

3 The amount of information recorded can become even more complex. Sometimes jurisdictions require that information also be recorded if holdings managed by professional managers move from one manager to another. This is referred to as **inventory accounting** and requires that the purchase price for each tax lot be maintained, but also the price at the time the management change occurred.

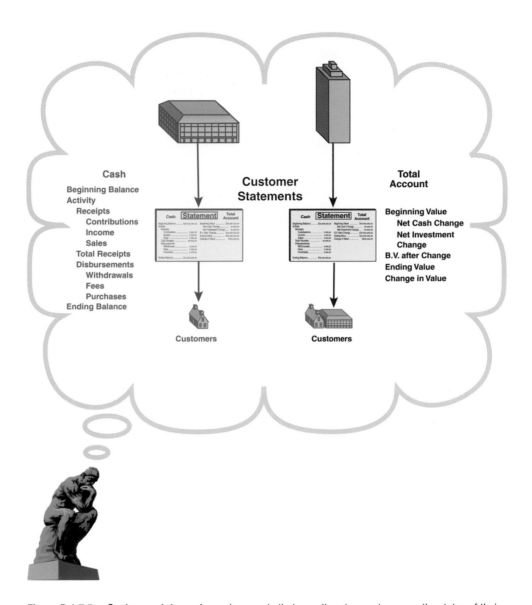

Figure B.1.7.5 *Customer statements* are documents that permit customers to assess the status of their accounts periodically.

The primary difference between P&L statements and customer statements is that a P&L statement provides a mechanism for allocating costs for the capital a trader commits. Therefore, the profit or loss includes a charge for the amount of risk the trader assumes.

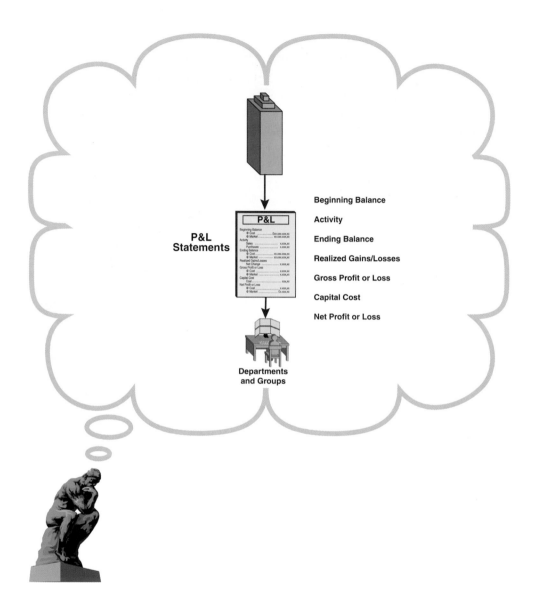

Figure B.1.7.6 *Profit and loss statements* are used by dealers to assess the performance of the positions for which they are responsible and to determine the bonuses they are due.

OTHER REPORTS AND PRESENTATIONS

We have focused on unit aggregations directly involved in the trading process. This is a small fraction of all information collected to support the trading markets. Many others are both directly and indirectly related to trading, but not the process of trading itself. For example, we consider the management of risk and compliance in Book 4.

HOW IT ALL COMES TOGETHER

Entities in the trading markets have customers. In Book 1, we examined a number of different types of entities, but for this book we focus on the buy and sell sides only. The mechanism that entities use to service customers is the account. Accounts also provide a linking mechanism to counterparties—other entities with which the buy and sell sides interact. These relationships are shown in the following figure.

Instruments are the assets in which entities and their customers trade and invest. Purchased instruments are grouped into holdings, which are controlled

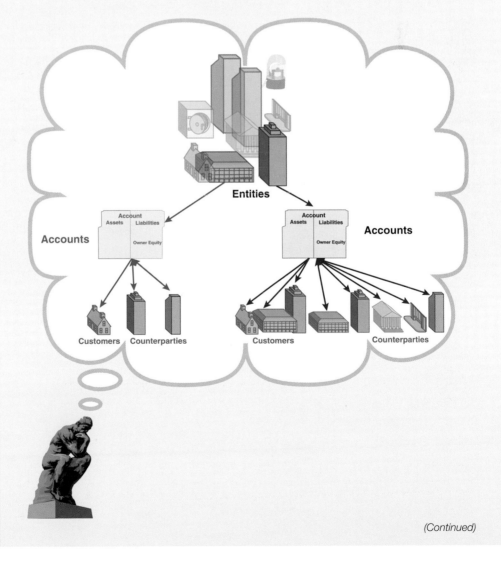

(Continued)

through the mechanism of the account. But instruments within an entity must be controlled in two different ways.

First, buy- and sell-side entities do not hold instruments directly. For the most part, positions or holdings controlled by an entity exist in other entities such as depositories, often through intermediaries such as custodians and agent banks. Buy- and sell-side entities must account for these aggregate positions, and reconciling internal accounts to accounts at custodians and agent banks constitutes an important part of the Street-side activities described in Books 1 and 2.

Aggregate positions as recorded by depositories, custodians, and agent banks must in turn map to holdings in accounts for customers, sometimes through intermediate accounts such as products. Managing customer accounts and mapping their holdings to the firm's aggregate positions are the business of customer-side accounting. These accounting linkages are shown in the next figure.

Entities are designed to engage in a number of activities and react to events affecting customers, counterparties, accounts, and holdings. The front office, shown earlier in Figure B.1.3.1.1, is responsible for acquiring new customers, selling them new investments and holdings, and managing direct interactions with them.

The middle office (refer to Figure B.1.3.1.2) maintains customer account information and controls the mapping from customer accounts to aggregate firm accounts. Finally, the backoffice (refer to Figure B.1.3.1.3) manages interactions with intermediaries and accounts for aggregate firm positions.

The accounts that are the focus of what we have described so far are the mechanism for owning holdings. Holdings can be in the form of cash or near-cash products such as money market funds, and other instruments or financial products. The holdings in an account are either owned directly or may be financed by loans, as shown in the following figure.

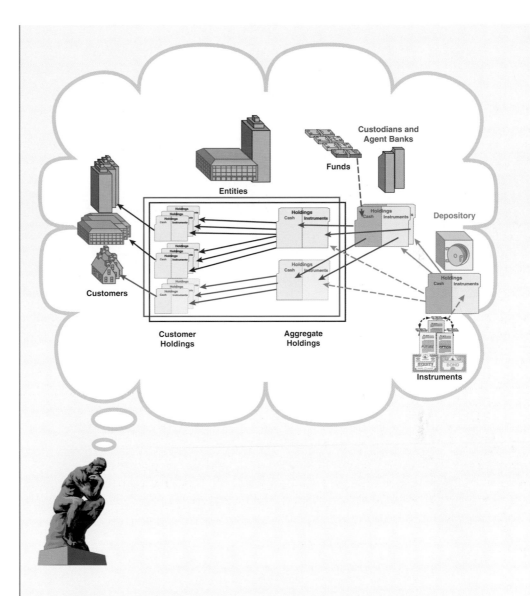

Accounts are managed through a number of activities and are subject to a number of events that we described previously. The holdings in accounts change because of actions by the entity and because of external events such as market fluctuations and corporate actions.

(Continued)

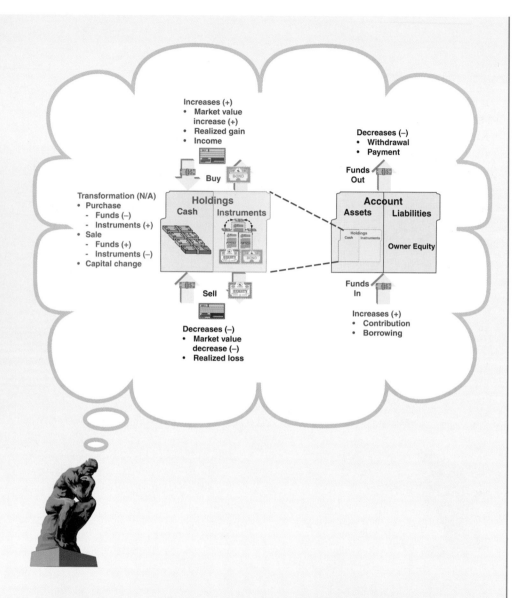

As we will see, the technology employed on the Street is designed to manage and report on these events and activities. Finally, at the heart of the processes supported by technology are holdings in both cash and instruments that represent the true purpose of trading in the markets.

This section explains some of the visual cues that are found in figures throughout this book in particular, but many are found in the other books of this set as well.

The entities on the Street all have different colors to differentiate them (see Figure VG.1). These colors are used throughout the set to distinguish functions, processes, and attributes related to specific groups of entities. Note that banks, while green, have either a blue or red stroke to denote that banks perform different functions for the buy side and sell side. The icons representing many attributes are color-coded to reflect the entity that they represent.

Figure VG.1   What the colors of the entities mean.

PREFACE

The book images with boxes indicating the major areas of content are used throughout the set to suggest areas of interest and to map sections with related content.
The current book (i.e., Book 3 in this case) is larger than the others (see Figure
VG.2). The content boxes do not include incidental sections such as the Preface
or Overview.

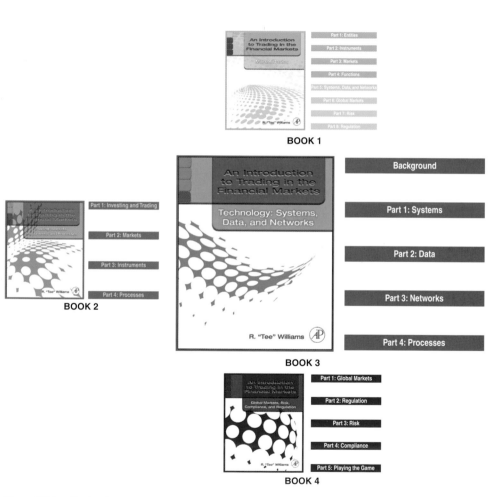

Figure VG.2   The book icons and content boxes indicate areas of interest and map related sections.

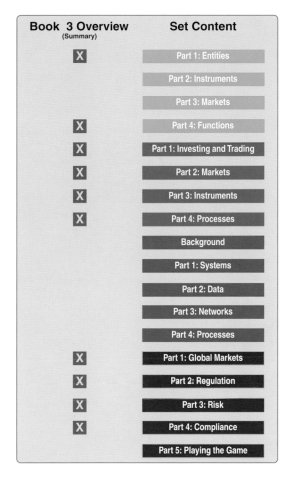

Figure VG.3   The relationship between content in the Overview and the set.

OVERVIEW

Figure VG.3 shows how subjects covered in this Overview to Book 3 relate to content in Books 1, 2, and 4.

We distinguish among markets in Figure VG.4 in two fundamental ways. At the top, we show that the primary market on the left creates new issues from issuers and distributes those issues to first-time owners.

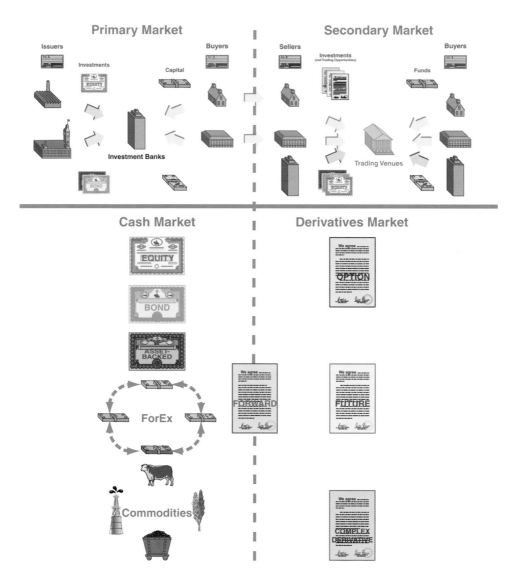

Figure VG.4   Two fundamental ways to distinguish among markets.

In the secondary market on the right, owners—both those who purchase an issue from an initial public offering (IPO) and subsequent holders—are able to sell to willing purchasers those holdings they no longer want. At the bottom, we distinguish between instruments in the cash market where instruments have intrinsic value in themselves and the derivatives that trade contracts, which may result in actions that have the potential to result in assets with intrinsic value.

We use the metaphor of the Street to define and categorize entities (see Figure VG.5). The Street runs north/south and is bisected by an east/west street. The left side of the Street is the buy side, and the right side is the sell side. Beyond the buy side and sell side, there are supporting entities. Entities north of the cross street are institutional entities, and those south of the cross street are retail.

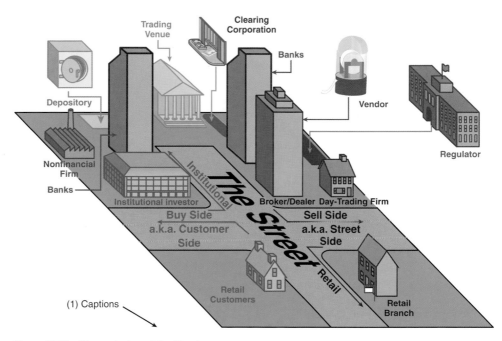

Figure VG.5   The metaphor of the Street.

Market entities include individuals and institutions that invest, intermediaries, and supporting organizations that together comprise the activities of the Street.

Each figure (except book maps) has a caption (1). The purpose of the caption is to distill into a simple declarative statement the meaning or purpose of the concept illustrated in the figure.

In Figure VG.6 we summarize the function of each entity first described in Part 1 of Book 1, *An Introduction to Trading in the Financial Markets: Market Basics,* using labels that point to the "footprint" of entities.

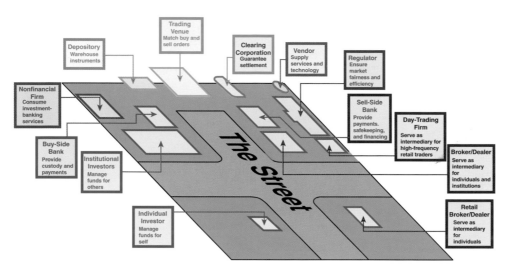

Figure VG.6 The functions of the entities.

BACKGROUND

We begin with a background that defines some of the concepts we use to serve as a foundation to understand the use of technology in the trading markets.

Throughout the set, we periodically present abstract concepts (see Figure VG.7). In these concept graphics, we use the image of "the Thinker" (2) to indicate that a graphic is presenting a concept. A "thought bubble" (3) surrounds the concept graphic. The graphic within the thought bubble in Figure VG.7 illustrates some of the icons we use frequently.

We use file folders to represent accounts (4). (This illustration demonstrates the recursive nature of accounts where a holdings account is held within a more general customer or product account.) We also see icons representing different types of funds (5) and instruments (6).

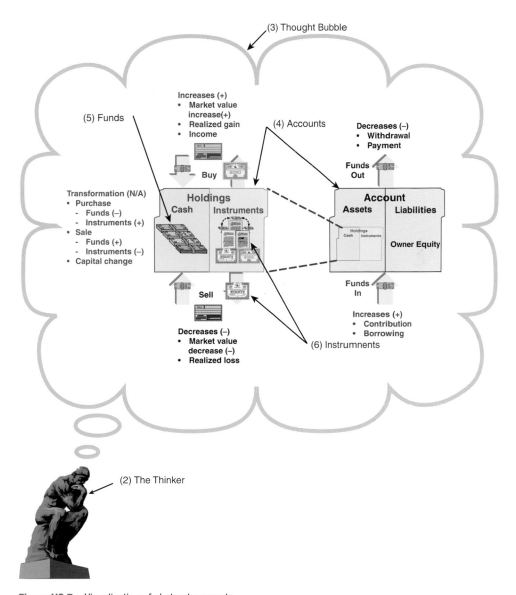

Figure VG.7   Visualization of abstract concepts.

PART 1: SYSTEMS

The first major part of the book is devoted to systems.

We use a device that might be thought of as a visual table of contents when a section presents a number of topics. In Figure VG.8 the topic groups relate to attributes of systems.

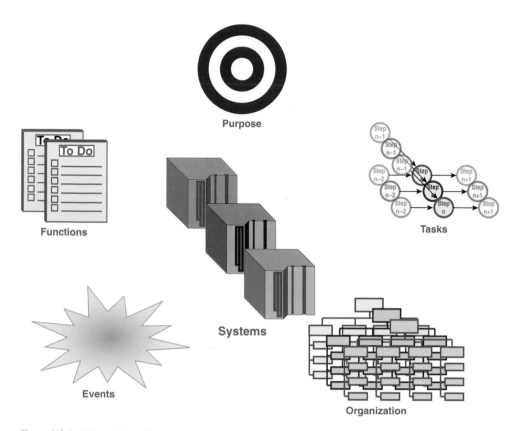

Figure VG.8   Visual table of contents that relates topic groups to system attributes.

In Figure VG.9 we show how the technology is presented throughout the first three parts of this book. We build on a descriptive device known as the Open Systems Interface, or OSI, model, which describes the levels in interentity communication in terms of layers that build to a complete communications definition.

The model depends on layers that are described in Part 3. However, we use the layer model to explain how a function (7) icon representing activities performed within entities, as described in Part 4 of Book 1, operates on a function layer (8) that is at the top of a four-layer stack.

Three successive layers support the function layer. There is one layer each for systems (9), data (10), and networks (11), which are represented as if they were situated below the function layer.

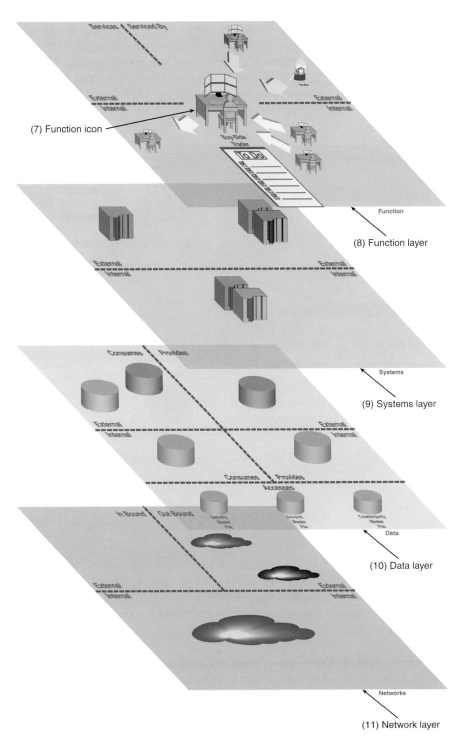

Figure VG.9 Visualization of how technology is presented in this book's parts.

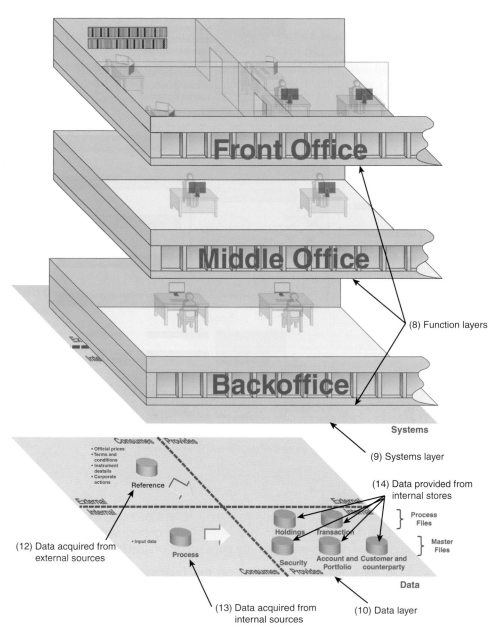

Figure VG.12   Data supporting the buy and sell sides of a firm.

On the figures showing the firm or one of the offices, the systems level (in Part 1) and data levels here show technology services that are provided broadly either to the entire firm or to most functions within an office. At the firm and office levels, we show the sources of systems or data on the left of the layer from external sources (12) or from internal sources (13), and the data stores provided throughout the firm or office on the right are from internal data stores (14).

In presenting data-supporting functions, we return to the graphics created in Book 1, Part 4, and used here to highlight systems in Figure VG.10. We highlight the data level in Figure VG.13 as we did in Figure VG.12, but show data that is consumed specifically by the featured function (15,16) as well as the data that function produces (17, 18). The data produced may be used to update internal data stores (17) (below the horizontal dashed line) or even made available to external users (18) (above the line).

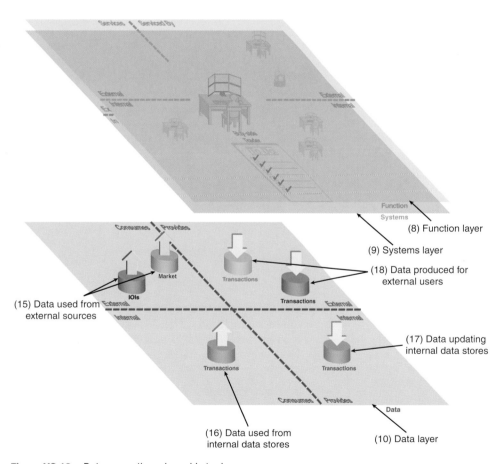

Figure VG.13 Data supporting a buy-side trader.

Figure VG.14 is a simple example of a process flow (19) used throughout the set. Steps in the process are presented on circular backgrounds (20) that are color-coded to indicate which entity group is involved. In many cases, "To Do" lists (21) describe the tasks performed.

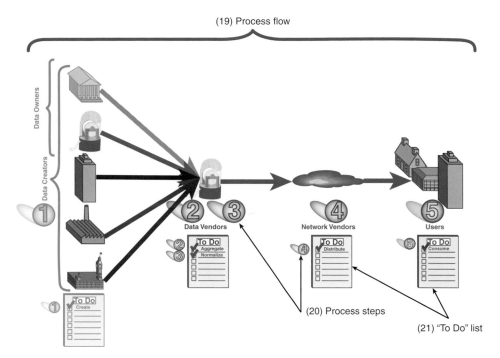

Figure VG.14   The market-data process flow throughout the set.

In Figure VG.15 we see another example of a process flow used to show different activities in a series of processes using three different participant groups (22): data owners, data vendors, and data users. Here, in addition to showing process steps (20) and "To Do" lists (21), there are also icons representing documentation exchanged (23) in the process.

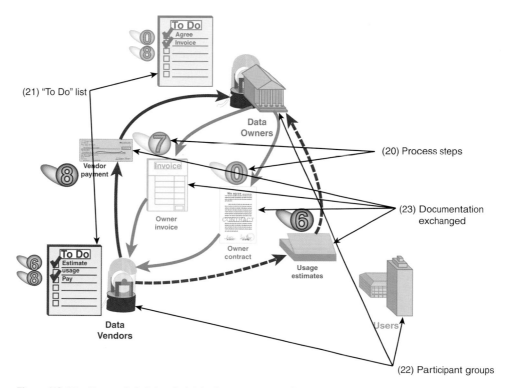

(21) "To Do" list

(20) Process steps

(23) Documentation exchanged

(22) Participant groups

Figure VG.15   The market-data administrative processes and documentation.

In Figure VG.16 we return to the business-process flow we used extensively in Book 2, *An Introduction to Trading in the Financial Markets: Trading, Markets, Instruments, and Processes*. This format helps describe a process that evolves through time as represented by the sequential step numbers at the top (24).

In addition to process step icons (20) and "To Do" lists (21), we employ participant channels (25) to separate the activities of different groups for clarity. Arrows serve as connectors (26), and connector icons (27) represent places where the process being shown interacts with processes in other figures.

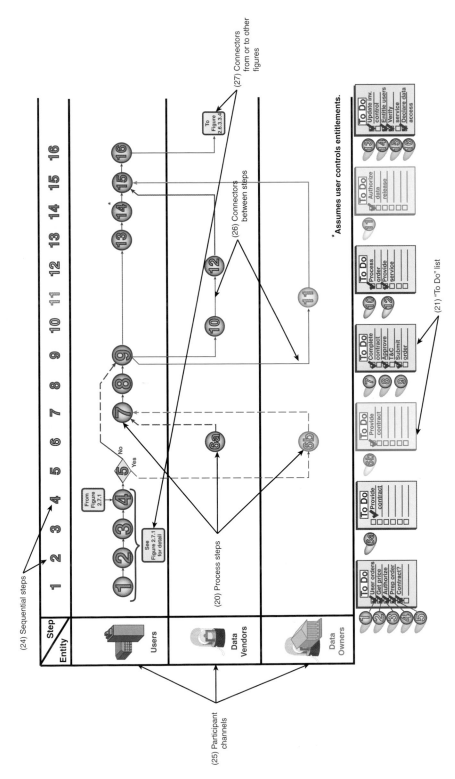

Figure VG.16 Business-process flow for market-data administration.

We show the structure of revenue calculations for market data in Figure VG.17. A cash register icon (28) represents revenue. Other icons represent different commonly used units of count (29); the unit selected in this example is placed in front of a circular icon (30). Units that are entitled are represented by a button icon that is "on" (31), and those that are not entitled are represented by a button that is "off" (32).

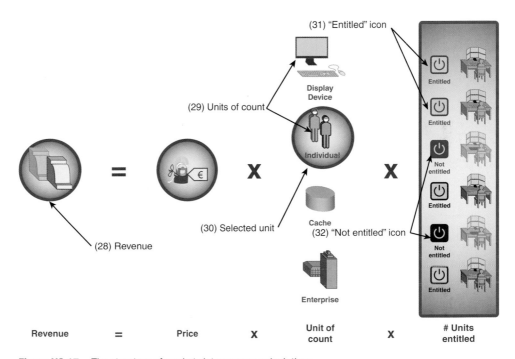

Figure VG.17   The structure of market-data revenue calculations.

Figure VG.18 shows a *conceptual* representation of the value of market data to a trader as a background to thinking about issues of pricing. *The graphical representation is conceptual and not the result of empirical research.*[1] The orange line suggests the perceived value of last-sale prices, and the red line represents quotes.

---

1   Throughout the books of this set, we continually emphasize that our purpose is descriptive and not quantitative. Our goal is to understand concepts such as "value," but not to measure it.

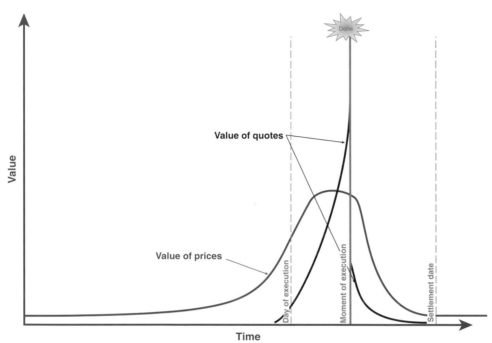

NOTE: Value estimates are both qualitative and conceptual and do not represent any quantitative analysis.

Figure VG.18 The value of pricing data to a trader.

Figure VG.19 represents the value two different user categories (33) place on data based on how the data is used. Different usages described in boxes (34) are arrayed along a two-dimensional axis (35). The vertical axis indicates that those tasks at the bottom do not involve trading, and those at the top do. Activities to the left involve people viewing the data through displays, and those on the right involve computers processing the data.

Value (36) increases from left to right and from top to bottom. The scale implies that trading commands more value than non-trading, and processing commands more value than non-trading. Even within the quadrants, we assume that not all tasks are evenly valued.

If different purposes for data have different values, then an entity pricing data needs to understand all the possible different group/purpose combinations that can

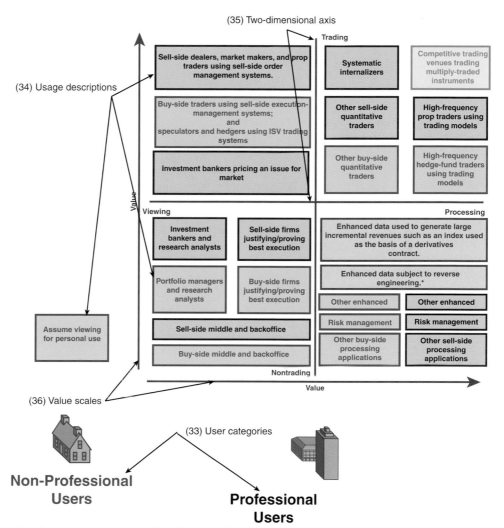

(35) Two-dimensional axis

Trading

(34) Usage descriptions

Sell-side dealers, market makers, and prop traders using sell-side order management systems.	Systematic internalizers	Competitive trading venues trading multiply-traded instruments
Buy-side traders using sell-side execution-management systems; and speculators and hedgers using ISV trading systems	Other sell-side quantitative traders	High-frequency prop traders using trading models
Investment bankers pricing an issue for market	Other buy-side quantitative traders	High-frequency hedge-fund traders using trading models

Viewing

Processing

Investment bankers and research analysts	Sell-side firms justifying/proving best execution	Enhanced data used to generate large incremental revenues such as an index used as the basis of a derivatives contract.
Portfolio managers and research analysts	Buy-side firms justifying/proving best execution	Enhanced data subject to reverse engineering.*
		Other enhanced / Other enhanced
		Risk management / Risk management
Sell-side middle and backoffice		Other buy-side processing applications / Other sell-side processing applications
Buy-side middle and backoffice		

Assume viewing for personal use

Nontrading

Value

(36) Value scales

(33) User categories

Non-Professional Users

Professional Users

* Data that can be returned to its original form through a known transformation.

Figure VG.19   The data's value is based on purpose.

access the data. The chart in Figure VG.20 shows possible user subcategories represented by different icons. The boxes surrounding the icons indicate groups using the data for trading (purple field) as opposed to those based on viewing (green field) using the same value concepts presented in Figure VG.19.

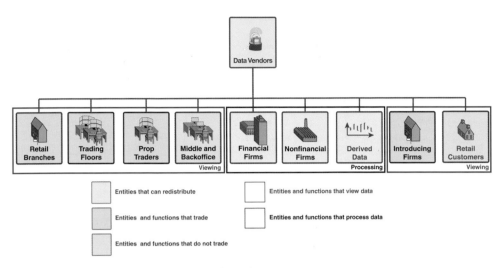

Figure VG.20 Distribution relationships based on value.

As an added piece of information, boxes with gray backgrounds indicate groups that may redistribute the data. Finally, we surround those groups that use the data primarily for processing with a red box with a clear field and those groups that view the data with a blue surrounding box.

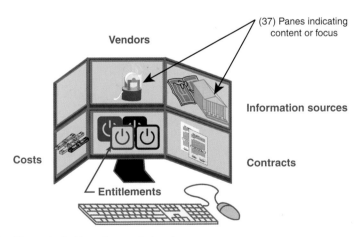

Figure VG.21 The content of inventory control systems.

In many graphics like the one in Figure VG.21, we employ the panes (37) in the display screens used by a function to describe the type of information that is the focus of attention for the function under consideration. Here, we use the panes to show the different types of content provided by inventory control services.

When describing technology organizations, we employ organization chart-like representations, as shown in Figure VG.22. The boxes (38) symbolize functions that need to be performed. We do not suggest that this is a good organizational arrangement or that any particular department within any existing firm is organized in this manner.

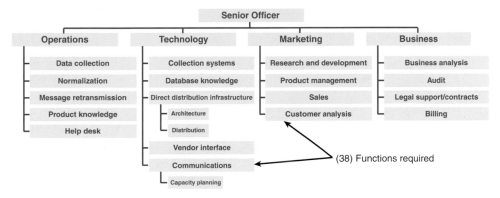

Figure VG.22 The functions an organization needs to perform.

Figure VG.23 shows a suggested model for measuring the maturity of the management process for firms that have to acquire and manage data.[2] The model presents a qualitative graph in which the level of maturity is represented by a five-level scale denoted by the rings on the graph. The bullets, which are grouped into color-coded categories, represent specific activities that should be measured. We present this as a useful way to represent data management.

2   This representation is adapted from a presentation made by Mr. Michael Atkin as a part of an EDM Council Briefing in New York on June 18, 2010.

Data Governance Strategy

Data Management Goals
- Objectives definition and verification by stakeholders
- Priorities and precedence of DM program
- Scope of data types, business areas, functions, and asset classes
- Long term and incremental outcomes (business context)

Corporate Culture
- Alignment of stakeholders on principles and objectives
- Confidence in IT, operations, and data management to deliver

Operating Model
- Executive sponsor and placement in corporate hierarchy
- Governance structure, reporting relationships, and implementation
- Measurement and benchmarking

Funding
- Total cost of ownership and funding requirements
- Business case and ROI evaluation
- Funding model, allocation, and financial accountability

Data Operations

Operational Requirements
- How business requirements are defined, verified, and translated
- Definition of core data elements
- Implementation and tolerance for disruption

Resourcing Strategy
- People, processes, and technologies needed
- Structure and management of resources
- Staff functions, skill sets, and IT resource mgt

Policies and Procedures
- Definition of functions and processes to be governed
- Promulgation and compliance

Business Process and Data Flows
- Coordination of attributes along transactions
- Dependencies, links, relationships and flow

Data Sourcing

Data Procurement
- Data requirements and mapping
- Procurement process
- Inventory of data and access points
- Usage monitoring

Vendor Management
- Contract negotiation
- Source comparison and selection process
- Quality control and vendor gap analysis
- Communication and escalation process

Data Quality

Data Quality Strategy
- Definition of levels of quality for each functional area
- Process for validating critical data attributes

Quality Assurance
- Profiling tools, tolerances, and validity checks
- Integrity monitoring and data standards
- Data cleansing and enrichment
- Data quality tracking and benchmarking
- Unique and precise tags and identifiers

Exception Management
- Management of change requests and source systems
- Error logging and root cause analysis

Data Platform and Technology

Architectural Framework
- Data storage and distribution methodology
- Architectural standards and implementation approach
- Platform for data storage and distribution
- Release management and rollback

Content Standards
- Semantic definitions and ontological relationships
- Data transformation and Extract, Transform and Load (ETL)/Enterprise Application Integration (EAI) standards
- Messaging formats and symbology

Figure VG.23 Visualization of how to measure an organization's management process maturity.

PART 3: NETWORKS

Part 3 on networks concludes what we describe as the three elements of technology. We do not believe it makes sense to describe a network for each function, unlike data and systems. Indeed, the purpose of networks is to link functions.

Therefore, in this part instead of having a subsection on functions, we present types of networks. At four points in the trading process described in Part 4, we describe the networks that link different functions engaged in trading and post-trade processing.

We return to the idea of concepts to describe information distribution strategies. In Figure VG.24 we show a strategy that involves sending all information to all users whether or not they are using the data. We employ communications symbols for routers to represent connecting nodes (39) whether or not the node is a router. (Many such nodes are routers, but we do not attempt to suggest what technology to use.) We use our "on" switch (40) and "off" switch (41) to indicate whether a user is interested in the data at the moment.

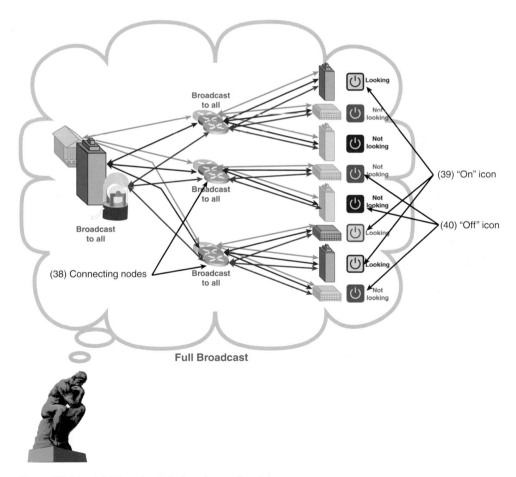

Figure VG.24   A full-broadcast strategy for sending data.

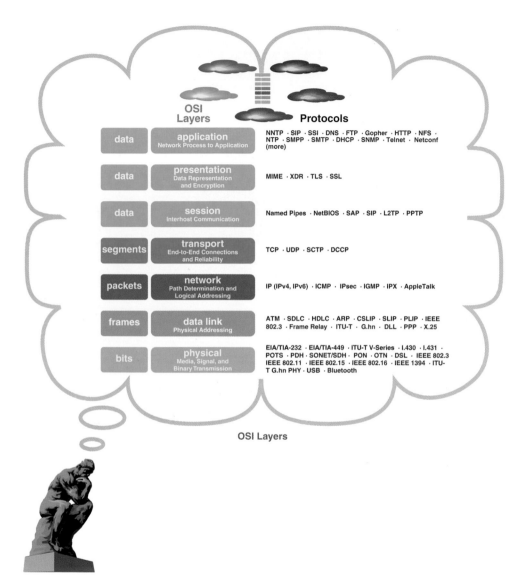

Figure VG.25 The OSI layers.

We illustrate the OSI layers in Figure VG.25. We found several different variations of this presentation method in research but could not find an original source to reference.

Instead of function-by-function representations for networks, we show different types of networks using the concept of levels. In Figure VG.26, we repeat the function (8), systems (9), and data (10) layers, all compressed with the network layer (11) below as the major focus.

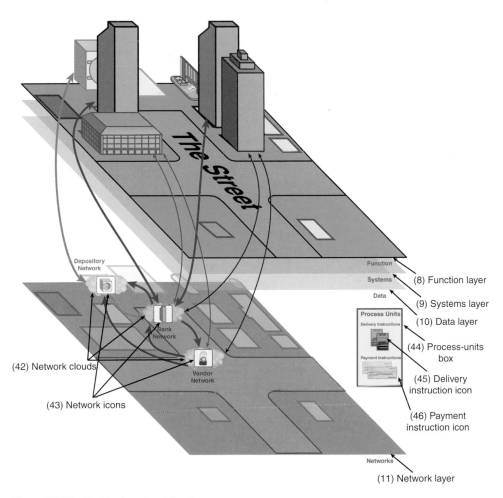

Figure VG.26 Post-trade network levels.

Network clouds (42) are color-coded and have a network owner icon (43). Each network type has a box highlighting the process units (44) that are the primary messages for networks of the type considered. (We define process units in the Background section.) In this example we have a post-trade network that carries primarily delivery instructions (45) and payment instructions (46).

We define three different types of capacity planning for networks using the illustration in Figure VG.27.[3] We use flowchart page icons (47) to represent the three

---

3   This approach to capacity planning was developed in 1997 in a project for CTA and OPRA under the oversight of the SEC. Mr. Alan Kolnik, the project supervisor, devised this planning approach. Mrs. Tamara de Dios was responsible for the graphics.

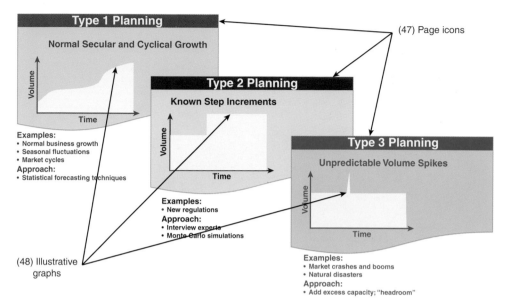

Figure VG.27   Definition of capacity planning for networks.

types of planning required. On each page there is an illustrative graph (48) showing roughly what the volume events being planned for would resemble.

PART 4: TRADING PROCESS

In the final part of the book, we examine the use of technology in the trading process. We consider only those functions directly involved in trading, and for those processes, only the technology related to the trading process.

In Figure VG.28 we return to the trading process first introduced in Book 1 and expanded in Book 2. Here, we add the systems (9), data (10), and network (11) layers below the function layer (8).

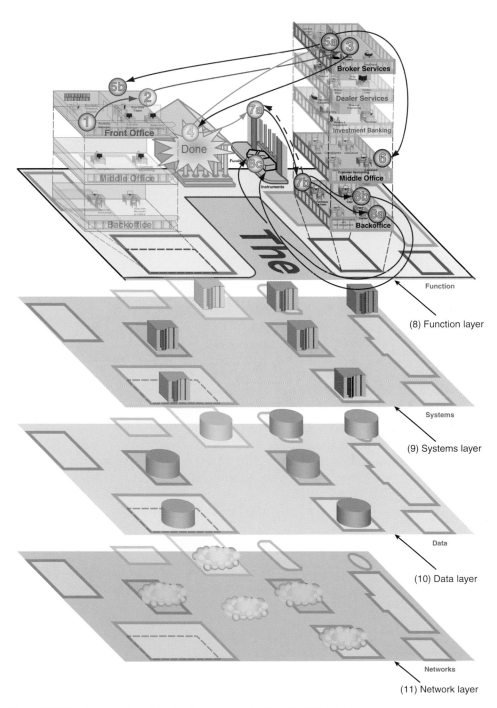

Figure VG.28   An expansion of the trading process introduced in Books 1 and 2.

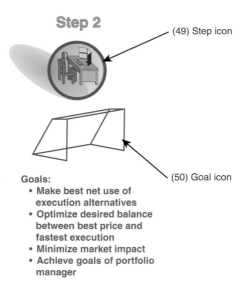

Step 2

(49) Step icon

(50) Goal icon

Goals:
- **Make best net use of execution alternatives**
- **Optimize desired balance between best price and fastest execution**
- **Minimize market impact**
- **Achieve goals of portfolio manager**

Figure VG.29   Graphical representations to explain buy-side trading goals.

For each step in the trading process, we have three different graphical representations to explain the technology. The first (see Figure VG.29) presents the step icon (49) that we have used elsewhere and a football (soccer for the United States) goal (50) to highlight the purpose of the step.

The next element in explaining each step in the trading process is to describe the subprocess involved in the step. Figure VG.30 presents the buy-side trading sub-process. An "in" box (51) and an "out" box (52) are in every diagram. Subject icons (53) are typically the focus of an activity, the process unit acted on or produced, or the data that is input to the process.

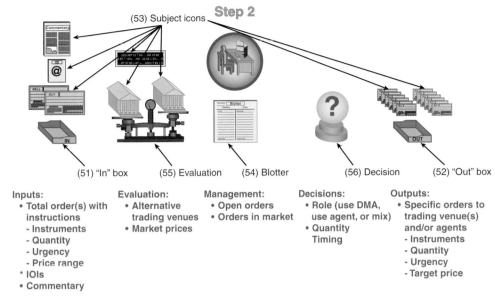

Figure VG.30 The buy-side trading subprocess.

Inputs:	Evaluation:	Management:	Decisions:	Outputs:
• Total order(s) with instructions	• Alternative trading venues	• Open orders	• Role (use DMA, use agent, or mix)	• Specific orders to trading venue(s)
- Instruments	• Market prices	• Orders in market	• Quantity	and/or agents
- Quantity			Timing	- Instruments
- Urgency				- Quantity
- Price range				- Urgency
* IOIs				- Target price
• Commentary				

There are usually icons representing the major tool for managing the process and often activity icons. The management tool here is a blotter (54), and the activity icons are a scale (55) representing an evaluation or comparison and a crystal ball (56) representing a decision.

The final element of the description of a trading process step is a summary figure like Figure VG.31 that shows the function icon (57) at the top and the systems (9), data (10), and network (11) layers below. (The function layer has been removed to simplify the graphic.)

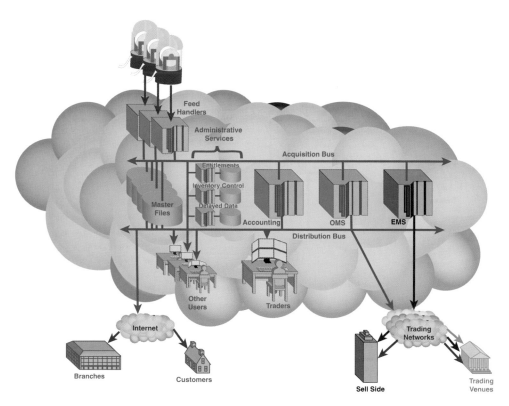

Figure VG.33 Illustration of an enterprise infrastructure.

Figure VG.34 shows a trading network. We return to the four layers highlighting the network layer (11). We show the process unit icons for orders (63) and trade reports (64).

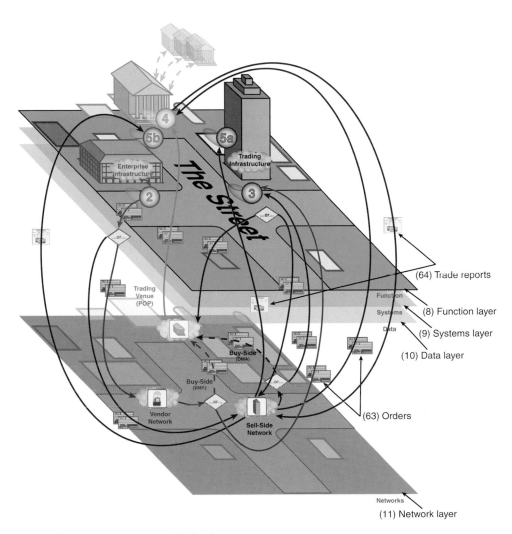

Figure VG.34   The trading network's four layers.

Systems

Part 1

For the purpose of this book, we define **systems** as the combination of computer hardware and software, usually organized for a specific purpose or to perform one or more tasks. These purposes or tasks are commonly referred to as **applications**, which individually and collectively produce the information in support of the markets. In Part 2, we explore the data that financial systems consume and produce. In Part 3, we look at networks linking systems and passing data among different functions and financial entities.

THE OPEN SYSTEMS INTERFACE MODEL AND OUR APPROACH

The International Organization for Standardization (ISO) is a global body that works toward creating standards that make all manner of commercial and technical interactions more efficient. In the late 1970s, the ISO created a model for defining how systems interact in an environment in which systems have to receive and provide information from and/or to other independent systems—a situation that is common in the trading markets.

Although we return to describe this model in Part 3 when we examine networks, we introduce it here because we extend this model to explain how systems, data, and networks interact with the functions they support.

In the next three parts of this book, we represent technology supporting the trading markets as if they are "floors" or levels that "underlie" the activities and functions they support. On the layer just below the activity, we present the systems supporting that activity. The next layer shows the types of data employed by the activity. Finally, we examine the networks connecting different activities. This representation is illustrated in the following figure.

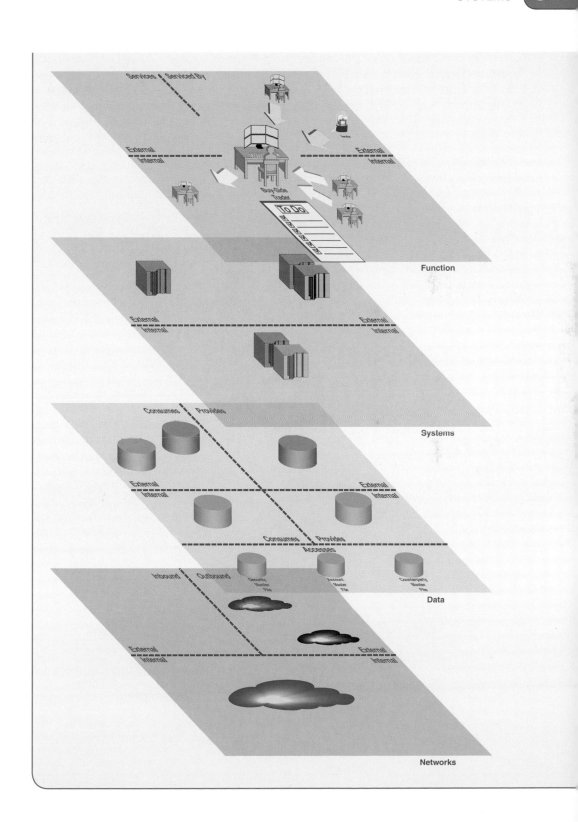

Services | Serviced By

External
Internal

External
Internal

Buy-Side
Trader

To Do!

Function

External
Internal

External
Internal

Consumes | Provides

Systems

External
Internal

External
Internal

Consumes | Provides

Accesses

Inbound | Outbound

Security
Number
File

Account
Number
File

Counterparty
Number
File

Data

External
Internal

External
Internal

Networks

As we have noted in other contexts, these distinctions among systems, data, and networks are arbitrary because they are inextricably intertwined. These three facets of the technology supporting the trading markets are extremely interdependent, and many things we put into one category arguably could be placed in one or both of the other parts.

Systems manage and produce data. Systems are linked by networks, and as the processing of data among entities in the markets becomes more tightly coupled, it is difficult to separate the networks from the applications they connect and the data they transfer.

Each time markets encounter problems the need for ever-tighter interaction among entities to permit market-wide **risk management** is demonstrated,[1] and the entire industry becomes increasingly akin to a huge interentity processing environment combining all three components.

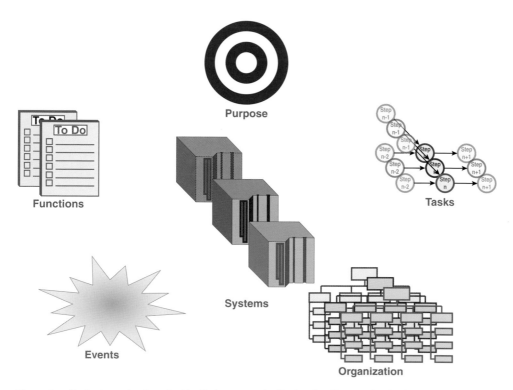

Figure 1   **Systems** can be described by their purpose, by the function they service, by the tasks they perform, by the events to which they must react, and by how an entity organizes to support the applications.

---

1   Risk management is defined in Book 4, *An Introduction to Trading in the Financial Markets: Global Markets, Risk, Compliance, and Regulation*.

Our strategy for describing systems is to group them into several categories. Our categories are but one of many ways to classify systems, and as we have said on multiple occasions in the books of this set, each schema serves to highlight some features but may mask others. Figure 1 shows the categories we use.

We examine the information (data) used for each of the functions in Part 2. Therefore, in looking at the systems in this part, we focus on what the systems *do*. The first method of categorizing systems is by their purpose. We define a **system's purpose** as the task the system must perform. We examine a number of broad purposes that might relate to systems in any industry and then relate these broad categories to specific purposes that are unique to the trading markets.

It is also useful to note that although many systems can be identified as separate applications that may be built in-house or furnished by a vendor, other processing capabilities may be a module provided by core services within firms or by procedures written using tools provided by **database management systems (DBMSs)** or using **scripting languages** to create **web applications**.

We next categorize systems by the **function** that they serve. The functional categories we use here are related to the functions we introduced in Book 1, *An Introduction to Trading in the Financial Markets: Market Basics,* such as **wealth management** (**retail brokerage**) and **buy-side traders**.

For each function we examine, we look at the systems each employs based on the system's purpose. Although we considered an array of functions in Book 1, we consider only the functions directly involved in the trading process for the buy and sell sides here.

Within our description of the systems supporting the trading functions on the buy and sell sides, we look at the specific activities that must be performed for the functions defined in Book 1. We also look at the events that can occur and that must be accommodated. In particular, we consider how the process units, introduced in the Background section, serve as inputs and outputs, and we describe the specific tasks performed on the inputs by applications supporting each function to produce the outputs.

After categorizing and describing the functioning of the systems, we consider briefly how organizations structure their systems departments to develop or purchase systems and then manage those systems on a continuing basis to make the markets function.

Purposes 1

We define eight major purposes that systems in the financial markets serve. These purposes, illustrated in Figure 1.1, are described in more detail in the other chapters of this part.

Many of the major systems within the trading markets are used, with slight variations, by entities on both the buy and sell sides. Therefore, we describe basic categories of systems and then use these categories to explain systems used by specific functions on the buy and sell sides. To the extent there are differences in systems used by the buy and sell sides, we explain those differences when we explain the systems used by functions in Chapter 2 of this part.

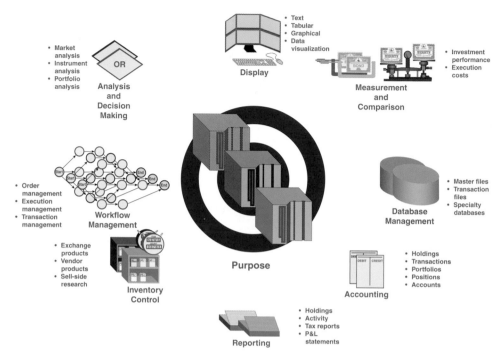

Figure 1.1 *A system's purpose* can be grouped into eight major categories.

DISPLAY AND PRESENTATION

Although display and presentation are important in many industries, the display of information on the markets and from the systems supporting trading is pivotal to decision making. A visit to an active trading room on either the buy side or the sell side shows traders and sales personnel sitting in front of workstations connected to multiple displays showing information broadcast news, tabular market data, graphical information—increasingly multidimensional ***data visualization*** presentations. The quantity of information that is a byproduct of the markets makes careful presentation of that information essential if traders and investors are to understand and act on it. Here, we break the presentation of information into four major categories.

Plain Text

The simple presentation of text from news stories, research reports, investment ideas, email messages, and many other types of information is critical to decision making and process management and control. Therefore, the presentation of raw text data and formatted text is the first presentation style.

Unlike text data in many other environments, the display of information is often presented in ***scrolling formats***. The principle is that someone directly engaged in the activities of the markets, particularly trading during frenetic periods, does not have the time to be distracted by positive actions required to access information.

Therefore, scrolling displays of prices and news are commonly provided as part of standard market-information displays.

In the 1970s, the U.S. military examined scrolling **ticker displays** and discovered that the pace of those displays tended to present information in the fastest format the human eye could distinguish. (The pace at the time was constrained by distribution technology limitations. Now much faster distribution technology requires that information be slowed to speeds that can be understood by **users**.) Moreover, the scrolling displays now popular around the edges of general news services originated with financial news services.

Tabular

The volume of quantitative information generated by the markets makes tabular displays in spreadsheet-like presentations important. Tabular displays presenting information from market-data services, databases, and workflow management systems are among the most frequently used means of presenting information on different instruments, orders, holdings, and other types of information.

Graphical

The **technical traders** as described in Book 2, *An Introduction to Trading in the Financial Markets: Trading, Markets, Instruments, and Processes,* were among the early users of stock price charts, often printed long after the end of trading. Now because of the ease and prevalence of high-quality graphical display systems, almost every user of information about any of the parts of the market depends on graphical displays to understand market events and changes. Even free services presenting information about the markets and web sites providing data on customer accounts rely on graphical displays to present information clearly and attractively.

Data Visualization

Data-visual presentation systems are increasingly being used to present complex concepts, particularly those in which many variables are at work simultaneously, in formats that allow users who understand the presentation rules to quickly grasp large quantities. Some displays represent information in three dimensions and add color, intensity, and even movement to represent the interactions of large numbers of variables.

These presentation systems, which evolved from the presentation of scientific data, are often referred to as **heat maps**, probably because of the similarity in their appearance to weather displays using different colors to represent differences in temperature and precipitation.

ANALYSIS AND DECISION MAKING

Decision-making systems are often closely linked to presentation, but decision making is increasingly being assumed by algorithms rather than by individuals acting based on information from displays. Therefore, the systems we describe here include both systems for display and systems that employ computer technology, data, and networks to implement programmed strategies. We categorize these systems in broad groups based on the philosophy of the users. These philosophies were described in Book 2.

The key to analysis and decision-making systems is the ability to assess holdings in an environment that is not affected by accounting changes that may be important for **statutory reporting**, but that do not affect or negatively affect the analysis of the portfolio or position.

PORTFOLIO ACCOUNTING VERSUS PORTFOLIO MANAGEMENT SYSTEMS

From the earliest days of automating portfolio management within organizations, there was a general belief that when accounting systems became effective, sophisticated portfolio management tools would be widely available. Early accounting systems were **batch-processing** systems that could update asset values only infrequently, often monthly.

In the past decade, accounting systems have improved dramatically. Most accounting systems process in real time and update their asset values frequently, often continuously. Nevertheless, portfolio management tools deriving their input from accounting systems have proven more difficult to create.

The major problem centers on the processing cycles introduced in the Background section. The fundamental difference between accounting and portfolio management is that the two types of systems measure results over different cycles. Accounting is focused on calendar periods—months, quarters, and years.

By contrast, portfolio management is more often focused on holding periods—the date on which the asset is purchased until the date when it is sold. Also, portfolio management often looks at market cycles that rarely conform to calendar periods. This is demonstrated in the following figure.

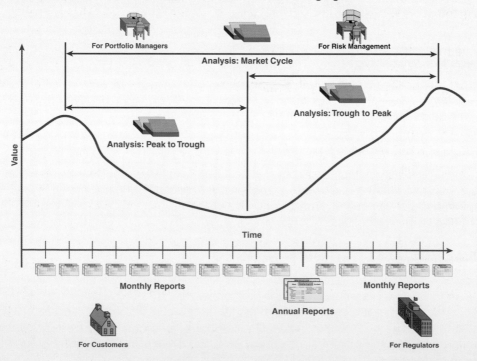

As a result of these different characteristics, portfolio accounting and reporting systems are related to portfolio management systems, but they are fundamentally different. We look at portfolio accounting and reporting in this chapter and also portfolio management.

Before we describe our three categories, it is important to note that spreadsheet software is beyond a doubt the most important analytical tool employed in the financial markets. For each of the analytical categories we discuss here, spreadsheets provide a way for users and analysts to construct bespoke analytical investigations quickly and without significant technical background.

Market Analysis

A huge variety of systems provides information about the markets that serves as input for both humans and algorithms. For humans, early market information systems were primarily designed for exchange-traded instruments (equities and derivatives), and the cost structure of these real-time systems limited them primarily to traders, and for both institutional and retail sales people.

These groups could justify the costs because the systems directly resulted in commissions and trading revenues. Beginning in the late 1980s, much more sophisticated market systems better suited to fixed income and for analytical purposes such as research, investment banking, and portfolio management began to be created.

Current market analytical systems combine the display of real-time data from the markets and supporting information such as news, research, and commentary with analytical tools that are able to evaluate situations based on a variety of strategies to support decisions "in-the-minute." Although we consider the meaning of the content in the next part on data, these systems combine information presentation with content to facilitate decision making.

For applications, particularly trading applications, there are two components to analytical systems. The first component is a set of tools that facilitates model building and testing. A number of specific tools fit within an **enterprise infrastructure** that provide these capabilities. Databases, to be described later, collect data in real time from the markets or house data sets purchased from vendors as the foundation of modeling.

Other tools provide the capability to feed data from these storage devices into models in the same asynchronous pattern found in the original feed. Complex-event tools may monitor the flow and use rules to interpret and react to the input flows. A specific model creation environment may provide the capability to develop and test new models and to tweak existing models as conditions change.

A separate environment needs to manage models in production, taking information from the markets into the models in real time and using the model(s) to generate orders back to the market.

ANALYTICAL TOOL PHILOSOPHY

Intentionally or unintentionally, most analytical tools used for either portfolio analysis and instrument selection have an underlying analytical philosophy built into the service. As we saw in Book 2, Part 1, a number of different investment strategies form the basis for portfolio analysis and/or instrument selection. These strategies tend to creep into the structure of programs; the tools available; and the way programs access, store, and manipulate information.

Although many tool vendors attempt to include the capability to employ multiple strategies, the construction of the tools frequently makes the core strategy or strategies most effective. As a result, most of the tools are optimal when the user adheres to the philosophy built into those tools.

Instrument Analysis

We noted in Book 2 that **instrument selection** is a common investment strategy, and a number of analytical tools permit users to analyze specific instruments using most common and many special tools as a part of their investigation. Many of these tools provide databases of fundamental and technical data on a wide variety of instruments. These databases permit users to perform analysis on both historical and real-time data.

For many traditional investors, instrument analysis may lead to the conclusion that specific instruments are over- or undervalued. These insights may then trigger investment decisions. In this environment, the analysis can be detached from any tools required to implement the decisions reached.

As a part of what has come to be known as high-frequency trading, quantitative investors or traders may model theoretical values for a group of target instruments, and based on these theoretical values, the models send orders to markets based on market **quotes**. When computers are involved in the trading process, the analysis and implementation tools need to be tightly coupled. Models, as they finish testing, may be quickly put into production because there is a strong belief that the new ideas will be quickly copied or neutralized by competitors.

Portfolio/Position Analysis

Portfolio managers and **position traders** need systems that provide information on holdings in a format that facilitates analysis of existing positions as well as a means to assess the impact of possible purchases and sales.

Portfolio and/or position analysis systems may offer a variety of ways to analyze a portfolio. Analysis can include the ability to perform **what-if analysis** and to assess the impact of existing and possible new positions on costs, profitability, and risks.

Portfolio management for firms engaged in some form of Modern Portfolio Theory (described in Book 2) may provide the capability to analyze **diversifiable risks** and **nondiversifiable risks** of the portfolio. Other types of analysis such as asset allocation may also be available. Analysis systems also provide the capability to compare portfolios to a **universe** of similar portfolios grouped by investment objective and investment style.

Position accounting systems and portfolio systems supporting proprietary trading and other activities involving commitment of a firm's own capital usually provide the facility to look at the profit or loss on positions. Position analysis systems often provide the ability to **roll up** the individual positions from traders within a group or department to provide managers the ability to oversee the aggregate positions in real time. Indeed, individual traders are often unaware of how their particular activities can affect or be affected by the activities of others in their trading groups.

MEASUREMENT AND COMPARISON

Perhaps more than any industry with the possible exception of sports, the financial industry and in particular the trading markets are obsessed with both the measurement of performance along a number of different dimensions and the comparison of that performance against like competitors.

Almost every publication dedicated to any phase of the financial markets provides one or more issues each year to some sort of comparison among both firms and individuals. One of the first and most well known such comparisons was created by *Institutional Investor* magazine that early in its life began to produce the "All America Research Team" based on the American football analogy. We have also noted the importance of "league tables" of underwriters using the rest-of-the-world football metaphor.

Beyond published comparisons, however, there are systems and services that perform measurement and comparison.

Investment Performance

Beginning in the late 1960s, the Association for Investment Management and Research (AIMR) issued a paper for its members in the United States recommending that customers be provided with information that measured the performance of the customers' assets in a standardized format that could be compared easily with the performance of other funds and accepted investment indexes. This initial recommendation has evolved into a global standard that many investment organizations employ.

In general, investment information—changes in asset values and income—are reduced to a periodic, usually monthly, percentage increase or decrease and/or an index based at 1.0 or 100% at the time of the origin of the management agreement. Current asset value adjusted for income can then be compared to the initial value of the assets as well as the month-on-month change.

In addition to simply measuring the investment performance of a given fund, vendors offer the ability to compare funds against groups of funds known as universes that permit a specific fund to be compared to similar funds based on investment strategy and other characteristics. We describe the nature of these universes in Part 2 when we describe different types of data.

Execution Cost

Execution costs for investors, like investment performance, can be measured and compared against universes of executions for comparable investor types. Since the concept of best execution has grown in importance because of regulatory pressures on buy-side firms, execution cost analysis has grown from a topic of incidental interest to a main concern for many fund managers.

WORKFLOW MANAGEMENT

Workflow management tools are designed to simplify a process or control the process to avoid errors, ensure deadlines are met, and track the status of activities as they unfold. In the trading markets, numerous processes involve multiple entities, and the impact of failing to complete any step in the process at the assigned time can have huge cost implications. (In Chapter 4 in this part, we describe the concept of **straight-through processing**, which requires that the trading process be carefully monitored.) Therefore, firms make extensive use of software both to control internal process steps and to monitor the steps controlled by others.

A second type of workflow control system is used both to manage complex decision rules in real time and to bind customers to intermediaries. Intermediaries provide customers with sophisticated systems for managing the execution of orders as a service that is attractive to the customer firm, but these systems also have the indirect benefit of generating transactions resulting in commission revenues. Similarly, banks, custodians, and prime brokers provide sophisticated tools for cash and settlement management. These tools are a method of service differentiation by the intermediary, and they also help in monitoring risks created by the customer.

Order Management

Order-management systems (OMS) are used by the buy and sell sides as a means of automating the process of handling orders as they are being released to the market.

The basic feature of these systems is a spreadsheet-like display of pending orders called a blotter, which we introduced in the Background section, that can be used to organize orders in whatever fashion the user finds most effective. Later, we describe more completely the unique functionality of these systems as they differ for the buy and sell sides.

Order-management systems are provided by a variety of vendors and may be developed internally at large buy- and sell-side firms. For firms, such as hedge funds and dealers, order-management software may have enhanced features (e.g., the support of internal markets) and/or AutoEx features.

Execution Management

Execution-management systems (EMS) automate the release of orders to execution venues based on rules defined by the user, by the intermediary, and/or by the trading venue that can be selected based on the user's preference or market conditions monitored by the software.

These systems permit the user to take advantage of **order-release algorithms** intended to achieve specific execution goals such as a **volume-weighted average price (VWAP)**, a **time-weighted average price (TWAP)**, or other defined targets. Moreover, the release of orders can further employ **order-routing algorithms** such as **rules-based routing** and **smart order routing**.

Transaction Management

After an execution is complete, systems monitor the successive tasks required during the clearing period up to and including settlement. Because a number of tasks must be completed, the major objective is to ensure that all these tasks are completed on time, and if not, to alert those who are in a position to initiate corrective actions.

DATABASE MANAGEMENT

In the Background section, we introduced the basic file types required by most firms in the trading markets. Some form of database management system is required to control the definition and maintenance of the details on these files. In addition to the standard master and transaction files, there are specialized database management systems optimized to handle the high-speed transactions required in quantitative trading.

Master and Transaction Files

All firms in the trading markets must have some form of database management capability related to the primary master files and transaction files required to support the activities in the trading markets. These database management systems can be internally developed, but most firms depend on systems from vendors to provide the basic capabilities.

Most major providers of generalized database management software used throughout the business community provide versions tailored to the trading markets. In addition, a number of firms provide specialized database software specifically designed for the master files employed by financial entities.

Specialty Databases

Beyond the common master files, database management systems are employed for customer information systems and for specialized research and trading data-bases. Analytical databases provide information in a format that facilitates analysis by specialized analysis tools or that easily feeds spreadsheets for bespoke analysis.

Trading databases are optimized for capturing market data that is broadcast from trading venues and storing this information for analysis and for input into trading models. Related software permits the data to be fed to trading models in the same asynchronous sequence produced by the trading venue for testing.

INVENTORY CONTROL

A number of vendors provide inventory control systems that help users track the information and services required to manage a trading operation. Related systems provide the capability to track **entitlements** that control individual users' and appli-cations' ability to access information and software. We return to these inventory systems and entitlements in Part 2 when we consider the economics of data.

ACCOUNTING

The accounting we examine in these books is accounting as it pertains to investment and trading.

We examine the holdings within an account split between instruments other than cash and cash. Moreover, the instruments other than cash are often further categorized by instrument type and sometimes by industry sector, depending on the needs of the users of the accounting information.

Investment and position accounting is the interaction of accounts and transac-tions during various processing cycles. At the beginning of a processing cycle, the value of the account is the market value of all holdings plus any cash. During the ensuing processing cycle, transactions that occur combine with changes in market values for the instruments in the account to create the value of the account at the end of the cycle.

Every type of event affecting the account typically has a unique transaction, and accounting systems are designed to process transactions and value holdings. In Chapter 4 in this part, we describe a number of important events affecting account holdings.

For investment/position accounting purposes, transactions affect the cash position, the instrument holdings, or both. Transactions for each kind of event must correctly reflect the changes in cash and/or the units of the instrument. When a purchase and sale occur, the transaction must also capture the cost of the units at the time of the purchase or sale to establish the cost basis for the transaction.

Purchase and sale transactions may also need to capture additional infor-mation or spawn subsidiary transactions to reflect commissions paid and/or the accrued interest received or paid when a fixed-income instrument is purchased or sold between interest payments.

Cash positions are influenced by contributions and withdrawals, by borrowings and repayments, and by income received for assets. Although accounts periodically have free receives or delivers of instruments, the most common changes in instrument holdings occur because of purchases or sales, maturities, deliveries, and expirations. Less commonly, holdings can change and/or increase as a result of warrants and options being exercised, by stock dividends, and by conversions.

Transactions reflect direct changes to account holdings, but the value of holdings is generally established based on market values at points established at the beginning and end of processing cycles. We describe the information used in valuations in Part 2 when we describe data. Important processing activities are required to record pricing information when valuing holdings. Moreover, when assets do not have an active market to establish fair prices, processing is involved in estimating prices such as **spreads** against **benchmarks**, as described in Book 2.

MULTI-CURRENCY ACCOUNTING

As the global economy becomes increasingly interdependent, investment managers find themselves investing more and more of their assets across national borders. This means that assets traded in different countries that are purchased with and pay income in different currencies must be integrated into a single picture of all the assets in a portfolio even if the assets are housed and denominated in different countries.

There are two major approaches to managing portfolios that span national borders. For those portfolios where the fund is primarily managed in one country and where assets from other jurisdictions are mainly an exception rather than the norm, assets purchased in other jurisdictions are generally converted into the currency of the home country at the time of the purchase, and subsequent activities such as income and capital changes are immediately valued in the currency of the portfolio for as long as the asset remains in the portfolio.

The second approach is to manage portfolios in the currencies of each asset group, handling the activities for each asset group in their native currency. When periodic reports are required, portfolios can be restated into any currency based on market values at the time of the report. This second form of accounting is much more common with large multi-national investment organizations with major portfolio holdings and often offices in multiple countries.

Within the general concept of investment and trading accounting, there are several distinct subcategories that are often serviced by the same systems. We consider these subsidiary purposes separately. The key to these categories is that each has unique accounting requirements. There is, of course, a broader concept of business accounting as is included in a general ledger for a buy- or sell-side firm, but that is beyond the scope of our investigation.

Customer

Accounting for a customer, particularly a retail customer, requires maintaining information about the customer and information about the customer's holdings within a firm. The information about customer falls into four major categories. First, the firm must document contact information that controls how the firm communicates with the customer.

Second, the firm must maintain information about the customer's preferences and requirements to ensure that all actions taken for the customer are consistent with those preferences. (For retail customers, there may also be governmental requirements that must be maintained.)

Third, particularly for institutional customers, there may be a complex array of details about the customers' internal accounts and accounts belonging to the customers with a variety of counterparties that must be maintained to allow business to operate smoothly.

Finally, many jurisdictions require that the firm maintain a record of communications with the customer that is there to satisfy both the demands of regulators and as protection for the firm if problems arise.

Customer holdings include units of instruments and products. Periodically, the holdings must be valued and the valuations must be maintained often for extended periods as required by laws and regulations.

Portfolio

Portfolios are typically pools of investment funds often managed centrally for a number of different investors. The pool can be purely internal to an investment manager as a **comingled fund** or can be the investment vehicle for a product defined below. As we define them here, portfolios are typically **long-only** investment accounts.

Position

From an accounting perspective, positions represent an investment portfolio that can have short positions and may also be leveraged in different ways. Positions are common to dealer activities. Positions require profit and loss reporting and may have tax responsibilities.

Product

Products are investment offerings in which an external investor or internal customer can invest and expect returns according to the charter or rules established for the product. A number of products have legal requirements that establish special accounting requirements for the products' customers. Mutual funds, unit trusts, and exchange-traded funds are examples of these products. But both buy- and sell-side firms may have other products that are available only for their existing customers, such as money market funds for managing excess cash balances.

Firm

Finally, all buy- and sell-side entities have to account for the holdings and cash on behalf of the firm itself. All funds and holdings for customers are grouped or pooled into accounts that exist in banks, clearing corporations, depositories, and other counterparties, and these accounts must be managed and reconciled. Moreover, holdings in these firm accounts must be mapped back to the customers, portfolios, positions, and products.

REPORTING

Remember that we have defined the generalized concept of a unit aggregation as the presentation of information that may be in either electronic or printed form. Whereas electronic presentations can take many forms determined by what is most useful and/or convenient to the user, required reports are generally specified by regulations or by the management of the organization. As such, reports have more defined characteristics.

The three primary types of reports created for customer accounts are holdings, activity details, and tax reports. Additionally, dealer positions require profit and loss reports and risk information, which is explored in Book 4, *An Introduction to Trading in the Financial Markets: Global Markets, Risk, Compliance, and Regulation*. In most cases, these reports conform to a format that is specified by regulators or is established by the management of the entity.

Holdings

Holdings reports present details on holdings, usually grouped by asset category listing the number of units of each separate asset and the market value of the asset at a specific time. Holdings reports may be in summary form listing the cumulative units and market value for each category.

Activity Details

Activity details generally provide the cumulative events occurring in an account. The initial holdings in an account adjusted by the financial events should produce the valued holdings in the account at the end of the period.

Tax Reports

Most accounts must produce documents that can be used by the beneficial owner of an account to file taxes in the jurisdiction(s) where the account is domiciled. In some cases (usually trusts and related types of accounts), the account itself is taxed and the manager must produce reports that are filed directly with the tax agent.

P&L Statements

Firms actively engaged in trading produce P&L statements to permit traders and their managers to assess performance on an ongoing basis. Moreover, these statements are usually the basis for bonuses and therefore are the basis of intense scrutiny by both traders and their managers. P&L statements are also closely related to risk analysis, described in Book 4.

Functions 2

As we noted in this book's Background section, financial entities are organized to perform the activities required in the normal course of business. Therefore, we examine the majority of the activities by examining the systems required to support the business functions defined in Book 1, Part 4. The major functions we examine are split between the buy and sell sides and are further divided among the front, middle, and backoffices on each side.

These functions are represented in Figure 1.2. Risk management and compliance are described in Book 4 and are not addressed here. Also, we do not focus on the needs of the functions involved with investment banking.

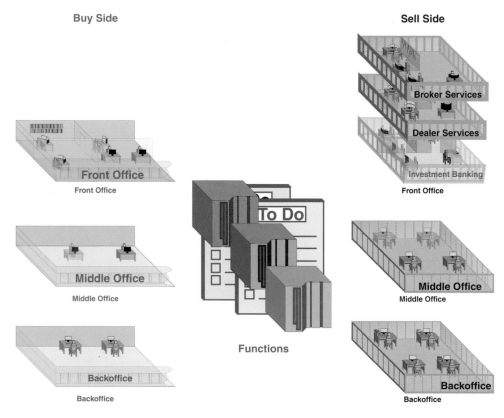

Figure 1.2 *Systems supporting business functions* enable the activities that functions are organized to accomplish.

At a more fundamental level, however, both the buy and sell sides engage in five basic activities that must be supported by technology. These activities include the need to

1. Make decisions

   a. About the attractiveness of existing holdings

   b. About the attractiveness of taking or holding principal positions

   c. About alternative holdings or positions

   d. About timing transactions based on market conditions

2. Control and monitor transactions

   a. Concerning impending and active orders

   b. Concerning the location, timing, and instructions of executions

   c. Concerning successful executions and unsuccessful orders

3. Maintain information

    a. On the instruments and holdings of the entity

        i. For static data about each instrument and holding

        ii. For activities that are planned for instruments and holdings

        iii. For instrument and holding events as they occur

    b. On customers and products

        i. For static data about each customer and product

        ii. For activities that are planned for each customer or product

        iii. For customer and product events as they occur

    c. On counterparties

        i. For static data about each counterparty

        ii. For activities that are planned for counterparties

        iii. For counterparty events as they occur

    d. On accounts

        i. For static data about each account

        ii. For activities that are planned for each account

        iii. For account events as they occur

    e. On holdings for each of the account

        i. For customers

        ii. For products

        iii. For both cash and instruments

4. Display and report information

    a. As required to support decision making and control

    b. As required for customer service

    c. As required by regulators and self-regulators

5. Manage sales and marketing

At the end of this chapter, we describe briefly generic activity-related tasks performed by systems supporting each function.

BUY SIDE

When we examine systems on the buy side, we are looking primarily at institutional investors (see Figure 1.2.1). For the most part, technology for individuals is provided on their behalf by the firms on the buy side and sell side, and is not purchased or developed by the individual.

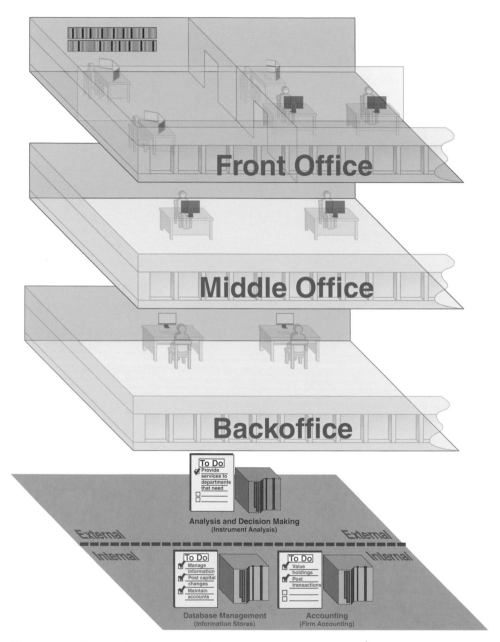

Figure 1.2.1 *The buy side* uses systems that can be grouped into support for the functions of the front, middle, and backoffices.

For institutional investors, there is much variation in the technology that is employed that depends on the regulatory regime for the particular type of firm. In general, the differences depend on the way the returns on the funds are treated for taxation and the statutory reporting requirements for the fund.

These factors vary from country to country and by type of fund. However, several basic types of systems are employed by buy-side firms that support the entire firm: the front office, middle office, and backoffice.

At a firm level, buy-side firms provide some level of analysis and decision-making systems to many functions throughout the firm. Mainly, these users get basic services such as real-time prices. Functions that need more detailed information and information related to investment style receive this directly or for the office in which they work.

Buy-side firms usually manage the information stores on a firm-wide basis. Master files are updated and changes are applied. Finally, firms manage the firm accounts with counterparties and service entities in the backoffice, but these accounting changes support accounting at every other level within the firm.

In this chapter, we are focused on the activities performed by the functions within buy-side entities. In Part 4, we return to the trading process introduced in Book 1 and expanded in Book 2 to explore how the specific systems used by each function are employed in the trading process.

Front Office

Buy-side front-office systems support the primary lines of business to facilitate investment and to provide direct customer interactions with the firm. In Book 1, we defined the functions of major entities including buy-side firms. Systems supporting portfolio managers and analysts are designed to assist in analysis and decision making.

Historically, information about customer accounts was provided through account managers who presented the information to customers and served to bind the customer to the entity. Now much information is available to customers directly through web sites providing accounting detail and information about the firm.

The buy-side front office is supported by analysis and decision-making systems. Typically, these systems are more detailed and provided in addition to systems provided firm-wide to most employees. In a small firm, these systems may be specialized based on the investment philosophy of the firm. Larger firms tend to have groups that employ many different philosophies. For these larger firms, generic services are provided to the entire front office, and specialized services are provided directly to the groups affected.

Workflow management links both portfolio managers and buy-side traders with pending and open orders, and exists at the office level.

Account systems focused on customers, investment portfolios, and products support many of the functions in the front office. We have mapped these activities across the functions defined in Book 1, Part 4, in Figure 1.2.1.1.

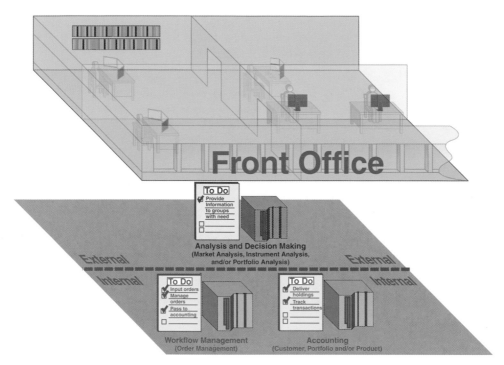

Figure 1.2.1.1 ***Buy-side front-office systems*** provide support for investment decision making and information on customer accounts as well as managing orders.

PORTFOLIO MANAGER

Portfolio managers continuously monitor the holdings that they control and consider possible changes they may make to improve the long- and short-term prospects for these holdings. The managers depend on ideas generated by the sell side, and internal research departments may engage in original analysis of their own. Changes are made taking into account customers' wishes, the views of their own firms, and regulatory requirements. Decisions, once made, along with any special instructions, must be transmitted to buy-side traders to be implemented.

To perform the requirements of their functions, portfolio managers depend on portfolio management systems to assess their existing holdings and on systems providing investment research information in electronic format from a variety of sources. Market-data vendors provide information from the markets, news, and other related information that is input to the trading process. Some portfolio managers may employ analytical software designed for instrument evaluation, portfolio evaluation, or both, but some firms prefer that portfolio managers not engage in direct analysis.

In a quantitative trading environment, the role of a portfolio manager is assumed by software. The software needs to access external sources similar to those of a human, but the way the decisions are implemented can be quite different. One

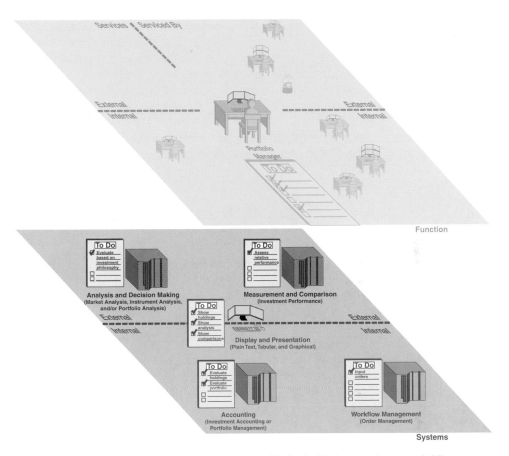

Figure 1.2.1.1.1 *Systems for portfolio managers* provide the facility to evaluate current holdings, investment ideas, and alternative investments.

manager we interviewed uses an algorithm that continuously compares existing holdings against real-time evaluations of all possible alternative instruments and decides on changes based on an evaluation of all possible alternatives using the comparison algorithms built into the model. Many different models and many alternative approaches are possible.

For those firms willing to dedicate unique functionality to portfolio management, ***portfolio management systems*** distinct from accounting represent specialized tools dedicated to managers (see Figure 1.2.1.1.1).

BUY-SIDE TRADER

Buy-side traders take decisions on *what* to buy or sell from portfolio managers and decide when, where, in what quantities, and what instructions to give to implement fundamental decisions. Moreover, because executing orders seldom occurs as a single event, buy-side traders are required to monitor the ongoing execution process and sometimes make decisions to modify or even cancel orders.

Buy-side traders depend heavily on ***buy-side order-management systems***, which are specialized versions of the general class of order-management system described in the earlier section on system purposes. Such systems that are dedicated to the buy side provide the ability to arrange orders into blotters as previously described, but also provide the ability to link to trading venues. An important feature of a buy-side OMS is its ability to filter indications of interest (IOI), searching for indications that relate to open orders. The OMS can then link the IOI to the blotters that hold the related orders and display the IOI in proximity to the related orders. Moreover, the OMS can flip the IOI, creating an order to be sent to the firm originating the IOI.

LINKING OMSs WITH DARK POOLS

An important approach to technology development occurred when ***dark pool*** *Liquidnet* used software giveaways as a means to achieve traction for its trading-venue concept more quickly. Throughout the early history of automated markets, the most difficult aspect of getting a new trading venue started was the difficulty of attracting order flow. The problem rested on the following conundrum: A new market has no existing orders on its book, but without existing orders on the book, no one will put new orders on the book.

The problem for *Liquidnet* was more daunting because the idea of a dark pool, as this type of trading venue form came to be called, was a totally new concept. (Dark pools were described in Book 2, Part 2.) The concept required that OMSs be linked to the dark pool, but OMS vendors are known for being unwilling to add new functionality unless there is strong demand from existing OMS users. Without the linkage, OMS users could not evaluate the capability of the dark pool; but without evaluating the capability, users could not demand the linkage; and without the demand, the OMS vendors would not build the linkage.

Liquidnet's solution was to build the linkages to major OMS systems for the OMS vendors, which was a radical approach for a startup company. The approach of building linkages to existing systems, including modules that have to run in those systems, suggests an important new way to gain approval for new systems and services.

In addition to OMSs, buy-side traders depend on execution-management systems that control the process of executing open orders. EMSs have become more widely used as buy-side firms increasingly depend on direct market access (DMA) to reach trading venues.

As increasing proportions of trading are electronic, the process of buy-side trading shifts from traders on phones to algorithms making trading decisions based

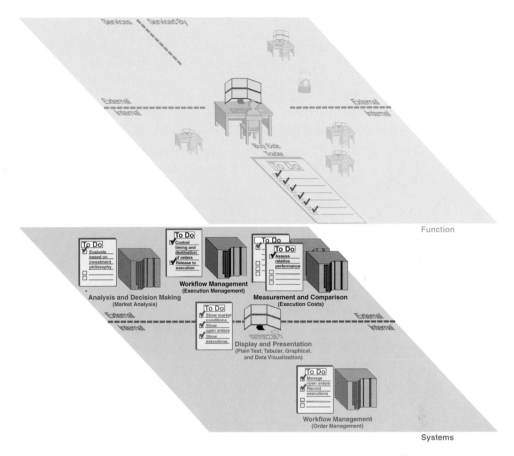

Figure 1.2.1.1.2 *Systems for buy-side traders* provide tools to assess market conditions, manage orders, and control the execution process.

on information gleaned from input streams into trading models. In this environment, it is the models that control and manipulate orders. Therefore, the conventional role of a buy-side trader changes, but the tasks of monitoring the markets, managing orders in the process of execution, and controlling the execution process continue in a different, electronic form (see Figure 1.2.1.1.2).

OMSs are usually provided by vendors or developed internally, but sell-side firms frequently provide EMSs. Because an EMS is tightly linked to executions, the required functionality is well understood by sell-side firms. Moreover, an EMS has the potential to generate commission revenues on behalf of sell-side firms.

Finally, an EMS has the potential to monitor the trading activity for firms engaged in DMA, and regulators are increasingly concerned about so-called **naked access** where **high-frequency traders** submit orders aggressively without adequate oversight. Therefore, many EMS vendors are sell-side firms that have either developed EMS products for their customers or have acquired firms to be able to provide the functionality to their customers.

RESEARCH ANALYST

Buy-side research analysts must review and synthesize ideas and research content fed to the firm by their counterparts on the sell side. In addition, they may help in the creation of buy lists that categorize the universe of potential instruments for investment into groups that are considered attractive, unattractive, and perhaps some that are unsuitable. As quantitative trading becomes a larger part of the investment process, analysts may also participate either in developing models or in creating the conceptual basis for models used in portfolio management and trading.

Research analysts need systems that provide broad and deep access to information about the markets coupled with tools that permit analysis of the information (see Figure 1.2.1.1.3). As we have noted, analysts make extensive use of spreadsheets for their analysis as well as systems that provide dedicated tools and data for evaluation of individual instruments and portfolios.

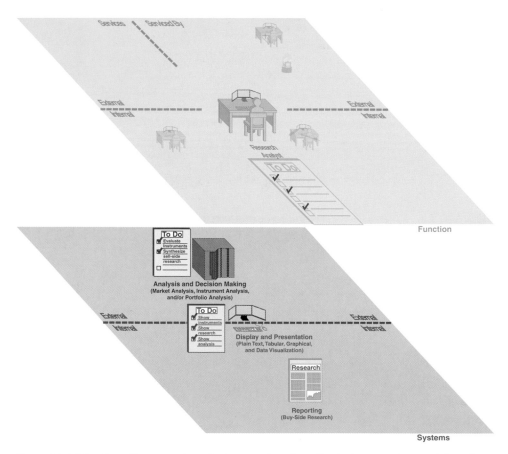

Figure 1.2.1.1.3 ***Buy-side research analysts*** use systems to synthesize investment research from the sell side, to analyze investment and trading opportunities directly, and to communicate ideas to the portfolio managers.

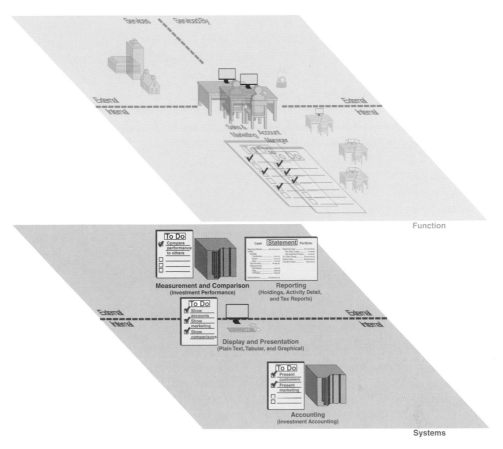

Figure 1.2.1.1.4 ***Marketing and customer managers*** use systems to interact directly with potential customers to bring them to the firm, and with existing customers to explain their holdings and answer questions.

CUSTOMER INTERACTION

Both the sales and marketing and the account management for both retail and commercial customers involve systems that present information on customers and their accounts in a form that permits easy interaction and discussion with the customers (see Figure 1.2.1.1.4).

Firms are increasingly using a software known as **customer-information systems**. This kind of software permits a process known as **data mining** to find information about customers that may be useful in order to provide additional services.

Increasingly, account managers are also under **know-your-customer obligations**. Know your customer is an evolving concept that suggests that a firm is responsible for knowing its customers well enough to be certain that a customer is not engaging in activities that might be damaging to the customer and/or that are illegal.

DATA MINING AND KNOW YOUR CUSTOMER

A classic example of the use of data mining and its implications occurred when a major national bank with offices along the Mexico/U.S. border discovered a number of simple checking and savings accounts with abnormally high values.

The finding could have signaled the opportunity to provide sophisticated investment products in retail branches to provide better returns than the checking and savings accounts offered. Alternatively, finding this pattern among accounts could also suggest the presence of either drug or terror-support funds that would need to be monitored and reported under regulations intended to stop **money laundering**.

Marketing personnel need to construct both presentations and collateral materials that explain the value and benefits of their firm's investment services and products. Unlike most commercial organizations, financial firms are under very strict guidelines to ensure that all claims made can be substantiated and that advertisements and representations are within the boundaries established by regulators.

To perform these tasks, account and marketing groups need tools that present information on customers and can analyze that information in a number of different ways. Presentation programs are used to construct one-on-one and group education on the benefits and uses of the firm's products and services.

Finally, information about the investment performance of a firm's funds and products must be available for input into publications, web sites, and presentations. For marketing, the performance of the firm's funds and products are compared to the performance of competitive funds using universes, which provide data on a variety of similar funds.

Middle Office

As we defined in Book 1, the middle office is dedicated to supporting customers through accounting/reporting and compliance (see Figure 1.2.1.2). We look at the accounting and reporting activities here. Compliance and the technology to support it are considered in Book 4.

Middle-office personnel manage the systems required by the front office. They update customer, portfolio, and product accounting systems. To do so, they employ

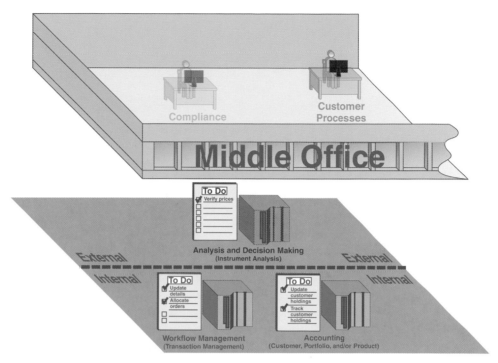

Figure 1.2.1.2 *Buy-side middle-office systems* provide information required to service customers.

information from instrument analysis systems (market data) to update transactions following execution.

CUSTOMER PROCESSES

Investment accounting and statutory reporting are aimed at informing the beneficial owner of instruments what those instruments are worth, how those instruments are performing, and what changes have happened in the account. There are two basic types of accounts, and those two types shape the type of reporting required. Funds taxed directly at the account level must report the details of account positions and activities to the taxing authority. Funds taxed directly include trusts and are often treated as if they are "individuals."

In addition to reporting to the beneficial owner, these funds must file tax returns in the jurisdiction where the funds are **domiciled**. The reporting systems for these funds often have integral tax-return-producing functionality or tax-return-producing applications that are tightly linked to the reporting software.

For non-taxed funds, any taxable income or capital returns are the responsibility of the beneficial owner after the income is distributed. Reporting to tax authorities is not required for non-taxable funds, but the fund usually reports any taxable income or gains to the beneficial owners of accounts for their personal tax preparation, often on forms required by the reporting authority. Figure 1.2.1.2.1 shows the systems supporting customer processes.

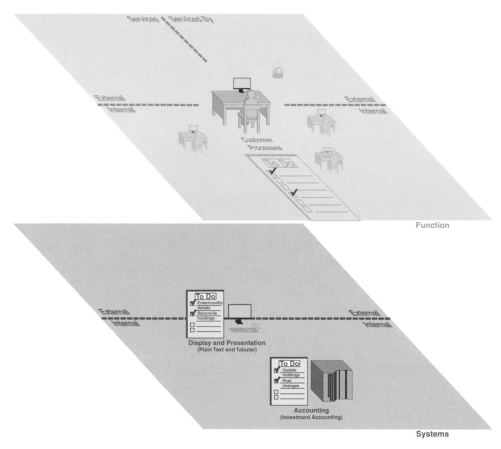

Figure 1.2.1.2.1 *Middle-office customer processes* require systems to value customer holdings and to process transactions generated by customers, by investment activities, and by corporate actions.

Funds often need to report to regulators based on the requirements of the statutes under which the funds are managed. The reporting may include the assets held by a fund, aggregate value of the fund, or units of the fund. Often funds offered to the public are required to file periodic formal reports that are registered with the regulators and sent to customers.

This information is similar in nature to the reporting required of public corporations. Over time, there is a general trend to require more reporting and for different regulatory authorities to copy one another's reporting requirements. There is often pressure from multi-national fund managers to make reporting more uniform from jurisdiction to jurisdiction so that reporting can be streamlined.

Although managers sometimes manage accounts for customers that hold individual instruments directly, most managers create internal comingled funds that manage the assets for many different individuals as if the comingled funds were internal mutual funds or unit trusts. Comingled funds are easier to manage than individual assets for investors with modest assets. From the customers' perspective, comingled funds offer the ability to diversify and to invest portions of their funds using different investment strategies with a flexibility that would be possible only for the very largest investors if the instruments were held directly.

For most types of reporting, managers must accumulate holdings for customers or accounts and then value those holdings based on market value. Funds such as mutual funds and unit trusts may be required to value units or shares daily. These valued units or shares may be published in newspapers and by market-data vendors. For most individuals and smaller pension and corporate funds, assets consist of investments in both public mutual funds and unit trusts, as well as comingled funds created by the institutional investment manager that manages the beneficiaries' assets.

Backoffice

Backoffice activities for buy-side firms require monitoring transactions and their effect on aggregate holdings in the name of, or on behalf of, the entity itself (see Figure 1.2.1.3). The aggregate holdings are then mapped to products and accounts by the middle office. Smaller firms may cede most of this activity to custodians (for traditional firms) or prime brokers (for hedge funds). Using our definitions, holdings accounting manages accounts.

Securities movement and control handles the processing of transactions between the decision to trade and settlement. Although both of these functions must be performed, there are many ways to organize the activities that comprise these functions.

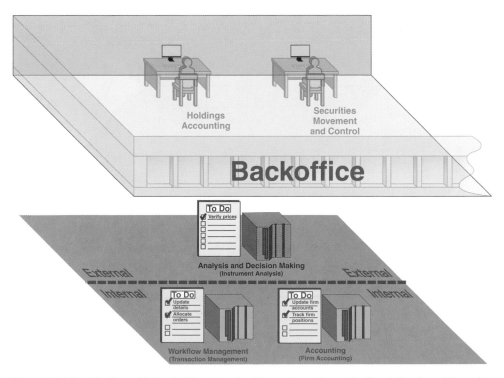

Figure 1.2.1.3 *The buy-side backoffice* interacts with counterparties on the Street directly and through custodians.

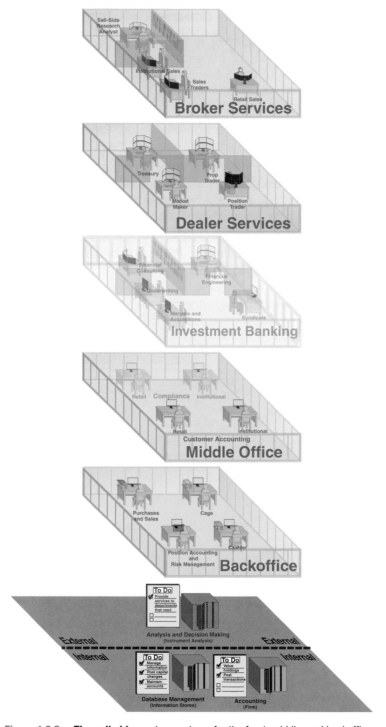

Figure 1.2.2   *The sell side* requires systems for the front, middle, and backoffices.

On a firm-wide level, sell-side firms provide instrument analysis (market data) information to all individuals who have responsibilities that require knowledge of market prices for individual instruments.

Many firms either provide database management services for the basic information stores (master and transaction files) on a firm-wide basis or coordinate regional management. A firm's accounts involve aggregate holdings, which must be related or mapped to the holdings of customers, trading positions, and products. We are defining this mapping as a middle-office activity.

Front Office

The front-office systems we investigate support the two primary roles of a broker and dealer (see Figure 1.2.2.1). We are not examining the support for investment banking. Although we defined a number of different functional tasks in Book 1, Part 4, many of those functions use the same or similar systems.

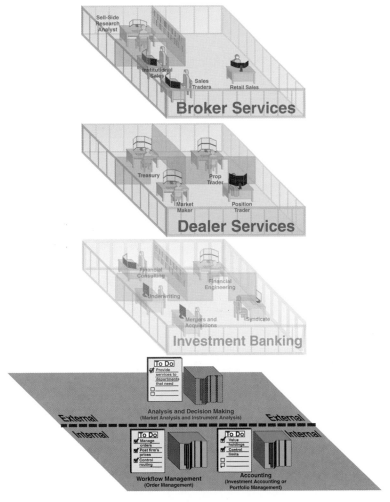

Figure 1.2.2.1 *The sell-side front office* employs systems supporting the roles of broker and dealer.

For the entire front office and particularly for broker and dealer operations, systems linking the two operations are provided at the front-office level. (Remember, we are not addressing investment banking systems directly.) Workflow management links all trading departments with the markets, often flowing through position traders who control aggregate positions and instrument prices the firm offers to customers. Position accounting at the front-office level manages overall positions and controls **limits** on principal positions.

BROKER

In the role of broker, there are functions that provide sales for both retail and institutional customers (see Figure 1.2.2.1.1). Sales traders manage the execution process on behalf of institutional customers. Research analysts investigate investment opportunities to create trading ideas for both retail and institutional customers.

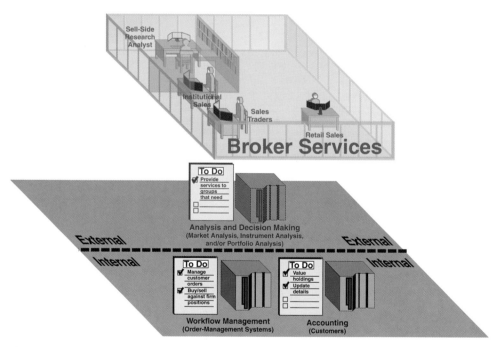

Figure 1.2.2.1.1 *The sell-side brokerage operations* require systems for those supporting customers primarily in an agency role.

Sell-side brokerage operations access information needed to understand and react to conditions in the markets on an ongoing basis. Order-management systems accept new orders and control how those orders are directed to the markets or against the firm's positions depending on the policies of the firm, regulatory requirements, and the customer's instructions or wishes. The brokerage operations focus primary accounting attention on customers.

Retail/Institutional Sales

Retail sales started as a way to sell stocks and bonds to individual investors for commissions. The business model has evolved to serve as an asset manager offering comprehensive money management services at lower costs to individuals usually with assets too small to be of interest to most investment managers. Therefore, retail investors must record and report the assets under the broker/dealer's management, including cash and money market funds, individual security positions, or packaged funds provided by the broker/dealer, and mutual funds offered by other packaged-funds providers.

Typical information is available on the Internet, and provides valued positions, summaries of transactions, and aggregation if the customer has multiple accounts, such as investment accounts and retirement accounts. In addition to normal reporting, the broker/dealer provides necessary information that permits tax reporting as required for the customer's tax jurisdictions.

Institutional sales departments of broker/dealers manage the relationship with institutional investors (see Figure 1.2.2.1.1.1). Institutional investors deal with multiple broker/dealers; therefore, they use custodians to maintain their holdings, usually at a depository, and consolidate their transaction information from multiple broker/dealers. Consequently, the broker/dealer is responsible for interacting with the custodian during the settlement process to ensure that funds and transfer instructions are in place to facilitate the settlement process.

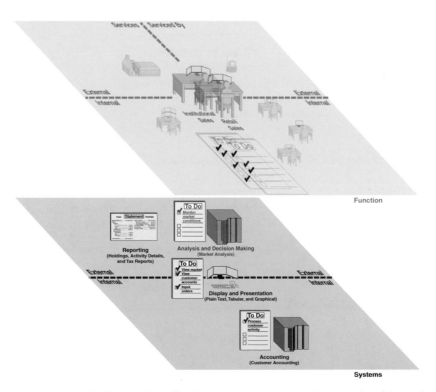

Figure 1.2.2.1.1.1 *Institutional and retail sales* use systems to support the promotion of the products and services of the firm to customers.

Institutional sales, although they do not need to manage the holdings of their institutional customers, nevertheless maintain detailed information on each customer, their account details, and all settlement instructions. Modern trading is far too intense to require this information be entered every time an institution trades.

In addition to managing account details, most sophisticated broker/dealers maintain records of the trades they execute with a customer, and sell-side firms attempt to keep a record of all communications the broker/dealers receive from the customer, indicating an interest in buying or selling a specific instrument. These records permit broker/dealers to identify potential counterparties whenever they get an order from one of their other customers. We see in the order routing portion of the trade process how this information is used to generate trades.

Sales personnel need systems to access customer information and the status of customer activities. One of the problems created by the structure of the sell side is an insular or silo structure of relationships with customers. As a result, groups selling derivatives, equities, and fixed income may have completely independent views of the same customer and may sometimes sell at cross purposes. Firms are working to build systems that help to remove these conflicts.

In addition to information on customers, the sell-side sales activities also need to monitor market conditions and the products and research recommendations of their firm. In some cases, the sales personnel are called upon to encourage transactions and in other situations to promote new investment banking offerings. All these activities have the potential for abuse and conflicts of interest, and we see in Book 4 that compliance actively monitors the sell-side selling activities.

Sales Trader

We distinguish the sales trader as the order-placement function within the selling processes at sell-side firms. A sales trader either directs a simple order to a trading venue using rules established by the firm or, increasingly, through an algorithm-driven routing system that can send the order to multiple markets using real-time data on market conditions to satisfy best-execution obligations (see Figure 1.2.2.1.1.2).

Larger, more complex orders are typically sent to position traders who coordinate executions using multiple markets, perhaps inviting participation by other customers as well. Buy-side traders need good information about market conditions, they need access to customer details, and they need input into the order-routing system for the firm.

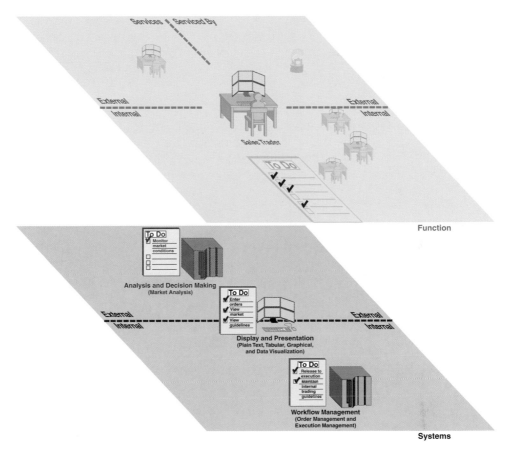

Figure 1.2.2.1.1.2 ***Buy-side traders*** use systems to route customers' orders to trading venues or position traders depending on the nature of the order.

Research Analysts

Sell-side research analysts perform many of the same functions as their buy-side counterparts, but they do not perform any synthesis functions and they have much more aggressive objectives to produce in-depth research reports and ongoing investment ideas for the firms they follow. They may also have the responsibility to communicate their ideas and analysis on a continuous basis using both in-person and electronic communications channels.

Although sell-side analysts employ many of the same systems tools as the buy side, they also need direct communications tools and document publishing capabilities (see Figure 1.2.2.1.1.3).

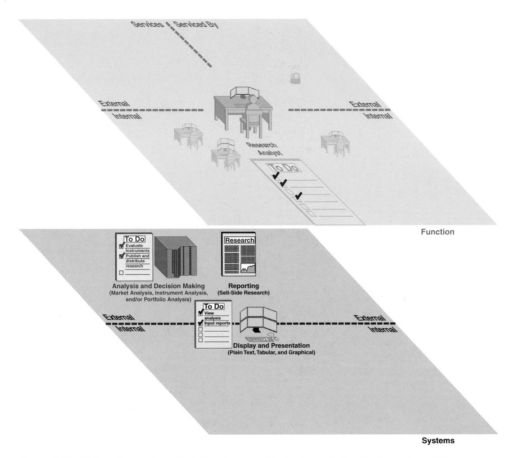

Figure 1.2.2.1.1.3 *Research analysts' systems* provide for the analysis of instruments and the distribution of ideas to customers.

DEALER

Here, we have separated the roles of dealer from those of broker because of the structure we established in Book 1 (see Figure 1.2.2.1.2). However, in actual trading environments, the two functions are not distinct, and in fact, the same person may move freely back and forth between the two roles throughout a trading day. The functions we list here are usually dedicated activities requiring dedicated systems support.

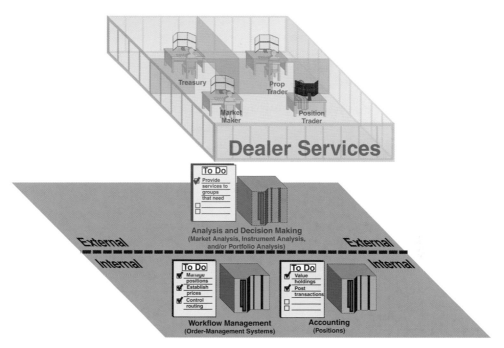

Figure 1.2.2.1.2 *Sell-side firms acting as dealers* require systems to support principal trading.

Sell-side principal or dealer operations access information needed to understand and react to conditions in the markets on an ongoing basis. Order-management systems accept new orders and control the firm's principal positions based on the requirements of the trading venue(s) if the firm is an official market maker.

The order-management system may also maintain the firm's official prices and inventory if the firm is acting as a dealer in individual instruments. The OMS may be connected directly to trading venues using transactional feeds (described in the Part 3 on networks) that permit orders and quotes to be entered directly onto the **book** of the trading venue. The dealing operations focus primary accounting attention on positions and instruments.

Position Traders, Dealers, and Market Makers

Position traders, dealers, and market makers are traders whose primary responsibility is to manage instrument positions on behalf of the firms they represent (see Figure 1.2.2.1.2.1). (Other traders are usually responsible for or focused on customers.)

In this role, they have the responsibility of establishing the price at which the firm is willing to buy (the bid price) or sell (the offer price) any instrument, and the maximum quantity the firm is willing to hold on both a temporary basis (usually intraday) and for longer periods.

Although we are considering trading support systems here, these functions are also involved in managing the risks for the companies' trading activities and are discussed again in Book 4. To this group, we add proprietary traders who have a role that seems similar to portfolio managers—managing portfolios—but unlike portfolio

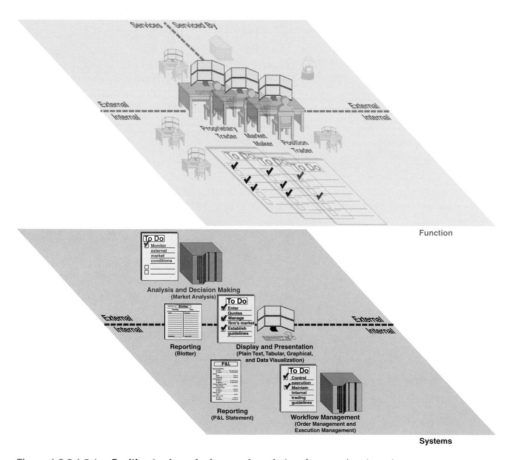

Figure 1.2.2.1.2.1 *Position traders, dealers, and market makers* need systems to manage open orders, to generate and distribute quotes, and to maintain and monitor positions.

managers, proprietary traders trade their positions much more aggressively, focusing on short-term, volatile opportunities arising from information the firm acquires from activities in the markets. Also, unlike traditional portfolio managers, proprietary traders often establish short positions.

Sell-side position traders, dealers, and others focused on instrument positions use **sell-side order-management systems** that are conceptually similar to those used by the buy side but differ in specific functionality. For example, sell-side traders managing firm positions and dealers may need to establish position limits, disseminate quotes, and monitor the aggregate positions of traders, which are functions not required on the buy side.

Middle Office

We define the middle office to include those activities in support of the front office that are oriented to customers (see Figure 1.2.2.2). We describe the accounting and reporting support systems here and leave compliance to Book 4.

Middle-office systems support the front office. Middle-office personnel may require market data to the extent they deal with instruments and in particular may use **time-and-sales** services to answer customer questions and validate trades. Transaction management systems handle the customer side of the clearing and

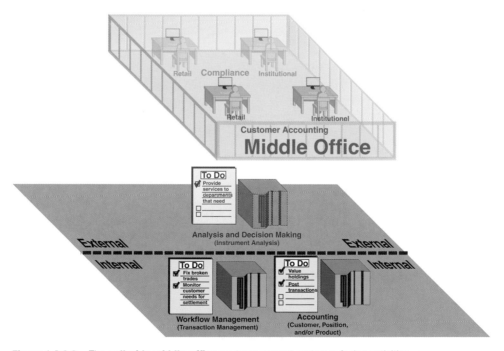

Figure 1.2.2.2 The **sell-side middle-office systems** support customer-facing activities.

settlement process and prepare customer accounts for settlement. Accounting systems support customers, positions, and products managed in the front office.

CUSTOMER-SIDE PROCESSES

Customer-side activities are very different for retail and institutional customers of the sell side. Retail brokerage or wealth management, as it is coming to be called, is increasingly focused on managing assets for a fee that is based on assets-under-management rather than for commissions for transactions. As a result, customer-side systems must manage and report on both instruments and funds owned by the customer and left in the **street name**.

Institutions most often either manage their own holdings or, more likely, entrust holdings to custodians. The sell side has a primary responsibility to institutional customers to participate in the **allocation process** and **affirmation process**. These two processes are explored in Part 4 when we examine how technology is employed in the trading process.

Wealth management requires software that tracks each customer's holdings, mapping those holdings to the aggregate positions of the firms at custodians and agent banks. The software must maintain and value holdings in cash and instruments and must be able to process trading activities, corporate actions, and **margin financing**.

One special service for retail customers is a **cash management account** that operates like a sophisticated checking or demand deposit account. For broker/dealers that are not commercial banks, these services are offered through commercial banks that manage the linkage to the funds transfer system that is usually open only to commercial banks.

The product system for these accounts must maintain additional (to normal trading account information) customer data to handle the information that customers demand and that the servicing commercial bank requires. For example, the system must manage ordering checks that the customer can use in normal commercial transactions.

The account may also offer credit or debit cards that can be used in normal retail transactions. The system must also permit linkage to commercial bank accounts to facilitate transfers of funds and other banking services (see Figure 1.2.2.2.1).

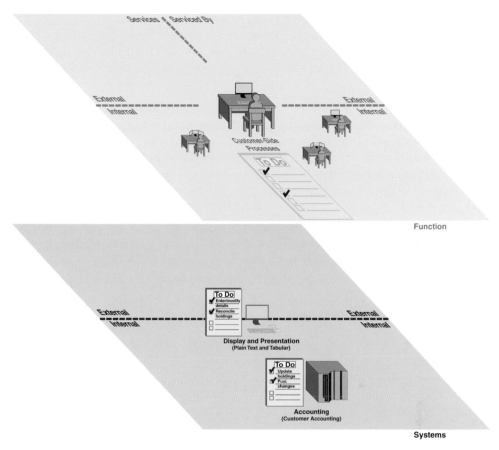

Figure 1.2.2.2.1   *The sell-side's middle-office customer-side systems* primarily support retail customers but must also handle the allocation of institutional executions to incoming orders and accounts.

We have noted that firms must handle allocations and affirmation, but there are two other types of specialty processing for customers. ***Prime brokerage*** is the name given to services provided by investment banks to hedge funds. ***Correspondent services*** are provided when an investment bank provides trading, clearing, settlement, and processing services to another broker/dealer.

PRIME BROKERAGE

Broker/dealers provide services to hedge funds that are analogous to those provided to regular institutional investors by custodian banks. The ***prime broker*** manages holdings for the fund either directly or through a custodian bank. The prime broker also consolidates trades done by the hedge fund through other broker/dealers. The prime broker helps finance the trading activities for the hedge fund, which is particularly important because hedge funds frequently employ leveraged trading.

A critical part of the role of a prime broker for a hedge fund is to monitor the risk undertaken by its hedge fund customers to ensure that the hedge fund does not endanger itself or the prime broker. Prime brokers often facilitate technology used by the hedge funds it services to ensure uniformity of technology and to reduce costs.

CORRESPONDENT SERVICES

Large broker/dealers often provide **correspondent services** to other, usually smaller, broker/dealers that permit the small broker/dealers to avoid part of the costs of being a broker/dealer. We noted earlier that a broker/dealer does not need to be a direct member of either an exchange or a clearing corporation. When a firm elects not to belong to either the exchange, the clearing corporation, or both, it relies on a correspondent to provide the services it does not want to perform directly.

There are also two major types of accounting services that can be offered. With **omnibus accounting**, the correspondent broker/dealer provides only Street-side processes, whereas in **fully disclosed accounting**, the correspondent manages the customer accounts as well. Next, we look at these two types of accounting in more detail.

Omnibus Accounting

In omnibus accounting, the correspondent provides accounting services that permit the customer broker/dealer to avoid some of the tasks required to trade in a market. In the case of a firm that is not an exchange member, the correspondent trades on behalf of the customer firm using the correspondent's exchange membership. The customer firm sends orders to the correspondent firm, and the firm handles all the trading processes for the customer firm.

If the customer firm is an exchange member, the customer has to meet all the capital requirements of trading in the market for its own account, but in the case of a physical market, the customer firm may not want to maintain an office in the exchange city and will use the correspondent firm's trading staff. If the customer is not a clearing member of the clearing corporation, the correspondent manages the clearing process on behalf of the customer firm.

If the customer firm trades but uses a correspondent for clearing, the customer firm **gives up** the name of the correspondent (i.e., adds the correspondent's clearing identification to the trade record) when the trade it is submitted for clearing. Finally, in the case of over-the-counter (OTC) transactions, the correspondent firm may do some or all of the trading and settlement process for the customer firm.

Fully Disclosed Accounting

Fully disclosed accounting means that the customer records are maintained on the books of the correspondent, not the firm that has the customer relationship. Therefore, the customer firm is known as an **introducing broker**, and the correspondent is known as the **carrying broker**. In the futures markets a carrying broker may be known as a **Futures Commission Merchant** or **FCM**.

When the individual customer receives his or her periodic account statement, the statement is on the letterhead of the correspondent (i.e., the carrying broker). When a firm chooses to act only as an introducing firm and does not carry customer accounts, its capital requirements are lower, and the firm does not have the expense of maintaining a customer accounting system.

Backoffice

In addition to accounting for customer holdings, a broker/dealer has to manage the relationship with the Street (see Figure 1.2.2.3). Street-side processing involves four primary relationships:

1. The direct relationship with all exchanges and market centers where the broker/dealer trades;

2. The relationship, usually as a customer, with market centers that are organized as a broker/dealer;

3. The relationship with other broker/dealers that trade in the market; and

4. The relationship with the clearing corporation.

As we saw in the section on correspondent broker/dealers, a firm can either provide for these services directly or choose to be serviced by a correspondent and thus outsource the responsibilities to the correspondent.

Sell-side firms provide market data to most groups to correlate market prices with the settlement process. Transaction management systems control the pre-settlement, settlement, and post-settlement process through successful completion or until problems are resolved. Managing the firm's accounts requires tracking holdings in instruments and cash held for the firm by counterparties and support entities.

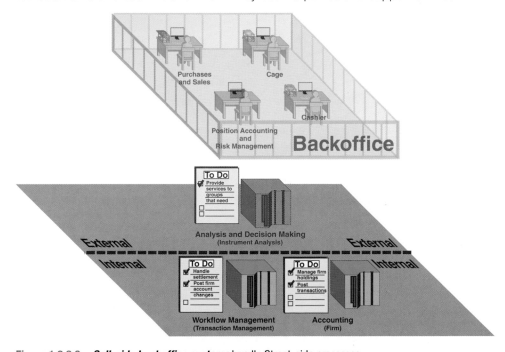

Figure 1.2.2.3   *Sell-side backoffice systems* handle Street-side processes.

PURCHASES AND SALES

In the Background section, we introduced the concept of a purchase or sale as an event because although a firm initiates a purchase or sale, the firm cannot control the actual execution of the price it receives or must pay. (We return to consider purchases and sales as instrument-related events later.) However, sell-side firms establish departments frequently titled purchases and sales (P&S) to handle the activities that are required immediately following an execution. The firm must relate the details of the actual execution (both price and quantity) to the order that precipitated the execution.

Moreover, when problems occur, such as errors in the details of the trade in physical trading or **trade breaks** for whatever reason, the P&S department is responsible for initiating corrective action. The tool that the P&S department usually employs to correct problems is to put the financial responsibility for the broken trade on the P&L of the group or department that is best able to correct the problem. Having a problem trade on the P&L of a department or group ensures swift action because the trade has the potential to negatively impact profits and thus bonuses.

The P&S department needs process control software to track trades through the clearing process to the point where other groups take responsibility for settlement. The system needs to interface with the OMS and with the clearing facility if one exists (see Figure 1.2.2.3.1).

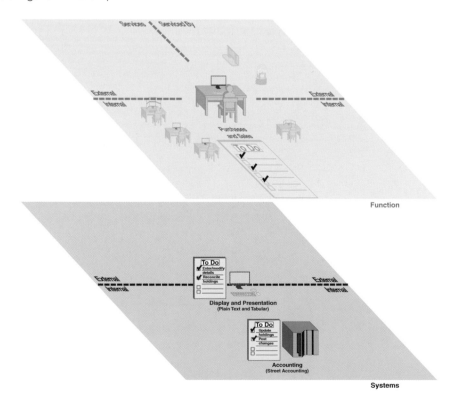

Figure 1.2.2.3.1 *Purchase and sales systems* manage orders and executions matching the order to the execution and tracking errors in details and trade breaks until they are resolved or allocated to the responsible department.

THE CAGE

The cage is responsible for instrument holdings for the firm, monitoring instrument positions both at the firm's bank(s) and at depositories. The cage must prepare instruments or delivery instructions in anticipation of settlement and may be called upon to borrow securities (a process known as a ***stock loan***) if customers do not provide instruments for settlement on a timely basis.

Most sell-side accounting software has a dedicated cage capability (see Figure 1.2.2.3.2).

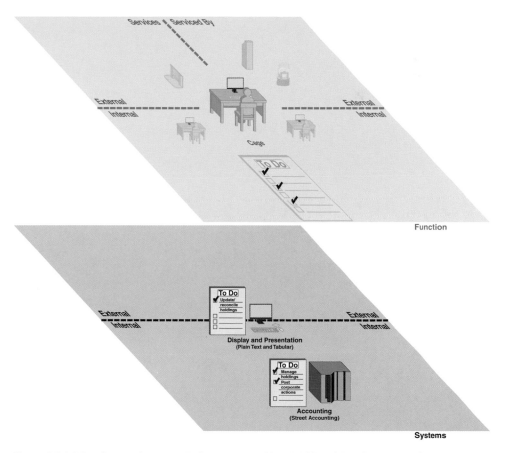

Figure 1.2.2.3.2 ***Cage software*** tracks instrument positions held in safekeeping at agent banks and manages instrument positions for delivery (a sale) or receipt (a purchase) during settlement.

THE CASHIER

The cashier is responsible for managing and monitoring cash positions. This includes monitoring all positions in the banks the firm uses as well as cash generated by and required for transactions, including projecting cash requirements or needs in advance of settlement. The cashier may be responsible for arranging cash loans from banks and coordinating borrowings with other financing techniques such as **repos** (see Book 2) in conjunction with the firm's **treasury department**.

Most accounting systems have cash management functionality, and many major banks that service the sell side provide **cash management services** and systems (see Figure 1.2.2.3.3).

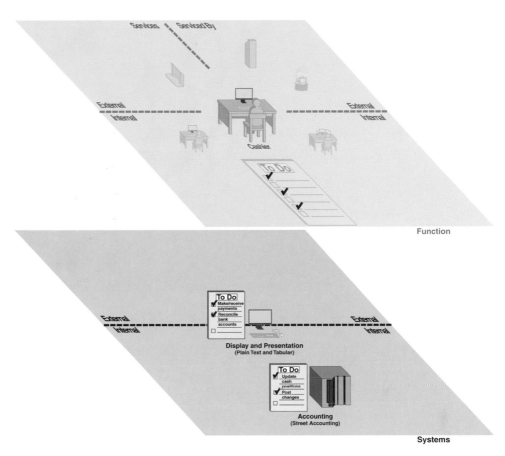

Figure 1.2.2.3.3 *Cashier systems* manage cash positions held by agent banks and prepare for receipts (a sale) or payments (a purchase) during settlement.

The tasks performed in conjunction with systems that support the functions developed to support the activities in the trading markets are common to all software systems, but financial firms have unique requirements for many of these tasks (see Figure 1.3).

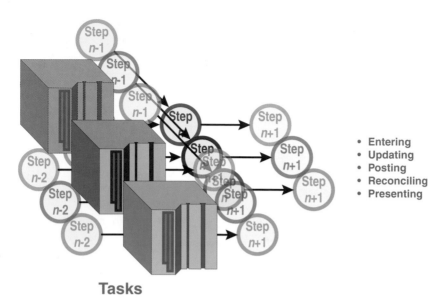

Tasks

- Entering
- Updating
- Posting
- Reconciling
- Presenting

Figure 1.3   **All software** performs five basic tasks in support of the trading markets.

ENTERING

Entering information into financial software is a source of major problems and the primary cause of data errors. (A sidebar in Part 2 on data recounts a problem that manual data entry created.) Therefore, firms invest in developing entry capabilities that check and verify the information entered, but more significantly there has been a long-running effort to source as much of the information required either from automated processes that can capture information without the possibility of data errors or from vendors that undertake the entry, verification, and update tasks as a primary business activity.

UPDATING

Obviously, after information is entered into the systems, the information must be updated. Much regulated information is required to be updated for filings and other reporting requirements; this is an indirect requirement to keep data fresh. As with data entry, updating information is a source of errors and is automated to the extent possible.

POSTING

All transactions, and many of the events described in the next chapter, must be posted to accounts, portfolios, and positions. Historically, the financial markets have operated assuming a processing day of a fixed length, and all the posting, updating, and maintenance required to support the systems used by the markets occurred after the processing day ended and prior to the start of the next business cycle.

There has been a slow evolution to business cycles of increasing lengths with after-hours trading and early trading sessions. This puts an intense strain on traditional methods of processing, and it is likely that systems will have to develop approaches that permit continuous cycles throughout the business week.

RECONCILING

Inevitably, multiple closely linked systems develop inconsistencies among data sets that should agree. A major system activity therefore consists of comparing these data sets, identifying inconsistencies, determining the reason or cause of the problems, and correcting those elements that are in error. As with all other tasks, the goal has been to minimize the number of situations in which errors can occur and to automate both the problem identification procedures and the error correction processes to the extent possible.

SYSTEMS PROBLEMS IN A CONNECTED WORLD

Reconciling has become ever more complex. Historically, systems were distinct, and it was a straightforward, if not simple, matter to find an error and trace the cause back to a flaw in data or of logic and then correct the problem. Now, as systems are more interconnected, problems may not stem from the system where the problem is observed but may come from other systems within the same organization or even in other organizations.

We noted at the beginning of the Background section that there has been layering of systems, some dating from the early days of market automation. In many cases, no one remembers the source of the logic of older systems, yet the cost of replacing older systems causes them to persist long beyond a reasonable life. The results are periodic bizarre occurrences that are never fully explained.

PRESENTING

Information, once it has been entered, updated, posted, and reconciled, is ultimately presented whether as a printed report, a visual display, or, ever more commonly, as input into some subsequent process that results in an automated reaction to its substance. It is this display or further processing that is the ultimate purpose of the systems that underlie the trading markets.

Events 4

As we defined them in the Background section, events are external happenings that an entity must react to but that are not controlled by the entity (see Figure 1.4).

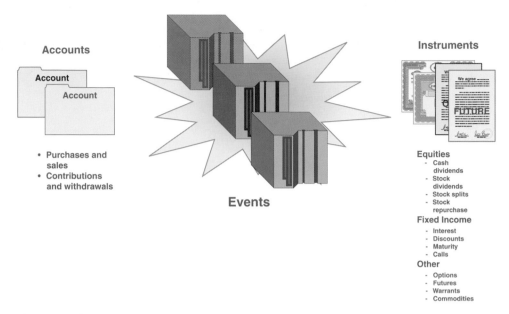

Accounts

Account

Account

- Purchases and sales
- Contributions and withdrawals

Events

Instruments

Equities
- Cash dividends
- Stock dividends
- Stock splits
- Stock repurchase

Fixed Income
- Interest
- Discounts
- Maturity
- Calls

Other
- Options
- Futures
- Warrants
- Commodities

Figure 1.4 *Systems in the trading markets* must handle events occurring outside the firm that affect accounts and holdings.

ACCOUNTS

When money is put into an account or paid out, the overall value of the portfolio changes by the amount of the infusion or payment, changing the overall value of the portfolio. Less commonly, assets can be contributed to a portfolio or removed from the portfolio directly. These are the only types of transactions that change the value of a portfolio *directly.* The value of the portfolio changes *indirectly* as the overall market value of the assets in the portfolio changes. In principle, these are the only events that change the value of the total account or portfolio.

Cash into or out of the portfolio generally has to be recorded based on how the money is received or disbursed. Differences are important for the management of the account, but for most accounts there are tax implications no matter whether the account is taxed directly or simply reported to the beneficial owner who handles taxes in some manner that is external to the account. In particular, income (from dividends and interest), capital gains (from the change in market price that is ***realized*** by a sale), contributions, and withdrawals are recorded and reported back.

INSTRUMENTS

All assets are affected when an instrument is purchased or sold. However, as we learned in Books 1 and 2, instruments are subject to a variety of other events, which are controlled by the issuing entity and affect every investing or trading entity that holds positions in the instrument. We consider a number of these events here.

Purchases and Sales

When an asset is purchased, the holdings of the asset increase by the units purchased, whereas the cash in the account or portfolio decreases by the value of the asset times the number of units plus any fees or commissions paid for the transaction. A purchase or sale results in an increase (purchase) or decrease (sale) in the quantity of the instrument in an account or a portfolio. There is a corresponding decrease (purchase) or increase (sale) in the cash account. For both purchases and sales, there is a decrease in cash equal to the amount of commissions or fees.

Equities

Common financial events affecting equities include **dividends**, **stock dividends**, **stock splits**, **stock repurchases**, and **warrants**. Each of these events must be recorded and may increase cash or assets. Equities are perpetual securities, lasting as long as the company that issues them. In principle, payouts from equities are deducted from the value of the instruments, and thus, the instrument and payout have the same value after the payout as before. Investors hope to participate in the success of a firm over time either through direct disbursements of income (dividends) or through increases in the market value of the asset.

CASH DIVIDENDS

A cash dividend is income paid by a company as a means of sharing profits with stockholders (owners). The dividend is treated as income.

STOCK DIVIDENDS

A stock dividend provides additional shares usually in a fixed ratio with the number of existing shares an owner has. The usual assumption is that if a company is doing well, in time the added shares will provide incremental value, yet the company does not have to pay out cash. Usually, the stock dividend increments the assets but is not treated as income unless it is sold.

STOCK SPLITS

Sometimes, when the price of a share of stock becomes too expensive, the stock splits in some ratio of old shares to new shares in an effort to lower the market price. Companies generally believe that share prices need to be at a level that makes wide ownership easy. Sometimes shares fall too low and there is a **reverse stock split** in which there are fewer shares after the split than before. This situation usually occurs when the price of a share nears or falls below the minimum share price required in an exchange where the shares trade.

STOCK REPURCHASE

A stock repurchase occurs when a company elects to buy back shares from existing shareholders. Often companies that believe their shares are undervalued buy back shares believing that doing so will restore a more appropriate price. The buyback also reduces the amount of equity outstanding. Typically, the company issues a tender offer to existing shareholders. The shareholder has the option to sell shares back to the company at a fixed price that is usually a premium over the market price when the tender is issued.

In terms of the mechanics, a repurchase is just like an asset sale; however, the portfolio or account manager must track the tender, decide how to respond, and file the necessary papers if he or she decides to accept the tender. From that point, normal sales procedures apply.

WARRANTS

Warrants represent contracts that can be converted into shares, usually over an extended period, that can themselves be traded in the period between when they are issued and when they expire. The receipt of a warrant creates a new asset for its duration.

Fixed Income

Fixed-income or fixed-interest securities are loans that exist for specific periods of time. At the end of that time, the security **matures** and is paid off. Also, a fixed-income or fixed-interest security pays agreed income to the lender either as a specific payment (**interest**) or as a **discount**, which means the borrower pays back more money than is borrowed at the beginning.

Sometimes the interest rate is tied to an established interest rate in the economy, and the interest on instrument has a **variable interest rate**. Some bonds provide the borrower the opportunity to elect to pay back the security before maturity or call the security under terms established in the bond.

INTEREST

When a fixed-income or fixed-interest security pays interest, the payment increases the cash in the portfolio and is recorded as interest.

DISCOUNTS

When a fixed-interest or fixed-income security is issued at discount, the borrower pays back the amount of the loan plus interest. The portfolio receives cash equal to the face amount of the instrument, but the cash must be recorded with the interest separate from the principal amount lent to the borrower.

MATURITY

When a fixed-income or fixed-interest security matures, the asset is removed from the portfolio, and the cash is increased by the amount of the instrument's face value times the number of units owned.

CALLS

When a fixed-income or fixed-interest instrument is **called**, the borrower pays off the loan under the terms established at the time the instrument was initially created.

The amount of the payoff is typically a function of the present value of the face amount at the time of the call.

Other Instruments

Beyond equities and fixed-income or fixed-interest securities, portfolios can contain options, futures or other derivatives, commodities, and real estate. In general, these instruments have their own events, but several are significant.

OPTIONS

Options have a fixed life and pay no income over the life. However, an investor with an options contract must be aware of the impending exercise date and decide whether to take action in advance of exercise or to let the option expire. If the price of the underlying security rises (for a **call option**) or falls (for a **put option**), the owner needs to decide whether to sell the option on the open market prior to the exercise date or to exercise the option and profit from the difference between the exercise price and market value. (An option with an exercise price less attractive than the value of the underlying less the cost of the option is worthless and will probably be allowed to expire.)

A **writer** of an option contract must monitor the implicit liability created by the option and be ready to buy the security (put) or sell the security (call) when the option expires.

The options contract is an asset for its life and may generate securities positions following exercise. There are also cash position changes that have to be recorded.

FUTURES

A trader that is **long** a futures contract must be prepared to deliver according to the terms of the contract. Alternatively, a long can liquidate his or her position in advance of delivery by purchasing a **short** position for the same number of contracts, effectively liquidating the long position.

A futures contract is an asset for its life and generates cash position changes depending on what delivery entails and how delivery must be made.

COMMODITIES

There are too many different types of commodities to consider each one. However, commodities positions can entail warehousing fees and other costs for ownership. Any income usually results from selling the commodity to liquidate the position.

HOLDINGS INFORMATION

Much like institutions managing a customer's assets, broker/dealers must maintain the holdings of customers, primarily individual investors. (In most cases, institutional holdings are under the control of a custodian.) Holdings may include both basic financial instruments as well as products developed by the broker/dealer or created by third parties.

Organization 5

In describing the organization of systems and other technology departments, we focus on the tasks that must be accomplished, not on the exact organizational structure that may differ greatly from firm to firm. Whatever the actual structure and lines of authority, there are similarities in the tasks required to develop, or acquire and then maintain, systems through all types of entities in the trading markets.

In the early days of technology, applications were developed to support specific functional activities. Among the first and most straightforward applications of technology was customer reporting. Slowly, most of the functions in the trading process were automated, but the process was complex because each market and each instrument type required unique features even though the underlying function or process step might be the same.

For example, a buy-side trader for equities is doing the same things as a trader for fixed income, but different tools are necessary. Indeed, we saw in Book 2 that fixed income is frequently traded by portfolio managers rather than dedicated traders.

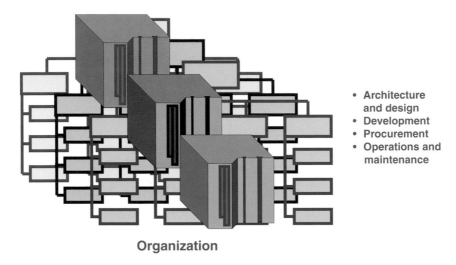

- **Architecture and design**
- **Development**
- **Procurement**
- **Operations and maintenance**

Organization

Figure 1.5   *The systems organizations within buy- and sell-side firms* can take many forms but need to satisfy four major objectives.

More recently, firms have worked to integrate insular technologies into a coherent whole. Four primary motivations have driven this consolidation (refer to Figure 1.5):

1. Firms have increasingly understood that there is a common, firm-wide risk exposure that requires information from all types of applications and functional areas be integrated to create a comprehensive picture.

2. Customers frequently use products from different functional areas within intermediary firms and vendors, and these customers are frustrated and irritated when sales personnel representing different areas compete with one another and/or are unable to provide a comprehensive picture of the customer's total business with the intermediary or vendor.

3. Related to risk, regulators are pressuring firms to shorten the time between execution and settlement, which requires the tight coupling of all the processes related to trading and settlement within firms. (In Chapter 1 in this part, we introduced tight coupling as the concept that is referred to as straight-through processing.)

4. Firms are unwilling to accept having the same information (for example, a customer's name and address) exist in multiple instances throughout the firm, which requires that each instance must be updated whenever details change; otherwise, the information quickly becomes out of control, making it impossible to determine which instance is correct and which is out of date.

Currently, there are ambitious activities underway to interconnect the applications among the different firms within the trading markets. As interdependent linkages are established among firms and supporting entities based on **standards**, it becomes possible to achieve industry-wide straight-through processing.

As systems have become interconnected, the management of applications and other technology has been centralized. Systems management was probably the first technical function to be centralized. The cost of early computer systems and the environments they demanded made a central "glass room" with special environments, power, and a support staff the only economically practical structure.

More recently, cheap processors and client–server architecture have permitted decentralized processing, but the management of the technology, or at least the infrastructure that interconnects the technology, remains coordinated if not centrally planned. Technology has been an important organizational department or division within the entities in the financial markets since the 1960s.

ARCHITECTURE AND DESIGN

We differentiate **architecture** and **design** in the following way: Architecture is the decision on how to allocate processing activities throughout an organization to accomplish the required tasks most efficiently. Design is the process deciding what tasks need to be performed, in what sequence, and using what processing techniques. Design frequently breaks into two separate stages.

Functional design focuses purely on how technology is to be used to perform the required tasks. If complex algorithms are employed in the processes, the details of the algorithms are explained in such a way that technical design can render the algorithm in specific computer instructions.

Technical design translates the functional design into specific programming instructions that permit the creation of the computer code required to execute the process.

DEVELOPMENT

Development is the process of converting the architecture and design into operating systems. In addition to the programming required, there may be extensive testing and error correcting in the period between the time the development begins and the system is implemented.

PROCUREMENT

In parallel with, or perhaps in lieu of, the design of a system, it is often necessary to purchase hardware, the supporting software, and in some cases the process software as well. The systems may need to be in place at the time the development occurs, and definitely by the time the application is implemented. If package software is used instead of bespoke design, implementation and training with the new software may represent significant activities.

MAKE, BUY, OR OUTSOURCE

One of the fiercest debates in technology management is whether to buy technology from a vendor, to build the technology in-house, or to outsource processing and even management to another firm or vendor. Strong proponents exist for each approach, and most organizations go through cycles in which they favor one solution only to change to another approach as a result of a problem or shift in the perceptions of value.

Proponents of building believe that it is not possible to buy a product that conforms to all the needs of an organization. Large entities in particular often believe that unique characteristics are not matched by generic products. Also, for many package applications, there are fundamental assumptions about how the function they are designed to automate is organized and operate that may be at odds with specific user needs.

Smaller organizations are often willing to modify their operations to conform to attractive software in ways that larger organizations will not. Finally, most vendors of applications are willing to add functionality such as linkages to markets or emerging instrument types only when there is broad-based demand from multiple customers. This approach is often too slow for entities that are moving rapidly into new product and service areas.

Purchasers of packaged applications or application components argue that it makes no sense to reproduce applications that are widely available from vendors. Packaged applications take advantage of a broad customer base, create user groups, and offer training on both the application itself and often on basic industry knowledge as well. Moreover, established vendors often have companion products serving other areas of technology that are tightly integrated.

By outsourcing, firms are able to offload almost all their technology operations. Some firms may believe that this is a low-cost approach to processing, or they might believe that the vendor or correspondent may be able to provide services that are not part of the strategic competence of the firm choosing to outsource. When outsourcing is to a correspondent, the outsourcing firm may also be able to offload regulatory and compliance costs as well.

Developing bespoke software or installing purchased software is expensive, time-consuming, and frustrating. After making a commitment to build, to buy, or to outsource a new application, managers sometimes come to the conclusion that any other choice would have been better. This feeling of angst usually persists throughout the development or implementation, but some managers never get over the feeling that the wrong choice was made.

Operations and Maintenance

After a system is programmed and tested, it is in a production stage, and there is an ongoing process to maintain the system, correct problems when and if they occur, and make minor and some major changes as new requirements emerge.

RELATED INFORMATION IN OTHER BOOKS

Systems for buy- and sell-side firms satisfy a variety of different purposes. Systems are used by each function within the firm, and those functions are designed to complete the activities required for customer acquisition and support, account maintenance, and transaction processing, as well as a number of collateral activities.

All software shares a number of common tasks and must be able to react to the events that affect accounts and holdings. Firms organize to solve these problems in many ways, but certain things must be accomplished to support systems however the organization is structured. Figure 1.6 summarizes the books in the set and the linkages between this part and the other books.

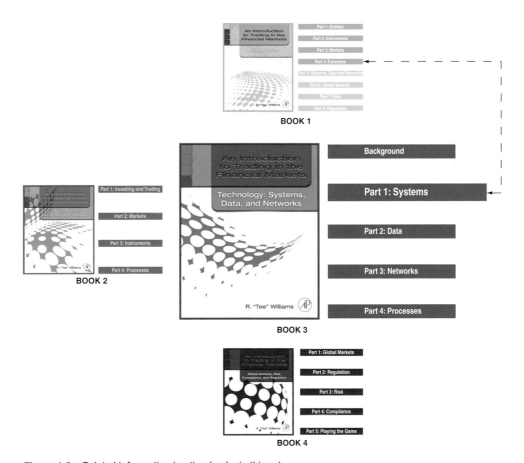

Figure 1.6 Related information in other books in this set.

Data **Part 2**

Data, or information, is both the fuel for and a major product of the financial markets. Robert Britz, who retired as co-president of the New York Stock Exchange (as it was then known) in 2005, is purported to have likened the NYSE to a factory that produces information. The same could be said for all firms involved in the trading markets including data vendors and data users.

In this part we explore the data used in and produced by the trading markets. We begin by describing the various types of data using several different methods of categorizing the data. We discuss how data is produced and how it is used. As we did with systems, we describe the broad purposes of data and describe how functions on the buy and sell sides consume and produce data. Data in the trading markets is also a business. We describe the activities required to produce, distribute, and consume data and the important groups involved in those activities.

The other part of the business of data turns on the ownership, pricing, and administration of data as a profit-making endeavor for producers and distributors and as a major cost for users. Finally, we describe a number of issues related to data and management. Figure 2.0 shows the features and attributes of data we examine in this part.

To begin, we define what is meant by data that is used and produced in the trading markets. Data can be categorized in a number of different ways, and each category presents some insights into its nature.

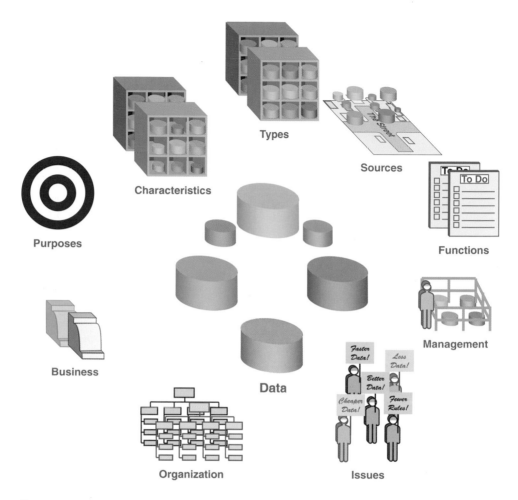

Figure 2.0 **_Data in the trading markets_** is classified by type and characteristic; constitutes a major industry; requires careful management and a dedicated organization; and generates a number of issues that participants in the industry must address.

Most participants in the market-data industry would identify two major types of data. One category is called **reference data**, and the other is called **market data**. We use these terms because they are widely accepted, but both terms are unsatisfying because they are subject to misunderstanding and also because they ignore important types of data that do not fit within the common definitions.

Most of all, these two data categories are used primarily for data that is commercially available from vendors and ignores data that is produced and then consumed within entities. Therefore, to these two categories, we add a third that we term **process data**—information that is generated and consumed within entities. Finally, we add a subcategory of **identifiers** to include data elements that allow us to uniquely label instruments, entities, markets, and registrars.

Figure 2.1 shows the major types of data we describe in this chapter.

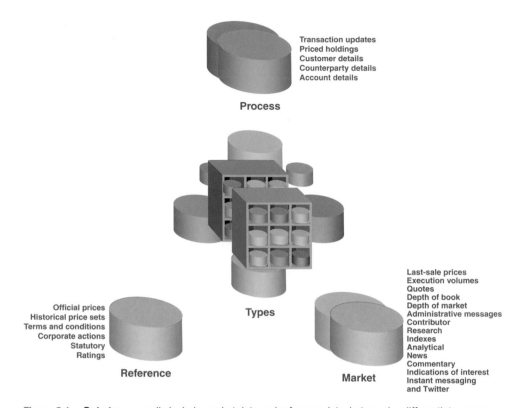

Figure 2.1 ***Data types*** usually include market data and reference data, but we also differentiate process data as well as identifiers and segments. ***Process data types*** (*top*) are generated and used within an entity and usually have transient value. ***Reference data*** (*left*) usually includes information that is less dynamic and is used primarily in processing activities according to most definitions. ***Market data*** (*right*) is a label applied to data that is dynamic and is used in trading decisions.

PROCESS DATA

Process data is our term for the information generated within an organization either manually input into systems or created as products, both final and interim products, from the processes required to operate the entity. Some process data exists as a separate category because the entities in the financial market are unwilling to share the information with others. Examples of this type of data include details about customers that would present the opportunity for competitors to attempt to capture the customer if the information was shared.

Other information includes interim products in the accounting and other processes within a firm, such as priced holdings. This information is generated and must be maintained but has no legitimate use to any other entity. Finally, some information is process data because vendors do not yet offer the information as a commercial product.

Both data users and vendors have a strong incentive to convert process data to information that can be purchased. Vended data represents a revenue source for the vendor and absolves the user of tedious and expensive effort to input and maintain the data. (We observe in a sidebar later in this chapter that much of what is now reference and market data was originally what we term process data.) The top part of Figure 2.1 shows the important subcategories of process data.

Transaction Updates

At each step in a transaction process such as a trade, the details of the transaction in its current state become information that needs to be input or generated, updated with each change, and maintained at least as long as the transaction remains open.

Priced Holdings

Any time the market price of a holding changes, the value of the holding must be computed by multiplying the number of units held by the price of each unit. If the purpose of the valuation is to present a response to transient inquiry, the value can be wiped out as soon as the inquiry is finished. However, if the valuation is the result of required periodic reporting, the valuation or the ability to re-create the valuation must be maintained for as long as it may be needed, perhaps several years.

Customer Details

Details about customers are important for both commercial and regulatory reasons and need to be maintained. The information is not typically available from any vendor, and the data must be input and maintained within the firm. However, information on customers is subject to change, and customers often have multiple places where they interact with a large buy- or sell-side firm. Therefore, maintaining this information can be extremely complex.

PROBLEMS FOR A LARGE INVESTMENT BANK

Some years ago we worked with a large investment bank that had a problem that typifies the difficulty encountered with managing process data. The firm estimated that it had more than 40 systems within the firm that required name and address information from retail customers. The firm had no way of knowing which, if any, of the 40+ possible instances of a single customer's name and address was correct or how to determine if different variations of a common name were a single customer or two customers with the same name. Finally, when different instances were at odds, there was no way to know which instance was correct.

Presumably, the firm has made some headway in resolving these problems, but they typify the difficulty of managing data and the reasons for the interest in enterprise data management that will be explained in Chapter 7 of this part.

Counterparty Details

Counterparties of all types represent business relationships that contain important information, making successful completion of transactions possible. Payments require knowledge of bank routing numbers, official office addresses, and account details. Likewise, the delivery of transfer instructions requires similar details. Every large counterparty can have dozens of departments, scores of independent trading desks or processing groups, and hundreds of accounts that must be tracked. Because there is less sensitivity to sharing this type of information, counterparty data is slowly becoming available from vendors, but extensive maintenance is still required.

Account Details

Accounts representing both customers and counterparties must be updated, and unique details must be recorded and maintained.

REFERENCE DATA

"Reference data" is a collective term for a variety of information that is generally important for managing accounts and securities. Several different types of data are generally referred to as reference data. We describe many of these in this chapter, but one component, which we have labeled "Identifiers," is sufficiently important to deserve a separate section later in this chapter. For the subcategories of reference data, refer to Figure 2.1.

As we noted previously, "reference data" as distinguished from "market data" is not a very satisfying term. The advantage is that before this term was coined, there was no common name for all the types of data we describe in this chapter. One problem, however, is that much of the information we term reference data actually comes from the markets.

Historically, a common feature of reference data was that the data was primarily static and delivered in bulk. In contrast, market data tended to be dynamic and could be delivered in streaming form. (These terms are explored in more detail in Chapter 2.) However, now much reference data is demanded in real time, so the distinctions blur even more.

The following sections describe most of the commonly agreed components of reference data.

Official Prices

In every market there is a need to establish a price that is used for official valuations for customer reports, regulatory reporting, risk measurement, mark-to-market, and a number of related activities. Traditionally, the official price was the price on the **last trade** of the day in the **primary market** or an established **reference market**.[1]

---

1 Note that we are using the term "primary market" to mean the dominant or major market for an instrument if the instrument is traded in multiple markets. Elsewhere in this set, we have used the term to mean the market where capital is raised. This is but one more example of the same words having different meanings, which underlines the importance of understanding the definitions and context in discussions.

Although there are a number of problems with the last price of the trading day (see the discussion in Chapter 9 on issues), there remains a need for an established official price for all instruments.

Determining official prices, even with the problems we have noted, is straightforward in cases where there is an active secondary market where prices can be determined. However, we noted in Book 2, *An Introduction to Trading in the Financial Markets: Trading, Markets, Instruments, and Processes,* that many instruments (e.g., some fixed income and commodities) do not have a source for market-based prices.

In these situations some means of developing an official price is needed. Historically, those needing a price for reporting purposes would call a group of dealers (often three were used) and get their best price estimates. An average of the dealers was then used as the price for reporting and other purposes. Now firms frequently use a spread against a benchmark security as the best price.[2] Determining official prices in **illiquid** markets often means adhering to local custom or conforming to guidelines published by regulators or **industry groups**.

Historical Price Sets

Historical data usually includes time series data on instrument prices. Although historical data sets represent information from the markets and are frequently used for analysis that is input to the trading process, historical data is commonly grouped as reference data. The reason is likely that the data is usually static and available in bulk form. Also, traditional vendors of reference data are frequently sources for historical data.

Terms and Conditions

Securities, particularly fixed-income instruments, have data defined in the documents that register the instrument for public sale. Details such as sinking funds, call features, and the details for resetting adjustable rate instruments are typical **terms and conditions** information.

Corporate Actions

Any information generated by a firm can be described generally as a corporate action. Some corporate actions affect the value of the instruments issued by an entity such as the issuance of important news about the entity, its senior officers, its customers, or products. An announcement of quarterly earnings is a common example of this type of news, but announcements of important new products can affect market prices as well.

Sometimes entities take actions referred to as **capital changes** in which the number of units of an instrument is changed or the instrument may be terminated.

---

2 See Book 2, Part 3 for a discussion of determining a price as a spread against a benchmark instrument.

Typical capital change information includes dividends, both stock and cash; stock splits; repurchase agreements; the issue of warrants; bond calls; and other activities that affect holdings of securities.

Vendors generally provide corporate information in bulk form, and the data is often collected directly from the entities that issue publically traded instruments. In many countries entities that are publically traded are required to make all announcements public to ensure that all instrument owners have an equal opportunity to receive and process the news.

Statutory

Many regulatory authorities require information on securities and investment portfolios to be made public. This information is important to investors and traders. **Statutory data** is collected by vendors and made available to interested users. Examples include corporate reports of their financial performance issued publically by companies that have publically listed securities.

Some regulatory jurisdictions require that holdings of securities in regulated institutional portfolios are required to be made public periodically. Both corporate reports and institutional holdings are examples of statutory data.

Ratings

Several firms review and rank instruments and the firms that issue them, passing judgment on the likelihood that the issuing firm will be able to meet the obligations established by the instrument. Ratings are critical to trading fixed-income instruments and play a role with other instruments as well. Ratings information is usually grouped with reference data.

MARKET DATA

Market information, or "market data," is produced by a number of different entities primarily involved in the trading process. (We describe some of the sources of market data in Chapter 3.) As was the case with reference data, the term "market data" is not truly satisfactory. Large portions of market data come from the markets, but other information such as news and research come from other sources.

The types of information commonly labeled market data are used to make and implement trading decisions but have broader impact. The right part of Figure 2.1 (page 78) shows major categories of data commonly referred to as market data.

Most industry professionals use the term "market data" to mean information that is broadcast or streamed to the user in real time. Thus, "reference data" refers to bulk data that is static or infrequently changing, and market data is delivered as individual messages asynchronously as they are generated in real time. Whatever the limitations of the labels, we use "market data" as a label for the group of information types that follow.

Last-Sale Prices

When trades occur, many markets publish the **prices**, but not usually the identities of the parties trading. The prices are also known as **last-sale prices** or **last sales**. Last-sale prices provide the historical record of trading over time.

Execution Volumes

Volume data records the size of each individual trade. Cumulative volume information provides a sense of the activity in the market. The combination of the price of a trade and the number of shares traded is known as a **last-sale report**. Last-sale reports include all the information in an execution report given by a market to the trade participants and to the clearing entity except for the identities of the participants.

Quotes

In Book 2 we defined quotes, and we described nine different types of quote-like price representations used to describe the market in different types of trading mechanisms. Earlier in this book, we defined a quote as a type of basic unit aggregation. In this section we address quotes as message types central to the trading process.

A quote is a paired offer to buy and an offer to sell with a quantity for both the buy and sell. The lower price is referred to as the **bid** and is the price at which a purchase can be made without any negotiation. The higher price is known as the **asked** or, alternatively, as the **offer**. The difference between the bid and offer is known as the **spread**.

In principle, the quote represents the best estimate of price of the next trade. An order to sell should occur at the bid price, or an order to buy should occur at the offer price. Depending on the rules in the market, an order that comes to the market priced between the bid price and the offer price may get an execution, but it is not guaranteed. If a trade occurs between the bid and offer, it is known as **price improvement**.

Quotes can have different meanings in different types of trading venues, as described in Book 2. Generally, in physical markets, quotes are advertisements posted by a market maker who stands ready to trade under the rules of the market. Although the dealer may be bound by the rules to trade at the prices he posts— a condition known as a firm quote—there is no absolute guarantee. By contrast, in an automated market, a quote represents two limit orders: one to buy and one to sell. In electronic systems an order priced to sell at the bid or purchase at the offer is automatically executed.

The purpose of an index is to reduce the activity in the instruments included in the index into a single number that helps investors assess the activity among the covered instruments. There are a number of different methodologies for computing indexes, and each method highlights some features of the covered instruments and may hide or distort other features. There can be fierce debate among academics and professionals as to which methodology is best.

The primary differences among index methodologies most often focus on two critical features. First, those charged with creating an index must decide which instruments to include and which to exclude. Broad-based indexes may give a better picture of a market but may be more complex to manage and may be affected by instruments that trade infrequently. Narrower indexes are less complicated and are usually dominated by large, active issues.

The second important feature of index design is the method of weighting. Those issues with high market prices dominate simple averages. The number of units outstanding for each instrument is used to weight many indexes, which is an attempt to reflect the relative importance of each component to the market. Other design refinements are possible.

Indexes are copyrighted intellectual property and, as we see in Chapter 6 on business, are licensed for use. Frequently, the copyright holder licenses vendors to distribute the index, and the vendor and not the copyright holder computes the index for distribution to users.

Traders frequently use indexes either as quoted numbers or as graphical representations to make decisions, as part of customer reports to permit the customer to assess performance, or as part of news and online financial reports. However, indexes have other valuable purposes as well. Many quantitative investors use indexes to help in constructing and managing portfolios.

Also, indexes form the basis for a number of important derivative instruments that permit investors to speculate or hedge future market performance. The market trading the contract licenses the use of an index when it is used as the basis for a derivative contract, and the holder of the copyright may receive license fees for each contract unit traded.

Analytical Information

Analytical information takes other data in the market and attempts to present the information in some format or employing some transformation that is intended to provide more insight into what the data means. The simplest type of analytical data may be price and volume graphs, but many more sophisticated types of analysis are regularly used. As a general rule, analytical information generally supports an investment or trading strategy. Therefore, different investors or traders have different preferences for various types of analytical data, depending on their strategies.

News

News is information, often from outside the actual markets, providing background and insight into individual securities and the broader economy. News information is generally held to be factual and is often presented in text form.

News information in electronic form is generally provided as **newsfeeds** or **newswires**. Newswires are often presented in streaming displays of **headlines** that show the most recent stories most prominently. In addition to the headlines, services provide access to complete stories on demand. Access to the full story is often provided both from the scrolling headlines and as links from displays for individual instruments when the story relates to the instrument.

Recently, news organizations have begun to embed triggers into news stories that permit automated trading models to generate orders based on the triggers. In addition, news is moving to a common XML standard (see the discussion of standards in Part 3, near Table 3.1.7, for additional examples of standards) known as NewsML. Using NewsML, users have the opportunity to write applications that can strip data and analytical information directly from news stories from any news provider and use it in applications.

Commentary

Commentary is closely related to news except that some respected expert has enhanced the news information or other data with insights that suggest meaning and possible actions. Commentary may be related to specific instrument types such as equities, fixed income, or foreign exchange; to systems—functions such as trading or portfolio management; or to economic issues. Although most business news grew from a journalistic tradition, where facts are kept separate from opinion, news organizations are beginning to link commentary more tightly to news.

Indications of Interest

We introduced indications of interest as a basic process unit in the Background section. Indications of interest are messages from a broker/dealer to institutional customers indicating that the broker/dealer has an actual order, known as a natural order, available if the customer is interested. A natural order means the customer can trade, often for reasonably large quantities, without announcing the interest to the market. This avoids market impact as described in Book 2.

An indication of interest from a broker/dealer indicates the instrument, whether it is a buy or sell order, and some indication of the size. Often IOIs are received into a firm's order-management system (OMS) where it can be displayed in the blotter where it might be of value. The order-management system often has the capability to flip the IOI, converting it into an order that can be executed by the broker/dealer.

IOIs are generally transmitted using the FIX protocol. IOIs are a standard FIX message.

Instant Messaging and Twitter

Instant messaging (IM) and **Twitter** are both social web services initially designed to permit casual, social interactions. The financial community has adapted these programs to pass research data and trading ideas. For the most part, these services are used to replace phone calls. These forms of interaction have the advantage that they do not require any action from a buy-side trader unless the trader chooses. Moreover, order-management systems described in Part 1 can be programmed to filter these messages to highlight only those of interest.

IDENTIFIERS AND SEGMENTS

A number of primary data elements are critical for all processing. They are used throughout the industry to manage processing and as vital components within the data files we will explore. These data elements are used both by external market and reference data services and internally in master, holdings, and transaction files.

Through standardization of industry-wide definitions of these elements, processing can move seamlessly among firms for transactions that affect multiple entities in the trading markets. We present important identifiers and segment labels in Figure 2.1.1.

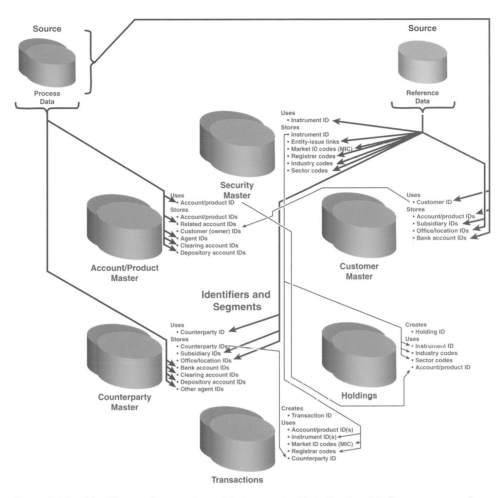

Figure 2.1.1 *Identifiers and segments* are data types embedded with other data files as a means of identifying instruments, entities, and individuals; and to group data into recognized categories.

Instruments

It is critical for all processing to be able to uniquely identify all instruments, and in many cases different instances of the same instrument. **Instrument identifiers** fall into two major categories. **Ticker symbol** is the common name for identifiers used by traders, salesmen, and investors to identify securities in the normal course on interpersonal interactions in the securities markets.

Processor symbols are used by computers to uniquely identify instruments when sending messages or performing accounting tasks. Because there are extensive interactions in the trading process among different entities, it is essential that all parties use a common means of identification to avoid confusion.

TICKER SYMBOLS

Ticker symbols are generally assigned initially by exchanges as a means for traders to send orders to the market. Market-data vendors extend exchange-generated symbols to identify the different markets where the instrument trades and other important information that helps to uniquely identify each specific type of instrument. Common examples of ticker symbols are "T" for AT&T, "BT" for British Telecom, and "S" for Sony.

PROCESSING SYMBOLS

The symbols used by computers generally depend on combinations of numbers and characters as identifiers. Typically, these processor symbols are not intuitive for humans and are used only for processing. The most widely used symbol numbering system is known as International Security Identification Numbers (ISINs).

As we will see in the Instrument Identifiers section in Chapter 9, there are problems with the ISIN number; therefore, there are proposals both to improve the current numbering system and proposals to replace ISIN numbers with a better system. One possible alternative is the SEDOL numbering system owned by the London Stock Exchange.

Counterparty

We noted in the Process Data section that a number of critical pieces of information about branch office addresses and accounts of counterparties at banks, clearing corporations, and depositories are necessary to process transactions. In addition to these details, it is also necessary to be able to uniquely identify all counterparties, often down to individual offices and departments. Counterparty identifiers are beginning to move from the process data category to reference data, as standards develop to identify entities operating in the markets.

Trading Venues

As instruments begin to trade in multiple venues in a process that we learned in Book 2 is known as market fragmentation, it is not sufficient for trading and settlement purposes to identify the instrument, but it is also necessary to identify on which market(s) the instrument trades. **Standards organizations** (described later) are developing **market identification codes (MIC)** that can be embedded in information related to quotes, trades, and settlement information to uniquely identify the market of trading or execution.

Registrar

Just as the same instrument can be traded in different trading venues, instruments from the same issuing or creating entity can be registered in different countries and/or listed on different markets. Typically, instruments registered in different countries are not exact duplicates, but they may be effective substitutes because they represent claims on the same underlying source of value.

Instrument Groups

Instruments are frequently segmented by type. The instrument types presented in Book 1 of this set, *An Introduction to Trading in the Financial Markets: Market Basics*, and expanded in Book 2, *An Introduction to Trading in the Financial Markets: Trading, Markets, Instruments, and Processes,* are commonly used groups.

Fixed-income instruments may be grouped as government issues, corporate issues, convertible issues, and municipal issues within portfolios and for research purposes. Equities may be grouped as common, preferred, and convertible issues. Futures can be segmented as agricultural, financials, index, as well as other groups, while options are frequently aggregated into equity options, index options, options on futures, and smaller categories.

Sectors

Instruments are commonly grouped into sectors composed of multiple industries with common underlying attributes. For example, the "industrials" sector includes many different types of manufacturing industries such as steel and aluminum production; finished goods manufacturing such as aircraft, automobiles, and appliances; and numerous other industries engaged in fabricating products. Examples of other sectors include energy (oil and gas, coal, and renewable energy industries) and transportation (auto, rail, trucking, and shipping industries).

Industries

We listed several industries in defining sectors, but many others exist such as fashion, consumer goods, pharmaceuticals, and the like.

Characteristics 2

We have looked at the types of data, so now we can look at the characteristics of that data. By "characteristics," we mean the different attributes that affect how the information is delivered and used. We present two major and several second-level characteristics of data in Figure 2.2.

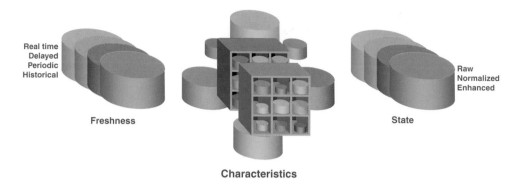

Figure 2.2 *Data characteristics* are attributes of data that tend to distinguish among data that is used for different purposes.

FRESHNESS

The freshness of information is a measure of how current the information has to be and how quickly information changes need to reach users. We know of no information set anywhere in the global economy where information has a wider dispersion in freshness than the trading markets.

Data on the freshest end of the spectrum includes **ultra-low latency** trading information where traders move trading models to reside at trading venues to avoid time lost because of the limiting speed of light.[3] On the other end of the spectrum, bond terms and conditions often remain static for the 30-year life of the bond.

In parallel to the differences in freshness requirements, there is an infrastructure of delivery capabilities to provide information with the required freshness. We describe the delivery tools in Chapter 2 or Part 3. In this section we describe common freshness categories and what they mean.

As a general rule, information is increasingly demanded and available with limited delay. Even information such as reference data, which was once delivered only weekly or monthly, is now demanded and increasingly provided in **real time**.

Real Time

Data required for trading is required to reach prospective traders as quickly as possible. This information has been delivered in real time since the creation of ticker machines during the 1850s. When trading information is requested, the most recently

---

3   Latency is an important attribute of data, but because it is more logically related to information distribution, it is addressed in detail with the discussion of networks in Part 3 of this book.

produced information is the information that is sent. This information is delivered in two different ways.

BROADCAST DATA

Much real-time data is broadcast from the source. "Broadcast" means that the data that is produced at the source is sent to vendors and other directly connected recipients continuously as it is produced. If the information is going directly to where it is consumed, it is used immediately. If the recipient is a vendor, it must be sent onward to successive users. Vendors use two different technologies to distribute information to secondary users: ***streaming*** and ***inquiry/response***.

Another term used to describe the ***streaming*** transmission of data from vendors to users is ***dynamically updated***. Streaming data is sent to the end user as soon as it is received. An individual viewing a display that is fed by streaming data would see prices or other information change on the screen as soon as it is received. This is very important to applications and humans engaged in trading and sales.

Streaming technology used to require highly sophisticated technology and was available only to the most sophisticated and demanding users. Now the information can be streamed over the public Internet and is widely available.

INQUIRY/RESPONSE

The alternative to streaming data is to provide real-time data as a ***single update*** only when it is requested. This delivery mechanism is known as inquiry/response and was initially employed for less demanding users to save cost. Now single update information is used to conserve bandwidth to those users who do not need continuously changing data. (We will discuss market-data message traffic in Chapter 9 on issues.)

Delayed Data

Market data is often delayed 10 to 25 minutes (15 minutes is common) before it is delivered to end users. Delayed information is not the result of user demand or technological problems, but because exchanges and other information creators treat their content as ***public information*** after a delay and thus the data is free. Fees for real-time market data can be substantial, particularly for individual investors, and the delay is preferable to paying for the data in real time.

Ironically, delayed data, although it is free to the end user, is very expensive for vendors and other data distributors. If information were delayed at the source, it would require a separate distribution mechanism with the same capacity as real-time information, but with a built-in lag as required by the ***data owner***. For this reason, delayed data is often broadcast in real time and delayed near the user to save duplicate distribution costs.

Periodic Information

Much information updates only periodically. An example of periodic information could be dividends on equities or announcements of corporate earnings only, which change once each quarter. Some information such as the terms and conditions for bonds is produced only once when an instrument is created. In the past, information that does not update continuously was only distributed infrequently and in bulk.

Increasingly, users are demanding this information as streaming feeds. The reason is that the information, although it changes only occasionally, has an immediate impact on trading when a change does occur. These changes are increasingly used as inputs to quantitative trading models.

Historical Data

Historical data includes databases of information available for research purposes. This information includes files of tick-by-tick price and quote information and historical files of corporate reports. Like periodic data (some might include historical files as a category of periodic data), historical data has traditionally been delivered periodically and in bulk form. Increasingly, quantitative trading firms are looking to technologies that can **replay information** to simulate real time. This information can be input into quantitative models to test their behavior with real market conditions.

STATE

The **data state** refers to what is done to data from the instant it is produced. Data, once it is produced, may be sent out "as is" with no modification. In other cases the information may be cleaned and made more useful by the creator or by intermediate vendors. Still other information may be significantly modified to provide added value. Different applications have different needs with respect to how the information is modified.

Raw

Raw data suggests that data is sent for consumption as it is produced with no attempt to transform it. Perhaps the best example of raw data is information from the automated trading system at an exchange or trading venue going to a trading application or trading terminal where the recipient will use the information to generate orders back to the market. For these applications speed is more critical than attempting to clean the data. Even in the case of raw data, minor **normalization** is performed. In particular, raw data has ticker symbols added.

Normalized Data

Normalization suggests that data has been examined and possibly cleaned. Information from exchanges and other data owners is often checked for consistency and erroneous entries. As we noted, ticker symbols are added at the exchange. Vendors take information from multiple exchanges and replace the exchange symbols with a consistent set of symbols across all the markets they carry. Exchange messages commonly include sequence numbers, and if messages are lost (i.e., there is a break in the sequence), vendors typically ask the exchange to **retransmit** the missing information.

Enhanced Data

Enhanced data has been supplemented or transformed to make the core information more valuable. Enhancement usually occurs at a vendor or the user firm, and often reflects the beliefs of the entity making the transformation as to what is important. We have described graphs as a means of enhancing information; however, market-data vendors often enhance quotes and last-sale information by providing information on the entity being traded. Supplemental information includes dividends, earnings per share (EPS), and related data. Enhancement generally increases the value of data and thus the price.

Firms in the financial markets both depend on and produce many different types of information (see Figure 2.3). In this chapter we examine the major producers of information used in the markets.

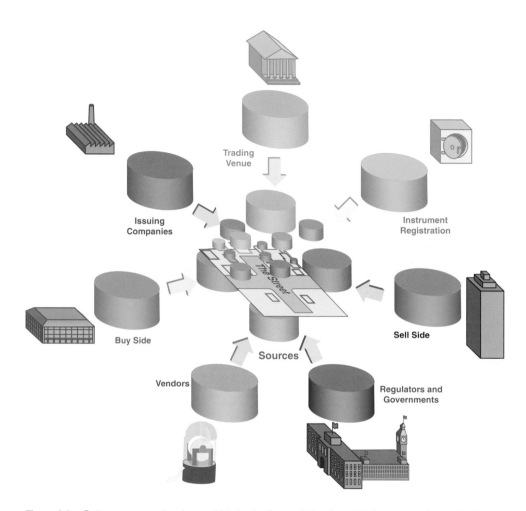

Figure 2.3 **Data sources** are the places within the trading markets where data is produced for use by others.

TRADING VENUES

Exchanges and other trading venues are the dominant source of last-sale information and a major source of quotes. In many markets, trading venues are required to make trade and quote information available, and increased transparency is a clear objective of regulators who believe widely available information makes markets more efficient and fairer. Finally, trading venues are sources of administrative messages and depth-of-book information.

ISSUING COMPANIES

Issuing companies are the source of information about any instruments they issue, including instrument features and terms and conditions for bonds. Moreover, companies in many markets are required to make public disclosure of important information that becomes part of the business and investment news. Firms also tend to report their *financial statements*, often quarterly, and this financial information becomes part of the analytical information used to assess instrument values.

INSTRUMENT REGISTRATION

We noted that corporations provide information on the instruments the firm issues, and much of this information is generated in the registration process. Registration information may come directly from the issuing firm, from an underwriter, from the regulatory authority, or from a trading venue when the instrument takes the form of a *financial contract*.

THE SELL SIDE

Sell-side firms are the source of quotes from dealer operations directly through trading venues, through dealer associations and other quote publication systems, and as contributed information delivered through vendors or through the Internet. Sell-side firms are major providers of research information and contribute to commentary services, particularly related to opinions on trading, execution, and the markets. Sell-side firms have been originators or major sponsors for a number of vendor services as a means to attract customers and have paid for many information products for the buy-side using *soft dollars*.

THE BUY SIDE

While the buy side is a major consumer of information, buy-side firms are sometimes required to publicize information that has commercial appeal. In particular, some categories of investment funds are required to report portfolio holdings on a quarterly basis, and *mutual funds* publish net asset values daily.

VENDORS

Although vendors have a major role in the aggregation and transmission of data, they are also the source of much of the incidental information provided to users. Vendors compute instrument measures that are provided along with prices from trading venues, they may compute indexes to provide context for prices, and they may be the source of news.

REGULATORS AND GOVERNMENTS

Governments require the collection and distribution of much of the information available in the trading markets. Governments are often the source of financial information on companies that must report their results to the public. In some cases governments require information collection and offer commercial vendors a franchise on the actual collection process, provided the vendors make the information available to their customers and through other vendors.

Purpose 4

Information can be employed for a variety of purposes within the trading markets as can be seen in Figure 2.4.

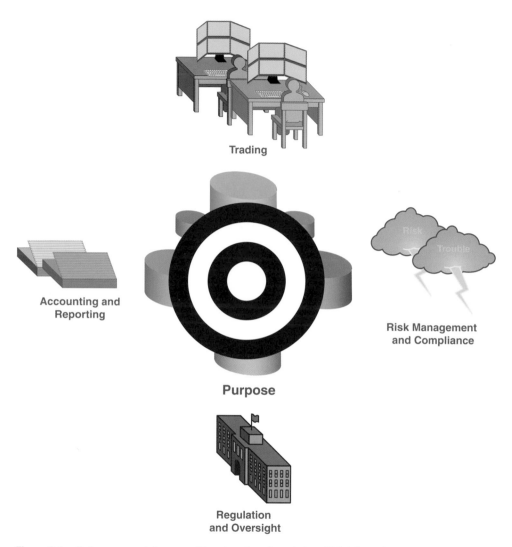

Figure 2.4 *Data purpose* defines specific categories of needs for which information is employed within the trading market.

TRADING

Data used as input to the decision to trade and/or to price an order sent to the markets in anticipation of an execution is extremely valuable. In addition to information on quotes and recent prices produced by trading venues, trading data includes news, commentary, and research information that helps in the decision to trade as well as in deciding what a *fair value* is for an instrument.

ACCOUNTING AND REPORTING

Data can be input into accounting and reporting services. For example, official prices are used to value portfolios and positions. The accounting information is input into decision making and to satisfy regulatory requirements.

RISK MANAGEMENT AND COMPLIANCE

Although we do not explore either risk management or compliance until Book 4, *An Introduction to Trading in the Financial Markets: Global Markets, Risk, Compliance, and Regulation*, we note that both activities require extensive data both from within the firm and from external sources.

REGULATION AND OVERSIGHT

Regulators, self-regulators, and firm management all require extensive sources of internal and external data.

Functions 5

Here, we return to the functions defined in Book 1, Part 4, to explain some of the major ways that data is used. We examine the same buy- and sell-side functions we used in Part 1 to understand systems. The functions on the buy and sell sides both consume and produce data (see Figure 2.5).

Moreover, this data is frequently accessed through the information stores introduced in the Background section. Therefore, we look at the information consumed and produced by each function from both internal and external sources.

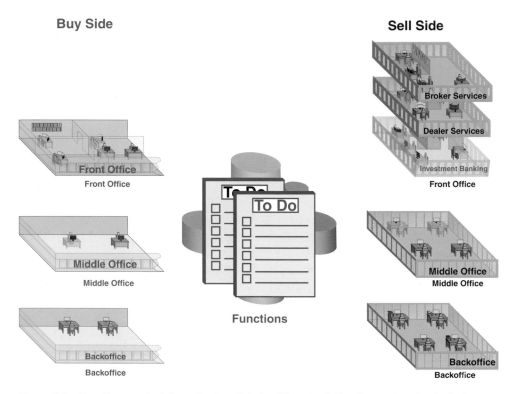

Figure 2.5 *Functions* require information to satisfy the different activities they each undertake in the trading markets.

In this chapter we will discuss how data is used by various functions on the buy and sell sides. We further differentiate data that tends to be used on a firm-wide or department-wide basis versus data that is specific to a given function or activity. After first describing firm-wide and then office (i.e., the front office, middle office, and backoffice) needs, we address each of the functions for the buy and sell sides.

BUY SIDE

Buy-side firms are major consumers of data and typically have dedicated technology staffs responsible for acquiring and managing data. There are needs for three primary categories of information in all parts of a buy-side firm, although how the information is employed differs from office to office. First, instrument pricing information is used throughout a firm from investment decision making in the front office to transaction updates, compliance, and risk management in the back.

Second, transaction processing from order management in the front office to trade settlement in the backoffice spans the firm. Finally, accounting occurs in each office even though the focus differs. The front and middle offices focus on customers, portfolios, and products, whereas the backoffice reconciles firm-wide accounts with accounts held by counterparties and support entities. The linkage in accounting is the mapping from gross firm accounts to individual holdings for customers, portfolios, and products.

The need for information stores as we described them in the Background section is necessary for all offices within a buy-side firm. Therefore, there is a need for a security master, an account master, and a customer master to service each office. Moreover, holdings files and transaction files affect and are affected by each office. Although there are similarities in need, the meanings of holdings and focus for transactions change from office to office.

Accounts and holdings tend to relate to customers in the front and middle offices while relating to counterparties and support entities in the backoffice. Transactions tend to originate in the front office and migrate to the middle and then the backoffice as time passes and a transaction nears settlement.

Although data to be used for analysis and decision making may go directly to specific offices or directly to individuals, many firms bring the analytical information into the firm centrally and make it available through an enterprise infrastructure, which is described in Part 3 when we examine networks. In particular, real time pricing data is used in every part of most firms.

Much reference data is used primarily as a resource to maintain and update firm-wide databases (see Figure 2.5.1). Official prices, corporate actions, instrument identifiers, and many other types of reference data are used to price holdings, modify information in security master files, and the like. They are not used by specific functions directly, but as input to the master files, they make the variety of information services used by different functions possible.

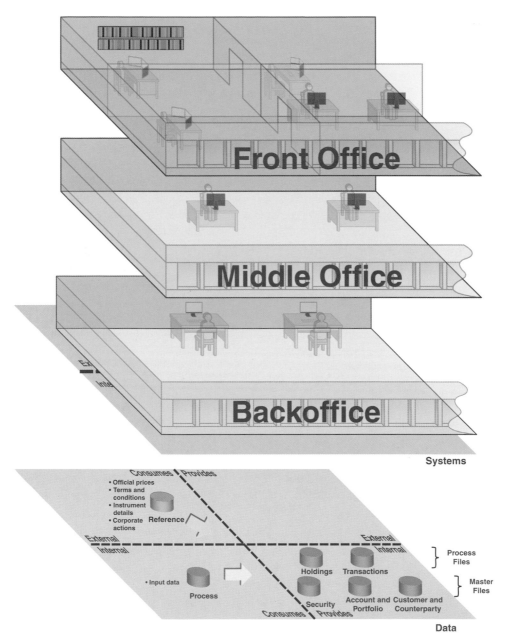

Figure 2.5.1 *Buy-side firms* provide market data to many of their employees and employ reference data to update data stores for use by all systems within the firm.

Therefore, at a firm-wide level, information is being managed for use in all parts of the firms. Data that is used by all offices is updated and maintained. Firms are attempting to solve problems like those of the investment bank with more than 40 instances of name and address files (described in the "Problems for a Large Investment Bank" sidebar in Chapter 1 of this part) through a concept known as **enterprise data management**. We explore this in more detail in Chapter 9 on issues.

Front Office

The functions within the front office are consumers of analytical data as well as information on portfolios, customers, and their accounts. Although specific functions have unique information needs, most functions receive at least some basic services.

There has been a significant change in the demand for market information services by the buy-side front office over the past several decades. For years after market information was mandatory for the sell side, it was common to visit a large buy-side firm and find only a single market data terminal, usually in the library of the research department. Many firms argued that they invested only for the long term, and therefore, moment-to-moment pricing information was unnecessary.

Beginning in the late 1980s, vendors encouraged by sell-side firms began to offer services focused on the needs of the buy side with particularly strong fixed-income offerings. Slowly, buy-side front-office users began to demand market information. Moreover, the sell-side sponsors of these services often offered them for soft dollars, making them even more attractive to the buy side.

Most front-office users receive a base level of market data including prices, quotes, and news. A number of firms attempt to define categories of users and permit users to choose from a menu of comparable alternatives. Those more actively involved with the markets choose from a more extensive menu of service alternatives.

Also, most front-office users need access to accounting and/or portfolio management information (see Figure 2.5.1.1). Investment managers focus more specifically on portfolios, whereas account managers receive customer account information. Whether for customer accounts or portfolios, the information typically consists of priced holdings, often broken into tax or cost lots that permit users to evaluate not only the absolute attractiveness of holdings but also the cost implications of changing positions.

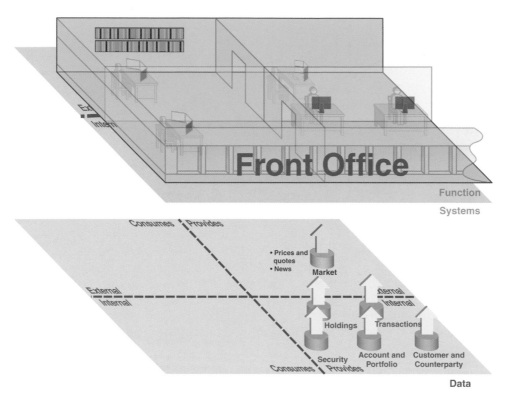

Figure 2.5.1.1 *The front offices of buy-side firms* provide detailed market data to traders and many portfolio managers; deliver accounting data on customers, portfolios, and products for analysis and decision making; and furnish order management information to facilitate the trading process.

PORTFOLIO MANAGER

Portfolio managers use information on holdings and access to details about the account or portfolio as a starting point for decisions. Holdings are updated based on changing market values for the component instruments, sometimes in real time. Some portfolio managers perform analysis on their existing holdings as well as evaluation of alternatives. Other managers leave all analysis to research analysts. We describe the analysis when we describe research analysts, but note that portfolio managers may have access to analytical data.

Portfolio managers depend on research from sell-side analysts and in-house analysts as well as "ideas" from personal investigation, salesmen, news, commentary services, and other sources when assessing existing holdings or considering new purchases. We noted in Book 2 that some firms have an ***investment committee*** that compiles ***buy lists*** stating what instruments are acceptable within the firm, what instruments should not be considered for purchases, and sometimes recommendations on recommended purchases and sales.

One additional issue was noted in Book 2: Portfolio managers often trade directly in less active fixed-income instruments such as corporate issues, provincial and municipal bonds, asset-backed issues, and other fixed-income instruments where trading is thin or illiquid. For these instruments portfolio managers require information comparable to buy-side traders.

Portfolio managers may generate a variety of data that is used to augment or modify information in internal accounting systems. However, for our perspective, their primary contribution of information is to generate new orders (see Figure 2.5.1.1.1). Portfolio managers generate the intention to buy or sell, the quantity of instruments, target prices, and a general sense of urgency. In the aftermath of their decisions to request trades, portfolio holdings ultimately change as well.

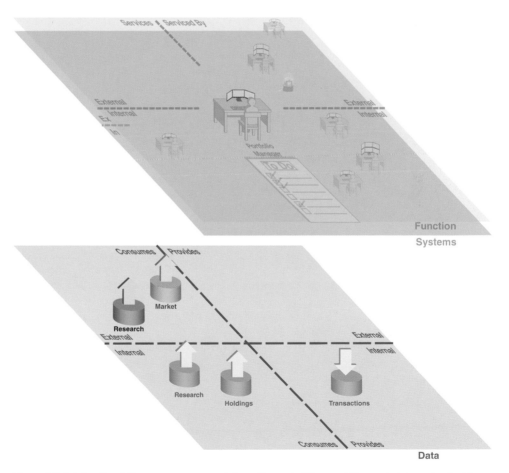

Figure 2.5.1.1.1 *Portfolio managers* access information on holdings and the markets to make decisions that affect those holdings and generate orders.

BUY-SIDE TRADER

Buy-side traders require extensive access to information about the markets in general and prices and quotes for specific instruments. The price and quote information may come from vendors or from sell-side services. Traders may receive indications of interest that may feed directly into an OMS. The traders may receive news and commentary as background for trading systems. Some research and market intelligence may also come from the sell side.

Traders are producers of orders and, indirectly, of IOIs going to other firms (see Figure 2.5.1.1.2). Also, traders are indirectly causes of position and holdings changes and trade reports both for internal processing and for broadcast to the broader market. As we noted in Book 2, the most important piece of information controlled by buy-side traders is the information about orders *that they do not disclose*. Knowledge of orders not released to the market represents undisclosed liquidity that

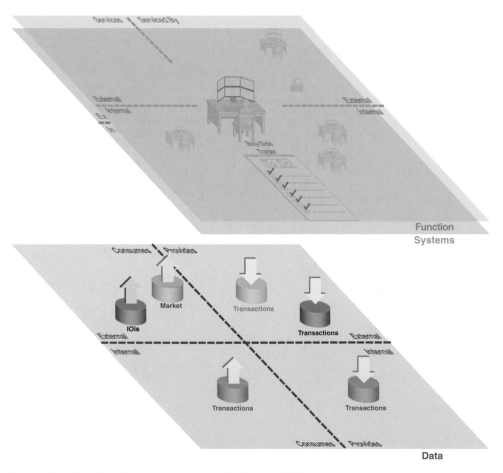

Figure 2.5.1.1.2 *Buy-side traders* receive orders from portfolio managers and use information from trading venues and the sell side to generate orders for execution and indications of interest.

trading venues and the sell side regularly barter for in important concessions and access to special services.

RESEARCH ANALYST

Buy-side research analysts are consumers of analytical data such as historical price sets and fundamental information on instruments, but also of universes of similar portfolios. They access research as documents and as ideas from sell-side analysts and from third-party research firms.

Analysts produce a stream of reports and ideas that are consumed by portfolio managers within the firm and sometimes by customers. Analysts may also provide input to buy lists (see Figure 2.5.1.1.3).

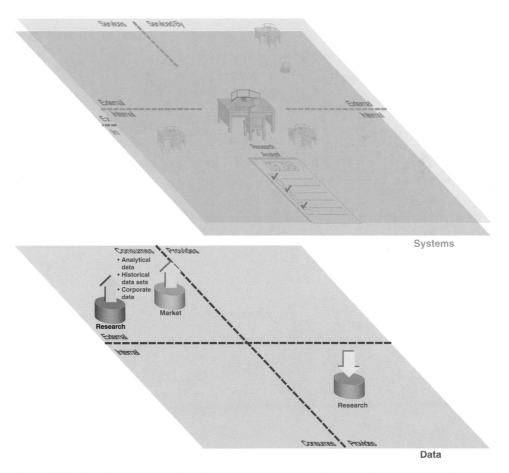

Figure 2.5.1.1.3 *Research analysts* synthesize research and ideas from sell-side analysts, analytical information, and market data to create research and ideas employed within their firms.

CUSTOMER INTERACTION

Account managers and sales personnel depend mostly on accounting information to service existing customers. They explain investment performance and sometimes compare returns on accounts with indexes and universes of comparable accounts. Sales personnel may use comparisons to universes in marketing materials, making sure they do not make any claims that exceed what is permissible by regulators.

Account managers provide updates to customer details as necessary and handle contributions and withdrawals. Sales personnel provide details for new accounts and establish the accounts by accepting deposits and transfers as needed (see Figure 2.5.1.1.4).

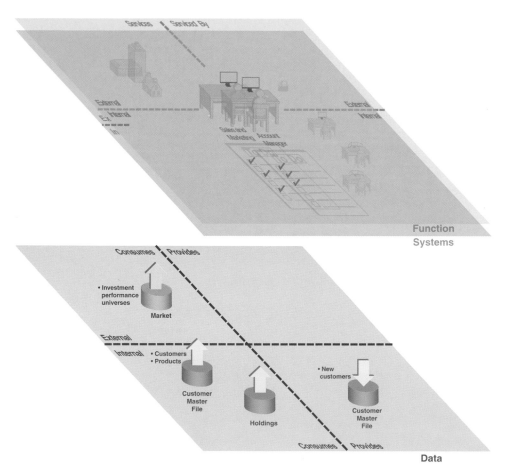

Figure 2.5.1.1.4 *Account managers and sales personnel* rely on customer accounting information to service existing customers and on comparative information with competitive services to attract new customers.

Middle Office

The middle office supports its staff with market information, particularly related to investigating problems and answering complaints. Time-and-sales information is an important source.

Information generated in the middle-office activities updates customer accounts (see Figure 2.5.1.2). Also, aggregate customer balances must be reconciled with positions held by the firm. As noted, we address compliance in Book 4.

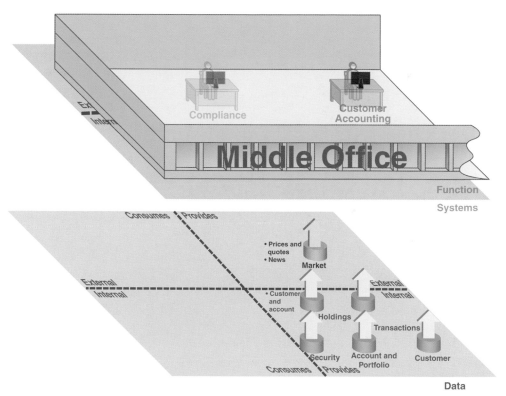

Figure 2.5.1.2 *The middle office* provides market information as needed and receives information to update accounts while producing updated customer master files.

Backoffice

The backoffice provides market information to support operations and receives notification of changes to firm accounts from custodians, counterparties, and other support organizations.

Activities in the backoffice produce changes to firm holdings and updates to pending transactions (see Figure 2.5.1.3).

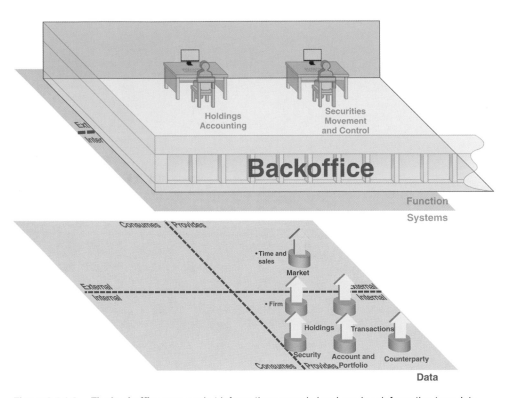

Figure 2.5.1.3 *The backoffice* uses market information as needed and receives information to update the firm's accounts while producing updated security master and transaction files.

HOLDINGS ACCOUNTING

Holdings accounting maintains accounts with banks, custodians, and depositories reconciling balances in cash and instruments and updating information as changes occur (see Figure 2.5.1.3.1). It is important for firm balances to map to aggregate customer balances plus proprietary firm accounts.

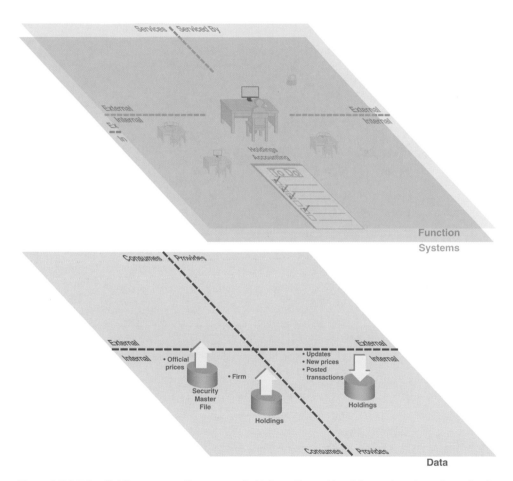

Figure 2.5.1.3.1 *Holdings accounting* uses market information and input from external counterparties to update accounts to generate changes to the firm's balances in cash and instruments.

SECURITIES MOVEMENT AND CONTROL

Securities movement and control depends on market data to resolve issues that arise during trading, clearing, and settlement (see Figure 2.5.1.3.2). Inputs from various counterparties update transaction details and status, and problems must be researched and corrected.

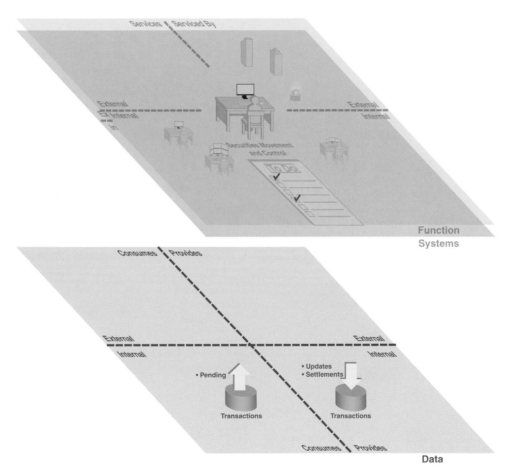

Figure 2.5.1.3.2 *Securities movement and control* employs market information and inputs from counterparties in the trading and settlement processes to update transaction files.

THE SELL SIDE

At a firm-wide level, sell-side firms provide most of the same classes of data functions as their buy-side counterparts, but the nature of the information differs. General market data is provided to substantial segments of the firm, and accounting information is used by or feeds many operations (see Figure 2.5.2). At a more basic level account,

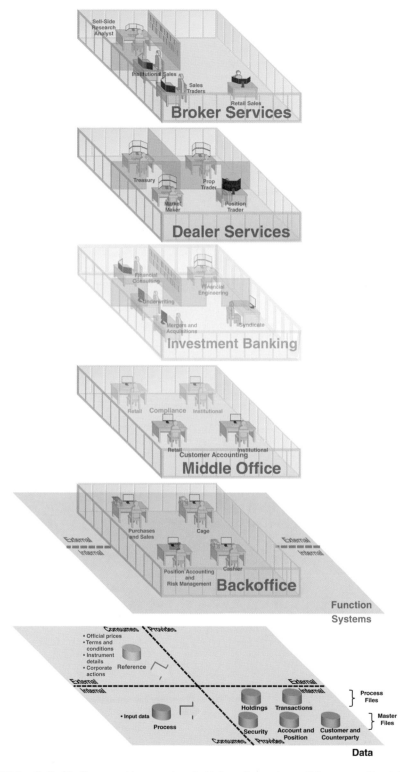

Figure 2.5.2 *Sell-side firms* provide general market information and overall firm accounting data to large segments throughout the firm and update the major information stores for use by all.

customer, and counterparty files are maintained and service many functions within the firm.

Sell-side firms are required to furnish data to regulators, trading venues, and support entities as part of ongoing operations. Although much of this information is generated by specific functions, it is presented to other entities as representing the entire firm.

THE "GREAT WALLS" OF THE STREET

Ironically, sell-side firms must also work to shield some parts of the firms from information produced in other parts. For example, firms are supposed to protect consumers of research information produced by the firm from the influence of investment banking, which may seek or actually represent firms covered by research.

Likewise, market-making operations and positions acquired by a firm are not supposed to influence agency recommendations to customers. To protect these possible conflicts, firms attempt to erect so-called **Chinese walls** intended to shield potentially conflicting groups from mutual influence. The obvious reference is to the Great Wall of China.

Front Office

The front office of sell-side firms provides prices and quotes, news, commentary, and assorted analytical information to large segments of the front office (see Figure 2.5.2.1). Order-management systems provide linkages that permit orders to move from portfolio managers to traders and for the status of pending orders to be viewed and updated as trading unfolds. Accounting for customers and positions is available both to sales personnel and dealers.

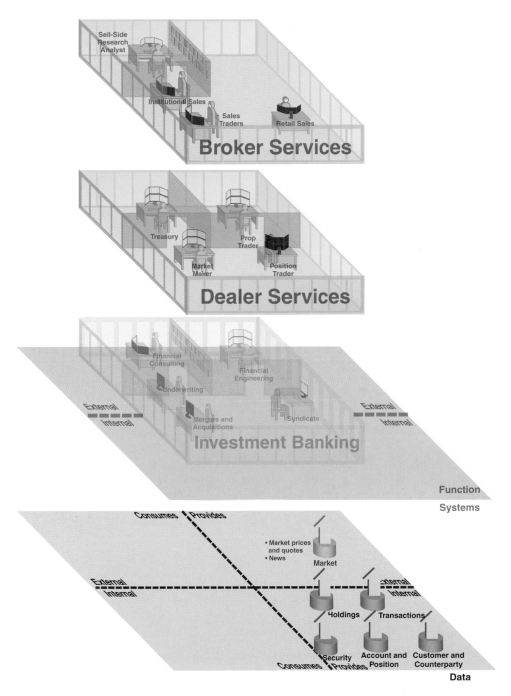

Figure 2.5.2.1 *The sell-side front office* provides specialized market information, order management data, as well as customer and position accounting data to large segments of the front office.

Increasingly, firms receive customer orders directly through execution-management systems from institutional customers, and active retail customers may send orders using sophisticated trading systems delivered through the Internet. Execution-management systems may also channel orders directly to trading venues by sponsoring customers' direct market access.

BROKER

Brokers, both institutional and retail, use pricing information, news, commentary, and research information to track the markets. They receive information on customer accounts, and firms may maintain systems to track customers' interests in trading opportunities.

Retail and institutional customers are provided with information about their accounts, general research information, market data, product information, and information to support trading. Typically, institutional brokers have access to market information that is broader and more detailed than the information available to retail brokers.

Both retail and institutional brokers may be responsible for generating customer orders, and institutional brokers may be responsible for routing indications of interest to firms and traders within firms that may have an interest in the instrument involved in the IOI (see Figure 2.5.2.1.1).

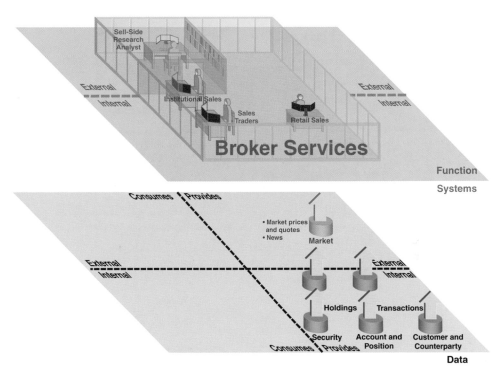

Figure 2.5.2.1.1 *The sell-side brokers* use information on the markets and from internal order-management systems to facilitate trades on behalf of customers and pass on indications of interest, research, and other intelligence to customers.

PRINCIPALS

Those engaged in principal trading (dealers, market makers, and proprietary traders) receive the widest assortment of information with detail on market conditions and prices for regularly traded securities (see Figure 2.5.2.1.2). Supporting information such as news and analytical information is available if needed. Whereas brokers receive information on customers and their holdings, principal traders receive information on positions.

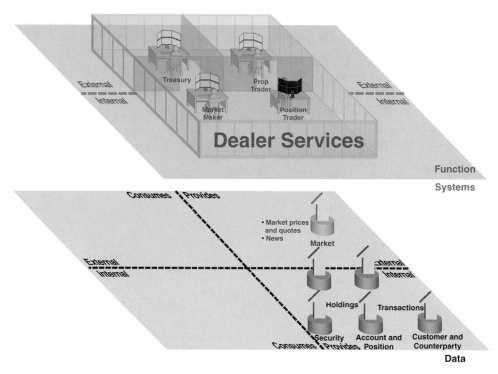

Figure 2.5.2.1.2 *Sell-side principals* consume market and other data as a basis for pricing orders and defining markets for both internal trading and to be advertised through trading venues and contributor information systems.

For principal traders engaged in quantitative trading, strategies information input into trading models may be required to have very low latency. (Latency is described in the Part 3 on networks.) Position information includes not only priced holdings but also information on profitability and data on leverage.

Dealers produce quotes on the instruments in which they make markets and may generate contributor data. They establish internal market quotes and produce guidelines followed by brokers trading for customers against customer accounts. The transactions generated update positions.

Middle Office

The middle office consumes information on markets to research and update holdings and transactions (see Figure 2.5.2.2). In particular, middle-office staff may use time and sales reports and other information as needed to research problems. They access and update information on customer accounts and positions. Changes and updates are posted to master and transaction files.

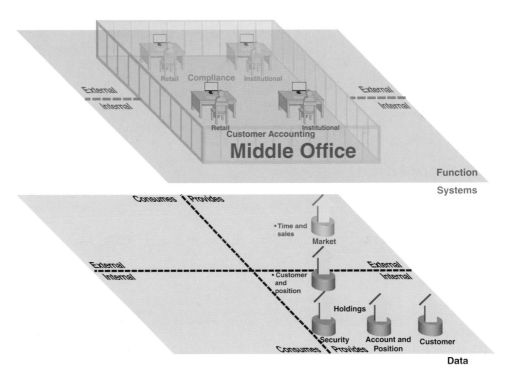

Figure 2.5.2.2 *The sell-side middle office* provides general market information and customer and position accounting data to middle-office staff who update and reconcile accounts and positions.

Backoffice

The backoffice of firms requires basic market information and access to the data from the firm's accounting information (see Figure 2.5.2.3). Information from counterparties is also available to specific functions within the backoffice.

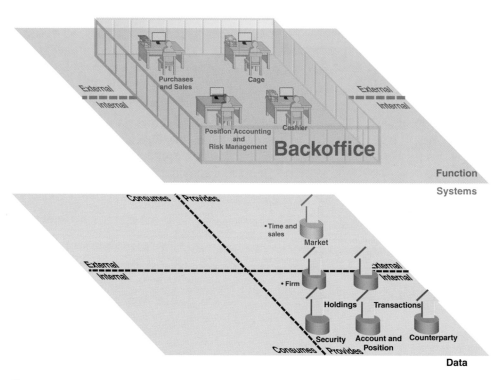

Figure 2.5.2.3 *The sell-side backoffice* provides general market information, transaction management data, as well as firm accounting to its staff.

PURCHASES AND SALES

The purchases and sales department receives trade reports from trading venues and/or clearing corporations, must map the executions to the orders that generated them, and must research and resolve any problems if possible (see Figure 2.5.2.3.1). For complicated problems, the trade is passed on within the firm to the department able to resolve the problem.

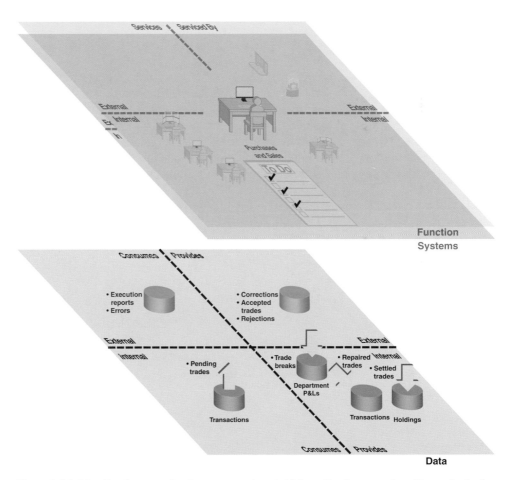

Figure 2.5.2.3.1 *Purchases and sales* use general market information for research and to receive trade reports and open orders that are matched or set aside for problem resolution.

THE CAGE

The cage is responsible for managing aggregate positions in instruments that may be maintained by agent banks, in open positions at clearing corporations, and at other counterparties (see Figure 2.5.2.3.2). Instruments supporting loans and short positions must be segregated in special accounts. All this information must be managed through the accounting system so it can map to individual accounts and positions.

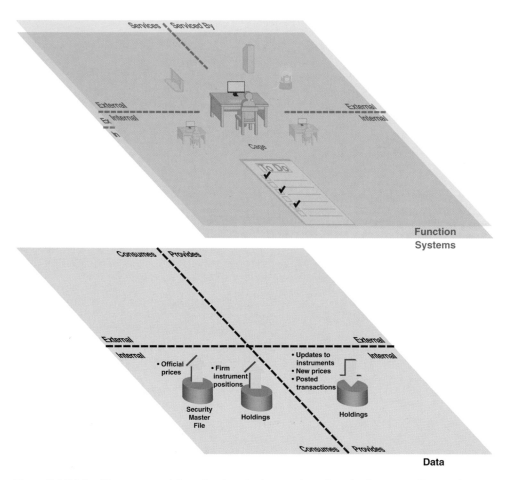

Figure 2.5.2.3.2   *The cage* uses information from banks, counterparties, clearing corporations, and internal sources to reconcile and verify aggregate firm holdings in instruments.

THE CASHIER

The cashier uses information from internal accounting, banks, the clearing corporation, and counterparties to manage aggregate cash positions (see Figure 2.5.2.3.3).

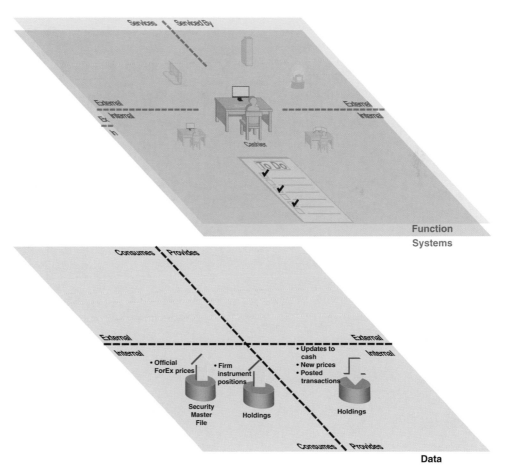

Figure 2.5.2.3.3   *The cashier* uses information from bank statements, clearing corporations, and counterparties to develop an aggregate value for all cash positions.

Except for what we have called process data, the entities that create data and/or vendors own substantially all the data used in the trading markets. The creation, collection, distribution, and use of data within the trading markets constitute a separate collateral business. In this chapter we consider all the aspects of the **business of data**.

Figure 2.6 illustrates many of the facets of the data business. We examine each of these facets in turn as we examine the business of data in more detail.

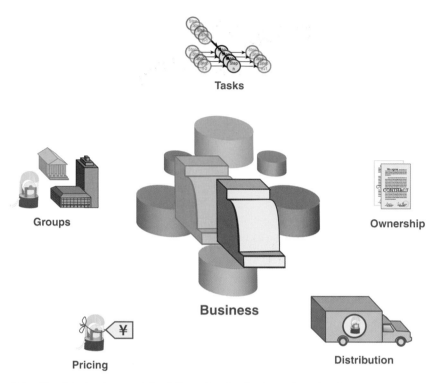

Tasks

Groups

Ownership

Business

Pricing

Distribution

Figure 2.6 ***The data business*** entails all the tasks of collecting and moving data from the place where it is created to the place where it is used and all the subsequent tasks required to subsidize those tasks.

TASKS

In this section we focus on the major categories of tasks required to provide information as a business. Figure 2.6.1 highlights these tasks.

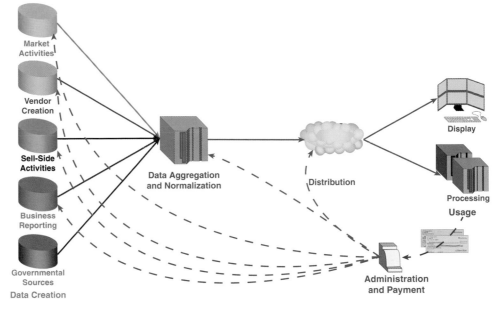

Figure 2.6.1 ***Data-business tasks*** involve creating, aggregating, normalizing, distributing, and using commercially available data.

Creation

Information and data products are created either as a byproduct of other activities or may be purpose-created to solve a specific need. The key difference between data creation and the process data we described previously is that data creation intends the content for sale and the creators take steps, described later, to ensure that they are paid for the data's use and to protect the ***intellectual property*** of the content.

Aggregation

Information intended for sale is aggregated into packages that are believed to be most valuable and attractive to those who may use the information. When vendors aggregate data, the process may require collecting information from tens or even hundreds of different information sources. The ***data aggregation*** process often requires a dedicated functional group within a vendor organization. The data aggregation unit is responsible for identifying data owners and performing all the business and contracting tasks required to permit the vendor to offer the data.

Normalization

We introduced normalization as a characteristic of data and suggested that **data creators** or owners sometimes normalize data. Vendors extend the normalization process. First, every **listing exchange** and many other trading venues assign ticker symbols to instruments they trade, but trading venues do not attempt to coordinate their symbols with other markets.

Each vendor develops a methodology for resolving instrument identification conflicts and also assigns market identifiers. Moreover, vendors add incidental information to the information they offer to make the information more useful to their customers. For example, a number of equity measures such as earnings per share and estimates of **alpha (α)** and **beta (β)** may be added for equities while yield might be added for fixed income.

Also, in the normalization process, information from different sources may be linked. For example, prices for a given instrument might be combined with news stories related to the instrument, often from different news sources.

Distribution

Data must be distributed from the place where it is aggregated to the location where it is consumed. We see in the next part that the process of deciding how to distribute data efficiently is a complicated task and may not be accomplished by the information vendor. Indeed, an important change that has occurred in the business of data has been the decoupling of the tasks we are describing.

Consumption

Information is consumed in one of two primary ways. Data may be displayed so human users view it as input to their work and decisions, or it may serve as input into a variety of system applications.

Reporting and Invoicing

Finally, because we are describing the information business, there are a number of tasks associated with the invoicing and administration of the business. Because they are such an important part of the process, they are described in more detail in a separate section.

GROUPS

The groups performing the tasks required to produce or acquire, to store, to **normalize**, to distribute, and to use information throughout the industry are shown in Figure 2.6. In Figure 2.6.2, we focus on the groups or roles in the data business.

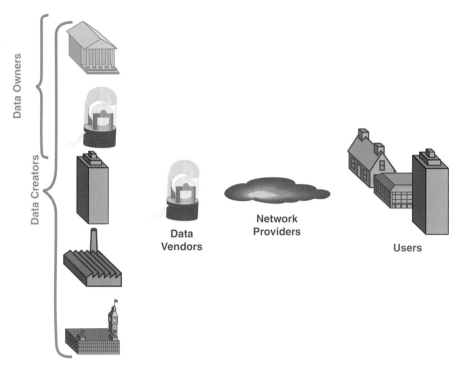

Figure 2.6.2 *The data-business groups* are the roles of data owner, data vendor, network provider, and user.

The major groups include data owner (or sometimes **content owner**), **data vendor**, **network provider**, and user. Note that these are actually roles and not specific industry functions or entities as defined in Book 1. For example, an exchange is an entity that is commonly known to be a data owner, but exchanges frequently serve as vendors, particularly for smaller members. Exchanges likewise consolidate and distribute information and are active users of information as a part of their operations.

Owner

Data owners have to generate and sell the data they produce. An alternate term might be "data creator," but in many cases the owner of data does not necessarily create the data.[4] In some cases the owner may also provide a preliminary level of normalization to the data before passing the data on to vendors. Some data owners, particularly exchanges and other trading venues, may distribute their data directly, bypassing vendors. We consider this business in this book's Part 3 on networks.

---

4   As an example, exchanges and other trading venues "own" the quotes they publish, but in most cases the quotes are generated by principals submitting orders through brokers and market makers quoting in their role of providing **liquidity**. Similarly, vendors that provide contributor pages to market makers often assert ownership of the information even though the market maker created the quotes. Invariably, when one entity asserts ownership of data created by another, friction results, particularly when the creator is asked to pay to see the data it helped to create.

Creators also have to invoice for the use of the data, either directly or using an outsourcing arrangement described later, and they must ensure that the use of their data is consistent with the rules they establish to govern usage.

Data Vendors

Vendors of data are responsible for arranging to acquire data from multiple sources, assembling and arranging the data in a form that permits easy access and/or delivery, normalizing the data yet again, and ensuring that the data is delivered to users.

Vendors of market data collect information from many different information creators; consolidate and normalize the data; sometimes provide additional information; distribute the data to end users; and may furnish tools for viewing the data, providing the data to applications, and monitoring and reporting usage.

Network Providers

Network providers arrange for the facilities to transmit information among various destinations as a part of the business of data. The network function may be a stand-alone business offered to others, a service provided by a vendor to customers to enhance the value of data that is sold, or a means of transmitting information within a user organization.

Users

Finally, users consume information for a variety of purposes, which gives the data value. As we noted, usage can mean individuals with access to displays of information and applications that consume data as part of the activities the application performs.

THE DATA PROCESS

In the figure shown here, we see how the groups perform the tasks involved in the data process:

1. *Data creators*, who may or may not be *data owners*, *create* information.
2. *Data vendors* then *aggregate* information from various sources.
3. *Data vendors* may also *normalize* the information to make it more useful.
4. *Network vendors distribute* the data.
5. *Users consume* the data.
6. *Users* must *pay* for the information they use.

Note that governments do not typically receive payment for the information they create except to cover any unique costs of production or delivery.

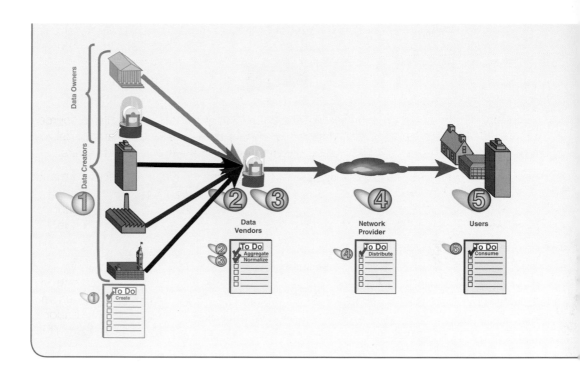

OWNERSHIP

The important underlying principle that is needed to understand the data business:

Substantially all data is not sold; it is licensed for use.

This principle implies that acquiring data neither enables the acquirer to use the data without restriction, nor pass the data to others without permission. Moreover, the user must undertake and/or submit to defined activities to ensure that the owner's (the data creator's) rights are protected and the owner receives all the revenues defined in the usage agreement (see Figure 2.6.3).

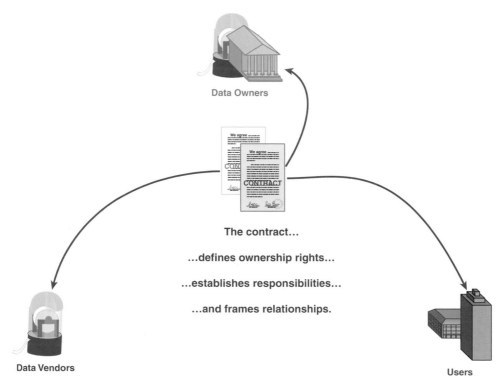

Figure 2.6.3 *Data ownership* involves contractual relationships among the data creator, any vendor, and the user.

Contracts

Data ownership and the details of how it may be used are established through contracts. The contract for the data asserts the ownership of the information, the conditions under which it can be used, and any responsibilities that must be assumed by the user.

INTELLECTUAL PROPERTY

The portion of the law that regulates intellectual property controls the ownership of data. The difficult problem with data is that a number of different entities may be involved in the creation and distribution of data. Each adds different aspects of the product that data becomes and it is difficult to assign relative importance to each component aspect. Moreover, for most important types of data, some entity established ownership early in the evolution of data as a business and now defends that ownership against later participants who now add incremental value to the information.

THE LIFE CYCLE OF A DATA PRODUCT

Most data products begin with little interest in the service. In fact, many data creators work very hard to attract users to new services. Not many years ago, an important Latin American market actually paid to have its market prices published daily in major U.S. financial newspapers. Now that information is highly valuable and is in great demand.

There is some tendency for information owners to overlook the need to establish the data's value and assert their intellectual property rights in their information when it is not in high demand. When the information becomes more valuable, it is difficult to reassert property rights if the information has been delivered free of charge for a time.

MECHANICS

To understand the discussions of relationships, process flows, reporting, and enforcement, one needs to understand the mechanics established in most data contracts. The contracts generally state that the owner of the data is willing to license the use of data to a user and the user is responsible for reporting back to the owner some units of usage that are known as **units of count**. A unit of count is some measurable quantity or number that is the basis for charging for the use of the information.

UNITS OF COUNT

A typical unit of count for market information is a **display device** or a **desk unit**. Early in the history of market data, information from the markets was distributed to primitive computers known as **controllers** that provided data to display devices that were simple video displays with no processing capabilities. As personal computers have become more common and users have increasingly demanded access to data using mobile devices, the concept of a display device has become problematic.

First, personal computers connected to the Internet permit users to redirect the information they receive in ways that are difficult for vendors and data owners to monitor or control. Second, users are angered by having to pay multiple times for the same data just because they access the data on different devices. We return to these problems in Chapter 9 on issues.

For reference data, the unit of count can be a market. For example, a user might buy the right to data on all fixed income from the United States. Alternatively, some data is available in set numbers of instrument identifiers known as a **cache**. An example of this might be a user purchasing the reference data for 10,000 instrument identifiers of the user's choosing spread over several different markets.

Many other types of units of count can be used. One possibility is an individual, but this requires a unique user identifier. Some data owners offer so-called enterprise licenses in which the user and owner negotiate, usually yearly, on an estimated number of units of count for the next year. Once they are agreed, the user pays for this number even if the actual numbers fluctuate. The next agreement can be modified to reflect actual changes.

The contracts state the user must **report** the number or quantity of units of count that are **entitled** to use the data, typically on a monthly basis. The contracts also state the way these entitlements are reported. (We describe the relationships next.)

Either directly or, more often, indirectly because of the requirements of the contract, a process is established for providing new data services, changing existing services, and ending the distribution process.

Finally, contracts usually have some provisions for policing the use of the data. The most common means of policing is an **audit** in which the owner or an entity chosen by the owner will visit the user to verify that all information is being used in accordance with the contract and by only those units of count that have been reported. This is illustrated in Figure 2.6.3.1.

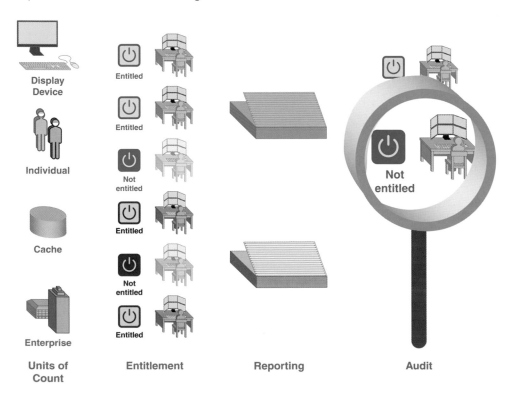

Figure 2.6.3.1   *Data ownership mechanics* define the units of count, as well as the methods of reporting usage, invoicing, and payment

RELATIONSHIPS

Most contracts establish a relationship between the content owner, vendors that may distribute information, and the user. Over time, three major types of relationships have evolved (see Figure 2.6.3.2).

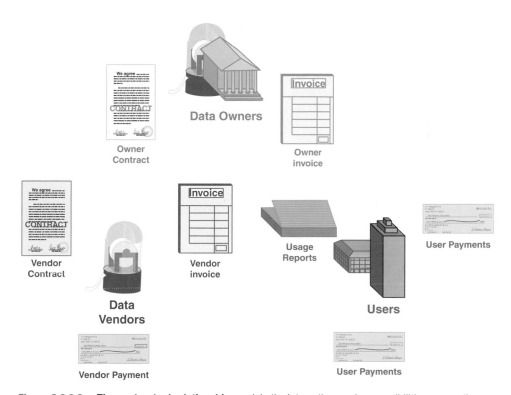

Figure 2.6.3.2 *The contractual relationships* explain the interactions and responsibilities among the data creator, the vendor (if any), and the user.

No Reporting

At first, small new data owners may not have any direct relationship with the user. These small owners can negotiate with vendors, selling a vendor the right to permit the vendor's customers to access the information for a specified period. The owner and vendor negotiate the expected number of units of count that will likely be distributed by the vendor or that will be entitled to use the information (see Figure 2.6.3.2.1).

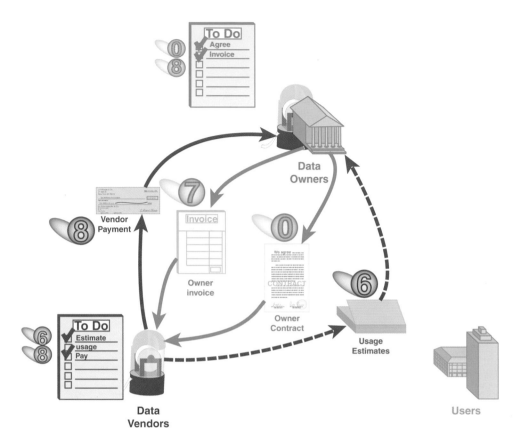

Figure 2.6.3.2.1   *The contract* requires no direct reporting of usage if the content owner licenses the data to a vendor for distribution based only on an estimate of usage.

Based on this negotiation, the vendor pays the owner for the right to distribute, and the user is not involved. This approach is simple and straightforward, but most content owners believe they do not receive as much revenue as they would like and there is no direct relationship with the user.

Vendor Reports

Many content owners use a system where they have a direct contractual relationship with the user, but all reporting and invoicing is routed through the vendor (see Figure 2.6.3.2.2). The vendor often provides the content owner's contract to the user, but the contractual relationship is between the user and the content owner.

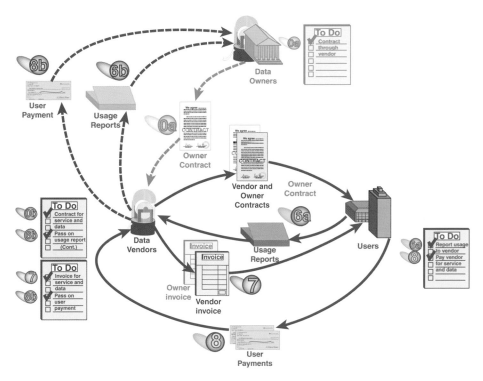

Figure 2.6.3.2.2 *The vendor* may be used to collect reports from and invoice the user on behalf of the data creator.

When the contract is signed, the user reports all entitlements to the vendor and the vendor passes the information on to the content owner. When the vendor invoices the user, it includes an amount for the fees charged to the content owner, and the vendor passes the fees on to the owner. This system absolves the content owner of the expensive invoicing requirements that billing directly would provide, but most content owners lament the fact that they are isolated from their users and do not have a clear understanding of usage trends.

User Reports

The final approach used by a few exchanges is to have a direct contractual and invoicing relationship with the user (see Figure 2.6.3.2.3). The owner may use the vendor for reporting, or the owner may permit direct reporting using a web site. This approach gives the owner much better control and a better understanding of the users' activities and needs, but the advantages come at the cost of an administrative and invoicing infrastructure.

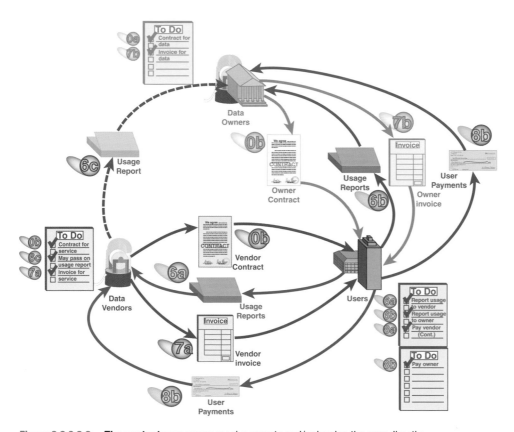

Figure 2.6.3.2.3   ***The content owner*** may receive reports and/or invoice the user directly.

ENTERPRISE LICENSES

A number of large entities on both the buy and sell sides are negotiating ***enterprise licenses*** in which the entity and the data owner negotiate a license for an aggregate amount to be paid over the next year. The amount is a function of actual usage and may be adjusted to anticipate probable changes. Each year the usage and the amount are adjusted, but there are no monthly changes as usage ebbs and flows. This reduces paperwork for both parties, and the data owner gets a more stable revenue stream.

PROCESS FLOW

We introduced the concept of a business process flow to show how the different steps in the trading process involved the interaction among entities over time. We return to this method of graphic representation to show the data business. Instead of the entities defined in Book 1, we use the groups defined for the data business previously. Here, we consider four major processes, as illustrated in Figure 2.6.3.3.

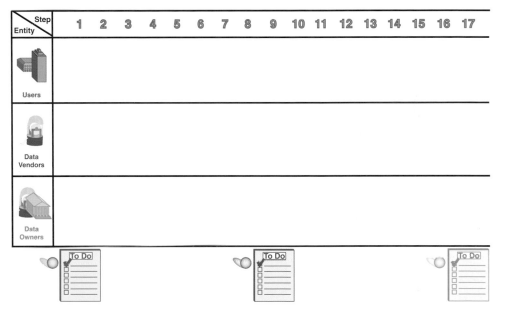

Figure 2.6.3.3   *The data business process flow* describes the steps required to provide new services, accommodate service changes, and manage reporting and the way invoicing occurs.

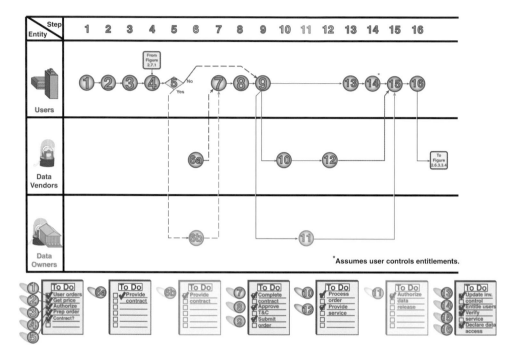

Figure 2.6.3.3.1 *A new service* requires an exchange of executed contracts, verification of the service, approval, and initiation of service.

New Service

When a user initiates a new service that requires the distribution of data that is owned by an entity other than the vendor of the service, a process is required to place the order, generate and execute the contracts required, verify the contract details, approve the contracts, order the service to be delivered, receive the service, and verify that the service conforms to both the contract and the order to purchase. This scenario is shown in Figure 2.6.3.3.1.

Change of Service

During the life of any data service, it frequently happens that the service must be changed. A frequent type of change occurs when an employee of a user firm requires a new service or an existing user employee cancels usage. When this occurs, the date on which the service starts or ends must be established. Both the vendor and data owner must be notified, the units of count must be updated, and the initiation or termination must occur (see Figure 2.6.3.3.2).

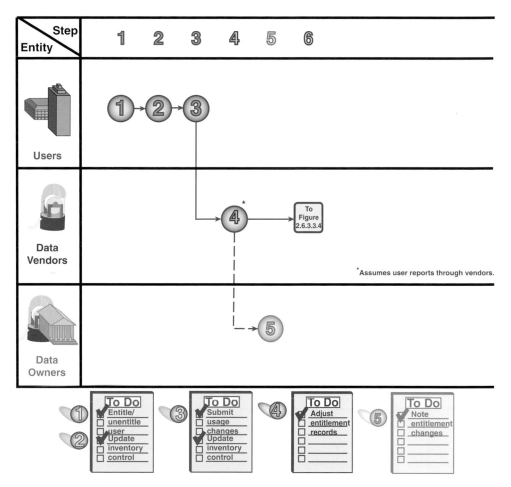

Figure 2.6.3.3.2 *A change of service* involves defining a start/end date, verification of the change, reporting, and the actual change.

Reporting

Periodically, usually monthly, for most data, users must report to data owners either directly or indirectly how many units of count are entitled to receive the data belonging to the owner. Both the data owner and/or vendor use the reports as a basis of invoicing (see Figure 2.6.3.3.3). The reports must be reconciled with existing information to create adjusted numbers of users. For changes in usage, there needs to be a date for each change that can be used for individuals using data for less than the whole period.

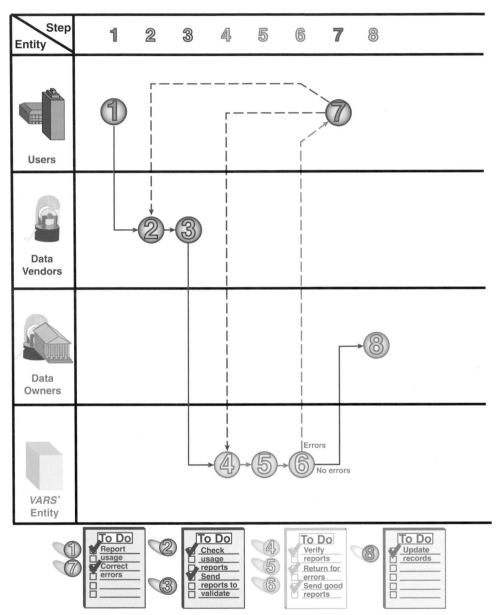

* A **Vendor Account Reporting System (VARS)** is a reporting format used by vendors to report information on usage to data owners.

Figure 2.6.3.3.3   *Periodic reporting* instructs all parties of the number of units of count actually receiving the service so invoicing reflects actual usage.

Invoicing

For each usage period, either the vendor or the data owner must invoice the user based on the updated units of count (see Figure 2.6.3.3.4). Almost always the invoice is a calculation based on the number of units of count times the price per unit. It is

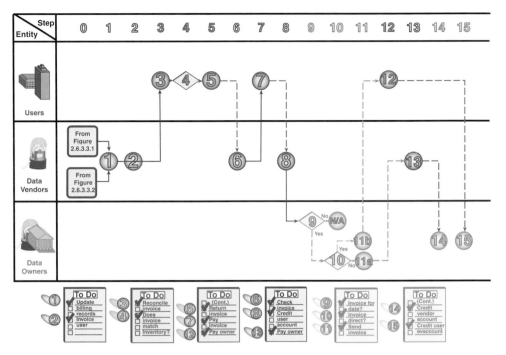

Figure 2.6.3.3.4 *Invoicing* involves the steps to produce and distribute an invoice that must be verified, adjusted if a problem is found, and paid.

possible, however, to have a ***unit of pricing*** that is different from the unit of count. For example, some vendors charge different amounts for different kinds of applications.

In this example the unit of count would be applications, and the unit of pricing is the type of application. (For example, the vendor or content owner might charge higher fees for applications involved in trading than for applications that generate customer reports.) Invoices once received by the user are typically vetted to make sure they are accurate. Inaccuracies are returned to the vendor and/or owner for corrections. Users and the owner or vendor then work out adjustments to correct errors.

ENFORCEMENT

In most data contracts, the owner establishes the right to visit the user periodically and verify that the data is being used as set forth in the contract and that the numbers of actual users are consistent with reports. Audits may be done by the owner's own staff or by a third-party auditing firm.

DATA THEFT

The FISD*, a association of exchanges, vendors, and users of real-time data has defined the problem of **misappropriated data**. The problem is a major concern to the members of the association now that technology in the form of powerful personal computers connected to the Internet is fully capable of retransmission of data without the data owner's approval or awareness.

The association defines three levels of misappropriation and theft:

- *Those unaware that they are misappropriating data*—The rules and contractual obligations of data users are complex and difficult to understand. Therefore, some users may be using information in ways that are in breach of their obligations but may not be aware they are misusing it.

- *Those trying to adjust for a perceived injustice*—Data rules sometimes create injustices or perceived injustices because the rules do not recognize differences in need or purpose. For example, a programmer who needs data not for its content but just to test a new application may be obligated to pay as much as a trader making huge profits from the data. In some cases firms try to circumvent rules because they believe the rules are unfair. Fair or not, owners expect the rules to be followed.

- *Simple data theft*—Some individuals and firms misappropriate data knowing full well they are breaking the rules.

---

*FISD stands for the Financial Information Services Division of the Software and Information Industries Association.

PRICING

Payments for data involve several dimensions or considerations. There is a general desire on the part of the data owner to get the maximum value for data, but substantially all the groups that profit from the sale of data prefer to simplify the pricing structure. Simple pricing makes invoicing easier to understand for both the customer and for the seller, but more importantly it simplifies the administrative burden for the seller. Unfortunately, simple pricing and maximum value are usually conflicting goals.

Typically, a price for data is a multiplier that is applied to the unit of count or the unit of pricing. The price is the charge for one unit, and the price times the number of units in use represents the total cost to the user (see Figure 2.6.4).

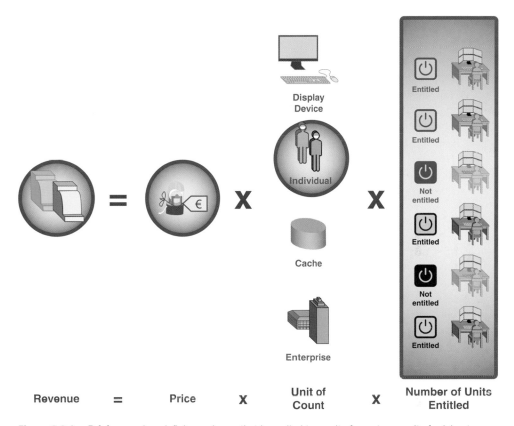

| Revenue | = | Price | X | Unit of Count | X | Number of Units Entitled |

Figure 2.6.4 ***Pricing*** requires defining a charge that is applied to a unit of count or a unit of pricing to determine the amount to invoice a customer for using data.

Typical charges have been the cost paid for a display unit, the monthly cost for an individual receiving information, the cost for a batch of data (e.g., North American fixed-income instruments), or the cost for a cache of prices on 10,000 instruments where the user chooses the ticker symbols of the instruments of interest. Other types of information beyond instrument prices such as news and research are frequently priced based on costs for a desk unit receiving the news or the cost for a given report.

Beyond the units for pricing, there is a complicated issue of determining how the actual unit prices are established. In the sections that follow, we look at some important factors that impact pricing.

Value

Value-based pricing implies that the same data may have different prices when sold to two or more different types of users who have different levels of need for the information and different abilities to pay (see Figure 2.6.4.1). (The "user" in the preceding sentence can be an individual, but also an application.) Value-based pricing typically means the content owner can sell the information for the maximum price to those who need it most, getting maximum revenue, but also getting incremental revenue from those who need it less. For the user, although those with high need for the information pay a premium, the user is able to provide important information to a number of other user categories that need the data but cannot justify a high price.

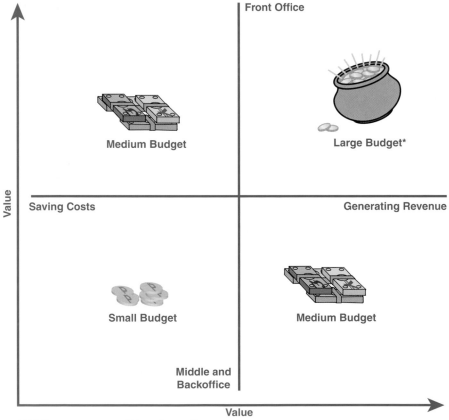

* Relative among groups within a given entity.

Figure 2.6.4.1 ***Value-based pricing*** creates packages of data and services that are priced differently based on the value of the package to the user.

The difficulty with value-pricing models comes in trying to enforce the separation of users into the correct group. It is often difficult to ensure that those with high need and the ability to pay are not signing up as members of a lower-price group. The most common solution is to package sets of information including different components into packages such that high-value users can get all of the information they need only if they sign up for the high-priced packages.

Vendors and content owners usually have rigid rules preventing users from selecting data combinations independently from an open menu of information. Vendors instead refuse to permit data combinations that do not conform to one of the packaged sets.

The value of data or a data service package depends on the purpose for which the data is used. Typically, data sets designed for traders command a premium. The value of information used for sales is almost as high as trading. Moreover, the sell side usually pays higher premiums for data than the buy side. Beyond trading and sales, investment banking and research data commands a premium. The middle and backoffice usually receive low-cost data services.

ASSESSING VALUE

One set of questions continually arises when trying to assess value for pricing purposes: What data is of value? How valuable is it? Which groups value the data? Why do the groups value the data? There are no absolute answers to these questions either on a relative basis or within any group of users. There are just too many different investment styles, approaches to trading, and methods of organizing the processes to be accomplished to make absolute statements. However, there are some relative obligations that can be helpful.

Chapter 5 on functions attempted to suggest what information is of value to different functions and also to suggest how the information is used. In the following paragraphs and figures, we try to show something of how important information is on a conceptual basis.

For a trader, and to a lesser degree a salesperson, the ultimate goal is to assess the price in advance of an execution, both to determine when to trade and in what quantity. The trader also needs to be able to price a limit order at the moment of the trade. Therefore, pricing information and, in particular, quotes are very valuable, and that value grows as the moment of the execution approaches.

(Continued)

When the execution is past, the value of the data drops dramatically but remains significant until the trade settles. At that point the value drops further but remains positive as the execution price becomes one more data point in a historical pricing set. This conceptual value is represented in this figure.

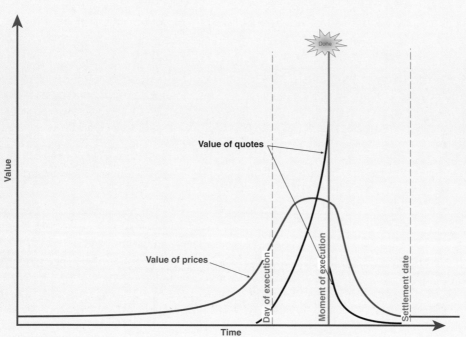

Note: Value estimates are both qualitative and conceptual and do not represent any quantitative analysis.

By contrast, investment banking and research personnel tend to value historical prices as a part of the analysis they perform valuing securities more than the moment-to-moment prices in the market.* This figure shows that.

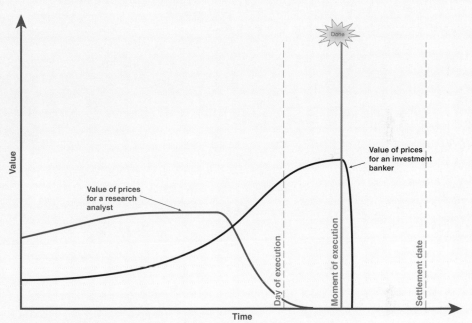

Note: Value estimates are both qualitative and conceptual and do not represent any quantitative analysis.

---

*   An investment banker at the moment a new issue is priced ends up valuing data much more like a trader, particularly if the issue is an addition to instruments already trading in the market. An overview of the investment banking process was presented in Book 2, *An Introduction to Trading in the Financial Markets: Trading, Markets, Instruments, and Processes*, Part 4.

(Continued)

Middle-office and backoffice personnel tend to value information only in the period following an execution and before settlement. Compliance people may be interested in prices just prior to an execution and just after. The reason is that compliance tends to assess execution prices in the context of trades in the same instrument just before and just after an execution either to justify the price or to determine a problem has occurred, as shown in the following figure.

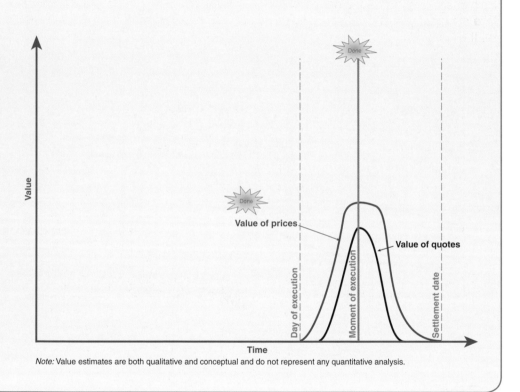

Note: Value estimates are both qualitative and conceptual and do not represent any quantitative analysis.

Purpose

We have already suggested that trading and sales functions place high premiums on information, whereas middle- and backoffice functions command low premiums. However, within and across functions, different purposes have different levels of benefit. For example, the act of trading commands a high premium, whereas reporting commands a lower premium.

Therefore, it is possible to price trading higher and reporting lower even if the reports are intended for a trader. One scheme in use defines four different purposes: trading, risk management, reporting, and operations. Each of these purposes is charged differently.

Using the concept of purpose, another method of segmenting usage is to distinguish between trading and non-trading purposes, and then to distinguish between applications using data in processing and individuals using data in viewed displays. This results in a segmentation scheme like the one in Figure 2.6.4.2, which represents one possible way to implement purpose-based pricing.

Looking at the structure in this figure, we can see that automated trading has higher value than any other purpose, and within automated trading, **actionable data** the most valuable data of all. Data that can be viewed for nontrading purposes has the least value.

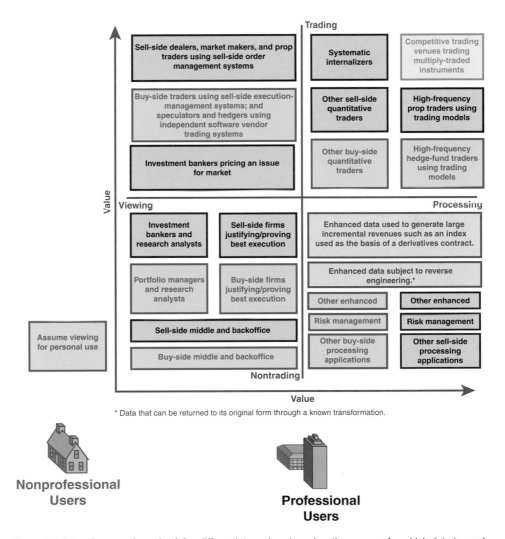

* Data that can be returned to its original form through a known transformation.

Figure 2.6.4.2 *Purpose-based pricing* differentiates prices based on the purpose for which data is used no matter who uses it.

Based on the approach in the preceding figure, data that is processed for nontrading purposes may have different subcategories of purpose. Simple processing such as reporting and operations is straightforward and commands a modest price. However, when data is being processed and resold in an altered form by an entity other than the content owner, the content owner has a problem in determining the amount to charge.

On the one hand, transforming and enhancing data in a way that makes the data more meaningful is desirable. The question is how much of the value of an enhanced data product should go to the originator of the base data and how much to the entity that enhances the data. The problem becomes extremely nettlesome when the enhanced data is used as the basis for a new trading product as happens when an index forms the basis of a derivative product.

In many cases each contract traded results in revenue to the index owner. Owners of the data used as a basis for the index believe they should share in the revenue from trading the derivative.

Professional/Nonprofessional

Many content owners provide a lower-cost service for users who are not "professional." The goal is to attract retail users to the markets. The big problem with professional versus nonprofessional as with other forms of value pricing is a mechanism that ensures that professionals do not sign up at the lower rates.

Discounts

Although most vendors and content owners have standard pricing structures, in reality pricing is chaotic because vendors and their sales personnel often grant discounts quietly to customers to win business or to keep customers from switching to another

---

FOR GOODNESS SAKE, DON'T SAY WHAT REALLY HAPPENS!

An exchange that sells its data reacted with horror to the suggestion that it publish a blog describing pricing decisions akin to case law. The suggestion arose that it would be useful for data owners to describe ongoing decisions related to pricing. The theory was that whatever an owner's pricing policies, those policies get modified in practice as users present unique situations that were not anticipated by the original policy.

Knowing these decisions in practice would help other users understand alternatives for their own problems. The exchange's horror came from the knowledge that its policies were riven with one-off decisions, which if widely known would likely reduce revenues sharply or even destroy the base policies.

source. Another form of discount is to permit "free trials" for periods of time that have the same effect as a discount.

DISTRIBUTION

A final factor in the business of data is to understand the relationships created by data distribution (see Figure 2.6.5). Each data owner has a limited number of types of entities to which it distributes its information directly. These direct recipients, however, frequently redistribute the data to other types of entities. Understanding these distribution alternatives is critical to understanding how the information can be used and therefore having realistic policies for usage.

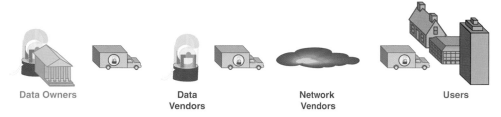

| Data Owners | Data Vendors | Network Vendors | Users |

Figure 2.6.5 *Data distribution* creates a problem for the content owner who must develop policies that permit all the contract mechanics described previously to operate effectively.

Direct

The industry term for an individual or entity that takes information directly from a data owner is a ***direct recipient*** (see Figure 2.6.5.1). Data owners distribute to as many as six different direct recipient groups. Five of the six types are entities that may, as we see in the next section, pass information on to their customers. The sixth category is composed of individuals. We assume that individuals are taking data for their own use.

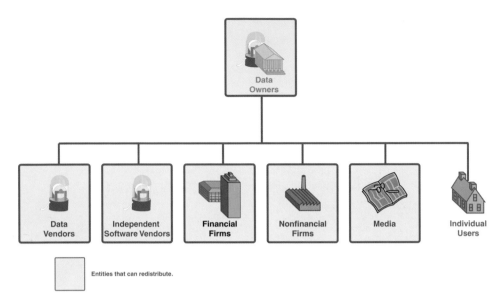

Figure 2.6.5.1   *Direct distribution* involves passing data from the content owner to recipient groups without any intermediary.

Direct recipients have a direct contractual connection relationship to the data owner and therefore establishing, administering, and enforcing the contractual mechanics between data owner and user are straightforward.

Redistribution

With the exception of individuals, each of the groups that receive data directly may pass that information on to subsequent groups of users. This process is known in the industry as **redistribution** (see Figure 2.6.5.2). As a result of the capacity of direct recipients to redistribute data, content owners must have policies not only for each category of recipient but also for subsequent or downstream users. Complexity comes in trying to monitor and control the onward transmission of data.[5]

---

5   In the following sections, we look at several different redistribution scenarios as we attempt to understand the different possible situations that can occur. The number of different logical distribution scenarios is a function of the number of direct recipients, whether those direct recipients can redistribute the data, and the different usage categories that can apply. For our purposes, we have limited the number of usage categories to two sets or two categories. Data can be either for processing or viewing, and data can be for trading or nontrading purposes. This corresponds to the categories in Figure 2.6.4.2 where we described pricing based on the purpose of the data.

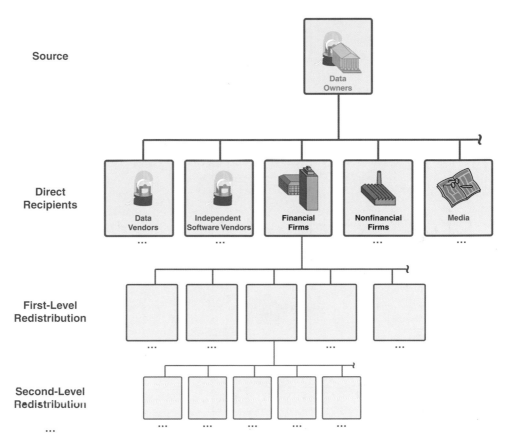

Figure 2.6.5.2 *Redistribution* occurs when a recipient of data directly from a source distributes that data to other recipients not directly connected to the source.

Redistribution interposes the redistributor (at least) between the data owner and the user. Moreover, because there is no direct contractual linkage, redistribution makes the administration of data usage more difficult for the data owner.

VENDORS

Vendors are the most significant and most straightforward redistributors of data. Vendors are in the business of redistribution, and the relationships among data owners, vendors, and users are well established (see Figure 2.6.5.2.1).

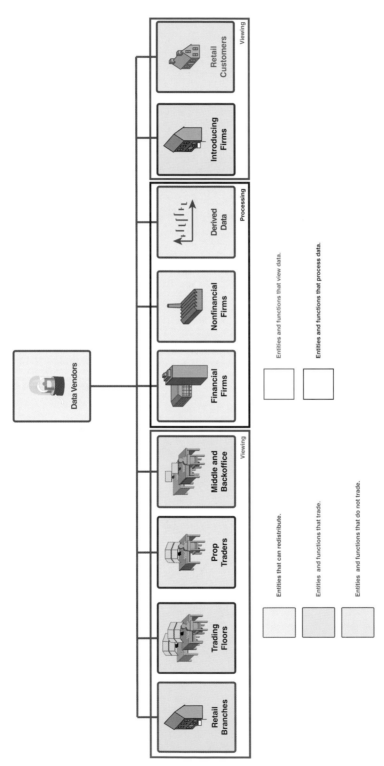

Figure 2.6.5.1 **Vendors** redistribute data to a wide variety of recipients on both the buy and sell sides, many of whom are further redistributors to subsequent users.

INDEPENDENT SOFTWARE VENDORS

Independent software vendors (ISVs) are vendors of software, usually for trading, that are most prevalent in the derivatives markets (see Figure 2.6.5.2.2). Early ISVs included data from markets as an incidental part of their service. As the futures exchanges began to automate in the mid-1990s, they encouraged the ISVs to link the new trading systems to more traders in the market to promote automated trading.

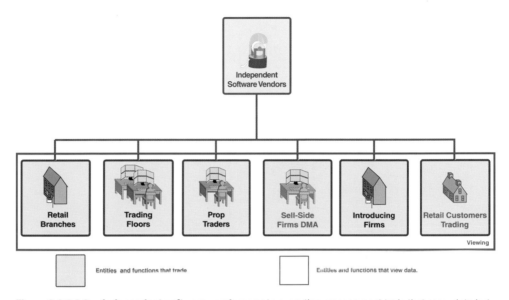

Figure 2.6.5.2.2 ***Independent software vendors*** create execution management tools that carry data but that may not be responsible for reporting and invoicing for that data.

     As an incentive, they did not make the ISVs or their customers report usage or pay for data. Now automated trading dominates the markets, and a substantial portion of the users of data do not report or pay for the information. Data owners are trying to close this loophole.

FINANCIAL FIRMS

We have noted at several different points that financial firms are actively engaged in providing services to their customers that make them *de facto* vendors (see Figure 2.6.5.2.3). Retail broker/dealers offer web-based information to their customers, and institutional broker/dealers offer execution management solutions to their customers. Both categories represent significant issues for data owners who must monitor usage.

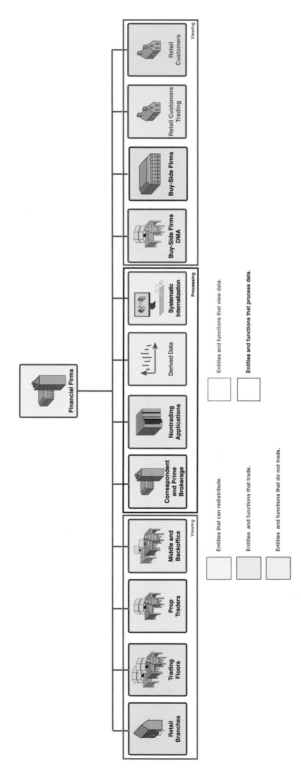

Figure 2.6.5.2.3 *Financial firms* are increasingly acting in roles that resemble vendors both as providers of execution-management systems to institutional customers and as vendors to individual investors who are customers.

NONFINANCIAL FIRMS

A limited number of nonfinancial companies, particularly commodity firms, engage in a number of roles that involve redistributing data to specific customer groups (see Figure 2.6.5.2.4). In these roles, they are redistributors.

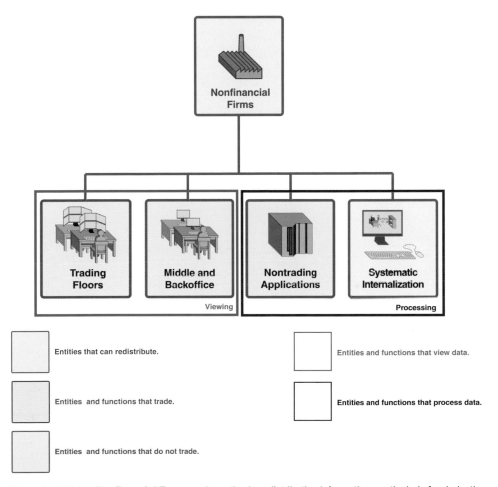

Figure 2.6.5.2.4   ***Nonfinancial firms*** may be active in redistributing information, particularly for derivative instruments.

MEDIA

Media outlets, particularly newspapers, have been major redistributors of market information through the established channels of print, radio, and television. These three channels created few problems for data owners because the information is naturally delayed and has limited trading value.

Moreover, none of the three channels creates the potential for redistribution. The emergence of the Web has created an immense new problem for data owners because it is nearly impossible to police and because it has the potential to erode market share from traditional products. The result has been a contentious standoff between site creators who want their sites to be more valuable by adding market information but who do not want the hassle and cost of monitoring usage, and data owners who do not want to give valuable information away and fear damage to existing products from low-cost or no-cost information channels (see Figure 2.6.5.2.5).

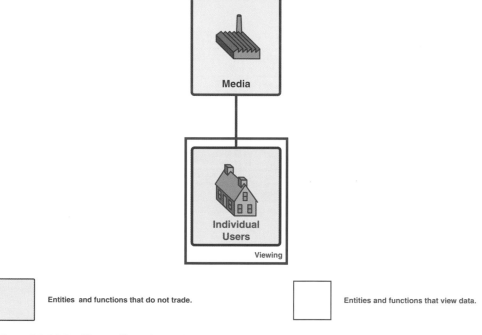

Figure 2.6.5.2.5 *The media* are increasingly acting as traditional vendors through web-based distribution systems.

INDIVIDUALS

Some exchanges permit users to access data directly from the exchange through a web site that provides exchange data. These individuals do not present a problem of redistribution except they like any recipient with a computer connected to the Internet can potentially steal data through unauthorized retransmission. (See the sidebar "Data Theft" earlier.) Note we are not considering several exchanges that have purchased or created full vendors. We treat those situations as any other vendor.

Management 7

All the groups described in Chapter 6 on business have to manage the data they own, vend, and/or use. Management involves acquiring or creating data, preparing the data for usage (if necessary) and/or ensuring its quality, databasing or maintaining the data, and entitling usage, reporting on usage, controlling the inventory of services and sources, and establishing rules for management.

These tasks are presented in the following sections. Although management affects all groups, we focus on the management issues of users (see Figure 2.7).

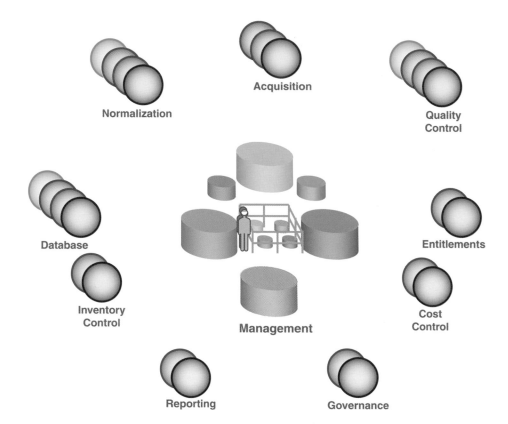

Figure 2.7 ***Data management*** is the internal control of data to ensure that users have good data where and when they need it, to satisfy the requirements of vendors and content owners, and to minimize waste and needless costs.

ACQUISITION

The complicated nature of contractual relationships causes the purchase of data to be complex and often time-consuming (see Figure 2.7.1). The purchase process is a legacy of the time in which the purchase of new products could take months and result in an exclusive relationship between the vendor and the user. Now those relationships are rare. A bigger problem occurs when users need information instantaneously, and yet contractual provisions extend the purchase process needlessly.

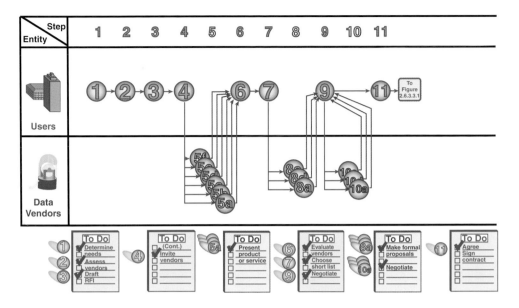

Figure 2.7.1 ***Data acquisition*** often involves a set of complex steps requiring extensive interaction between vendor, data owner, and user, particularly related to the contractual provisions involved in a purchase.

NORMALIZATION

Normalization is primarily a task performed by data owners and vendors, but users also sometimes engage in normalization. In particular, because there is no coherent form of ticker symbols, users often choose to create their own vendor-independent form of security identification. They must thus map all vendors to the internal identification scheme. Even if they use a vendor's security identification scheme, they must map the information from other sources to the internal scheme. Other data attributes may also be adjusted to fit internal standards.

QUALITY CONTROL

In addition to normalization, users may adjust for missing messages and lost ticks. Most trading venues permit retransmission of lost data, and most vendors perform this function for users. However, those users who take data directly must perform this function. Beyond missing ticks, users must also adjust their master files for corporate actions and any other adjustments to information.

DATABASE

For access by internal systems, information from whatever source must be put in a coherent database that can be accessed as needed. Standard database programs are used for the vast majority of information, but for information related to historical price sets used in quantitative trading, special-purpose high-performance databases are required.

These databases not only capture tick data or store the data from vendors, but also play back the data in the same asynchronous pattern as when they originally occurred. This permits models to operate in a simulated environment and permits the creators to assess the model's behavior under real conditions.

ENTITLEMENTS

Firms must be able to actively manage the individuals and applications within the firm that have access to data from various data owners. These entitlement systems permit specific devices and/or users to be turned on and off and to maintain a record of active and deactivated entitlements, which can be audited and verified by data owners.

INVENTORY CONTROL

Inventory control systems permit firms to maintain a comprehensive list of entitled users, data sources (e.g., owners), all active contracts, and vendors. These systems now link to entitlement systems so that changes to entitlements in the inventory control systems can physically activate or deactivate entitlements (see Figure 2.7.2).

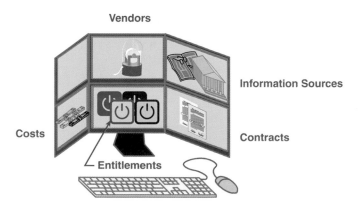

Figure 2.7.2 *Data inventory control* provides data users with a tool that tracks contracts, data sources, entitlements, and vendors and may be linked directly to the entitlements system.

We noted that many firms use profiles for different functions that determine a menu of possible information services available to each functional category. The inventory control systems are tools that permit the human resources department of a firm to implement these profiles among users.

COST CONTROL

Although inventory control systems can help in managing the cost of data usage, another type of system has been developed to help assess the usefulness of existing entitlements. These systems track the frequency with which users actually use the entitlements they have. The systems can help isolate entitlements that are not used or that are used infrequently to target those that can be removed.

REPORTING

Owners and vendors primarily control reporting. The New York Stock Exchange developed a method for reporting using a spreadsheet known as the VARS (Vendor Account Reporting System) during the 1990s and other exchanges have adopted this reporting system. More recently, the NYSE developed an **eXtensible Markup Language (XML)**-based reporting structure known as **VRXML** (i.e., Vendor Reporting XML) that permits reporting through web sites.

GOVERNANCE

We have raised the idea of enterprise data management and describe it in more detail later in this part. An important concept in the management of data is the idea of **data governance**. This term describes a system of rules and policies within an entity that determines how data is managed. The idea of data governance is to systematize the process of managing data such that everyone in the organization knows what data is used as part of the **strategic data stores** of the firm; who is permitted to add, delete, or modify that information; and what tools can be used. Moreover, data governance defines the mechanisms for how existing policies can be extended or modified and how exceptions are handled.

Organization 8

Although the management of technology is largely similar among the different groups in the data business, the data produced and the management of that data exhibits important differences depending on the group (role). Data creators need to have business units to price and sell data, whereas users do not.

Users need to account for their usage, and data creators do not. Differences in both the data and how it must be managed are illustrated in Figure 2.8.

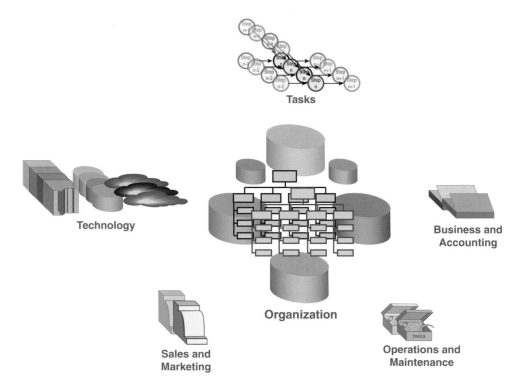

Figure 2.8 *Entities organize* to accomplish the activities unique to each entity type that are required to manage and consume the data they produce, market, and/or consume.

There are many ways to structure the management of data within an organization, ranging from highly centralized to highly decentralized operations. Our descriptions neither represent the exact way specific firms actually operate nor suggest that our description is how they should operate.

TASKS

In Figure 2.8.1 we have produced an organization-like chart showing the basic categories of tasks required for controlling data during creation, distribution, and usage.

The three primary functional roles defined earlier require different types of tasks. Each group—data creators, vendors, and users—have different sets of tasks

Figure 2.8.1 *Organizational tasks* are required in the creation, sales, distribution, and consumption of commercial data.

depending on the activities in which they engage. Every group performs some of the tasks, but some tasks are unique to a specific role.

In the next three sections, we examine the activities or tasks performed by each group. We do not mean to imply that any specific entity is organized in this specific way. But rather these are the tasks that each type of group must perform whatever its exact lines of authority and responsibility.

Owners

Data creators have technical, operational, marketing, and business functions (see Figure 2.8.1.1). Within these broad functional categories, we note in particular the responsibilities of legal support and contracts as well as audit.

Figure 2.8.1.1 *Data owners* must manage the creation or acquisition of data, develop and maintain the technology required, market it to users and vendors, and manage the business aspects of the service.

Vendors

Vendors have the same basic functions as owners, but we break out product management as a separate major function (see Figure 2.8.1.2). Whereas owners may create data products, vendors are often organized by product category. Frequently, the categories conform to the value groups we described in the pricing section earlier (e.g., buy-side front office, sell-side front office, investment banking and research, and middle and backoffices.)

Figure 2.8.1.2 *Data vendors* must manage their technical infrastructure, acquire data from owners, maintain the data, develop products, market it to users, and manage the business.

Users

Users do not have marketing or product management, but vendor and owner management represent major activities because they both adhere to the reporting and entitlement requirements of contracts and also attempt to optimize the use of the purchased data (see Figure 2.8.1.3). We described data management in more detail in Chapter 7.

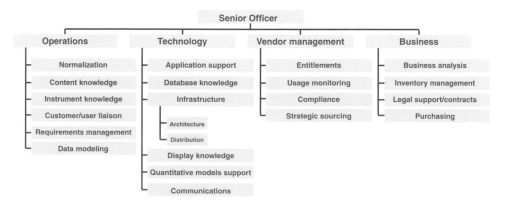

Figure 2.8.1.3 *Data users* must manage the data they acquire and the infrastructure that supports it as well as support those who use the data.

TECHNOLOGY

The label "technology department" is often used to mean "systems" as we have defined it, but also is used in the broader sense of the title to this book—that is, meaning systems, data, and networks. It is this broader sense of technology that is implied in this section and the figures. Each of the groups has different technology needs as shown in the functional charts, but in general, database specialists, architecture, and communications capabilities are required.

Specialty services are required by data owners and vendors to collect information from various sources, vendors may need special groups to program for products, and vendors may require network designers and administrators to plan distribution even if distribution is outsourced to specialty network vendors. Users may have distribution and maintenance support needs and, along with vendors, may need to provide presentation suites.

BUSINESS AND ACCOUNTING

Business and accounting have different meanings for each of the three groups, but each has either to administer the license and sale of data or to administer its acquisition and use. These tasks can include reporting and/or collecting reports, administering entitlements, producing or receiving invoices, and paying or receiving payments.

SALES AND MARKETING

Data owners and vendors are primarily involved with selling and marketing products, including developing attractive products and packages. Users' organizations, however, often employ a marketing-like activity involving specialists who evaluate and understand the available services and who help end users employ products effectively.

OPERATIONS AND MAINTENANCE

Finally, each of the groups must have operational and maintenance functions for receiving, normalizing, and storing information; applying updates such as corporate actions; processing retransmissions when data is bad or missing; and correcting other problems when they occur.

A number of issues affect the business of data. They include problems ranging from the rapid growth of data volumes to ownership models that hamper the use of data in forms that complement rapidly changing methods of trading. In this chapter we consider some of the issues affecting the business of data (see Figure 2.9).

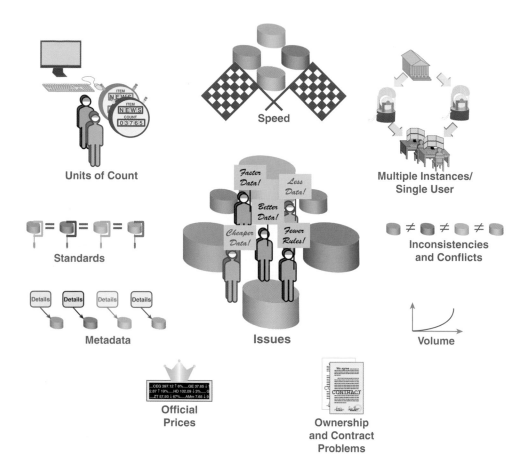

Units of Count

Standards

Metadata

Speed

Faster Data!   Less Data!

Better Data!

Cheaper Data!   Fewer Rules!

Issues

Multiple Instances/ Single User

Inconsistencies and Conflicts

Volume

Official Prices

Ownership and Contract Problems

Figure 2.9   *Data issues* are created by the complex requirements of data usage, the nature of how data is sold, and the huge volume of information generated by and consumed in the trading markets.

DATA MANAGEMENT EVOLUTION

In the earliest stages of the automation of the trading markets, data to be used in applications was purchased for that application only (see figure). Data produced by applications was stored on punch card decks, in sequential tape files and, for information that was most valuable, in random access disk files. Data from either internal or external sources was presented mostly in printed reports or sometimes on video displays.

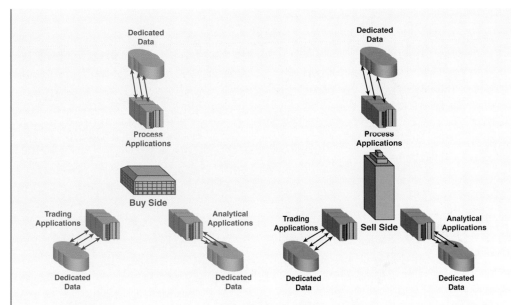

Firms slowly began to centralize data acquisition as a means to bring costs under control and to reduce duplication. As databases began to replace older, limited data files, more sophisticated data management became possible. To manage data, firms began to separate data management from the applications that use the data. This reduces the duplication of data and permits information to be used, created, and modified by multiple applications.

In the sidebar titled "Problems for a Large Investment Bank" in Chapter 1 of this part, we described the chaos of independent data stores for multiple applications. We introduced the term "enterprise data management" to describe centralized control.

The concept behind enterprise data management is the notion that each enterprise should strive for the goal of a single instance of each data element firm-wide for any given purpose (see next figure). This single instance often goes by the name **golden copy**. If there is a single instance or golden copy for each data element, there will be no duplicated data or confusion over which data element to use for any application. Earlier we described the related concept of data governance that describes the rules controlling how a golden copy is maintained.

(Continued)

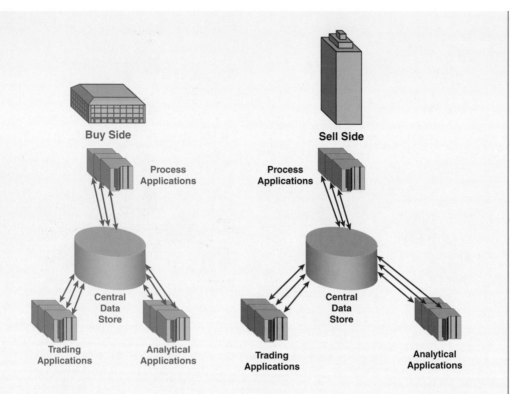

While the process of rationalizing data usage is well under way, it is far from complete. A group known as the Enterprise Data Management Counsel, which focuses primarily on reference data, has in cooperation with Carnegie Mellon University developed a so-called Data Management Maturity model.

The figure on the next page shows a graphical model that an organization can use to measure its evolution toward effective data management. The concentric rings in the circular graph represent successive levels of maturity from least mature at the center to most mature at the outside. The radii represent different features of data management that can be measured grouped into five categories.

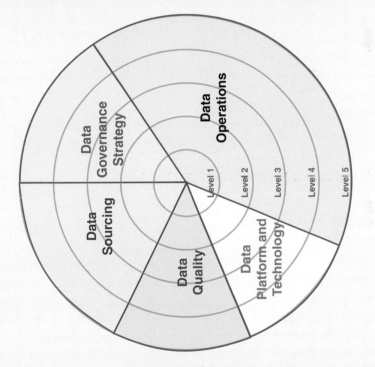

Data Governance Strategy

Data Management Goals
- Objectives definition and verification by stakeholders
- Priorities and precedence of DM program
- Scope of data types, business areas, functions, and asset classes
- Long-term and incremental outcomes (business context)

Corporate Culture
- Alignment of stakeholders on principles and objectives
- Confidence in IT, operations, and data management to deliver

Operating Model
- Executive sponsor and placement in corporate hierarchy
- Governance structure, reporting relationships, and implementation
- Measurement and benchmarking

Funding
- Total cost of ownership and funding requirements
- Business case and ROI evaluation
- Funding model, allocation, and financial accountability

Data Operations

Operational Requirements
- How business requirements are defined, verified, and translated
- Definition of core data elements
- Implementation and tolerance for disruption

Resourcing Strategy
- People, processes, and technologies needed
- Structure and management of resources
- Staff functions, skill sets, and IT resource

Policies and Procedures
- Definition of functions and processes to be governed
- Promulgation and compliance

Business Process and Data Flows
- Coordination of attributes along transactions
- Dependencies, links, relationships, and flow

Data Sourcing

Data Procurement
- Data requirements and mapping
- Procurement process
- Inventory of data and access points
- Usage monitoring

Vendor Management
- Contract negotiation
- Source comparison and selection process
- Quality control and vendor gap analysis
- Communication and escalation process

Data Quality

Data Quality Strategy
- Definition of levels of quality for each functional area
- Process for validating critical data attributes

Quality Assurance
- Profiling tools, tolerances, and validity checks
- Integrity monitoring and data standards
- Data cleansing and enrichment
- Data quality tracking and benchmarking
- Unique and precise tags and identifiers

Exception Management
- Management of change requests and source systems
- Error logging and root cause analysis

Data Platform and Technology

Architectural Framework
- Data storage and distribution methodology
- Architectural standards and implementation approach
- Platform for data storage and distribution
- Release management and rollback

Content Standards
- Semantic definitions and ontological relationships
- Data transformation and Extract, Transform, and Load/Enterprise Application Integration standards
- Messaging formats and symbology

SPEED

As quantitative trading strategies have become more important for users and as automated trading has become more important for markets, the issue of the speed with which information reaches users from the markets and orders reach markets from users has become increasingly important. We discuss the concerns of latency in the next part, but we note here that the speed with which data reaches users from all sources has become an important feature for information related to trading.

UNITS OF COUNT

For several decades, first display devices and more recently individuals have been the primary unit for measuring usage of real-time data. This measure is flawed on several levels. First, users increasingly receive information from a variety of different devices, even from the same vendor, and thus, they are no longer tied to a device as they once were.

This would seem to suggest that an individual, not a device, is the best measuring tool. However, there has been no accepted way to identify an individual.[6] Problems with traditional units of measure and rapidly expanding uses for information suggest that historic units are unsatisfactory, and in all probability, there is no single measure that can meet all needs.

MULTIPLE ENTITLEMENTS/SINGLE USER

Related to units of count is a problem that is troubling for data users. It is very common for high-need users such as traders on the buy and sell sides to have more than one display device from different vendors, each displaying data from the same exchanges. Because the different vendors do not know anything about the entitlements of other vendors, users with devices from multiple vendors pay for multiple entitlements to the same data. This can represent a significant cost for large user firms.

This problem is known as *multiple instances/single user (MISU)* or *multiple entitlements/single user (MESU)*. The fact that each vendor reports entitlements independently has made this problem unavoidable. Some trading venues permit users to file for rebates after the invoice is received, but the rebate process is cumbersome, time-consuming, and expensive. Two possible solutions have been suggested. First, there have been continuing discussions for several decades of a mutual processing entity that would handle reporting for multiple vendors and data owners. This could solve the problem if the mutual entity eliminated the double counting.

The second alternative would be to have data owners, not vendors, control the entitlement process. Users would submit a list of users and applications that are

---

6   Mark Schaedel of NYSE Euronext has suggested using corporate email addresses as an unambiguous means of identifying individuals. This seems to be a simple, universal, and useful identifier.

entitled, perhaps using email addresses for individuals and URLs for applications. The exchange would then present the list of entitled users and applications for each user–firm to each vendor. Note that for this solution to work the data owner would need to invoice directly rather than invoice through vendors.

STANDARDS

As the pace of trading accelerates, as demands for straight-through processing increase, and as the costs for errors grow, the need for standards is rapidly increasing. Almost every form of information used in the trading markets has an existing or emerging standard. Representative standards are shown in Table 3.1.7 in Part 3.

Standards permit data owners, vendors, and users to develop new products and applications, and as long as each uses an accepted standard the others can adapt to the new data and/or service with little or no bespoke development.

Three primary types of standards exist. First, there is the International Organization for Standardization (ISO) that is in the primary business of developing standards for all types of commercial applications, including issues surrounding the trading markets. Second, there are ad hoc industry groups that come together in an effort to solve a problem.

These groups may be formed in the aftermath of regulations to solve a problem identified by the regulation. (The exchanges in the United States formed working groups in the aftermath of RegNMS to develop a methodology to allocate revenues among the exchanges that are part of the **Consolidated Tape Association**, **CTA**.) Alternatively, groups such as the Financial Information exchange (FIX) are begun completely spontaneously. Finally, a commercial product such as Microsoft Windows® may become so dominant that it becomes a standard.

THE EVOLUTION OF THE FIX PROTOCOL

The creation of the FIX messaging standard began when Solomon Brothers (then an independent company) and Fidelity Research agreed in the early 1990s to develop a messaging standard to permit orders and confirmations to be exchanged between the two firms electronically. Ironically, the most common error that can occur between a buy-side trader and an intermediary is for the intermediary to misinterpret a buy order as a sell order or vice versa. This is the most expensive type of mistake. Prior to the adoption of FIX, sell-side firms frequently taped discussions with customers to figure out which side made the error.

When word of the emerging standard spread in the market, many firms wanted to participate, and the standard spread not only through the United States but globally. The organization is now global and has a governing body: the FIX Protocol Limited (FPL).

INCONSISTENCIES AND CONFLICTS

Related to standards are the problems created by the absence of standards. Several major areas of conflict exist in data that cause major operational problems and that are roadblocks to the development of straight-through processing.

Instrument Identifiers

The absence of consistent instrument identifiers is a major problem for the trading markets. At the most fundamental level, instruments are identified in two ways. First, ticker symbols (usually short letter groups such as IBM or BT) are used by humans to identify instruments on trading venues and market information from vendors. Processor symbols are usually extended number and letter combinations that are used by computers for processing.

This dichotomy creates the first level of problems. The second layer of problems occurs because the structure of processor symbols dates from the 1960s, because trading venues act independently, and because of defensive actions by vendors.

Processor symbols evolved from the earliest days of computerized processing using primarily number-based identifiers on a country-by-country basis. ISO adapted the country identifiers by adding a two-character country code to the front of national numbers and adding enough zeros to the country numbers to create a number of consistent length (two-character country code *plus* nine digits *plus* a check digit). Numbers conforming to the ISO standard are collectively referred to as **International Securities**[7] **Identification Numbers (ISIN)**.

Each country has a **national numbering agency (NNA)**,[8] which chooses the identifiers for instruments within that country. The difficulty occurs in that an instrument with a single ISIN number can be registered to be traded in multiple countries and can be listed to trade on multiple markets. The ISIN numbers do not have any intrinsic mechanism for identifying either the market where the instrument is traded or the country or countries in which it is registered.[9] Additional symbols such as market identification codes (MICs) in addition to ISIN are required to identify both an instrument and the market where it is traded.

Second, each exchange assigns ticker symbols for that market, and ticker symbols are a source of pride and branding for listed companies. Therefore, markets are more concerned with attracting listings than ensuring that symbol conflicts do not occur. Therefore, it is common for simple, easy-to-remember ticker symbols to be repeated for different companies in multiple markets.

---

7   We have found both "Security" and "Securities" in the title of ISIN numbers. Because the singular is often used to mean "protection" we elect to use the plural for clarity.

8   The Swiss markets call their numbers Valor numbers, and the NNA is SIX Telekurs. The United Kingdom uses Sedol numbers administered by the London Stock Exchange. The U.S. markets use Cusip numbers administered by Standard & Poor's.

9   The Sedol numbers of the London Stock Exchange do have the ability to identify both markets and registrations, but they apply only to those countries and/or markets that use Sedol.

There is some attempt at consistency within countries under pressure from regulators, but there is no mechanism to ensure consistency across national markets. Figure 2.9.1 shows the potential problems that occur because processor symbols do not completely identify instruments that are globally traded.

Issie	In-The-Ether Networks, BV			
ISIN	NL999999999*			
Registrar	Germany		Netherlands	United States
Market	Frankfurt	Zurich	Amsterdam	New York
Ticker Symbol	ITEN.DE.F*	ITEN.DE.Z*	ITEN.NL.E*	ITEN.US.N*
SEDOL	1111161*	1111162*	1111171*	1111181*

*All numbers and symbols as well as the company are fictitious to show the general structure and are not intended to represent any real company.

Figure 2.9.1 *Instrument identifiers* fail to uniquely identify all instances of an instrument because they do not include a means to identify instruments traded in multiple markets and registered in different jurisdictions.

Vendors have developed proprietary ticker symbol systems that solve the problem of instruments registered in multiple national markets and traded in multiple countries. However, vendors have treated their symbol methodology as proprietary and have attempted to keep customers by making the transition to a new symbol structure so difficult as to discourage customers from leaving.

The result of these problems is that straight-through processing is limited because of inconsistent symbols. Firms spend significant resources mapping different symbol structures to one another. Finally, it is inordinately difficult in times of stress to identify related securities across a global organization, which increases the overall risk for the firm.

Counterparty and Customer Information

Just as inadequate instrument identifiers create problems for straight-through processing, difficulties with customer and counterparty information create similar problems. The difficulties of maintaining up-to-date information on customers and counterparties such as addresses for offices and departments, bank and clearing corporation account numbers, and identities used within trading venues all slow processing. Moreover, when this information is inadequate or wrong, errors can occur, causing substantial costs.

Linking Entities and Subsidiaries

In the modern economic environment, combinations among companies both within countries and across national borders are increasingly important. In the trading markets, firms need to be able to understand these corporate linkages both to understand the overall economic attractiveness of linked companies and to identify all points of exposure when problems occur.

Linking Entities and Issues

Directly related to companies and subsidiaries are the linkages between complex organizations, and all of the instruments related to entities have issues. When problems occur, it is also critical not only to link parent companies to subsidiaries, but also to identify all of the instruments of all types related to the entity if trouble occurs.

METADATA

Metadata is data that defines or describes data. As the quantity of data related to the trading markets grows, and more importantly as the people who use data are more removed from the source of the data, it is increasingly imperative that the user and the systems the user employs be aware of any assumptions that go into the data that may affect the implications of how the data should be used. Many firms have adopted tools and strategies to create consistent metadata to support their operations.

VOLUME

One of the most complex operational problems facing entities in the trading markets is handling the huge and growing volume of message traffic coming from the markets. Data volumes from all types of instruments and from all markets challenge the ability of firms to handle the information. In many cases, firms spend more money and resources discarding information they do not need than they spend processing the information they want.

There are three primary reasons for the explosive growth in messages. First, as more and more markets automate, the average size of orders has decreased as the total number of shares traded has increased. This means many more smaller trades for any given share volume, but the share volume is itself growing rapidly.

The second factor is the rapid increase in quantitative trading. The primary method that quantitative traders use to implement their strategies is known as a **cancel/replace order** or strategy. Traders enter orders into trading venues as so-called **marketable limit orders**.[10] A marketable limit order is a limit order

---

10   Using marketable limits implies that the goal of the trader is to execute an order. There are many other possible strategies in which the prices might be just above (for an offer) or just below (for a bid) the market quote. In these types of strategies, the trader's orders are in the market but do not execute. Whatever the strategy, as prices change, these traders generate cancel/replace orders as frequently as those trying to get an execution.

priced at the price of the bid or offer in the market at the time it is submitted (i.e., a bid is entered at the price of the standing offer or an offer is entered priced at the standing bid).

In principle, these orders should execute. However, if the orders do not execute instantly, they are canceled and replaced with a new order at a slightly different price. In an environment of high-frequency trading, many orders do not execute and are subsequently canceled and replaced with new orders. Most markets suggest a cancellation rate that exceeds 90%. This suggests that for every trade, more than nine orders were entered and then canceled.

Finally, for a number of instruments, including options and warrants, those known as market makers use a technique known as an **autoquote** to generate quotes. The autoquote employs a model such as the **Black-Scholes Model** (see Book 2) to generate a quote based on quotes received for the underlying instrument. Remember that for every option there are both put and call options, and there can be several active strike prices for several expiration months for each put and call.

There can be several market makers for every options trading venue, and there have been five to seven trading venues all trading the same instruments in the United States. Therefore, when an underlying instrument quotes, then each active strike price for every month for both puts and calls times the number of market makers on each active market times the number of total markets all requote instantaneously.

Options and warrants represent but one example of the mechanisms in which models generate quotes multiplying the number of messages transmitted through vendors and processed by users. These volumes have been growing exponentially for several decades.

OFFICIAL PRICES

As we noted previously, many markets use the last trade in a reference market, usually the primary market for an instrument, as the official price. As markets have fragmented, it is no longer certain that the primary market is the most active market, and the last price in the primary market may not be representative.

Moreover, many markets have multiple trading sessions, and the definition of the last price raises questions of which session. Finally, for trading around the end of fiscal years, the ends of reporting quarters, and on dates when futures deliver or options expire, the last price may not be representative of trading prices earlier in the day.

Beyond issues of whether prices are representative, there is much uncertainty about what prices to use as the official price. In the late 1990s, the team of Messrs Craig Shumate and Herbie Skeete (both cited in the preface to the set at the beginning of this book) attempted to simply chronicle the definitions of the official price in a wide number of international markets. They finally had to give up the project because it was not possible to get firm answers in many markets.

OWNERSHIP AND CONTRACT PROBLEMS

Much data, as we noted earlier in this part, is owned by data owners and is licensed for use. It is not sold to be used in any way the user wishes. This fact means that the user is at the mercy of the data owner and must hope that the owner understands and will approve the many diverse uses to which data can be employed. In a marketplace that is changing as rapidly as the trading markets, this is impossible.

Consider the many different direct and indirect user categories that we examined in the section on redistribution we explored in Chapter 6 in this part. Comprehensive policies assume that the data owners not only understand each of the different ways direct recipients use their information, but also all the ways indirect recipients use the data as well. This is not a realistic assumption. Moreover, even if we assume that data owners fully understand the possible uses from all the direct and indirect users, there will be some uses that the user believes to be reasonable that the data owner will not approve.

Therefore, the problems of contractual permissions for usage are fraught with potential conflict even in a world where everyone has a clear understanding of potential uses and crafts reasonable policies to address them. In reality, the problem is much worse. Data owners have policies that were crafted in a much simpler technical environment and much less complex markets.

These policies, while completely out of touch with current usage, are easy for the owners to understand and seem safe. Therefore, many contractual provisions do not reflect modern needs and usage.

RELATED INFORMATION IN OTHER BOOKS

In this part, we have both defined and described data as it is used in the trading markets, and we have described the business of data. Data is frequently categorized as "market data" and "reference data," but we have seen that there is also much process data created by and within firms that is often ignored in the other types of descriptions. We have seen that neither the term "market data" nor "reference data" adequately describes the breadth of data in common usage. Moreover, many different attributes are needed to fully define the data used in and by the markets.

Beyond simple definitions, there is a complex business for the creation, distribution, and usage of data that must be understood to appreciate data in the trading markets. The value of data about the markets makes the business of data a very important industry on its own. The business of data, the management of data, and the way firms organize to control data at all levels are important and are evolving.

Finally, a number of important issues ranging from problems with data message volumes and inadequate identification methods to problems with contracts and usage rights makes managing and using data less effective than the markets require.

In the next part (see Figure 2.10), we look at networks. Understanding networks will complete the picture of technology in the markets and will help further the understanding of systems and data.

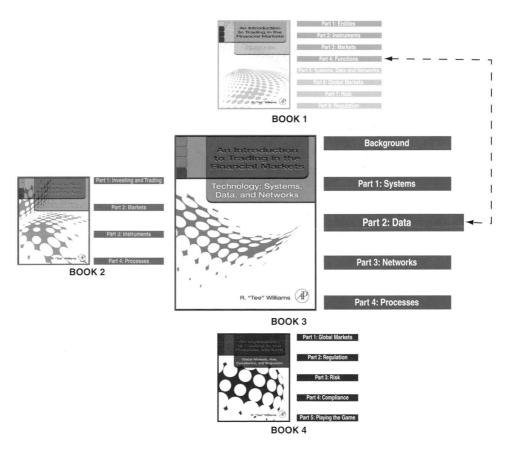

Figure 2.10 Related information in other books in this set.

Networks

Part 3

One of the most dramatic changes in the trading markets has been the creation of linkages among different entities permitting seamless processing and data transfer. Most of the major types of networks we describe in this part evolved from bespoke communications linkages developed for specific purposes, often at great cost.

From the 1850s through the 1980s, the two earliest forms of networks were telephones and market data developed in parallel. Most brokerage firms had phone connections directly to the floors of major exchanges, to customers, and to important counterparties. International connections replaced phones with telex or Teletype machines. Most market-data transfer was point-to-point over closed networks first to ticker machines, then to dedicated video displays, and finally to dedicated personal computers.

In the late 1960s, firms began to develop dedicated order-routing networks from branches to headquarters and from headquarters to points of execution. These dedicated networks have been joined or replaced by specialty order networks from network vendors and from some trading venues as well.

At about the same time a company in Boston called AutEx began offering dealers the opportunity to advertise potential trades to their institutional customers. This system was a precursor to current indications of interest. AutEx's linkages among firms in the trading community permitted it to create a system that offered a mechanism for institutional affirmation of trades. Also, Telerate for fixed income and Reuters for foreign exchange began to offer dealers the opportunity to advertise to customers through dedicated networks.

Beginning in the 1980s, firms developed information distribution systems designed primarily for high-end trading desks that employed local area networks to link all traders in the trading room. To support these trading terminals, vendors had to develop highly efficient methods of message transfer to support the high data message volumes. Vendors also began to develop message structures that were unique to the local network.

All data formats from external vendors were converted to the common internal format. This meant that applications using data within the firm could write programs using the common internal format without programming to each different data source. The internal distribution systems that evolved out of trading-room systems have come to be called **middleware**.

Early private, point-to-point networks have evolved into general connectivity. Bespoke networks now employ standards that make connection faster and cheaper. Many networks originally developed by market-data vendors have been spun off as specialized networks serving all parties in the trading markets.

All networks serving the trading markets are optimized for the content they deliver and activities of the Street. Also, networks tend to be concentrated in the geographic areas where major financial centers are located.

In the chapters that follow, we look at some of the concepts that underlie networks and their design. We examine networks categorized by type and consider how networks support the functions within both buy- and sell-side entities. We examine some of the major activities required to support networks and consider some current network issues. Figure 3.0 shows the components we cover in this part.

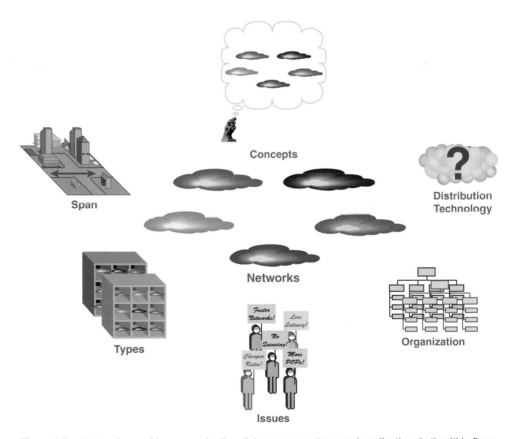

Figure 3.0 **Networks** provide communications links among systems and applications both within firms and among the entities that comprise the Street to perform processes that proceed nearly seamlessly.

Concepts 1

Our goal in this chapter is to describe some of the common concepts related to network design for the financial markets (see Figure 3.1). This is not a comprehensive exploration of network design. However, as automated execution and high-frequency trading have become more important in the markets, certain ideas related to networks have become critical for those who wish to understand trading. We introduce those trading-related concepts here.

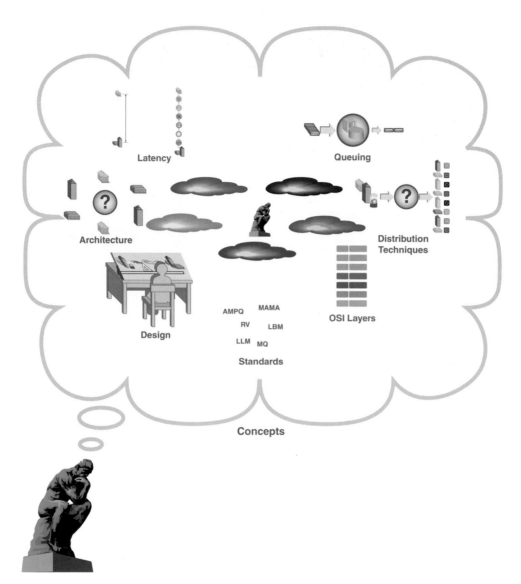

Latency

Queuing

Architecture

Distribution Techniques

Design

AMPQ MAMA
RV LBM
LLM MQ

Standards

OSI Layers

Concepts

Figure 3.1 *Network concepts* are important to understanding the workings of networks employed by the Street.

LATENCY

Before discussing some of the other concepts we will introduce, we want to define the notion of latency, which was introduced in earlier discussions. Simply put, latency is a function of the physics of message transfer. We know that the speed at which a message can travel is limited by the speed of light.

Therefore, the longer the distance between an event such as a trade and the individual or application that may need to react to that event, the higher the latency and the longer the delay before a response can happen. There is a comparable level of latency between the time the person or application reacting to the event enters a message in response and the time the responding message can reach the trading venue or any other location to which the message is directed.

Second, latency is increased when a process performed *en route* delays the message until the process is completed. In particular, most of the processes in data aggregation, normalization, and distribution involve large numbers of activities that require placing messages in so-called **buffers** where the data is held until a process can be completed. The cumulative effect of these actions is to create latency (see Figure 3.1.1).

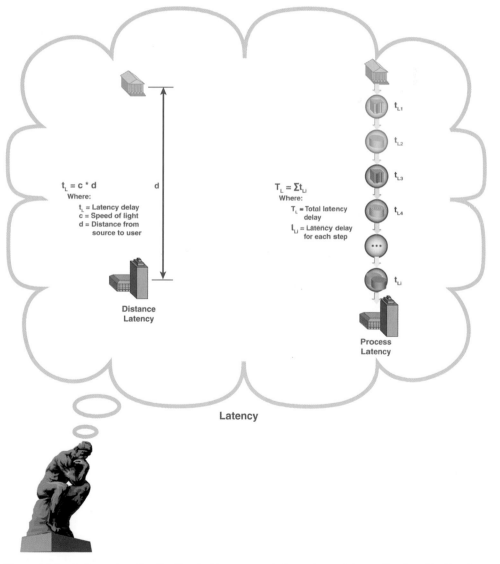

$$t_L = c * d$$

Where:

t_L = Latency delay
c = Speed of light
d = Distance from source to user

Distance Latency

$$T_L = \Sigma t_{Li}$$

Where:

T_L = Total latency delay
t_{Li} = Latency delay for each step

t_{L1}
t_{L2}
t_{L3}
t_{L4}
t_{Li}

Process Latency

Latency

Figure 3.1.1   **Latency** describes the time lost in messages between two points resulting from the time the message takes to travel the distance between the locations and the time lost to processing *en route*.

THE SOURCES OF LATENCY

Ms. Kirsti Suutari, then of Reuters (now Thomson Reuters), provided the following list of the events in the transmission of information through a vendor network.

Communications

- *Serialization*—Delay caused by clocking data into any circuit
- *Distance*—Laws of physics, rule of thumb is 1ms per 100 km
- *Switching*—Routers, number of hops, typically microsecond
- *Queuing*—Incorrectly sized bandwidth for message bursts

Computer Processing

- *Processor*—Raw CPU speed
- *Devices*—Bus, I/O devices, memory, disk
- *Platform*—Operating system overhead
- *Application*—Software architecture

Design and Integration Complexity

- *Normalization*—Translation, verification, and symbology
- *Native interoperability*—Data loaders

In the time when most trading took place manually, individuals had to notice, consider, and react to new information. The inherently slow nature of human reactions meant the limitations of the speed of light, and the necessary processes required to store, process, and distribute data were trivial *most of the time*. (See the sidebar titled "Queuing on October 19, 1987.")

Beginning with the creation of functional automated trading systems in the late 1980s, the idea of latency as a problem began to be considered. An early trading system for the London International Financial Futures Exchange (LIFFE) proposed only permitting connections to the system in the areas surrounding London.[1]

More recently, trading venues generally permit traders to make their own choices on location but offer so-called **colocation** services for those concerned with latency. In a colocation service, the user is permitted to have a processor and trading models located in the same facility as the trading venue's processors.

---

1 The exchange was subsequently renamed the London International Financial Futures and Options Exchange when it merged with the London Traded Options Market, but retained the mnemonic LIFFE.

QUEUING

Before we leave the idea of latency, it is important to introduce the related notion of **queuing**. Queuing, mentioned in the "The Sources of Latency" sidebar, can be thought of as "bad latency." Queues are the sequences of messages in the buffers mentioned previously, but "queuing" is the term for abnormally long delays caused by poorly designed processes that cause the buffers to fill needlessly (see Figure 3.1.2). In extreme cases, queuing can result in messages being permanently lost.

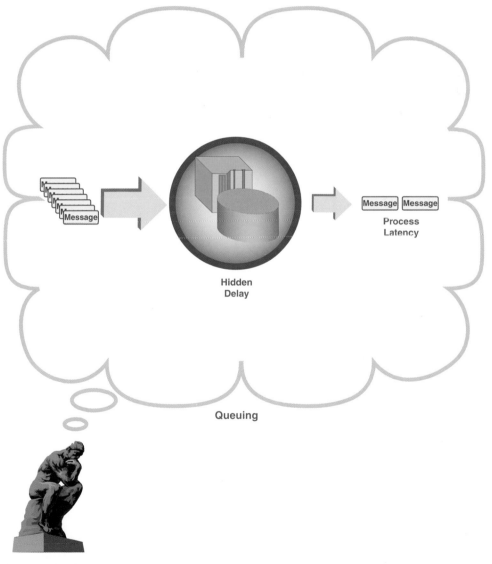

Figure 3.1.2   **Queuing** is defined as time wasted in message transmission because a process along the path either lacks capacity or is poorly designed.

QUEUING ON OCTOBER 19, 1987

On Monday, October 19, 1987, there was a dramatic selloff of securities that resulted in significant losses for investors. The Dow Jones Industrial average began trading at about 2246. A number of factors have been cited to describe how the market had behaved prior to what has come to be called "Black Monday," and we are not concerned with the economic and market forces that precipitated the selloff. What we describe here relates to the impact of queuing during that trading day.

Early in the trading day, the pace of trading quickened as more and more orders were routed to the markets. Traders frequently use marketable limit orders to achieve executions. These orders are priced at the current bid or offer from the trading venue and should execute immediately, provided that no earlier order has reached the market first. However, on October 19, 1987, the volume of orders, trading, and market data completely overwhelmed the systems of the exchanges and dealer associations as well as the market-data vendors.

One anecdote from an executive at one of the then-existing data vendors estimated the delay from queuing at about four minutes. That did not include the delays on the trading floors and in dealing rooms.

At about midday the mix of orders changed from marketable limit orders to **market orders**. We believe this occurred because traders had stopped believing their market-data services and wanted to make sure their sell orders were executed.

We conducted a statistical analysis for the U.S. Securities and Exchange Commission evaluating the data and concluded the order patterns were consistent with the problems resulting from queuing.* The day ended at 1738 for the Dow Jones Industrial index, a loss of 508 points, or roughly 23%. (Other indexes could be used as well with comparable results.)

The market rebounded sharply the next morning, suggesting that at least some part of the total fall may have been the result of the panic created by being unsure of where the market actually was during the trading day. We believe that economic forces caused the markets to fall, but when the selloff was underway, queuing in the systems that existed at the time was an important contributor to the magnitude and speed of the fall.

The reason that this type of queuing is so pernicious is that it is difficult to detect. In 1987, traders looking at their market-data screens would have seen prices changing and news updating and would have had no reason to suspect that the numbers they were seeing were several minutes old. Today, the data goes into trading algorithms. Great care is now taken to minimize all forms of latency, but if queuing were occurring, it would remain difficult to detect.

---

* Private investigation conducted by SRI Consulting, a subsidiary of SRI International.

ARCHITECTURE

Functional network architecture, as we define it, is an attempt to explain how all the nodes in a network are interconnected in a manner that is most efficient from the perspective of the task to be performed. Almost every financial network employs unique strategies and architectures to increase efficiency. In this section we examine a few basic architectures, and in the next we look at distribution techniques frequently used to handle financial market network tasks.

We consider four major architectures that are important to the financial markets. We describe them as *point-to-point*, *hub-and-spoke*, *hierarchical*, and a *ladder* (see Figure 3.1.3).

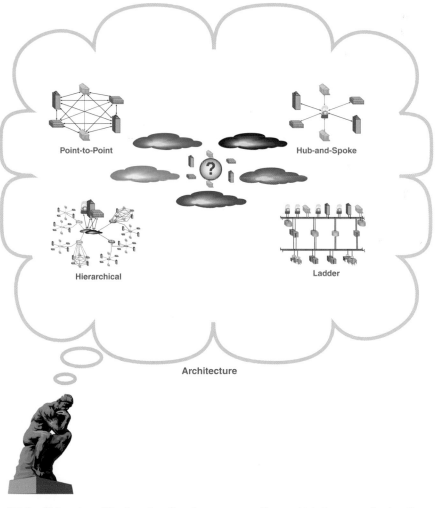

Figure 3.1.3 *Network architecture* describes the way connections and interim processing junctions are laid out to accomplish a message transfer task.

As a final note, the design of networks is highly sophisticated and employs many types of both physical and logical structures. Moreover, beneath the logical and physical structure of most purpose-built networks lies a telecommunications network where packets of information are physically routed; this network is completely separate from the network designs that underlie our discussion.

HOLES IN THE CLOUD

Network designers like to build **redundancy** into their networks so there is no **single point of failure**. To do this, they frequently construct completely separate redundant networks using different network vendors. In the mid-1990s, a tractor operator working in the state of New Jersey across the Hudson River from Manhattan dug through a telephone cable taking out a substantial portion of the networks servicing the financial community in New York.

Network designers discovered that although they had carefully chosen different network vendors, many of those vendors depended on the same telephone network for connectivity. Since that event, careful designers have demanded to look beyond the network design companies to ensure that their "redundant networks" actually use different telecommunications pathways.

Even an elementary exploration of network design is well beyond the scope of this book. Our goal is to describe how network design can affect trading and how trading can dictate how supporting networks are designed.

Point-to-Point

The simplest means of connecting a number of locations through a network is to link each node to every other node by a direct connection. This structure may also be referred to as a **fully connected network**. If speed is the primary concern for messages traveling between any two nodes, then direct connections minimize the latency created by distance and most likely from processing as well.

However, except for relatively small numbers of nodes or for situations in which many of the nodes do not need direct connections with many other nodes, point-to-point connections quickly become complex as the number of nodes grows. Figure 3.1.3.1 shows this complexity for a relatively simple six-node network.

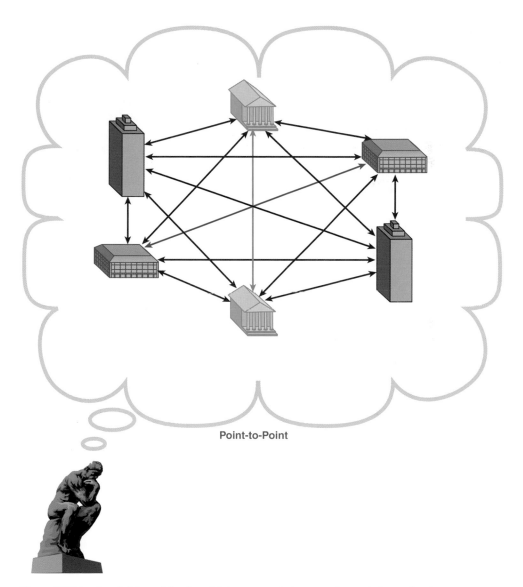

Point-to-Point

Figure 3.1.3.1   A **_point-to-point network_** links every node to every other node in a network.

Hub-and-Spoke

A more economical structure in terms of the number of links is to connect each functional node to every other functional node through a central **hub**. The hub has the advantage of reducing the number of linkages, and also the hub can provide a location where important activities can take place.

For example, a trading venue or a clearing corporation is a natural hub for trading or clearing. Separately, the hub can be a home for translation services among different message **protocols**.

One of the purposes of middleware is to provide a translation among different message structures. One means of performing the translation is using a facility known as a **message broker**. A message broker makes it possible to link different nodes each using different message structures providing only one point where translation must take place. (By contrast, a point-to-point network would require that every linkage between nodes with different message structures needs a translation algorithm.) As messages become more standardized, the need for message brokers is diminishing.

THE COMMON MESSAGE SWITCH

In the late 1970s, the New York Stock Exchange implemented the Designated Order Turnaround (DOT) system. At the time substantially every member firm had its own order-routing network, and most were bespoke using non-standard protocols. To accelerate the adoption of the DOT system, the Exchange created the Common Message Switch (CMS).

The CMS system served as a *de facto* message broker that was programmed to accept the then-existing network formats of all major order-routing networks. CMS made it possible for firms to begin to use DOT more quickly than if the Exchange had required each firm to program connections to the DOT message format. This is very similar and much earlier than the strategy used by Liquidnet that was described in the sidebar "Linking OMSs with Dark Pools" in Part 1 of this book.

Figure 3.1.3.2 shows a hub-and-spoke structure for the same six nodes used in Figure 3.1.3.1.

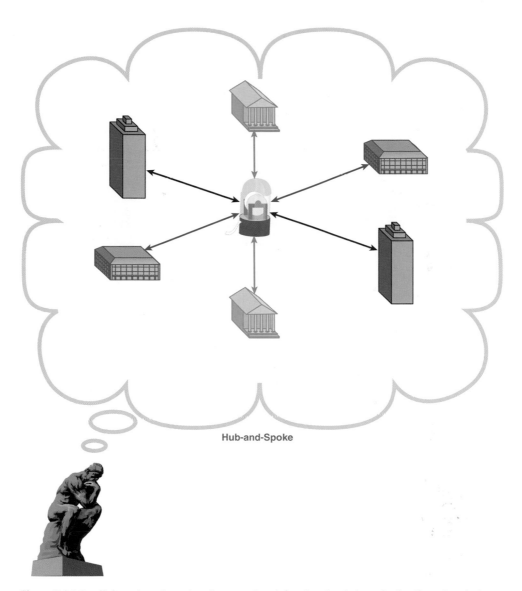

Hub-and-Spoke

Figure 3.1.3.2 ***Hub-and-spoke networks*** connect each functional node to each other through a single, central hub.

Hierarchical

The simple network structures such as point-to-point and hub-and-spoke are rarely satisfactory to solve real-world problems. Frequently, these simple structures are linked together in more complex hierarchical networks where subnetworks, perhaps employing point-to-point and/or hub-and-spoke structures, are combined into a larger network.

Most actual networking problems are solved linking different subnetworks, often from different vendors. Figure 3.1.3.3 shows earlier structures combined with additional subnetworks to create a hierarchical network.

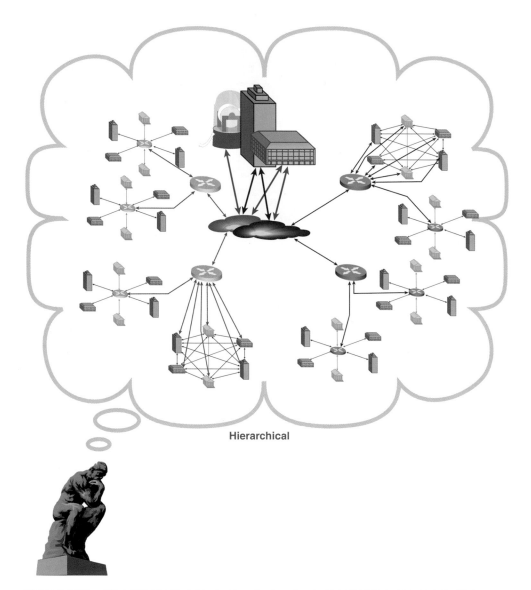

Hierarchical

Figure 3.1.3.3 *Hierarchical networks* combine simple network elements into a more complex higher-level structure.

Ladder

We coin the term a "ladder network" to define a common structure currently used in enterprise or middleware distribution systems. The ladder employs two layers that independently would be labeled a **bus**. (A bus is a network structure wherein nodes are each connected to a single delivery channel termed the bus.) In a ladder structure, external information sources are brought into one bus, and each source is converted to the format used within the internal network.

The other bus provides connections to users, both individuals and applications. Between the two busses (corresponding to the rungs on a ladder) are support applications and services provided within the enterprise that employ data from the external sources that enhance the usefulness of the external data for internal users. For example, analytical services might be used to transform data for users within the organization.

Alternatively, an internal service might store data to be used for models, or services could entitle users and monitor usage. Figure 3.1.3.4 shows a hypothetical ladder-style network.

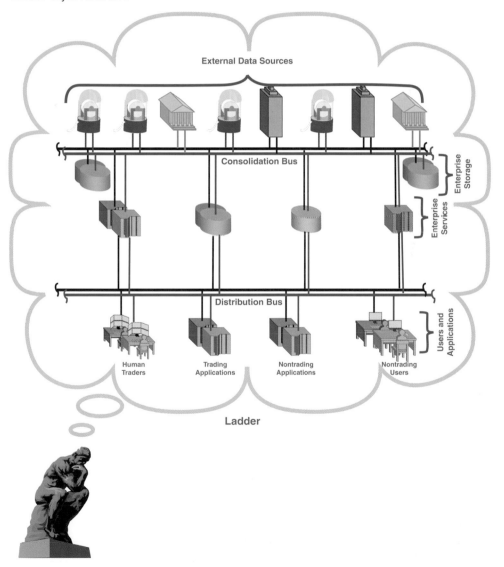

Figure 3.1.3.4 *Ladder-style networks* employ two busses, one to manage data from external sources and the other distributing services to users, while in-house services are located between the two busses.

DISTRIBUTION TECHNIQUES

Whatever the structure of a network, there are strategies or techniques for delivering data that make maximum use of the available **bandwidth**. These distribution techniques usually take advantage of the nature of the network or the demands of the nodes on the network (see Figure 3.1.4). The techniques presented here are used to facilitate streaming delivery of information.

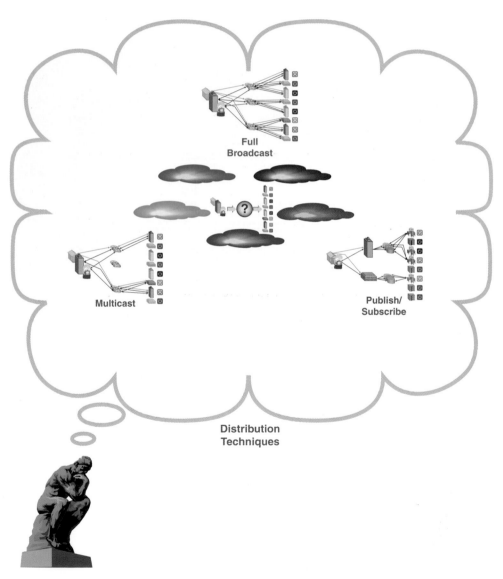

Figure 3.1.4 **_Distribution techniques_** refer to strategies for delivering messages so as to minimize redundancies that are not useful and to make the most economic use of network resources.

Full Broadcast

Early streaming data employed a simple strategy of continuously sending a *full broadcast* of all information to every node in a network (see Figure 3.1.4.1). In this environment the source of information broadcasts all information throughout a network as the information is received or produced without regard for whether nodes on the network are interested in the information. Each node then "listens" to the continuing messages as they pass the node and picks off those messages that are of interest.

This technique is relatively simple to create on a network-wide basis and does not require sophisticated processing at interim nodes. However, unless substantially all nodes on a network need most of the messages sent, full broadcast is wasteful of network bandwidth.

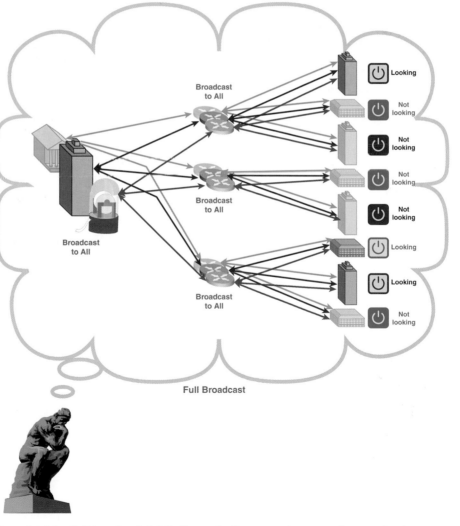

Figure 3.1.4.1   *Full-broadcast distribution* sends all messages to every node on a network.

Multicast

In multicast distribution each node in a network sends information only to successive nodes that want the information and not to nodes with no interest (see Figure 3.1.4.2). Therefore, the network does not waste bandwidth by sending information where it is not needed.

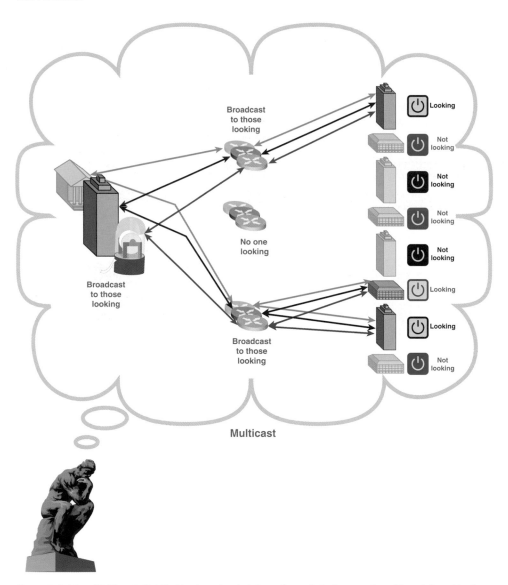

Figure 3.1.4.2 *Multicast distribution* broadcasts information only to those nodes with an interest in the information and not to those with no interest.

Publish/Subscribe

Publish/subscribe (sometimes called "pub/sub") is something like the inverse of multicast. Pub/sub **publishes** data at a source, but only those nodes that want the information **subscribe** to the information and therefore receive it (see Figure 3.1.4.3). The advantages of this distribution format are that the head end does not need to know who will need the information and the users can control what they receive.

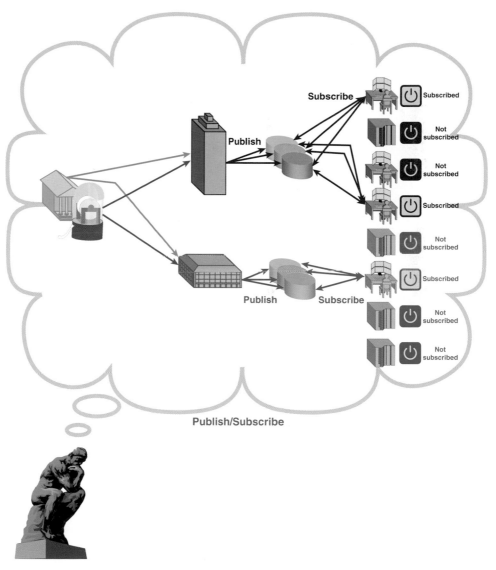

Figure 3.1.4.3 **Publish/subscribe** makes information available (publishes) at the source, and those users with an interest subscribe to the published data.

DESIGN

Network design involves the actual layout of assets such as hubs and data-storage facilities in geographic locations that facilitate the distribution of the information that must be transmitted. Some elements of design are constrained by factors beyond the designers' control. For example, customers are where customers are, and so the terminus of the distribution is constrained.

If the network employs the telecommunications infrastructure, then it is necessary to locate facilities near switching centers. However, designers do have control over decisions of where data is stored, how requests are handled (i.e., must they be routed back to the main processing facility or can they be satisfied by data stores at nodes closer to the user), and how data is distributed.

A number of clever strategies can be employed to make a network efficient. We have already described some distribution techniques, but the design of a network is important to efficiency as well. Some early vendors managed to simplify their networks and reduce distribution costs dramatically by focusing only on institutional customers that were concentrated in major financial centers rather than retail customers who were more widely dispersed.

Another technique is to split data streams into channels and to allocate different instruments to channels based on historical message volumes. The goal is to make sure no channel is overly burdened by volume.

Specific distribution strategies aside, modern network vendors need to understand how data is used to provide users with the information they need but not provide information that is not needed. As networks evolved, most early network designers assumed that the information they delivered needed to get to every location.

Likewise, those charged with acquiring information at user firms often elected to "take everything" rather than be caught without information that was needed. However, as the volumes of data that are produced in the markets have grown, as we will discuss in Chapter 6 on issues, both users and vendors have come to understand: "Not everyone needs everything everywhere all the time."[2]

Figure 3.1.5 shows the major components of a network and provides some of the terminology that is commonly used.

---

2   This phrase summarizes the conclusions of a study conducted for a major vendor that was trying to understand how to make the most economical use of its network asset.

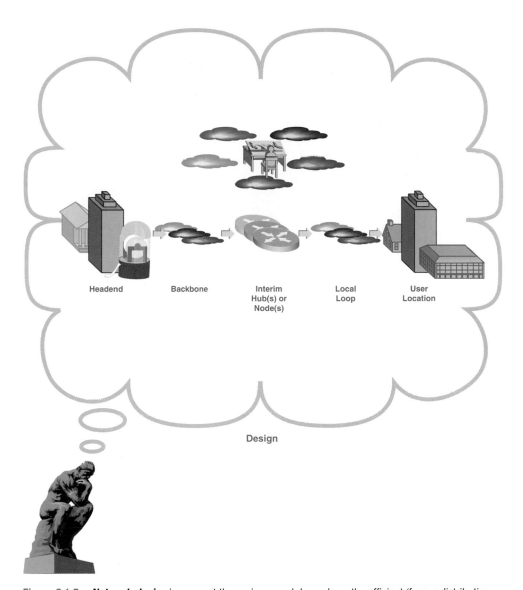

Headend Backbone Interim Hub(s) or Node(s) Local Loop User Location

Design

Figure 3.1.5 ***Network design*** is more art than science and depends on the efficient (from a distribution perspective) deployment of services such as hubs and data stores geographically to satisfy the network's purpose.

Location choice for data stores in a network involves balancing the advantages and disadvantages of different storage locations, taking into account the nature of the information being stored (see Table 3.1.1).

Table 3.1.1 Location of Data Stores in a Network.

	Headend		Interim hub(s) or nodes(s)		User location	
Location of primary data storage for users	• All data maintained at central site • Broadcast dynamic data and respond to requests • Interim nodes only route data • User locations only display		• Broadcast dynamic data • Data distributed to sites near users • User locations only display		• Broadcast dynamic data • All requested data distributed to user sites • User locations both store and display	
	Pro	**Con**	**Pro**	**Con**	**Pro**	**Con**
Advantages/ disadvantages	• No redundant data • Simpler design • Lower network maintenance • Highest control over content	• High bandwidth use at local loop • High latency (i.e., data request roundtrips)	• Latency reduced • Interim nodes store data • Can optimize data locations	• High backbone bandwidth • Much redundant data if not optimized	• Lowest latency • Low local-loop bandwidth • Less redundant data	• Requires sophisticated management tools • Least control over content
Network protocols	**Use proprietary protocol(s)** • All messages use protocol designed by the owner and/or user • May superimpose proprietary standards with industry standards for lower layers; see layers in OSI and TCP/IP models				**Use industry standard protocol(s)** • All messages employ industry standards	
	Pro	**Con**			**Pro**	**Con**
Advantages/ disadvantages	• Existing situation optimized for content and network design • Defends against competitive inroads	• Usually inefficient (i.e., does not take advantage of new design techniques and tools) • Expensive for customers (i.e., each source is a different design effort) • Often requires adaptation of hardware and/or software from outside vendors			• Latency reduced • Interim nodes store data • Can optimize data locations	• High backbone bandwidth • Much redundant data if not optimized

AN ELEGANT OLDER DESIGN

Quotron Systems, one of the early quote vendors, had a highly efficient design for its network. The entire network was based on a single processor that Quotron designed and built: the *Quotron 800*. The company used the Quotron 800 in clusters at the main processing facility, to serve as the processor for interim storage and distribution in network nodes, and as controllers distributing data to display devices at customer locations.

The entire Quotron maintenance staff was able to work on any processor in the network, and for its useful life the system was scalable. As volumes grew, new processors could be added to process data in parallel.

OSI LAYERS

We introduced the OSI layers in Part 1 in the sidebar "The Open Systems Interface Model and Our Approach," describing our method for presenting technology in this book. However, the OSI model presents a sophisticated method for describing how different components of network communications interact in an orderly fashion. More important, the model provides a framework in which different layers can construct standards for efficient information delivery in a single layer only without affecting existing or emerging standards in other layers.

Within each layer of the OSI model, there are component standards as highlighted in Figure 3.1.6 and described briefly in the following section. Each of these component standards has differing characteristics that permit a layer to assume the functionality required.

Some of these standards, such as the Transmission Control Protocol (TCP), the Internet Protocol (IP), and the Dynamic Host Configuration Protocol (DHCP), are familiar to anyone who has ever had to configure a computer to work on the Internet or a network, although few of us ever come to understand their meaning. Other protocols are not widely known but provide specific communications characteristics.

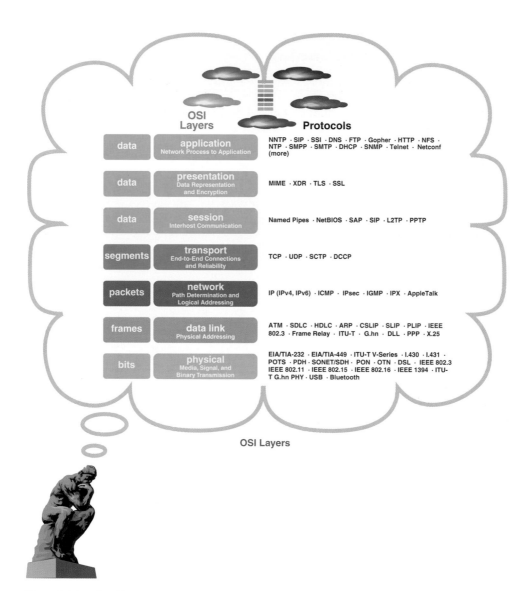

data	**application** Network Process to Application	NNTP · SIP · SSI · DNS · FTP · Gopher · HTTP · NFS · NTP · SMPP · SMTP · DHCP · SNMP · Telnet · Netconf (more)
data	**presentation** Data Representation and Encryption	MIME · XDR · TLS · SSL
data	**session** Interhost Communication	Named Pipes · NetBIOS · SAP · SIP · L2TP · PPTP
segments	**transport** End-to-End Connections and Reliability	TCP · UDP · SCTP · DCCP
packets	**network** Path Determination and Logical Addressing	IP (IPv4, IPv6) · ICMP · IPsec · IGMP · IPX · AppleTalk
frames	**data link** Physical Addressing	ATM · SDLC · HDLC · ARP · CSLIP · SLIP · PLIP · IEEE 802.3 · Frame Relay · ITU-T · G.hn · DLL · PPP · X.25
bits	**physical** Media, Signal, and Binary Transmission	EIA/TIA-232 · EIA/TIA-449 · ITU-T V-Series · I.430 · I.431 · POTS · PDH · SONET/SDH · PON · OTN · DSL · IEEE 802.3 · IEEE 802.11 · IEEE 802.15 · IEEE 802.16 · IEEE 1394 · ITU- T G.hn PHY · USB · Bluetooth

OSI Layers Protocols

OSI Layers

Figure 3.1.6 The *OSI Layers* break data communications into seven layers with each layer depending on the layers below and supporting the layers above so that communications can operate efficiently.

THE INTERNET PROTOCOL

The Internet Protocol has a data model that has four layers that are similar but not the same as the OSI model. We suspect but could not confirm that the similarities come from the fact that both models developed at about the same time. The Internet, which grew out of an effort by the Defense Advanced Research Projects Agency (DARPA), actually predates the OSI model. This figure shows the Internet layers.

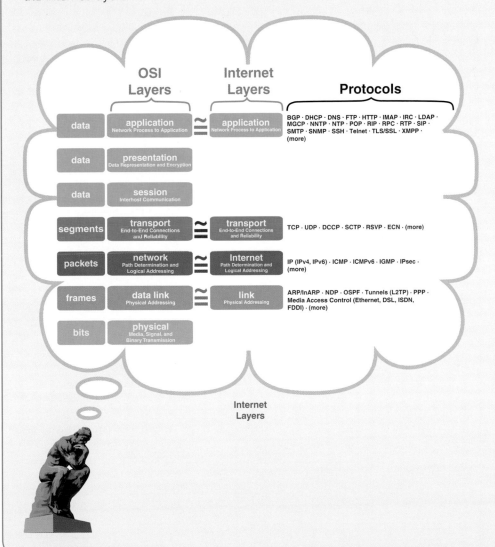

	OSI Layers	Internet Layers	Protocols
data	application Network Process to Application	≅ application Network Process to Application	BGP · DHCP · DNS · FTP · HTTP · IMAP · IRC · LDAP · MGCP · NNTP · NTP · POP · RIP · RPC · RTP · SIP · SMTP · SNMP · SSH · Telnet · TLS/SSL · XMPP · (more)
data	presentation Data Representation and Encryption		
data	session Interhost Communication		
segments	transport End-to-End Connections and Reliability	≅ transport End-to-End Connections and Reliability	TCP · UDP · DCCP · SCTP · RSVP · ECN · (more)
packets	network Path Determination and Logical Addressing	≅ Internet Path Determination and Logical Addressing	IP (IPv4, IPv6) · ICMP · ICMPv6 · IGMP · IPsec · (more)
frames	data link Physical Addressing	≅ link Physical Addressing	ARP/InARP · NDP · OSPF · Tunnels (L2TP) · PPP · Media Access Control (Ethernet, DSL, ISDN, FDDI) · (more)
bits	physical Media, Signal, and Binary Transmission		

Internet Layers

Financial networks are becoming much faster and more robust because developers are creating financial applications that are optimized at each layer of the OSI model.

STANDARDS

Data communications are dependent on a series of standards that are used as an integral part of the data transfer process. The standards are grouped at each layer of the OSI model, and evolving business message standards such as the Financial Information eXchange (FIX) protocol operate on top of the OSI layers. Some of the important standards affecting financial networks are listed in Table 3.1.2. Communications standards facilitate new services by allowing developers to focus on the capabilities they are trying to provide without having to be concerned with the characteristics of the applications and/or the structure of messages with which they interact.

Table 3.1.2 **Important Financial Network Business and Technical Standards**

Focus	Standard		Governing Organization	Access	Short Description
Business-Level Standards[a]	ISO 15022	FIX	FIX Protocol, Ltd.	Open	Message standards aimed primarily at pretrade activities
		SWIFT	Society for Worldwide Interbank Financial Telecommunication	Closed	Message standards aimed primarily at posttrade activities
	NEWSml		International Press Telecommunications Council (IPTC)	Open	A standard designed to be a media independent message standard for news and related information
	RIXML		RIXML.org	Open	A markup language for XML-based presentation of investment research
	XBRL		XBRL International	Open	An XML-based standard for electronic transmission of business and financial information
Technical Standards	AMQP		AMQP Working Group	Open	Wire level protocol for interoperable message exchange
	MAMA		NYSE	Closed	Middleware Agnostic Messaging API developed by Wombat and later acquired by NYSE Euronext
	RV		Tibco	Closed	Message bus technology primarily used for market data redistribution and front office integration
	LBM		Informatica / 29West	Closed	Latency Busters Messaging API(s) developed by 29West
	LLM		IBM	Closed	Low latency messaging API(s) offered by IBM
	MQ		IBM	Closed	Message queuing software that has been used primarily for backoffice integration

[a]Technology standards provided by Richard E. Shriver of R. Shriver Associates. Business standards are summarized from the Web sites of the sponsoring organizations.

Standards within the OSI layers permit those crafting networks to tailor each level to the exact characteristics needed for the network. Moreover, business-level standards permit entities to develop applications sure in the knowledge that they will mesh seamlessly with other entities provided all users adhere to the same standards. In addition, various groups work continuously to incorporate new functionality into standards that permit them to apply to new instrument types and different participating entity groups.

Networks can be grouped by their scope, or **span**, of coverage (see Figure 3.2). Two primary categories include internal networks that we have termed "enterprise infrastructure" and "interentity networks" linking firms.

Enterprise

The enterprise network tends to link line activities in the front, middle, and back-offices. Although not having the same demands as a trading room, substantially all the functions we introduced in Book 1, Part 4 are connected through the enterprise network. This means that most users have access to market-data services (as we described in Part 2), in addition to the ability to process transactions as they move toward completion, to review and update accounting and holdings information, and to share other work files.

Middleware that began as trading-system infrastructure, as described previously, has evolved into what we have referred to as "enterprise infrastructure." The difference between current middleware applications and early networks arises from both broader geographic span and more diverse content.

Enterprise infrastructure permits firms to take information into their infrastructure at any point globally and transmit the information to any other global location using a network owned by the firm. This lowers the cost of distribution for large firms and permits the distribution to be optimized for the way the information is used within the firm.

Internal information distribution is generally organized into what we referred to previously as a "ladder-style network." Information is brought into a basic consolidation layer that puts all information from any source into a common format and maintains that information wherever it is used. A separate distribution layer feeds all information to both individuals and applications that need to access the information.

Between the consolidation and distribution layers are any number of internal applications that need access to external information and that feed internal users. Thus, the infrastructure provides enhancements to external information and adds information generated within the firm. This structure is shown in Figure 3.2.1.b.

Administrative

Within financial entities, large numbers of users do not need and/or cannot justify the costs of market-data or other entitled services. These individuals are usually serviced by **local area networks** that are conceptually similar to local area networks in other commercial firms.

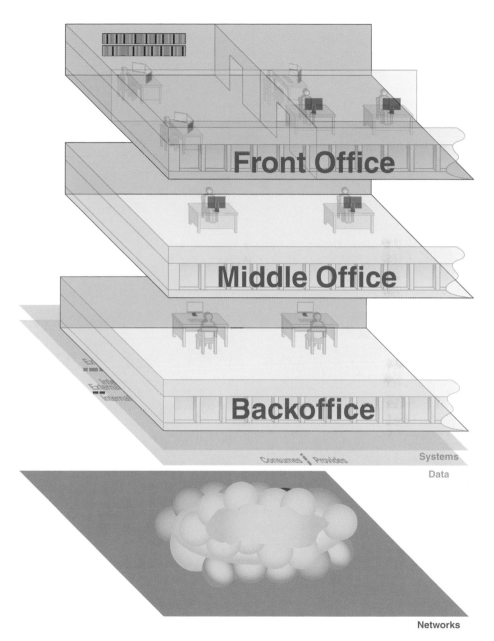

Figure 3.2.1.b *Enterprise networks* provide linkage among functions but also provide an organizing structure for the systems and data used within a firm.

INTERENTITY

A wide number of networks of the types described in the next chapter link entities throughout the Street (see Figure 3.2.2). The major distinction here is the geographic span of these networks.

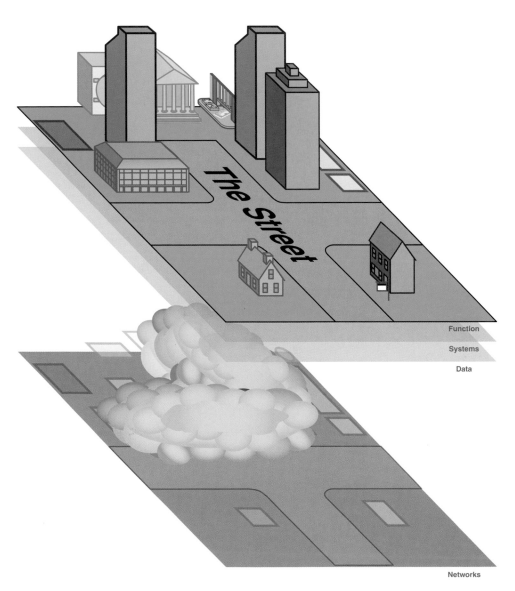

Figure 3.2.2   *Interentity networks* connect different firms within the same city, among cities in the same country, and globally.

Many financial centers have dedicated local (to the financial center) networks that permit firms to link to other firms (and to their own offices) by connecting to the network, which often uses high-speed **fiber-optic cables** with huge bandwidth. The networks often go by the name **extranets** and frequently provide a level of dedicated services for the financial community beyond that which would be typically offered by standard communications networks used by general commercial firms.

For example, these networks may provide the hardware and software (termed **FIX engines**) that permit FIX messages to be transferred freely by participants. (This is sometimes referred to as a **FIX dial tone**.)

National financial markets may include multiple financial centers in the same country. Therefore, extranets often link major centers providing a **point-of-presence (POP)** in each center where firms can connect either through the intracity networks or directly. By connecting to these POPs, the user is effectively connecting to any office, firm, or entity connected to any POP in other financial centers.

Finally, international networks are emerging, linking financial centers and countries globally.

Networks on all levels may be provided by commercial vendors; government-provided **postal, telephone, and telegraph (PTT)** agencies; industry associations; and/or by support entities such as exchanges.

Networks transmitting information among entities have evolved significantly from the early closed networks dedicated to a specific function or content set. First, in many cases the networks serving the trading markets are separate entities from the organization that initially created them. Second, networks increasingly employ standard protocols that permit applications that interact with the network to be completely independent of the networks they use.

Third, networks are optimized for the purpose(s) to which they are targeted. Finally, all networks are challenged by the total volume of information they must handle and by growth in message traffic because of conditions in the markets.

Distribution Technology 3

As we have noted, distribution networks in the trading markets are usually dependent on the underlying telecommunications infrastructure. In countries where there is competition in telecommunications, the costs are low and this form of distribution serves all types of networks. In countries where there is a state-run PTT monopoly, the costs of local distribution are sometimes quite high. In these countries, except for networks where performance is critical, vendors that operate networks look for lower-cost alternatives.

There are four primary means of distribution (see Figure 3.3). First, the basic telecommunications network is usually preferred for most distribution unless the cost is prohibitive. Second, without respect to cost, cellular distribution of informational (as opposed to transactional) information is becoming increasingly important as a means of reaching a broader user base, but also for professionals who want to operate from anywhere.

Third, the public Internet is the preferred method of reaching those for whom cost is a concern and where their location is remote from major financial centers. Fourth, direct, two-way satellite delivery to fixed locations is used where cost is a primary factor in providing information and where other delivery methods are not practical.

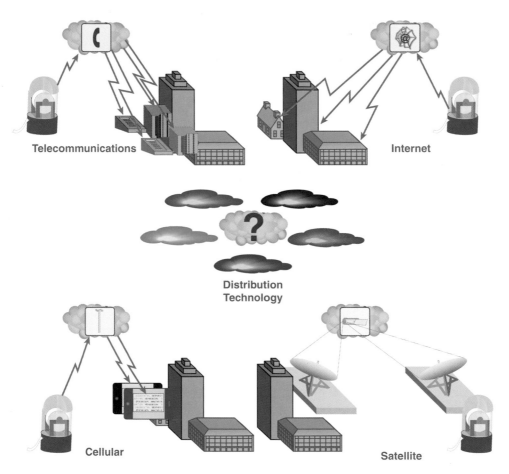

Figure 3.3   The ***distribution technology*** used for networks in the trading markets includes four major distribution strategies.

TELECOMMUNICATIONS

The basic telecommunications infrastructure in most countries is pervasive, often cost effective, and most often provides the most effective means of high-capacity delivery. Even the creation of extranets in local financial centers often uses the local communications infrastructure or employs a telecommunication vendor to build the network.

CELLULAR

The explosion of mobile technology has permitted users to access information from networks serving the trading community from anywhere. Because cellular networks are integrated with land-based networks, designers of networks for the trading markets can mix both technologies in network design.

Also in developing areas, the implementation of cellular networks is much faster and less costly than wired networks. Therefore, some markets elect to depend heavily on cellular communications for some trading functions instead of trying to build land-based networks.

INTERNET

The public Internet has evolved into an important delivery channel for some trading functions. This is particularly true for those activities involving retail investors. Also, network structures based on the Internet can be implemented quickly for those functions that work effectively with the structure of Internet communications.

SATELLITE

Direct satellite delivery has been the alternative delivery methodology where connection to wired networks is expensive and for remote delivery locations. Satellite delivery works in any location where there is clear line-of-site access to existing telecommunications satellites. This distribution method is particularly appealing where a local PTT charges high costs for access to data networks.

One liability is the noticeable *propagation delays*, which occur when requests are made for information that requires a round trip to the satellites and then to the data centers, with a return trip to deliver the information. Satellites orbit at about 22,000 miles altitude.

Types 4

We classify network types primarily by their fundamental purpose. Purpose generally refers to the reason for the network's existence. We define eight major types of networks:

- Telephone and verbal messages
- Market-data networks
- Advertising
- Trading
- Post-trade networks
- Funds and payments
- Email and text messaging
- Video

Within these major categories, distinctions among networks are generally predicated on content and performance. The reason is that network distinctions tend to be logical rather than physical because nearly all networks depend on the same physical telecommunications infrastructure. Networks that route market data tend to be logically separate from order-routing networks.

Likewise, market-data networks that transmit information for viewing by individuals sitting at video displays require substantially less performance than networks that are routing information employed in automated trading decisions. We discussed some of the issues related to network performance in Chapter 1 on concepts. Figure 3.4 shows logically different information distribution networks in the trading markets.

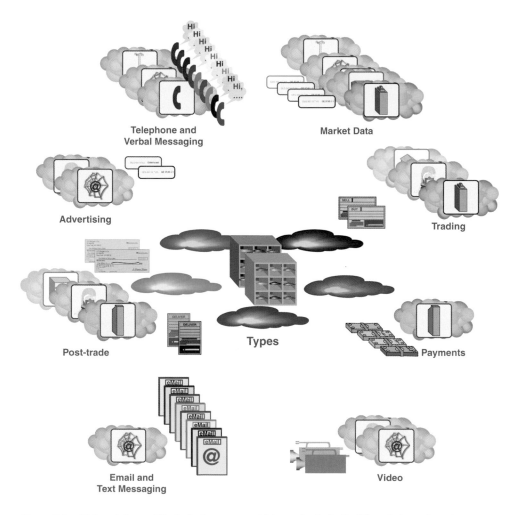

Figure 3.4 *Network types* differ in their purpose, which creates logically different channels and may require differences in capacity and points of connection as well.

TELEPHONE AND VERBAL MESSAGING

Telephone networks have connected firms in the trading markets as well as provided linkages to trading venues. Many of the networks provided direct telephone lines from buy-side personnel to sell-side trading desks to provide instantaneous access on demand.

Telephone communications has slowly been replaced with first email and then instant messaging and Twitter. Buy-side traders generally prefer to have messages that can be processed and to avoid the interruptions a phone call creates. Recently, **Voice over Internet Protocol (VoIP)** has replaced traditional telephone circuits for many applications.

Telephone communications often caused different recollections of the content of messages in the heat of trading, so many telephone circuits were recorded as a means for replaying conversations when problems occurred. In the transition to electronic messages, the need for archiving messages is a consistent regulatory theme.

MARKET-DATA NETWORKS

Beyond telephone networks, the oldest and most extensive networks that permeate the trading markets are those distributing market data. Market-data networks date from the creation of **ticker machines** in the mid-1800s. (A representation of a ticker machine is the icon we use to represent market-data vendors in our graphics.)

As data communications became more standardized and as enterprise infrastructures became more robust, many large global users of market data elected to distribute their own market data in the late 1980s and through the 1990s. Thus, data vendors were left with networks with the costs required for global distribution but with their revenue base dramatically reduced because large firms were no longer willing to pay for distribution.

Therefore, around 2000, two of the major vendors, Reuters and Bridge, elected to spin off their networks as independent network vendors. Now some vendors have proprietary networks, and others rely on independent network vendors.

An important distinction in the distribution of market data is the method of access. We have considered data broadcast to users viewing the data on terminals, but the way that data reaches applications, even some applications that produce data for viewing is through a distribution method known as a **data feed**. Data feeds describe the distribution of bulk data to applications in real time. Two major forms of feeds are **consolidated feeds** and **direct feeds**.

Consolidated Feeds

A consolidated data feed transmits information to individuals or to applications through the normal vendor network distribution channel used to provide information to visual displays. Indeed, there is no difference in the information coming to a user viewing a screen-based service or to an application that is processing the data. In each instance information flows either to the user firm's enterprise distribution system or to a node close to the user where either the display service or the application accesses the data for use.

Consolidated feeds mean that the vendor brings together information from all sources and makes the data available to the application using it. Early feeds provided high volumes of information with little to mitigate the quantity. Indeed, many users likened accessing the information to drinking from a fire hose. Vendors now offer users the opportunity to select only the information they wish from a feed. (We described purchasing a cache of information as a device in pricing in Part 2 when we described the business of data.)

One liability of consolidated data feeds is all the processes the vendor applies to the data that create latency and slow down distribution. This is not a problem for many different applications, but is a problem when an application is used for trading.

Direct Feeds

Trading applications depend on **direct data feeds** to handle pricing and to evaluate best execution decisions. For these applications in an environment where high-frequency trading is a fact of life, the inherent latency of a consolidated data feed is not acceptable. Therefore, most users for whom latency is an issue take feeds directly.

If a firm takes a feed directly from the trading venue, then both the user firm and trading venue have the issue of managing the relationship. As we have seen, most trading venues depend on vendors for most administrative functions such as managing usage reporting and invoicing.

Moreover, most trading venues do not have the technology support staff to handle connections from many different users (as opposed to a few vendors), and so connecting directly to trading venues presents a complicated technical problem with limited support. Therefore, vendors offer both administrative and technical support for users that wish to take the feed directly from the trading venue. The vendor provides a standard, supported interface to the user, provides the administrative support to both parties (trading venue and user) if they choose, yet the physical connection is still direct from the trading venue to the user firm with little if any vendor-induced latency.

ADVERTISING

In the introduction to this part, we mentioned AutEx, Telerate, and Reuters as companies that began the process of advertising and publishing contributed data from dealers. These networks were unique at the time they were created because they linked participants that were not connected in any other way. Indeed, AutEx became the basis for an affirmation service because it linked sell-side firms to their buy-side customers.

Bespoke IOI messages have been replaced by FIX messages, and contributor data is now carried by a combination of traditional vendors and the Internet. Therefore, advertising has become more of a service type within broader vendor offerings rather than a unique network type.

TRADING NETWORKS

Specialty order-routing networks provide secure connections among institutions, the broker/dealers either executing or guaranteeing trades, and the markets and trading venues where trades are executed. These networks often provide a reverse route for trade confirmation, but they do not typically support post-trade processes such as trade affirmation, clearing, and settlement.

Order routing evolved from telex and Teletype networks that were developed by large broker/dealers and used to route orders to trading venues. Indeed, early national broker/dealers in the United States were known as **wire houses** because they maintained these networks. Smaller firms depended on vendors or correspondent brokers for routing networks.

Order-Input

Order-input networks route orders from users and their agents to execution venues. We make a distinction between order-input networks and **transactional networks**. Order-input networks are **unidirectional**, linking a user to a trading venue. The presumption is that an order-input network requires some other source for the information that leads to an order being entered such as a direct feed.

Transactional

A transactional feed operates in two directions although likely with separate channels. Actionable market data comes from the trading network to the user, and the user sends orders back in the other direction.

Colocation

Finally, **colocation services** are not so much a network type as a service that makes other types of networks unnecessary. Trading venues offer high-frequency traders and others the ability to place their trading models in the same facility as the trading venue's processors (to colocate), often on a local area network connecting the two. This minimizes the latency caused by routing distance. There may be a separate channel or connection between the user and the model for updates and to monitor operations.

POST-TRADE NETWORKS

A number of networks have been developed to link buy-side firms, sell-side firms, custodian banks, clearing corporations, and depositories. The genesis of these networks arose from the fact that buy-side and sell-side firms did not have access to the networks linking banks for payments.

Yet there was a need to provide a linkage that permitted institutional investors to affirm trades in multiple markets globally. These networks also have the functionality to facilitate the affirmation process described in Book 2, *An Introduction to Trading in the Financial Markets: Trading, Markets, Instruments, and Processes.*

PAYMENTS NETWORKS

Like the geographic span of networks described previously, funds transfer networks exist on three levels: in financial centers, within countries, and globally.

Financial Centers

In major financial centers, banks often band together to form a **clearinghouse** to net payments and to reduce the costs of funds movements. In London, the **Clearing House Automated Payments System (CHAPS)** and the **Clearing House Interbank Payments System (CHIPS)** in the United States are two such systems. These systems tend to be **mutualized**, and this can reduce the cost of each payment.

National

Most countries provide an internal wire transfer facility either as a service of the central bank or as a mutualized facility of the banks in the country. In the United States, FedWire is run by the Federal Reserve.

In Europe, there is a pan-European International Bank Account Number (IBAN) that provides users with a EU-wide account number that is recognized and can facilitate transfers among member countries as if they were within the same country. However, while the IBAN simplifies the transfers, it is dependent on national payments networks to actually complete the transfer.

Global

The dominant payments network for global transfers is the Society for Worldwide Interbank Financial Telecommunication (SWIFT), which is owned by member banks and processes funds payments among members. In the past two decades, SWIFT has moved into the securities settlement area.

EMAIL AND TEXT MESSAGING

Email using the public Internet has become an important means of communications both on a professional and retail level. For professionals, instant messaging and the newer Twitter networks offer the ability to communicate new ideas quickly and to process those ideas at least in part.

The problem with most commercial versions of these technologies is the lack of a guaranteed archiving facility that can be monitored and/or audited by regulators in the event of problems. Therefore, market-data vendors offer instant messaging that is archived, and independent companies have stepped in to provide archiving for all electronic messaging.

VIDEO NETWORKS

Beginning with the first Gulf War, particularly in the spring of 1991, political events had a dramatic effect on the markets, and trading rooms began to provide traders with access to cable news channels. More recently, financial news networks have also become standard services for traders.

Beyond news, many buy-side and sell-side firms use videoconferencing as a means for professionals in different offices to communicate. A few firms have considered the use of "video walls" as a means of linking multiple trading floors into a single virtual environment.

Organization 5

Many entities in the financial markets maintain a network organization separate from other technology groups, but other organizations simply have a single technology group. Whatever the structure of the organization, the tasks required to manage all communications within an entity require unique skills and training.

The major categories of network activities include network architecture, procurement, finance, and operations. This conceptual structure is shown in Figure 3.5.

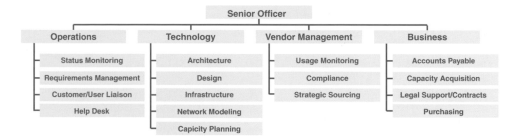

Figure 3.5 The ***network organization*** must accommodate functional needs to maintain day-to-day operation of the network; to provide any technical assistance in the design and development; to manage vendors providing services; and to make payments and perform other administrative tasks.

We also included some of these activities in Part 2 as well to indicate that those entities engaged in the business of data require network skills that are essential to data creation, distribution, and consumption.

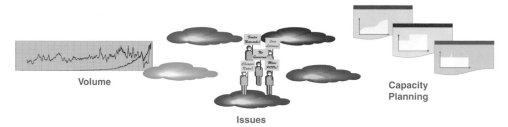

Figure 3.6 ***Network issues*** center on message traffic that has been growing exponentially, as well as discussions on how to plan for the growth that will occur.

MESSAGE TRAFFIC

When we discussed growing data volumes in the preceding part, we described the process of autoquoting for options, and we noted that other instruments autoquote as well. However, autoquoting is not the only cause of exploding message volumes. Specifically:

- In 1999, the United States moved from trading in fractional units to trading in decimals. Quoting in decimals would not have had a huge impact if the ***minimum price variation (MPV)*** had not been fixed at one penny.

- The movement to one penny as an MPV had an immediate impact on options and autoquoting.

- Nearly simultaneously, the U.S. Securities and Exchange Commission caused the end of a moratorium that had seen options contracts on equity issues traded by only one exchange at a time. Immediately, multiple exchanges started to quote the same very active options contracts.

- Regulators also ended the practice of competing market makers on the same exchange developing a composite quote for all market makers in each options contract. Each competing market maker was required to develop an independent quote for each contract.

- A separate impact of penny MPVs was a dramatic drop in the size of orders on major exchanges and an increase in the number of orders required to complete an initial order.

- Other instruments began to use automated quoting to generate orders, and execution was automated in those markets as well.

The cumulative effect of these and other changes has been that traders have felt the need to automate the order submission process with a resulting impact on the pace of trading. This has meant a classic ***feedback loop*** in which traders need automation to cope with the pace of trading that in turn accelerates the pace of trading, which results in the demand for more automation.

Many traders now engage in what has been labeled "high frequency trading" as a result. These trading strategies, as we described previously, generate many orders for each execution.

More recently, the MiFID changes in Europe in November of 2007 legitimized the idea of systematic internalizers with a similar impact in encouraging quantitative trading as occurred with decimals in the United States. More specifically, when global trading firms invest in quantitative trading in one country, they tend to employ the same strategies in the other market where they regularly trade, and the pace of trading reinforces the loop in those countries as well.

The increasing pace of trading generates a demand for big, fast networks and close proximity to trading venues. It also generates interest in how to mitigate volume growth and how to plan for that growth.

CAPACITY PLANNING

One of the major challenges facing network managers in an environment where volume grows seemingly without bound is to develop a methodology that maintains adequate capacity in the face of huge message volumes. In a project for the Consolidated Tape Association (CTA) and the **Options Price Reporting Authority (OPRA)** in the late 1990s, Mr. Alan Kolnick, then of SRI Consulting (a firm mentioned earlier in a footnote) suggested a useful model for capacity planning. The model we proposed to CTA and OPRA is described next.

In the development of a capacity plan, three types of growth must be anticipated. First, much growth is secular, normal growth that sometimes includes cyclical patterns as well. Most firms that have a reasonable history can forecast this type of growth using normal statistical forecasting tools, often augmented by qualitative assessments concerning markets, the economy, and other factors.

The second type of growth occurs when known events can be anticipated and evaluated in advance of the events. Examples of these types of events include the conversion to decimals in 2000, RegNMS in 2005 and 2006, and MiFID in 2007. Each of these events was announced more than a year before it was enacted or implemented, and there was time to assess and forecast the implications of the change. This type of forecasting results in a step function increase and requires different forecasting techniques.

Finally, there are completely unforeseen events that result in huge spikes that cannot be anticipated. Forecasting for these types of events cannot occur directly because they are unforeseen. What can occur is that planners can look at similar past events and estimate the percentage increase above normal volumes that have occurred. When this historical percentage is used, and some additional headroom is provided, an increment above the forecast changes from the other two methods of forecasting can occur.

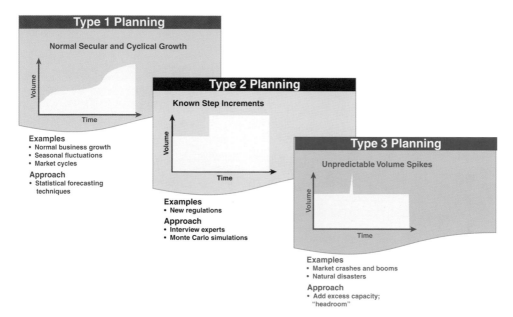

Figure 3.6.1 ***Network capacity*** can be forecast by employing three different types of forecasting to create a cumulative projection.

The result of these three forecasting strategies is a cumulative forecast that combines the three projections. This is represented in Figure 3.6.1.

RELATED INFORMATION IN OTHER BOOKS

This part describes networks, beginning with some concepts related to them; the scope of coverage for networks; and types of networks based on their primary purpose, organizational requirements, and network issues. Here, we did not attempt to fully describe the requirements of network design except to the extent that a fundamental understanding is necessary to fully understand the trading markets and how entities in those markets are linked to perform their primary functions. Figure 3.7 shows where additional information can be found.

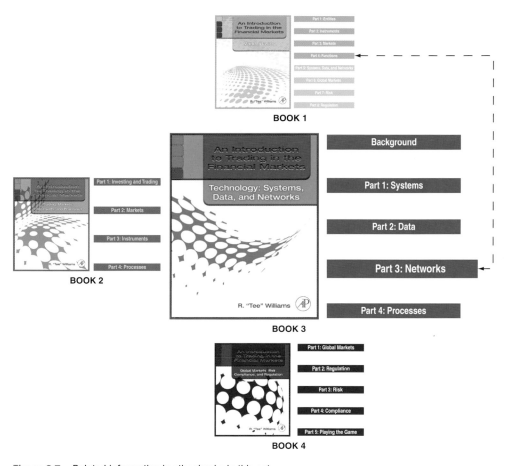

Figure 3.7 Related information in other books in this set.

The next part concludes our exploration of technology in the markets by following the use of systems, data, and networks through each step in the trading process. We introduced this process in the Preface to Book 1 and expanded on it in Part 4 (Processes) in Book 2.

Trading Process

Part **4**

In this part we return to the trading process as we defined it initially in Book 1, *An Introduction to Trading in the Financial Markets: Market Basics,* and as we described it at the beginning of the secondary-market process subsection: Chapter 2, Part 4 of Book 2, *An Introduction to Trading in the Financial Markets: Trading, Markets, Instruments, and Processes.* This simplified flow focuses on the eight primary steps involved in most trades but exempts the subsidiary steps introduced in Book 2. The overall flow is shown in Figure 4.0.

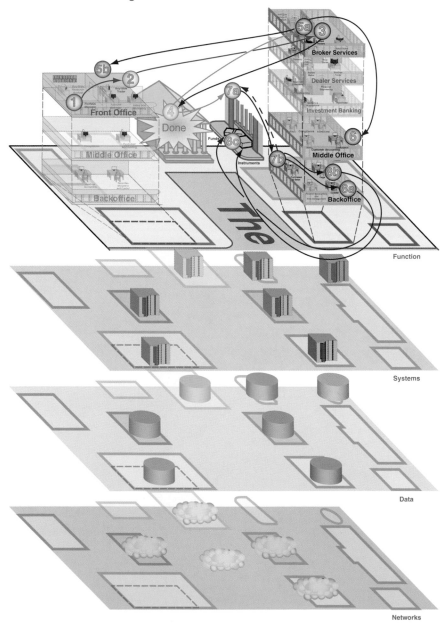

Figure 4.0 *Technology in the trading process* provides the systems, data, and networks to support each process step and complete a transaction.

TRADING-PROCESS BUSINESS-PROCESS FLOW

In Book 2 we introduced the concept of a business-process flow to make the interactions among the different entities easier to understand in a complex process described in Part 4 of that book. The figure that follows is the final flow for the secondary market presented there. For clarity, we have enlarged the process steps that we will consider here.

(Continued)

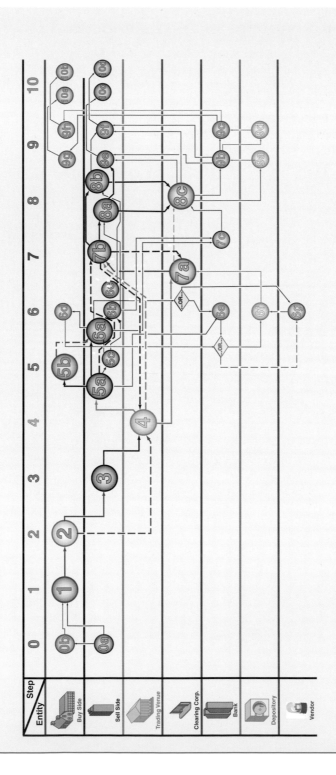

For each step, we begin with an introduction that summarizes the purpose of the step. (If you want more detail about the purpose of the steps, you may want to review the appropriate parts of Book 2.) We then describe briefly the inputs that may precipitate actions taken in the step. (For the most part, the inputs to each step are the outputs from previous steps, and we do not repeat the descriptions unless there are additional factors or external inputs.)

We then define the major data inputs within the step and the systems employed. We conclude by identifying any data that is produced and the process units that are updated and/or produced. After groups of steps that are linked by networks, we pause to outline those networks and describe the movement of the process units.

In Book 2 we described both the different styles of investing and other motivations for trading. We noted a number of specific causes such as new funds or a change in the assessment of the attractiveness of specific instruments that might be the cause of specific trading decisions.

Here, we are not concerned with the exact cause of a trading decision, but we are interested in understanding some of the systems and information employed in that decision. Figure 4.1 shows how portfolio managers employ systems and data to generate decisions to trade.

Step 1

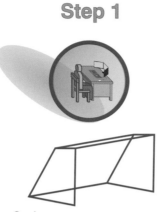

Goals:
- Optimize the returns on the portfolio
- Satisfy the needs of the beneficial owners
- Conform to firm's policies, owner's wishes, and regulatory mandates

Figure 4.1 *Step 1: Pre-trade decisions* employ internal systems and market and reference data to arrive at a decision to buy or sell instruments.

From our perspective, pre-trade decisions are the source of the trading process. Other decisions no doubt occur upstream that may result in the decision to change the holdings in a portfolio or an account, but those decisions are external to our investigation. Therefore, we are not concerned with any inputs into the pre-trade decision.

PROCESSES

The portfolio manager controls the assets in portfolios and decides how to implement the strategy for managing the portfolios through additions to and sales from existing holdings. In addition to the data and systems described later, many portfolio managers try to stay up to date with current theory for the portfolio management philosophy to which they or the portfolio's charter subscribes. (As we noted in Book 2, large portfolio management companies typically have portfolios or funds that subscribe to many different philosophies to satisfy customers' varied preferences.)

Outside our focus on technology, therefore, portfolio managers frequently attend seminars, and there is a wide array of different investment strategy publications that they can read to stay current in their specific field. Indeed, many portfolio managers contribute articles to these publications.

More specifically, the portfolio manager needs to monitor general business and economic conditions to be able to decide how the overall climate is likely to affect the existing portfolio and what changes should be made. The manager must monitor expectations for the products or accounts that are tied to the portfolio to judge what adjustments may be needed to satisfy those expectations.

Finally, the manager must also monitor both existing holdings and potential additions to assess the effect of possible changes. The manager's actions may be circumscribed by guidance provided by the firm and by the charter of the fund being managed. Figure 4.1.1 shows the portfolio process in overview.

Step 1

Inputs:
- **Customer requests**
  - Policy
  - Contributions
  - Withdrawals
- **Research and ideas**

Evaluation:
- **Alternative investments**

Decisions:
- **Changes (If any)**

Outputs:
- **Order(s) with instructions**
  - Instruments
  - Quantity
  - Urgency
  - Price range

Figure 4.1.1 *Pre-trade processes* involve analysis and then actions portfolio managers take that result in trading instructions based on information from portfolio management systems and information from the markets.

Data Consumed

Although we are not focused on upstream decisions that precede the portfolio management process, it is important to understand that both internal and external data sources contribute to the pre-trade decision process. From external sources, market data, including real-time pricing information, news and commentary, historical data sets, and most particularly research, contribute to the decision-making process.

From internal sources, priced holdings either in portfolio management systems or from the portfolio accounting systems require prices that come from the firm's priced holdings file. Priced holdings in turn use inputs from the security master file and the account and/or product master file.

Systems

Portfolio managers depend on two different types of systems. Portfolio management systems focus on the holdings in the portfolio. Analytical systems help to evaluate either individual securities or the attributes of the portfolio depending on the investment strategy of the fund.

To make effective decisions, the portfolio manager needs a management system that provides information in a format optimized for the strategy of the fund he or she manages. Information presented in this way can be easily compared to alternatives presented by research and the output from analytical systems.

Finally, the portfolio manager is the initiator of orders using order-management systems.

OUTPUTS

Pre-trade outputs are primarily orders specifying the instruments to be traded, the quantities required, the urgency of the transactions, and any other instructions required.

Data Produced

The pre-trade decision-making process does not contribute significant data to either internal or external systems. It may provide updates to statuses in accounting, portfolio management, OMS, or other systems.

Process Units

The pre-trade process is the source of the most important process unit in the trading process: the order. Coming from the pre-trade decision process, an order is simply an indication of intent to buy or sell, a sense of a target price or price range, and a sense of the urgency of the transaction. In Step 2, this general intent is converted into a specific order or orders submitted to trading venues.

SUMMARY

In the pre-trade decision process, systems providing portfolio management and/or portfolio accounting present holdings data to a portfolio manager. The portfolio manager, perhaps because of new inputs or withdrawals, or because of changes in market conditions or analysis comparing alternative holdings, makes a decision to alter a portfolio. That decision, entered as an order into an order-management system, instructs a buy-side trader to execute the order in accordance with the portfolio manager's instructions (see Figure 4.1.2).

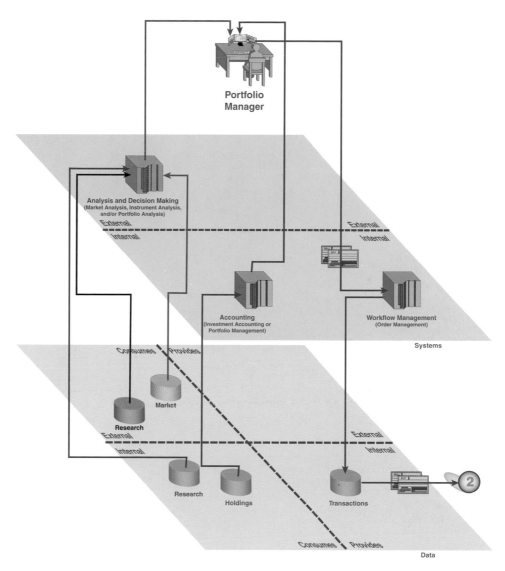

Figure 4.1.2 The ***pre-trade step*** uses analytical systems and data with portfolio and/or accounting systems and holdings data to produce orders and instructions processed in order-management systems and held in transactions files.

Step 2: Buy-Side Trading 2

Investing institutions must manage orders prior to releasing them to the market; they must track orders in the markets before they receive confirmation of an execution; and they may need to cancel all or part of an order before it is executed. In many situations orders are not simply handed off to the sell side as might have occurred in the past.

Instead, orders are actively managed during the execution process. This can involve monitoring and actively engaging multiple trading venues as well as the sell side in a changing process while the order remains active. Several different pieces of technology assist in this process. Figure 4.2 shows the buy-side trading process.

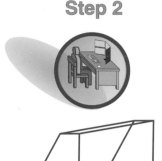

Step 2

Goals:
- **Make best net use of execution alternatives**
- **Optimize desired balance between best price and fastest execution**
- **Minimize market impact**
- **Achieve goals of portfolio manager**

Figure 4.2   *Step 2: Buy-side trading* implements the trading decisions expressed as orders from portfolio managers.

PROCESSES

A buy-side trader receives an order with general instructions, wishes, and possibly, advice from a portfolio manager.[1] The buy-side trader then has to decide how to implement those instructions and to execute the order. To do this, the trader depends on a wide variety of information and several systems to manage the order through the execution process.

The buy-side trader can employ stealth, hiding the true size of the order, and can employ multiple sell-side agents and dealers to execute the trade. In addition, the trader may use execution-management systems independently or in concert with the sell side to achieve the objectives set for executing the total order. Figure 4.2.1 shows the overview of this process.

---

1   We noted in Parts 1 and 3 of Book 2, *An Introduction to Trading in the Financial Markets: Trading, Markets, Instruments, and Processes,* that for less liquid securities such as some bonds and other instruments without an active secondary market the portfolio manager sometimes acts as the buy-side trader as well. These instruments typically do not trade frequently enough for this to be a major problem. Moreover, because bonds frequently cannot be purchased based on a specific issue, the portfolio manager may be in a better position to choose among alternatives than a trader.

For equities and other liquid instruments, many firms view the separation of portfolio management and trading as an important risk management policy. We describe risk management in Book 4, *An Introduction to Trading in the Financial Markets: Global Markets, Risk, Compliance, and Regulation,* but the general idea is that if the roles are separated, there is less likelihood that decisions can be made without the decisions being widely known and possibly reviewed.

Step 2

Inputs:
- Total order(s) with instructions
  - Instruments
  - Quantity
  - Urgency
  - Price range
- * IOIs
- Commentary

Evaluation:
- Alternative trading venues
- Market prices

Management:
- Open orders
- Orders in market

Decisions:
- Role (use DMA, use agent, or mix)
- Quantity Timing

Outputs:
- Specific orders to trading venue(s) and/or agents
  - Instruments
  - Quantity
  - Urgency
  - Target price

Figure 4.2.1 The **buy-side trading process** manages orders generated by portfolio managers controlled by order-management and execution-management systems aided by market data and indications of interest from the sell side to create orders for direct market access or execution through the sell side.

Data Consumed

The buy-side trader is primarily responsible for gauging conditions in the market on a moment-to-moment basis to judge the right timing for submitting orders and the best trading venue to use. From often multiple external sources, the trader receives market data. News and commentary, often directed specifically at traders, provide an assessment of likely market conditions and how those conditions are likely to change in the event of anticipated economic and market events.

Indications of interest from the sell side alert the trader to possible sources of **hidden liquidity** that can permit an order to be executed with minimal **market impact**. (Hidden liquidity and market impact were the subject of a sidebar discussion titled "Hidden Liquidity" in Book 2, Part 1.)

Systems

The primary systems employed in buy-side trading include market-data and analytical systems primarily from vendors, internal order-management systems, and execution-management systems from vendors and the sell side. The market-data and analytical systems are often tailored specifically for buy-side users, and some market data and/or analytical services are provided in EMS offerings.

ORDER MANAGEMENT

Order-management systems (OMS) created for the buy side are designed to automate and streamline the workflow of receiving requests to buy or sell instruments from portfolio managers and converting the requests into specific orders with instructions to be submitted to the markets. After the orders are released to the market, the systems monitor the orders, recording executions when they occur, and receive and book allocated trades from broker/dealers.

Buy-side OMS typically are organized into blotters that appear as spreadsheets with rows representing orders and columns displaying details of the order (buy or sell, security identifier, number of shares, and so on), details of instructions (limit price and constraints on agents), as well as the status of each order.

The term "blotter" is a holdover term from the time when traders would write the status of orders on a desk blotter that would be collected at the end of the day and used in either a manual or rudimentary automated accounting system. Traders typically have the flexibility to structure blotters in whatever format they prefer.

Examples might be a blotter for buys and another for sells; a blotter for orders that are urgent and another for less critical orders; orders that are to be used for soft-dollar payments (see Book 2 for a description of soft dollars); or orders being managed directly versus orders that are to be managed indirectly.

In different firms, traders may use specific structures, and individual traders may organize blotters to conform to their style of trading. Some order-management systems are optimized for specific types of firms such as hedge funds, whereas others are targeted at specific asset types such as equities, fixed income, or derivatives.

Order-management systems may also have access to market data (different kinds of data are described in Part 2); for example, the OMS probably shows the price of each security in an order as of the moment based on market data feeds that update prices in real time. In addition, buy-side OMS often receive inputs from other feeds such as capital changes where events such as stock splits and dividends can affect both the value and perhaps the advisability of pending orders during the period when an order for an instrument is pending.

Other information (e.g., indications of interest (IOIs),[2] instant messages (IMs), and brief Twitter messages) may provide the opportunity to find an execution at a better price. Buy-side OMS often provide the ability to filter incoming messages provided in FIX format, showing potential opportunities to trade when the incoming message represents the other side of a possible execution for one of the active orders in a blotter.

Some order-management systems permit trading by dragging an order in a blotter to an icon representing an execution venue and dropping the order onto the

---

2   As we noted at the beginning of this part, most of the input to each process step is an output from a previous step. However, IOIs emphasize the fact that the trading process that we have portrayed as a linear process is actually a feedback loop. Existing orders left with the sell side (Step 3) become IOIs that feed into the buy-side trading process (Step 2). Less directly, prices generated by trades (Step 4) are fed back as market data into the decision process of buy-side trading (Step 2) and order routing (Step 3).

THE EVOLUTION OF AN IOI

We introduced the notion of an IOI in Book 2, Part 1, and discussed it as an important process unit in the Background section. However, with the background of the subsection on OMS, we want to point out that an IOI is really an "immature" order. An IOI, if fairly used by a sell-side firm, is an indication from the sell-side firm to its buy-side customers that a natural order exists that can be executed.

For a buy-side firm with an order on the other side of the IOI, this means that it is possible to execute with little market impact by flipping the IOI. Thus, an IOI implying the existence of an order can be converted to a firm order with a strong potential to create an execution.

icon. Although some OMS have trading capabilities, a separate class of execution-management systems is described in the next section.

EXECUTION MANAGEMENT

Although buy-side OMS provide some execution capabilities, they are often more suited to infrequent trading and less sophisticated execution strategies. Therefore, specialized capabilities have been developed for more aggressive traders and for those traders employing sophisticated strategies.

Execution-management systems permit the trader to manage the process of execution. These systems are linked directly to execution venues such as dark pools, electronic communications networks (ECNs), multilateral trading facilities (MTFs), and exchanges that permit direct market access (DMA).

A sophisticated EMS enables the trader to employ all the different order types for each of the different trading venues the trader uses. Finally, the trader may use an EMS to break large orders into smaller pieces to be submitted in an automated fashion to different trading venues simultaneously.

This capability is known as smart order routing, and the process is known as ***sweeping the Street***. In this process the order is broken into pieces that correspond to published orders displayed by trading venues at any given moment. The orders are sent to the venues where they are executed, or if no execution is received, the order may be canceled to be sent to a different market or resubmitted at a different price.

SWEEPING THE STREET

The next figure shows conceptually how smart routing systems are employed to sweep the Street. The system takes pending orders to be executed and scans all available trading venues for exposed orders on the **other side** from the pending order. The system then begins to break the pending order into executable sizes and routes those orders to all possible venues with standing orders that

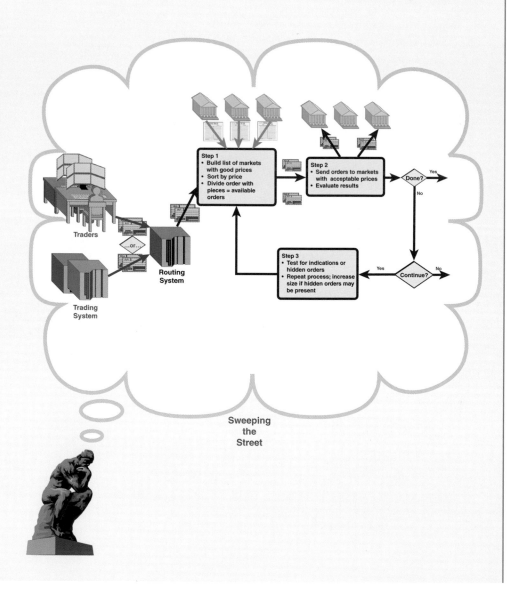

Sweeping
the
Street

are attractive. The system may monitor the process in the hope of deducing automated strategies that may be exploited.

For example, if an execution immediately results in an order being replenished, the system may assume that a hidden order is operating in the venue. When orders do not execute, the price may be adjusted in pursuit of executions. These algorithms can employ great sophistication and must be modified frequently because others will adapt to strategies to gain an advantage.

OUTPUTS

Buy-side trading produces the orders and is responsible for market data although we do not address the data until the execution is completed in Step 4.

Data Produced

The trading process does not produce any data either internally or externally except for status changes to both the OMS and EMS. Those updates that result from successful executions are addressed later.

Process Units

The major output from the buy-side trading process are orders as they are submitted to trading venues and to the sell side for execution and/or management. These orders may remain in their original form until they are completed or canceled, but many orders change based on dynamic market conditions. Therefore, part of the role of the trader and the order-management system is to relate initial orders to subsequent changes as they occur.

SUMMARY

The buy-side trader uses the order-management system to manage orders during the execution process. The trader may use indications of interest from the sell side and market data from vendors to assess the best way to execute existing orders. The system updates the status of orders until the order is fully satisfied or canceled. The trader may also use an execution-management system to handle the release of orders into the market (see Figure 4.2.2).

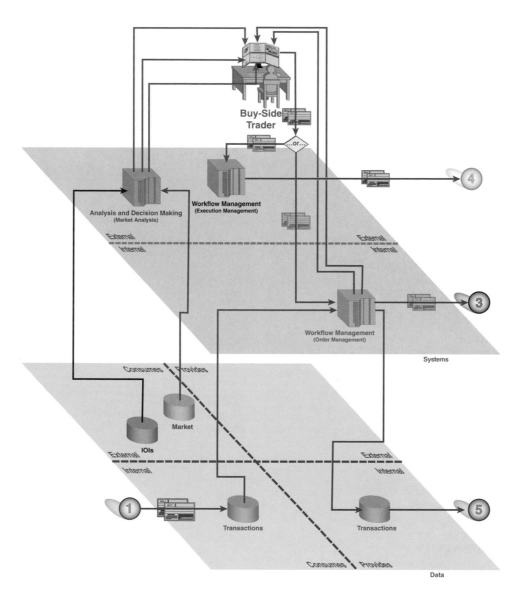

Figure 4.2.2   The **buy-side trader** receives aggregate orders from portfolio managers stored in transactions files and employs market data and workflow control systems, both OMS and EMS, to determine the best place and timing to release orders into the market.

NETWORKS WITHIN THE BUY SIDE

The primary network affecting the buy side is the enterprise infrastructure network, which was described earlier in Part 3. These networks may be implemented internally, but larger money managers are usually the only people able to afford these systems. Vendors often offer "virtual" networks in a hosted environment that provides most, if not all, of the features of an in-house system.

The enterprise network takes in all the feeds, which are employed both for market-data display and to support the OMS. An execution-management system may also be fed by the network but may also be offered as a semi-independent service from a sell-side firm. The structure of the enterprise network and its linkages to other systems is shown in the figure.

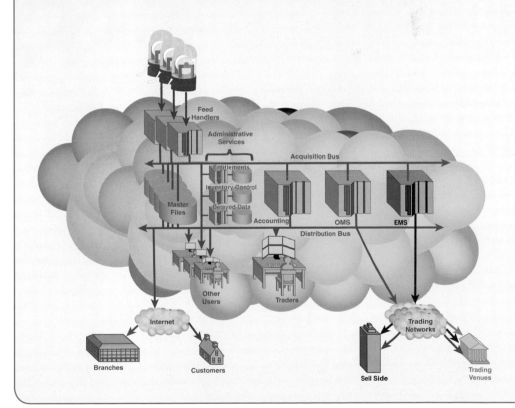

Step 3: Order Routing 3

We have treated order routing primarily as the activities of a sales trader operating on behalf of a buy-side customer. However, we have labeled this step "order routing" instead of "sales trading" because the order from the buy side can be handled in either of two ways (see Figure 4.3). The order can be handed off to the sales trader who acts in many ways as if the buy-side trading function has been outsourced.

Alternatively, we have noted the potential for the buy-side trader to employ DMA to submit the order directly to the trading venue for execution. It is important to

Data Consumed

The sales trader representing the sell-side firm uses commercial market data plus the information accumulated in the trading room from active participation in the markets as an agent and/or as a dealer to evaluate where and when to execute some or all of the customer's order.

Systems

Order-management systems on the sell side provide all the functionality of those on the buy side but may also provide the functionality of an internal market and dealer support. This added functionality might mean that a customer can choose an ***internalized execution*** in combination with or instead of using an independent trading venue.

RULES-BASED SYSTEMS

Traditionally, sell-side forms have used order-routing systems that employ fixed rule sets. These rules might dictate that all orders be routed to a specific market or that orders be routed to a dominant or primary exchange. The advent of better technology and regulations requiring best execution has made rules-based routing largely obsolete.

SMART ROUTING SYSTEMS

Smart routing systems employ algorithms to choose the place and timing of executions. We described the concept of smart routing in the earlier sidebar titled "Sweeping the Street" when discussing Step 2.

OUTPUTS

The order-routing process is, as we have suggested, structurally similar to the buy-side trading process, but order routing has a slightly different focus and employs different relative advantages. Except for IOIs discussed later, the outputs of order routing are similar to those of buy-side trading.

Data Produced

Like buy-side trading, order routing produces no major data for the categories described in Part 2. There are updates to system statuses, but they occur mostly when events have occurred.

Process Units

As was the case with buy-side trading, the most important process unit produced by order routing is the order(s) sent to trading venues for execution that becomes part of quotes published by the trading venues, creating an important part of market data.

Broker/dealer institutional sales departments use information on customers' holdings and interests to generate potential sales both as a result of other customers' orders and as a result of the firm's own dealing and market-making activities. The institutional sales departments send out structured IOI messages using the FIX protocol (see the following sidebar) to all customers that are likely to be interested in a pending order. As we noted previously, one order from a customer may generate an IOI sent to other customers. Those customers receiving an IOI may use it as input to their trading decisions.

ORDER ROUTING AND THE FINANCIAL INFORMATION EXCHANGE PROTOCOL

In the early 1990s, Solomon Brothers (then an independent investment bank) and Fidelity Research and Management (a large investment institution) agreed to develop standardized messages that would permit the two firms to exchange orders, confirmations, and other trading-related messages in a standardized format. At the time most messages were handled over the phone and required information to be transcribed, often resulting in errors.

In fact, the most common mistake was for the broker to "hear" or at least write down "buy" on an order when the customer wanted to "sell." That type of error on a large order was extremely costly to whichever party made it. (Many trading rooms record the calls between the buy side and sell side so that such errors can be assigned to the person responsible when an error like this occurs because of the potential cost.)

The Financial Information eXchange (FIX) protocol established a series of standardized messages that could be built into orders and related messages to ensure that the messages could be handled electronically and without transcription errors. The following list presents representative FIX message types.

Allocations	Reference data: instruments
Communications control	Reference data: markets
Event notification (news and email)	Registration instructions
Indications (IOIs)	Requests for quotes
Market data	Settlement instructions
Multileg orders	Single orders
Order cancellation including mass cancels	Trade capture
Program trading	Trade errors
Quotes and negotiations	

(Continued)

From two firms, FIX has evolved into a global organization involving substantially every firm that trades actively. It began primarily for equity securities but has grown to handle most traded instruments. The FIX organization was initially a completely informal association of technical and operations people meeting to solve a problem, but FIX has developed a more formal structure.

Most computer systems that employ the FIX protocol employ a so-called FIX engine that is furnished by several different vendors. FIX engines take FIX messages and handle all the administrative parts of communications processing. For example, there are different versions of the FIX standard, and firms tend to adopt the most current version as their standard.

If a firm does not need some of the later message types, it may not update to newer releases of the standard. The FIX engine permits two firms to communicate even if they are using different versions of the standard.

SUMMARY

In order routing, a sell-side order-management system is employed to control orders as they are received (see Figure 4.3.2). The OMS may include an internal market to execute orders against the firm's inventory or may provide order-routing algorithms to send the order to execution venues.

The system may also provide support for a dealer trading firm if the customer requests and the firm agrees to commit capital to complete the trade. Order status is maintained until the order is completed or canceled. Orders going to trading venues are frequently formatted as FIX messages for routing.

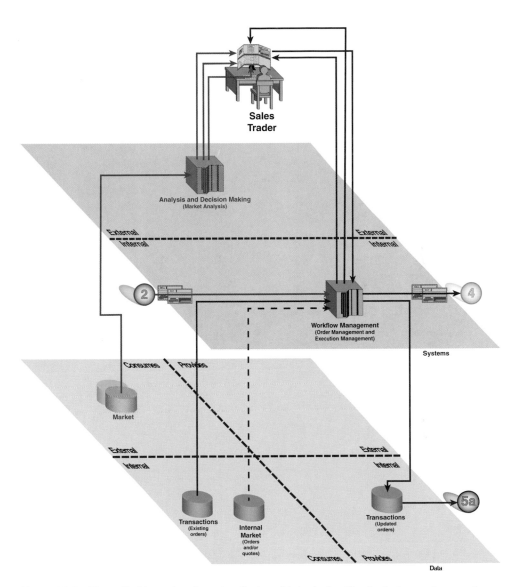

Figure 4.3.2 The *sell-side* receives the orders the buy-side trader is willing to disclose and uses order-management systems to execute orders internally, if the customer wishes, or uses the sell-side firm's skills and knowledge of the market to find the best execution(s).

TRADING-ROOM NETWORKS WITHIN THE SELL SIDE

Sell-side firms, like their buy-side counterparts, employ enterprise infrastructures to manage their internal communications and to distribute much information from external sources (such as market data) in a common message format. Although there are differences in these enterprise networks, their functions are similar. Therefore, the figure in the earlier sidebar, "Networks within the Buy Side," also works for the sell side.

There are, however, dedicated internal networks supporting trading that are common among large sell-side firms; they may also be found at large buy-side firms that trade aggressively, such as hedge funds. These networks are known as **trading-floor platforms** or **trading-room infrastructure**, or similar names (see figure).

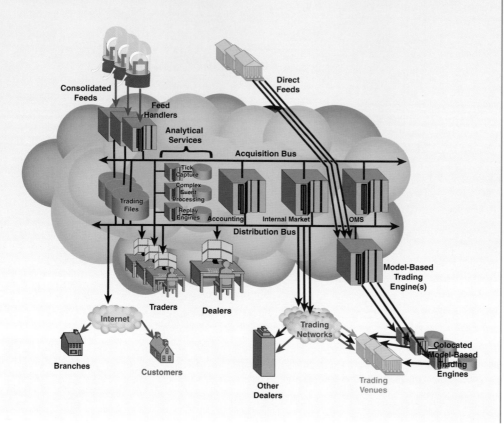

These networks are a class of middleware optimized for trading and are the latest stage in the evolution described in the sidebar "The Evolution of Enterprise Infrastructures" presented in Part 3, Chapter 2. The key factor in the design of these networks is to minimize latency and to be able to host trading models and testing environments for model development.

Although vendors of enterprise infrastructure frequently offer total solutions serving the needs of large organizations with diverse needs, trading-floor platforms may consist of an assembly of component parts from different vendors. Modeling software, database hardware and software, message structures, and other components may all come from different vendors that are either sold separately or as part of joint solutions and offerings.

Step 4: Execution 4

If you think of a body or an organism as a metaphor for the trading process, then execution is the heart pumping trades and market data throughout the Street and the component functions within the trading process. However, because of **fragmentation**, which was described in Book 2, Part 1, execution as we mean it in Step 4 does not occur in a single entity or even location in most markets.

Instead, competing trading venues, often in different cities or even countries, trade the same instruments simultaneously, and trade reports and quotes frequently come either from a reporting exchange, mutualized reporting organization, or third-party vendor. When we describe Step 4, we are therefore talking about all these competing and cooperating entities working in concert (see Figure 4.4).

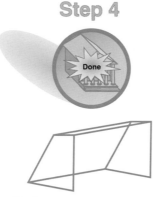

Step 4

Goals:
- Execute orders according to rules
- Satisfy regulatory obligations
- Satisfy customers/members
- Generate profit for firm *or* minimize cost for members

Figure 4.4 ***Step 4: Execution*** employs technology to match orders either electronically or physically according to the rules of the trading venue.

PROCESSES

The execution process involves orders from buy-side traders (through DMA) and orders from the sell side being received by a trading venue or venues. The trading venues combine orders to form quotes, which we defined earlier as a unit aggregation in the Background section; the venues distribute these quotes as market data to the Street, perhaps to generate even more new orders or modifications to existing orders. When an order to buy and an order to sell occur at the same price, employing any of the matching mechanics described in Book 2, Part 2, then a trade report is produced, and that report enters the market-data distribution cycle.

This process, described graphically in Figure 4.4.1, is complex because of the feedback loops created by market data, but the process becomes even more convoluted in a world that is fragmented. Fragmentation requires rules and systems that permit an order to buy on one trading venue to interact with an order to sell on another trading venue.

Figure 4.4.1 **Step 4: Execution processes** employ technology to match orders either electronically or physically according to the rules of the trading venue.

The quotes produced in this environment may also result in crossed markets and locked markets, as described in Book 2, Part 1, when the best bid is in one trading venue and the best offer in another. Reporting rules or strategies may be required to resolve these anomalies. When some trading venues are organized as brokers and others as exchanges, brokers may not be allowed to officially report their results and may publish through **reporting exchanges**.

If there is no requirement for the creation of a consolidated tape, vendors or users may have to create their own displays for decision making and/or order routing, and duplication can result in complex algorithms.

Finally, even the method for sharing revenues among trading venues can be complex in a fragmented marketplace where the sources of a consolidated tape involve multiple venues as described in the following sidebar.

IT TAKES REAL MATH TO SHARE MONEY

The method of representing quotes devised by Lee Greenhouse that was described in the sidebar "Locked and Crossed Markets" in Book 2, Part 1 was developed as part of a project to allocate revenues among the participating markets in the U.S. Consolidated Tape Association. Reg NMS enacted by the SEC in 2005 and 2006 had mandated a new method of revenue sharing.

The complexities of allocating several hundred million U.S. dollars based on both trades generated on participating markets and quotes generated by markets in an environment featuring high-frequency trading resulted in a set of algorithms involving the mathematical methodologies generated in gaming theory.*

---

* The methodologies were first proposed to the project committee by Frank Hathaway of Nasdaq and interpreted in a functional specification by George McCord of the project team.

Data Consumed

In general, the execution process is a primary producer of data, but if the market involves a **physical trading floor**, then the market must provide market data information to support the requirements of the floor traders. Also, if trading is fragmented, then each trading venue may be required to access information from its competitors to feed **intermarket order-routing** capabilities.

Systems

A number of different types of systems are available in support of execution. We described the functioning of each of the different major types of execution systems in some detail in Book 2, Part 2. Moreover, we described the ways that each system presents the conditions in the market through quote-like prices. We do not attempt to repeat these steps here; however, several points are important to remember.

Most trading venues have different, distinct order types, and although most of them follow the general forms we described in Book 2, the technology linking traders to markets including OMS and EMS linkages must accommodate the specific implementation of these order types for each connected trading venue.

We also noted that the prices of transactions vary from venue to venue, and these prices, and in some cases accompanying rebates, affect the profitability of trades. These, too, must be included in the logic that chooses among markets. These details change frequently, and notices of the changes must be used to update the systems.

When the decision to execute a trade using whatever execution rules apply to the market requires any action from a human, such as yelling "sold" or pushing a button on a computer screen, we call the process **physical execution**. When the process happens without a human's intervention, even if the execution is predicated on rules a human determined, we categorize the process as **automated execution**. Order- and execution-management systems must accommodate the variations that arise from differences in the structure and timing created when instruments are traded in both environments at the same time.

Finally, when there are multiple trading venues, there may be differences in the way each venue reacts to unusual events such as trading halts and abnormal trading processes. Therefore, systems that interact with the systems in trading venues must also allow for some rules-based actions that may occur and may need to monitor administrative messages to recognize when these events have occurred.

In addition to systems to facilitate trading, venues may require some level of system to support the collection, distribution, and administrative functions required by the market data business. Except to note their existence, we do not describe these systems further.

OUTPUTS

The execution process is a major producer of information. Indeed, early markets were not only the producers of trade reports, but also the vendors of those reports through networks of **ticker-tape machines**. Some trading venues now own vendor organizations to participate in the revenues that arise from the publication of the information generated by the trading process, and other venues may participate in price-mutualized price-consolidation entities.

Data Produced

Three major pieces of market data are produced by the trading process: quotes, last-sale prices, and administrative messages. The first, and in many ways the most important, piece of market data is a quote, which is most often, as we noted, a composite of a buy order and sell order. A quote is not a process unit and in reality exists only within the trading venue(s). The quote message delivered as market data is therefore a report on the state that exists within the trading environment at any moment.

Second, last-sale reports are public representations of the information on trade reports output from the trading process. The trade report is a process unit input into the post-trade processes described in the four steps that follow in Chapters 5 through 8.

Finally, as we noted in Part 2, administrative messages are a byproduct of the trading process. As trading becomes more automated, these messages are likely to become critical to ensuring that automated trading can function effectively in rapidly changing markets.

Process Units

Trade reports are a critical output from the trading process. The reports provide details to operate clearing and serve as critical input to both the confirmation and allocation steps.

SUMMARY

Trading venues and firms acting as dealers employ systems to support or execute orders from members and/or their buy-side customers. The systems maintain orders until they are executed or canceled, and employ algorithms based on the trading rules established by the market to effect trades. The systems return trade reports to the principals or their agents and may generate market data messages for use in the trading process (see Figure 4.4.2).

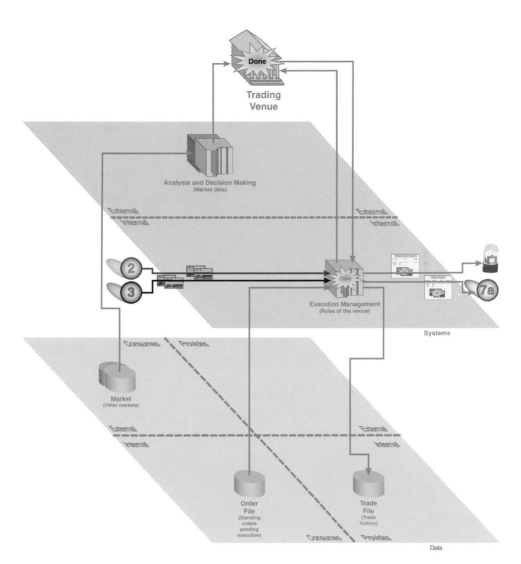

Figure 4.4.2 **_Execution_** employs systems to implement the execution-support tools described in Book 2 to match buyers' orders with sellers' orders, producing market data as a byproduct.

Step 5: Trade Confirmation 5

Trades must be confirmed so that the principal is aware of whether an order has been executed and, if the trade is successful, how much has been executed and at what price (see Figure 4.5). Many, if not most, markets require an official confirmation, but confirmations make business sense even if they are not required. The confirmation notifies the customer of a successful transaction but also puts the customer on notice if actions are required prior to settlement.

Institutional trades often involve a separate affirmation by the customer institution as a positive acceptance of the trade as confirmed. (The affirmation was described in Book 2, Part 4, and is not described here.)

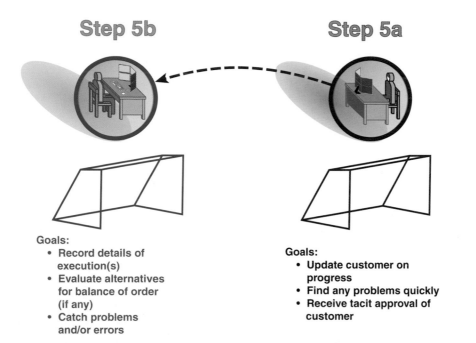

Step 5b

Step 5a

Goals:
- Record details of execution(s)
- Evaluate alternatives for balance of order (if any)
- Catch problems and/or errors

Goals:
- Update customer on progress
- Find any problems quickly
- Receive tacit approval of customer

Figure 4.5   *Step 5: Trade confirmation* employs any technologies authorized by local regulations to notify an investor or trading customer of the completion of an execution.

PROCESSES

Most institutional trades are handled using electronic systems, and the confirmation may be part of the order-routing and/or EMS mechanism (see Figure 4.5.1). Increasingly, both institutional and retail confirmations are generated and transmitted electronically. Automating the confirmation process was an important step in the movement to straight-through processing.

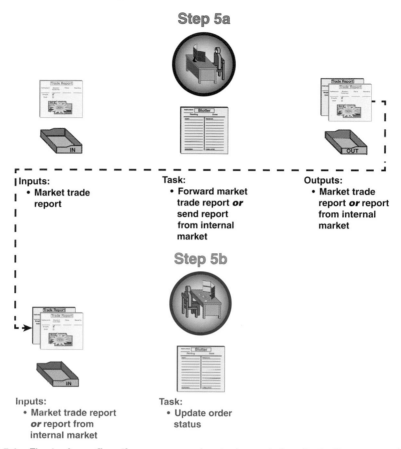

Step 5a

Inputs:
- Market trade report

Task:
- Forward market trade report *or* send report from internal market

Outputs:
- Market trade report *or* report from internal market

Step 5b

Inputs:
- Market trade report *or* report from internal market

Task:
- Update order status

Figure 4.5.1   The *trade confirmation process* receives trade reports from the trading venue and forwards the details to the customer.

The transmission is often routed back to the customer using the trading networks described in the "Trading Networks" sidebar that follows. Retail confirmations may involve only an email notice. Older requirements of postal (physical mail) confirmations are sometimes used as an alternative or as an additional notice, depending on the regulator.

Data Consumed

All information required for a confirmation is generated in the trading process and is reported to the sell-side firm through the trade report. Provided that the trade report is an automated message, then the trade confirmation can be generated and trans-mitted automatically as well.

Systems

Most confirmations are handled as a byproduct of other systems such as customer reporting and do not require dedicated, independent systems.

OUTPUTS

The trade confirmation is both a process step and a notification message sent to the customer. The message may be only an email or other electronic notification, but a printed notice may be mailed by post as well.

SUMMARY

Sell-side firms use either existing OMS or accounting system capabilities, or email-based notification systems to alert customers to successful executions or order execution status (see Figure 4.5.2). Buy-side firms use the notifications to update their own OMS systems and as input to the affirmation process.

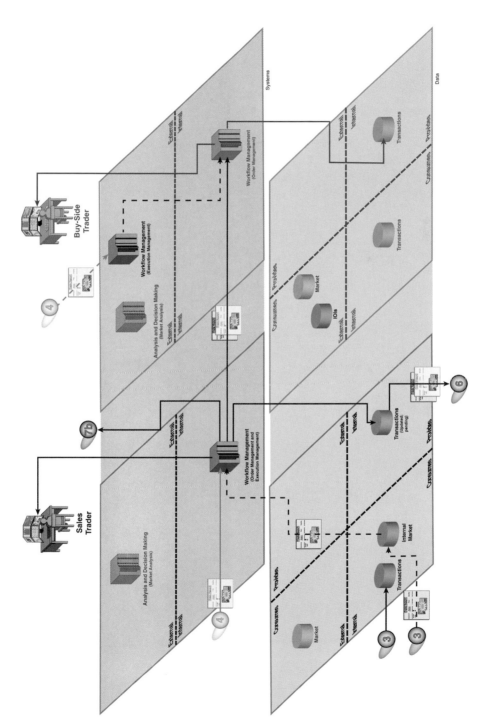

Figure 4.5.2 *Trade confirmation* requires the sell side to use dedicated systems, email, or the telephone to pass trade reports to their buy-side customers.

TRADING NETWORKS

Trading networks come in three major variations. For trading, many large banks maintain private networks that connect directly to all the important trading venues. These networks are the lineal descendents of the teletype networks that earned nationwide broker/dealers in the United States the name "wire house."

In addition to internal networks, a number of vendors have developed networks that permit customers to connect to trading venues using standard protocols. The development of the FIX protocol has accelerated this trend of making networks less complex because they do not need to accommodate as many proprietary interfaces. Finally, several trading venues have begun to develop order networks in an effort to permit customers to trade from major market centers that may be remote from the location of the trading venue.

These locations, or points-of-presence, permit customers to enter orders locally (to the customer). A customer that enters an order in a local POP has the same status as a customer with an office in the trading venue's home location. Now these networks are being opened to competitive venues and their customers, making the networks *de facto* global trading middleware (see figure).

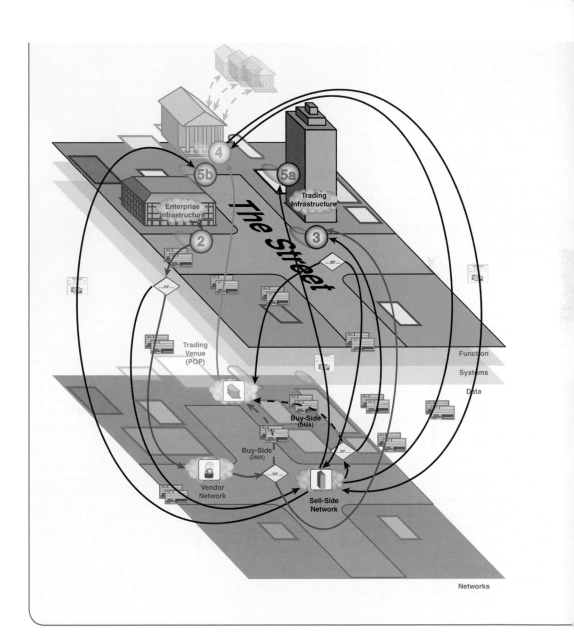

p0045 Trade allocation is a service usually provided by sell-side firms for their customers (see Figure 4.6). The goal of the process is to map orders received from the buy-side firm to executions created in the markets. Computing an average price can be complicated in several ways. For example, more than one buy-side account may participate in a single order.

Step 6

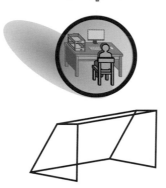

Goals:
- **Find average price**
- **Allocate executions to customer accounts**
- **Satisfy customer wishes**

f0010 **Figure 4.6** **Step 6: Trade allocation** employs data from a trade report, or reports, and account details from the customer to compute an average price for transactions and apportion the average prices to the accounts involved.

p0050   When multiple accounts are involved, the accounts may not remain part of the order for its duration. That is, some accounts may join an **open order** after it is initiated and after executions have occurred, or an account may cancel the remaining, unexecuted portion of an order before the total order is completed or before the other participating accounts choose to cancel.

p0055   In the latter case, executions may occur after some accounts have chosen to cancel their participation in the order. The order may also take more than one trading day to complete. For multiday orders, it is usually required that an average price be computed at the close of each trading day when the order is active. In the "Allocation Example Concluded" sidebar that follows, we complete an allocation example that we began in Book 2 to show the computations required for a specific example.

s0010 ## PROCESSES

p0060 Trade allocation requires that orders as they were received from the buy side be mapped to executions generated by the trading venue(s). Each execution typically occurs at a different price. Moreover, as we have noted, prices may be further allocated to accounts that may have different periods of commitment to the order (see Figure 4.6.1).

Step 6

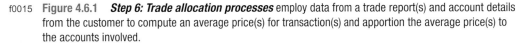

Inputs:
- **Trade reports**
- **Customer instructions and details**

Calculations:
- **Average price**
- **Apportionment to each participating portfolio**

Outputs:
- **Allocation report**

f0015 **Figure 4.6.1 *Step 6: Trade allocation processes*** employ data from a trade report(s) and account details from the customer to compute an average price(s) for transaction(s) and apportion the average price(s) to the accounts involved.

p0065   If there are multiple execution prices, an average price needs to be computed by multiplying the number of shares completed at each price times the price. These products are summed, and the sum is then divided by the total number of shares executed. This process can be complicated if the entire order is not executed or if part of an order is not executed until the next trading day.

p0070   In addition to computing the average price, portions of an order may be allocated to multiple accounts. Usually, all accounts participating in an order get the same price unless an account joins an order for which some executions are already completed, or if one account cancels the remaining shares not executed in an order while other accounts leave the order open. The rules for such events are typically handled by policies of the firm and/or by regulations.

s0015 ## Data Consumed

p0075 The primary inputs to the trading process are the original order(s) received from the buy-side trader (Step 2) and the trade reports that come from the trading venue(s) (Step 4). The prices and numbers of shares at each price come from the trade reports; and the total size, identifiers for accounts, and duration of each account's participation in the order are derived from the original order(s) with possible modifications over the period when the order was active.

p0080   Trade allocation requires the broker/dealer to either maintain the details for the customer account(s) for which the trade is executed or use the order messages as the source of that information. Many brokers maintain details of customers' accounts because that data helps form an understanding of where possible liquidity may occur that can be valuable in executing orders and making markets.

s0020 *Systems*

p0085 Trade allocations may be performed by standalone systems or by systems associated with the order-management system for the sell-side firm. Although systems to track customer interest and positions in various instruments are often maintained by the institutional sales and dealing groups, allocation can contribute important intelligence to understanding customers' histories and intentions.

b0010 **ALLOCATION EXAMPLE CONCLUDED**

p0090 In a sidebar titled "The Concept of Trade Allocation" in Book 2, we began the trading part of an example to explain how trades often become complex. We summarize the assumptions in our example as follows:

u0045
- An institutional investment firm has three portfolios: XYZ, XXX, and YYY.

u0050
- At 9:30 a.m., the portfolio manager of fund XYZ initiates a purchase order for 50,000 shares of In-The-Ether Networks, BV (ITEN), and the portfolio manager of fund YYY places a separate order to purchase 30,000 shares of ITEN.

u0055
- The buy-side trader combines the orders into a single order of 80,000 shares.

u0060
- At 9:30, 10,000 shares are executed for €50.00.

u0065
- At 10:00, 5,000* shares are executed at €50.05.

u0070
- Portfolio XXX submits an additional order of 20,000 shares at 10:30.

u0075
- The buy-side trader adds to the existing order, resulting in an unexecuted total of 85,000 shares from the 100,000 total shares to be executed.

u0080
- Subsequent executions are as follows:
u0085
    - 10,000 shares at €50.04
u0090
    - 5,000 shares at €50.06
u0095
    - 15,000 shares at €50.08
u0100
    - 10,000 shares at €50.09
u0105
    - 15,000 shares at €50.10

u0110
- The manager for portfolio YYY elects to cancel the remainder of that order.

u0115
- Portfolios XYZ and XXX remain in the order.

u0120
- An execution is made at-the-close for 10,000 shares at €50.07.

u0125
- At the end of the trading day, 20,000 shares of the total 100,000 possible shares were not executed.

---

* In editing this example, we discovered an error in the text of Book 2. There it says: "Another 50,000 shares are executed at €50.05 at 10:00...." It should have read: "Another 5,000...." The numbers in the chart were correct.

p0180   The following describes the calculation of the average prices *from the perspective of the buy-side trader*. (Note that the sales trader at the sell-side firm is not made aware of the total order at the start of the trading day. In the example the buy-side trader did not reveal all the order for reasons of trading strategy—a common technique. Therefore, if the buy-side firm expects the sell-side firm to compute the average prices based on the *total order*, then the buy-side firm would have to provide additional information.)

p0185   We are making simple and straightforward assumptions. The average price is calculated based on strict percentages of each portfolio's portion of the outstanding order at the times of each execution. (That is, while portfolio XXX was 20% of 100,000 total shares, 15,000 had already been executed when it entered the order. Therefore, we will not give that portfolio credit for the prices of the two early executions.)

p0190   Although our assumptions are reasonable, there is nothing to say other assumptions could not be used instead. The only caveat is that whatever the assumptions, the buy-side firm has to provide the sell-side firm with the details it wants used for the allocation.

p0195   In our example the following percentages apply at each point in the day. Prior to Portfolio XXX joining the order, the percentages are

u0130   • XYZ   62.50
u0135   • XXX   0.00
u0140   • YYY   37.50
u0145   **Total**   **100.00**

p0220 As the order is executed, the percentages remain the same until Portfolio XXX joins. Then we have a question: "Should the 20,000 shares be counted as a percentage of the total of 100,000 shares or as a percentage of the 85,000 shares outstanding at the time the portfolio joins the order?"

p0225   Either is possible, but in our example in Book 2, we assumed that the percentages would be computed based on the total shares available for execution (i.e., 80,000 shares until XXX joins; 100,000 shares when all three are active; and 70,000 after YYY drops out). The percentages after XXX joins are

u0150   • XYZ   50.00
u0155   • XXX   20.00
u0160   • YYY   30.00
u0165   **Total**   **100.00**

p0250 And after YYY drops out, the percentages are

u0170   • XYZ   71.43
u0175   • XXX   28.57
u0180   • YYY   0.00
u0185   **Total**   **100.00**

(Continued)

p0275   In Book 2, we proposed the formula

$$P_{avg} = \sum_{1}^{n} \frac{[P_e S_e]}{S_e}$$

where

u0190 P_{avg} = Average price for order or partial order

u0195 n = Number of executions

u0200 P_e = Price for execution e

u0205 S_e = Number of shares for execution e

as the calculation required to compute the average price. Note that each portfolio has a different average price because each participates in a different number of trades. For Portfolio XYZ, we compute

$$P_{avg} = \frac{\begin{array}{l}(€50.00*6,250)+(€50.05*3,125)+(€50.04*5,000)+(€50.06*2,500)\\ +(€50.08*7,500)+(€50.09*5,000)+(€50.10*7500)+(€50.07*10,000)\end{array}}{6,250+3,125+5,000+2,500+7,500+5,000+7500+10,000}$$

$$P_{avg} = €50.06$$

p0310   The average for Portfolio XXX is €50.08, and the average for Portfolio YYY is €50.06. The average price for all shares actually traded is €50.07. Again, please note that a different set of assumptions (e.g., computing percentages based on the shares remaining at each execution) would have resulted in different average prices.

s0025 OUTPUTS

p0315 Trade allocations provide inputs to post-trade systems in preparation for settlement and the information required for postings to accounting systems once settlement is completed.

s0030 Data Produced

p0320 The primary output from trade allocation is the average price for each participating account or portfolio in the order over the course of the trading day when the order is active.

s0035 Process Units

p0325 No specific process units as we define them result from trade allocation although the average prices are important input to other systems.

s0040 **SUMMARY**

p0330 In trade allocation, systems are increasingly replacing manual calculations of average prices and the allocation of executions back to the orders that generated the execution(s) and to the accounts from which the orders were generated (see Figure 4.6.2).

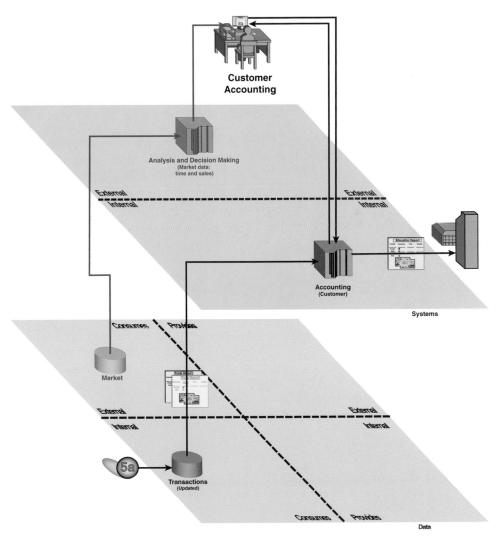

f0020 **Figure 4.6.2** *Trade allocation* is a process of allocating executions against orders and participating accounts to compute an average price for each account for the orders executed.

Step 7: Clearing 7

Clearing includes those processes following a trade in which the details of the trade are agreed among all the parties and when a clearing corporation or some other form of central counterparty is present to guarantee settlement to the extent that a guarantee is feasible. The tasks required to accomplish both agreement among parties and some level of assurance that settlement will occur vary widely from market to market. For trading in liquid securities on automated markets, little error can creep into the process, and clearing corporations are usually able to ensure settlement in all but the most extreme situations.

In less liquid instruments, most transactions are bespoke; valuing the transaction between execution and settlement is difficult; and few counterparties are willing to accept the potential liability implicit in a guarantee of settlement. Therefore, our description of clearing is extremely general in that we describe the processes found in liquid instruments (see Figure 4.7).

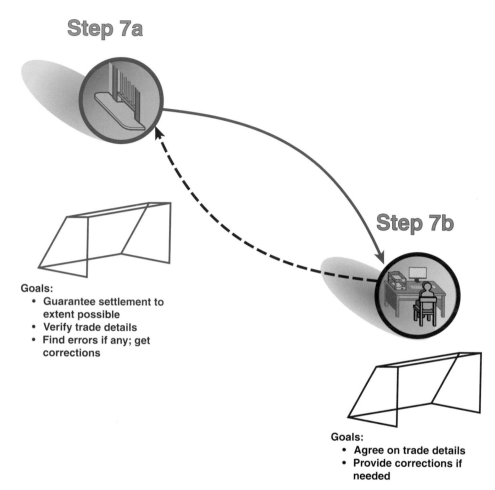

Figure 4.7 *Step 7: Clearing* matches the details from the buyer and seller, solicits any error corrections, and attempts to guarantee successful settlement.

PROCESSES

Clearing involves first ensuring that all details of the transaction are correct and are agreed on by all parties (see Figure 4.7.1). Next, the transaction may need to be formally accepted by the customers or principals if regulated institutions are involved.

The process of formally accepting an execution is known as affirmation and was described in Book 2, Part 4. If there is a clearing agent involved in the transaction,

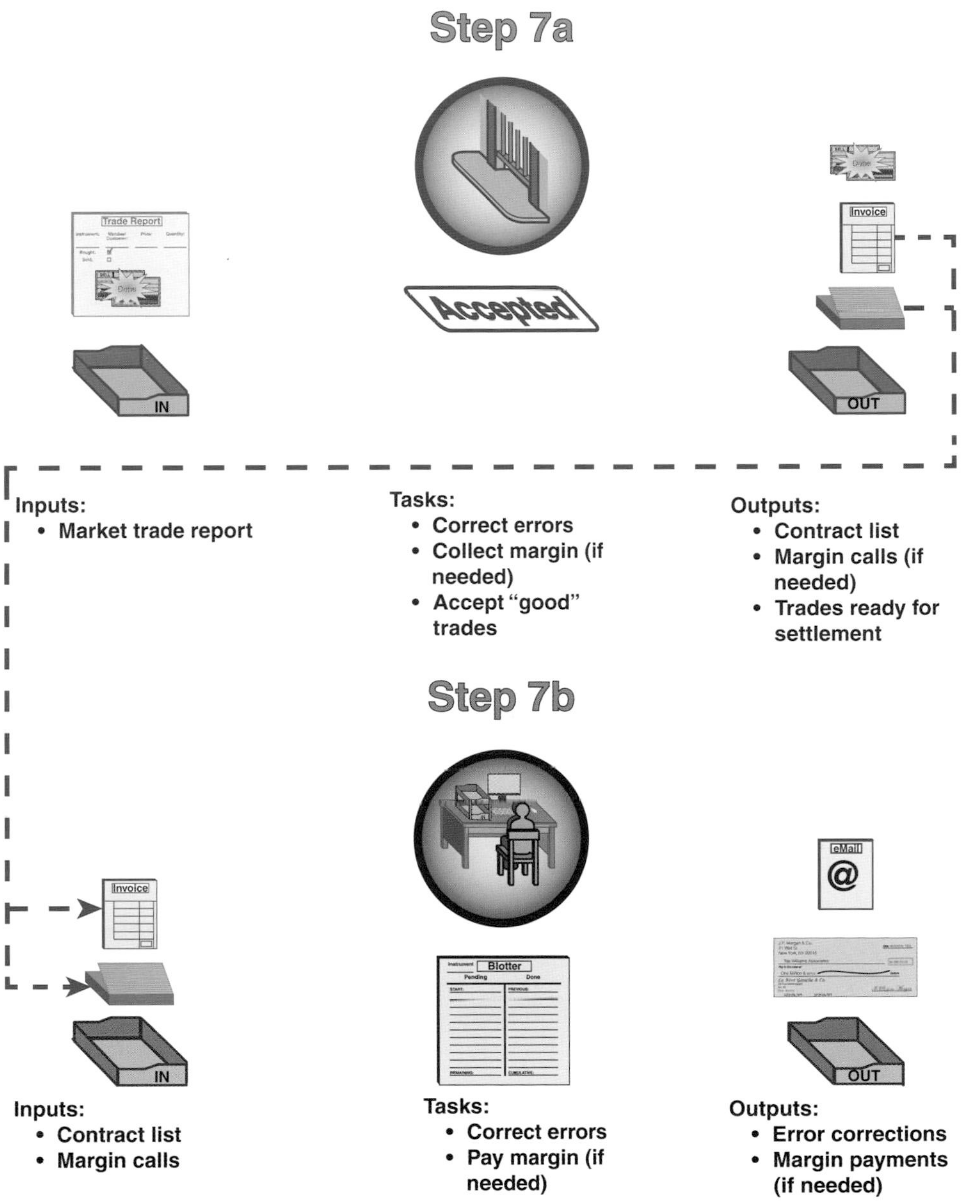
Step 7a
Trade Report
Accepted
Invoice
IN
OUT
Inputs:
• Market trade report
Tasks:
• Correct errors
• Collect margin (if needed)
• Accept "good" trades
Outputs:
• Contract list
• Margin calls (if needed)
• Trades ready for settlement
Step 7b
Invoice
Blotter
eMail
@
IN
OUT
Inputs:
• Contract list
• Margin calls
Tasks:
• Correct errors
• Pay margin (if needed)
Outputs:
• Error corrections
• Margin payments (if needed)

Figure 4.7.1 The ***clearing process*** provides a list of executions and their details to participants requesting corrections for any errors and may make margin calls, if needed, to guarantee settlement.

the counterparty may break the link between buyer and seller and assume the role of counterparty to each side. Finally, the agents (if any) in the trade must ensure that the principals are prepared to perform at settlement. (That is, the buyer must have ***good*** *funds* available for settlement, and the seller must provide **certificates endorsed for sale** or delivery instructions.)

Data Consumed

In addition to information that comes from the trade reports, clearing requires market prices throughout the period prior to settlement. For most equities, positions are market-to-market at the end of each intervening trading day based on the official price for the instrument.

Finally, important information includes data on counterparties and the accounts affected by each execution. Details are required to be supplied for the accounts of the principals and/or their agents at supporting entities (e.g., banks, custodians, clearing corporations, and depositories). Supplying this information to the supporting entities in a timely manner is critical to the settlement process. This information must be accumulated during the period before settlement if accurate information does not exist in the master files of the participants.

Systems

Each participant in the trading process requires important systems. Systems required in preparation for settlement were among the first applications of computer technology on the sell side and are known as Street-side systems. Buy-side firms depend heavily on their custodian banks to perform the tasks required for affirmation and settlement. In the case of hedge funds, prime brokers perform these tasks.

Institutional investors frequently monitor the activities during the period between execution and settlement even if they cede active responsibility to an agent. We referred to the systems that monitor the period between execution and settlement as "securities movement and control" in Part 1. Finally, banks maintain systems for their custodian operations to control the activities in advance of settlement while clearing corporations maintain systems to manage the clearance period.

Although we are not focused here on the roles of agent bank and custodian, we need to consider the tasks required of custodians and their systems. The bank that serves as the custodian for assets managed by an investment manager does most of the processing of trades. The bank custodian interacts with the depository and the broker/dealers that executed the trades and reports back information to the manager when the trade is settled.

The bank also facilitates the affirmation process by ensuring that the manager affirms the details of the trades as may be required during the settlement process. At settlement, agent banks make payment (for the seller) or receive payment (for the buyer).

OUTPUTS

A number of intra-process outputs are required during the period between execution and settlement. Trade corrections are requested and made; trade details are presented, and affirmation is made; and settlement and payment details are requested, and formal instructions are provided. However, the output from the clearing process as a whole is instructions to pay and deliver.

Data Produced

Although we have noted execution instructions, affirmations, and requests for settlement instructions, no specific information is generated outside the process itself.

Process Units

The process units from the clearing process are instructions to the buyer's bank to make payment and for the seller's custodian to make delivery at settlement. These instructions, or the actions they produce, are presented to the clearing corporation or to any other entity or location where settlement occurs.

SUMMARY

Clearing employs systems at a clearing corporation to identify problems with trades and to manage the resolution of the problems (see Figure 4.7.2). To the extent there is a central counterparty, the systems assist in interposing the counterparty between the trade participants and monitoring the period prior to settlement to ensure that all parties are able to perform at settlement.

This can include collecting margin and/or maintaining a clearing fund as a guarantee. For the parties to the trade, systems monitor funds and delivery instructions to ensure the preparations for settlement proceed satisfactorily.

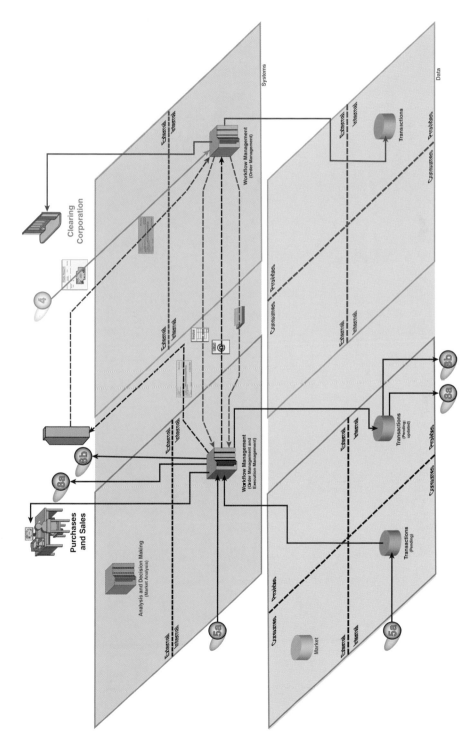

Figure 4.7.2 *Clearing* refers to a group of tasks undertaken by agents and clearing facilities to ensure the successful settlement of instrument trades.

In settlement, the instrument involved in the execution in Step 4 is exchanged for the funds agreed in the transaction (see Figure 4.8). As noted, the exchange frequently takes place at a clearing corporation but can occur in any forum that is established either by custom in the market or that the parties agree upon. Although any arrangement can be negotiated, most markets standardize the process as much as possible to reduce costs and to avoid possible problems.

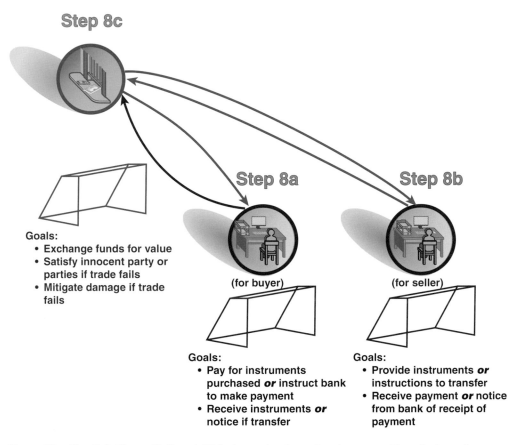

Step 8c

Step 8a

Step 8b

Goals:
- Exchange funds for value
- Satisfy innocent party or parties if trade fails
- Mitigate damage if trade fails

(for buyer)

(for seller)

Goals:
- Pay for instruments purchased *or* instruct bank to make payment
- Receive instruments *or* notice if transfer

Goals:
- Provide instruments *or* instructions to transfer
- Receive payment *or* notice from bank of receipt of payment

Figure 4.8 *Step 8: Settlement* is the established procedure for exchanging payment from the buyer for ownership from the seller at a place and in a manner established by the market or by local regulations.

PROCESSES

Settlement can usually be reduced to a simple description: Good funds are provided in exchange for acceptable delivery. This statement describes a situation known as ***delivery versus payment (DVP)***. Other methods of settlement are possible, but most markets employ DVP to avoid complexity, confusion, and cost (see Figure 4.8.1).

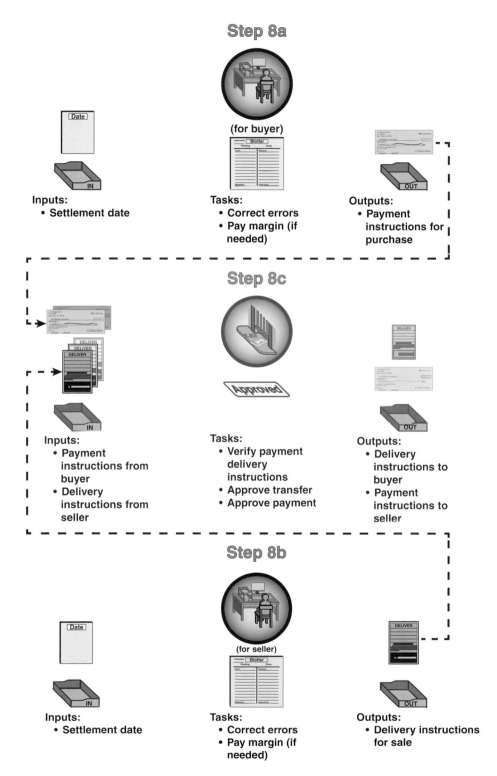

Step 8a

(for buyer)

Inputs:
- Settlement date

Tasks:
- Correct errors
- Pay margin (if needed)

Outputs:
- Payment instructions for purchase

Step 8c

Approved

Inputs:
- Payment instructions from buyer
- Delivery instructions from seller

Tasks:
- Verify payment delivery instructions
- Approve transfer
- Approve payment

Outputs:
- Delivery instructions to buyer
- Payment instructions to seller

Step 8b

(for seller)

Inputs:
- Settlement date

Tasks:
- Correct errors
- Pay margin (if needed)

Outputs:
- Delivery instructions for sale

Figure 4.8.1 The *settlement process* is a mechanism for receiving funds or payment instructions from a buyer, and certificates or delivery instructions from a seller and then verifying the details and delivering them to the appropriate party.

Data Consumed

No external data is required for the systems of the buy side and sell side for settlement using the DVP settlement process as described. However, the settlement process results in updates to the status of process control systems and also initiates a number of accounting updates when the process is complete.

Systems

Settlement is typically a function or feature of accounting and process control systems rather than a standalone system.

OUTPUTS

The outputs to settlement include reductions in cash holdings and an increase in instrument holdings for the buyer and the opposite transactions for the seller.

Data Produced

The primary data produced in settlement is status updates.

Process Units

The settlement process produces both payments from the buyer to the seller and delivery instructions that result in the transfer of ownership in the instrument(s) traded. Subsequent changes in accounting systems result as described in Book 2, Part 4.

SUMMARY

For settlement, systems at the clearing corporation interact to receive funds from the buyer and delivery instructions from the seller; they then pass the information necessary for the buyer to acquire formal recognition of ownership and for the seller to acquire its funds (see Figure 4.8.2).

Systems at the participating principals or their agents must provide the necessary instructions to the clearing corporation and be prepared for receipts when they are ready for transfer. This may require the participation of agent banks and/or custodians.

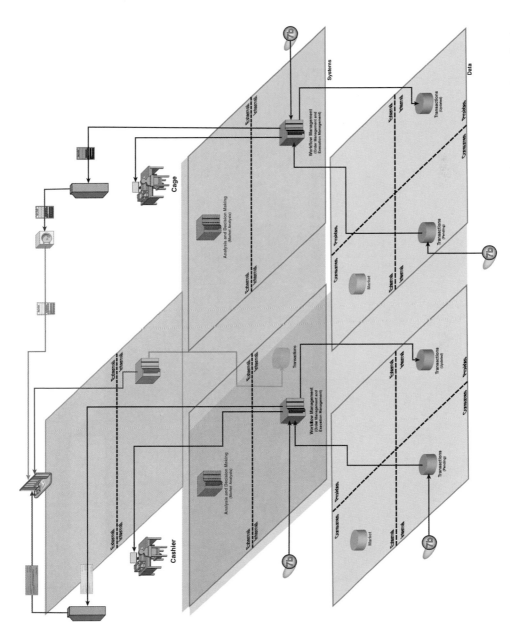

Figure 4.8.2   **Settlement** defines the actions required of agents and clearing corporations supported by systems to exchange funds from a buyer with instruments or transfer instructions to successfully complete a transaction as described in Step 4.

POST-TRADE NETWORKS

A number of networks have developed to facilitate the post-trade processes in the industry. Many of the networks evolved because bank and depository networks excluded broker/dealers and institutional investors that were not affiliated with banks.

In fact, one of the important networks evolved from a vendor system that provided an advertising system that was a precursor to IOIs. That system exploited its existence, linking the buy and sell sides to fill a need that bank networks did not provide.

Now banking networks are actively engaged in providing post-trade support networks to the trading markets, but the existing vendor networks continue competing on features and price. This figure shows these post-trade networks.

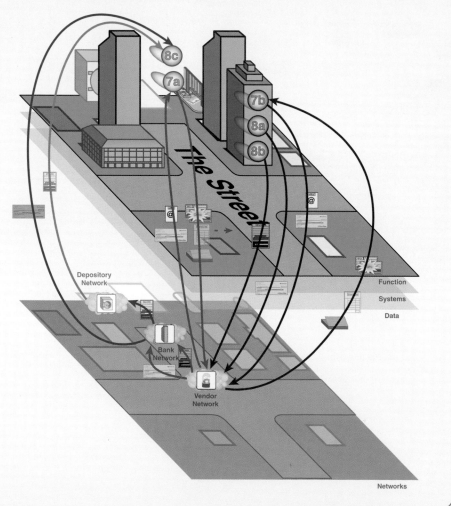

RELATED INFORMATION IN OTHER BOOKS

In this part we examined how technology—systems, data, and networks—supports the trading process for the buy and sell sides. We focused on the eight primary steps in the trading process as originally introduced in the Preface to Book 1. The added steps described in Book 2, Part 4, also use technology, but an exploration of those activities is outside the scope of this set. (See Figure 4.9.)

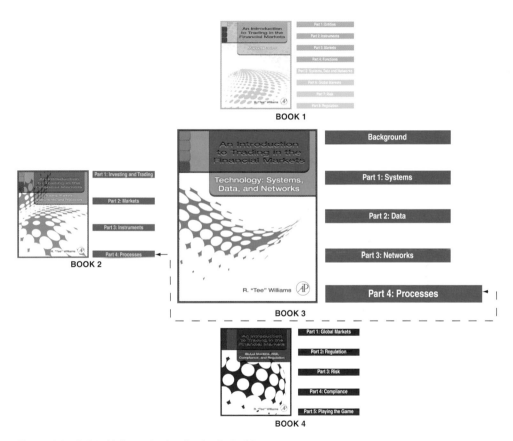

Figure 4.9   Related information in other books in this set.

This book described technology, which we have further segmented into systems, data, and networks. We also reexamined the major steps in the trading process to understand the role that technology plays in trading. With this book we complete the structural and functional exploration of the markets.

In Book 4, *An Introduction to Trading in the Financial Markets: Global Markets, Risk, Compliance, and Regulation,* we investigate the way that markets interact in a global environment and how entities operate in a globalized market. We also examine the roles of regulation, compliance, and risk management.

Finally, in Book 4, we return one final time to trading with a complex example showing how different entities and functions employ technologies to interact in the trading process in a risky, global environment subject to regulatory oversight. We call this part "Playing the Game."

BOOK 1: *AN INTRODUCTION TO TRADING IN THE FINANCIAL MARKETS: MARKET BASICS*

Book 1 presents the foundation for understanding the trading markets (see Figure C.1). It begins with an overview that is necessary to understand even the basics and, in particular, provides the first description of the steps in the trading process. Book 1 also includes a section on the history of trading that puts current practice in context.

Detailed sections of Book 1 begin with an introduction to the entities that operate in the trading markets. It then introduces the instruments that are traded, providing basic definitions that are then expanded in Book 2. Book 1 describes markets with a focus on how markets are organized that complements descriptions of market processes and the operation of markets presented in Book 2 also.

Book 1 ends by describing the functions that are required in the financial markets. The functions can be thought of as the tasks that must be accomplished for the markets to operate.

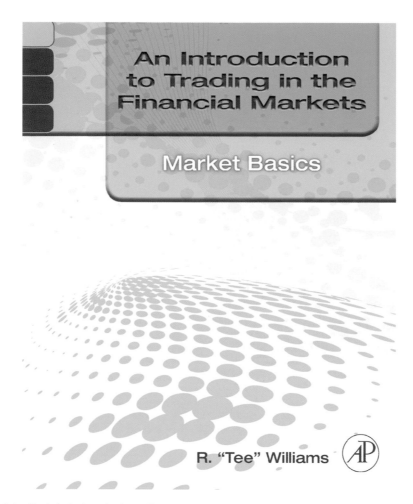

**An Introduction
to Trading in the
Financial Markets**

Market Basics

R. "Tee" Williams

Figure C.1 Book 1: *An Introduction to Trading in the Financial Markets: Market Basics*

BOOK 2: AN INTRODUCTION TO TRADING IN THE FINANCIAL MARKETS: TRADING, MARKETS, INSTRUMENTS, AND PROCESSES

Book 2 begins with a description of the trading process from the perspective of investors and traders using the markets as well as the different structures, formats, and mechanics found in alternative types of markets (see Figure C.2). It next provides a more detailed look at securities and instruments, focusing on the features that different instruments can include, the measures used to evaluate and compare instruments, the participants that invest in and trade instruments, and the characteristics of the markets in which each instrument trades.

Finally, we look at some of the important processes that enable the trading markets, focusing on how the functions presented in Book 1 permit the processes to be completed. The focus is on the primary market process and the trading (secondary market) process but other types of important processes are investigated as well.

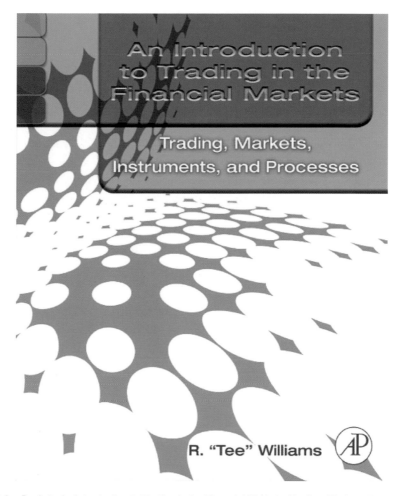

Figure C.2   Book 2: *An Introduction to Trading in the Financial Markets: Trading, Markets, Instruments, and Processes*

BOOK 4: *AN INTRODUCTION TO TRADING IN THE FINANCIAL MARKETS: GLOBAL MARKETS, REGULATION, RISK, AND COMPLIANCE*

The final book of this series, Book 4, begins with a description of important global trading markets and how the entities in the trading markets interact across national borders (see Figure C.3). It then introduces the concepts of regulation, risk, and compliance.

The goal is not to examine every regulation or provide a "how to" of risk management. We want to show how regulation, risk and compliance facilitate the markets and ensure their smooth operation. Finally, we end with a part we call "Playing the Game." The goal is to show how a trade occurs from the inception of the idea to settlement. We try to explain how each of the intervening steps occurs with entities performing functions, employing the market's processes using technology while abiding by regulations, evaluating the risks, and ensuring compliance.

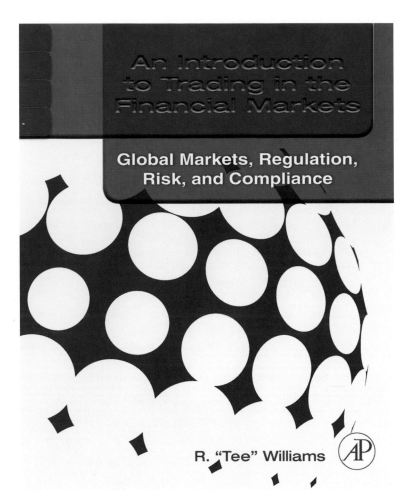

Figure C.3   Book 4: *An Introduction to Trading in the Financial Markets: Global Markets, Regulation, Risk, and Compliance*

Glossary

Account master file   One of the primary master files employed by many firms in the trading markets. The account master maintains mostly static details about each account. The static information combined with holdings makes reporting possible.

Actionable data or Actionable market data or Actionable prices or Actionable quote   Information from a market center (or centers) that can be converted to an order ready for transmission through simple actions such as a mouse click or a drag-and-drop operation. Actionable market data implies an electronic linkage between the trader and the market or trading venue. Actionable market data is typically available only to those authorized by a firm or the market center to enter orders.

Activities   Actions or processes that take place within an entity that is under the control of the entity. Activities are in contrast to events that are the result of a situation that the entity cannot control and to which the entity must react. (See also "Event.")

Adobe Acrobat   A file format developed by Adobe Systems Incorporated that enables authors and vendors to present information in electronic form that retains fonts and rich graphic materials such as logos that are important to branding. The format uses the file identifier ".pdf" and is widely used for financial reports and research documents where corporate branding is important to the producer of the file. Reader software is available free to users for all commonly used computer operating systems.

Affirmation or Affirmation process or Affirm   Investment managers are required to acknowledge, or affirm, to a depository that trade details on the confirmation provided to the investment manager are correct. Brokers provide the trade details to the depository.

Agent   A legal term for a broker who acts on behalf of a customer in finding a buyer or seller for the customer's order. An agent receives commissions for work and generally has a fiduciary responsibility to act in the best interest of the customer. (See also "Broker.")

Agent bank   A bank that provides services for an entity for a fee or commission, just as "agents" described above. (See also "Agent.")

Allocation or Allocation process   The process, typically for large institutional orders, of reconciling multiple executions that are part of one order as well as multiple funds or investors that are blocked into a single order. The broker/dealers they use typically provide the allocation process to investing institutions. The term "allocation" is also applied to the process of providing an average price to multiple accounts receiving executions through a single order.

Alpha or α   The y-axis intercept in a regression of returns on an individual security against the returns on the market, usually represented by a broad-based index. A non-zero value for α suggests that the security may have a return (either positive or negative) even when the return on the market is zero. A number of strategies attempt to find securities that "capture" a positive α.

Analytical information   A general term related to data and processed data that can be used to compare instruments, evaluate instruments, or analyze portfolios and the like. Analytical information is highly related to investment philosophy and strategy.

Applications   A generalized term for computer systems and software dedicated to a specific purpose. Often used interchangeably with "software" and "programs," but usually referring to software and programs aimed at a specific purpose or process.

Arbitrage   A trading strategy in which two economically equivalent securities are simultaneously purchased and sold to lock in a small discrepancy in their relative prices. Typically, the higher priced security is sold short, and the lower priced security is purchased.

Architecture   In systems development, the decision on how to allocate processing activities throughout an organization to accomplish the required tasks most efficiently.

Ask or Asked or Ask price   The price at which a market maker or any other seller prices an instrument to be sold. (See also "Best bid/offer.")

Audit   A procedure in which a data owner visits directly or uses a third-party auditing firm to verify that entitlements and actual usage are consistent with reported usage.

Automated execution or AutoEx or AutoEx system   A general name for a widely used type of application in which a dealer provides electronic connections to clients or its own sales force. AutoEx systems permit automated executions. Functionally, the user is trading against the dealer's inventory.

Autoquote   To engage in using algorithms to generate quotes, either by a person or system. (See also "Autoquote system.")

Autoquote system   A computer system that generates quotes based on parameters supplied by a market maker and uses inputs from other markets or data feeds. For example, there are autoquote systems for equities, used by third market dealers, and autoquote systems for options, used by options exchanges.

Backoffice   The several departments of a securities firm concerned with the operations aspects of trading, such as comparing, confirming, and settling trades; providing credit (margin); and creating and distributing dividends, proxies, and statements.

Balance sheet   An accounting construct used to measure the value of an enterprise. The balance sheet is usually presented with the "things that are owned" or assets on the left, or a statement grouped by categories of like items or assets. On the right, the balance sheet shows who owns the assets and how. This is usually a combination of equity (the ownership by the company's owners or shareholders) and investment using borrowed funds or liabilities.

Bandwidth   A measure of the capacity of a network or communications line. The measure is usually the quantity of information that can be transmitted in a given unit of time.

Banks   Supporting entities that facilitate market processes. Although many banks own either buy-side or sell-side divisions (or both), we are interested only in banks as providers of commercial banking services in support of trading and the markets.

Batch processing   A largely antiquated computer processing technique in which all the inputs to the computer process are entered at the beginning of the process, and no additional inputs are permitted after processing begins.

Benchmark   A security that is used as the basis for pricing other securities. Typically, U.S. government securities are used to price many other fixed-income securities globally.

Bespoke   A general term that is most commonly employed in British English. The term means customized or purpose built, and is useful to distinguish items that are one of a kind as opposed to a product or something that is mass produced.

Best bid and offer (BBO)   The BBO consists of the highest bid and the lowest offer from all market participants. Thus, it represents the most favorable terms for buying or selling at a particular point in time. (See "National best bid and offer" and "Top-of-book")

Best execution   The concept of trading an order to get the optimum combination of execution price and transaction cost to meet the demands of the funds being managed. The concept is an outgrowth of ERISA, which requires that pension funds achieve best execution on trades.

Beta or β   The slope of a line; it indicates the extent to which a security moves in response to a movement of the market. β is a measure of volatility. If β is greater than one, the security is more volatile than the market. If it is less than one, the security is less volatile than the market as represented by the index. A β of exactly one is considered to have a volatility that equals the market.

Bid or Bid price   The price at which a market maker will buy a security. In the marketplace, this is the "demand" price, as contrasted to the "supply" price. (See also "Best bid and offer" and "Quote.")

Big Bang   The term for the major market changes on October 27, 1986, for the UK market. Many of the changes paralleled the changes in the United States on May Day (May 1, 1975). For the most part, the changes created a new, more competitive market. The term "Big Bang" was subsequently applied in other markets where dramatic market structure changes occurred.

Black-Scholes model   A pricing model created by Fischer Black, Robert C. Merton, and Myron Scholes to price options. This model made exchange-traded options much more popular, facilitated autoquoting by market makers, and earned a Nobel Prize in economics for its creators. The Black-Scholes model prices "European-style" options.

Blotter   A collection of orders with a common characteristic within a trade order-management system. The name comes from desk blotters where traders recorded and tracked trades before automation became available.

Bond   A securitized debt instrument, usually packaged into instruments that have a face amount of $1,000.

Book   A general term for a physical or electronic file where a market or dealer stores orders pending execution. The term and concept evolved from actual books maintained by market makers on physical exchange floors.

Broadcast news   News sent out in streaming or broadcast format to feed scrolling news displays on market-data displays. Also a term for "television news." Business news particularly from cable news providers has become an important part of the information supplied to traders.

Broker   (See "Agent.")

Broker's broker   (See "Correspondent" and "Interdealer broker.")

Broker/dealer   An overarching term used to describe multi-function companies that provide a variety of services in financial markets, including acting as brokers and as dealers. "Brokers" act as middlemen, arranging sales between parties and receiving a commission for this work. "Dealers" buy and sell stock out of their own inventory. Rather than charging a commission, dealers, sometimes called "market makers," make money on the "spread," or difference between their buying price and selling price.

Buffer   A short-term storage area, often in a computer's memory, where data is stored between activities in a process or as the data is moved from one device to another. When a buffer is not sufficiently large to handle the volume of information being transferred, the data can back up in phenomenon known as queuing. (See also "Queuing.")

Bus   An information distribution device in which data is transferred among systems or processes. Buses are found in the distribution of data within computer processors and among functions within certain types of networks.

Business of data   The issues related to the commercial ownership, distribution, and use of data in the trading markets. Components of the data business include ownership rights, pricing, usage rights and obligations, and the administration and management that a commercial sale implies.

Buy list   A list of recommended or permitted investment holdings established by the investment committee of a (mostly traditional) institutional investment firm that serves as guidance or requirements for the firm's portfolio managers.

Buy side   The institutions and individuals that buy brokerage services from the securities industry. Institutions include professional money managers, insurance firms, and state and local governments.

Buy-side order-management systems   Order-management systems designed to be used by institutional money managers. Order-management systems are workflow control devices designed to assist traders as they manage orders pending execution. Although they are similar in intent to sell-side OMSs, those for the buy side have features that are of particular value to the buy side, such as managing incoming IOIs. (See also "Sell-side order-management systems" and "Order-management system.")

Buy-side trader   A trader working for an institutional investor charged with managing decisions to trade generated by portfolio managers and deciding how to structure the order(s) required to complete the desired trade, which broker/dealer(s) to use, and what instructions to use to manage the trade. Buy-side traders are often charged with ensuring best execution and repaying broker/dealers for soft-dollar obligations. (See "Portfolio manager.")

Cache   A small area of storage space in computers and in applications.

Cage   The department at a broker/dealer responsible for managing securities and other instruments. The name comes from the fact that securities used to be housed briefly (before they were sent to banks for safekeeping) in cage-like rooms for protection. Securities were received and dispensed from windows much like the teller cage of a bank. (See also "Cashier.")

Call   (1) A feature in fixed-income instruments giving the firm that issues the debt the right to buy it back or "call" it on demand if it chooses before the debt matures. The feature must be written into the bond contract. (2) A slang term for a call option. (See also "Call option.")

Call market or call-market process   An execution mechanism in which a market maker or system attempts to establish a new market price by soliciting bids and offers. The initial bid and offer (generated by the market maker or system) are frequently very far apart. As prospective traders submit their own bids and offers the side of the quote that has the least size is adjusted to attract more interest. The execution price matches all active bids and offers at a single price intended to match the maximum number of shares.

Call option   An option contract in which the owner of the contract has purchased the right to sell a fixed-amount security at a predetermined price up until a set date when the contract expires without value if nothing has been done.

Cancel/replace order or a Cancel/replace   A single order sent to a market that cancels a previously sent standing order and simultaneously replaces the canceled order with a new order with different details. Typically, the change is to the price of the original order. In some markets, a cancel/replace order may retain the priority or precedence of the original order.

Capital changes   Activities undertaken by a company that can result in changes in the structure of the company. These changes include stock dividends, stock splits, cash dividends, mergers, and other events that can affect the book value of securities and/or market price of a security. (See also "Corporate actions.")

Carrying broker   Another term for a clearing broker or a correspondent providing fully disclosed brokerage services for another broker. The term comes from the fact that the carrying broker maintains, or "carries," the actual accounts of the customer of the smaller broker using the carrying broker's services.

Cash management accounts   A general term for accounts offered by broker/dealers that have the same services as checking accounts offered by a commercial bank. Because a broker/dealer usually does not have access to the bank payments system, a cash management account usually is serviced by a commercial bank.

Cash management services   Commercial services provided by banks for their corporate customers that provide both management of cash balances, collection services for payments, and, if the customer requires, foreign exchange transactions. Most banks in financial centers offer specialized cash management services designed for both the buy side and the sell side.

Cash market   A market in which a physical commodity, security, or instrument is traded.

Cashier   A department in a securities firm responsible for receiving and delivering cash. (See also "Cage" and "Purchase and sales.")

Central counterparty   An entity, usually a clearing corporation, that is designated as the counterparty to all trades facilitating netting and centralizing risk management. (See also "Clearing corporation.")

Certificates endorsed for sale   In markets where physical certificates are used for instruments, there are usually specific provisions on the certificate where the seller endorses the certificate for sale. The endorsement may need to be notarized. A properly endorsed certificate is usually considered to be "good delivery" at settlement.

Chinese walls   A slang term for rules and sometimes physical separation that is intended to prevent interactions between groups where there is a high potential for conflicts of interest if information is shared.

Clearing corporation   An organization historically affiliated with an exchange or market center that serves to manage the process between execution and settlement. Many clearing corporations take the position of the counterparty to every trade in order to permit trades to be netted, reducing the number of deliveries required at settlement.

Clearing House Automated Payment System (CHAPS)   The bank payments system that is owned by the banks in London for the purpose of settling payments among members and their customers. (See also "Clearing House Interbank Payment System.")

Clearing House Interbank Payment System (CHIPS) The bank payments system that is owned by the banks in New York for the purpose of settling payments among members and their customers. (See also "Clearing House Automated Payment System.")

Clearinghouse or Clearing house General concept of an entity, often mutually owned, where financial transactions among participants and their customers are resolved (if there are problems) and settled, usually employing rules established by clearinghouse members.

Colocation or Colocation services Services offered by a trading venue in which quantitative traders are permitted to house their trading models in the trading venue to reduce distance latency.

Comingled funds Internal investment funds within an institutional investor that puts funds from many individual accounts into a single investment fund, or more commonly a set of investment funds with different investment objectives. This practice makes managing customer investments more efficient.

Commentary Information closely related to news that generally involves a recognized expert who comments on the meanings or implications of market or news events. Commentary is generally intended to give investors and traders the added perspective based on the knowledge and understanding of the individual providing the commentary.

Commodities Goods such as agricultural products and natural resources that are traded as both cash assets and futures or forward contracts.

Communication standards Protocols that are broadly accepted norms for transmitting information either among entities or within entities. By adopting these, systems that need to interact with other systems can be developed without the need to know anything about the systems with which they interact.

Compliance The departmental function within both buy-side and sell-side firms that assures trade compliance with both statutory regulations and constraints from customers and/or charters.

Consolidated data feed or Consolidated feed A data feed from a quote vendor that makes available prices from multiple exchanges and other data sources in a single feed, permitting the user to receive the data without having to negotiate with and program for multiple sources. The problem with consolidated feeds is that considerable latency is created in producing the feed. (See also "Direct data feed.")

Consolidated Tape Association/Consolidated Quote Operating Committee (CTA/CQOC) The operating committee composed of the American Stock Exchange, the Boston Stock Exchange, the Chicago Board Options Exchange, the Chicago Stock Exchange, the Cincinnati Stock Exchange, the Nasdaq Stock Market, the New York Stock Exchange, the Pacific Exchange, and the Philadelphia Stock Exchange that oversees the operations of the Consolidated Tape System (CTS) and the Consolidated Quote System (CQS).

Content owner The owner of information that is sold to others either directly or using a vendor. (See also "Data owner" and "Data creators.")

Contingent claim An obligation created by a contract in which certain actions or commitments may be required or are possible provided certain conditions are met usually during a future period. The contingency generally creates value for the owner of the claim, which increases in proportion to the likelihood that the conditions will be met during the life of the contract. Derivatives are typically contingent claims.

Contract list   A list, produced by a clearing corporation, particularly in support of physical trading markets, that shows trades where both buyer and seller (or their agents) agree on the trade's details, and highlighting those trades for which there are disputes concerning details. Such disputes must be resolved before settlement.

Contributor data   Data, typically from dealers, that provides information on securities that are not actively traded in venues where market data is produced. Typical examples are bond dealers providing indicative quotes for instruments that do not trade frequently and where price reports may not be public even when trades occur. Contributed data is an area of contention between the contributing dealer and the vendors that provide the collection and distribution services. The issues concern ownership of the data and the division of revenue it produces.

Controllers   A largely antiquated term for the dedicated computers that reside in user locations to support the display devices offered by market-data vendors.

Corporate actions   Activities undertaken by a company that can result in changes in the structure of the company. These changes include stock dividends, stock splits, cash dividends, mergers, and other events that can affect the book value of securities and/or market price of a security.

Correspondent or Correspondent broker/dealer or Correspondent firm   A term used in both banking and brokerage to mean a firm that acts on behalf of another (often smaller or remote) firm. A correspondent broker may clear on behalf of the other firm; it could execute trades or handle transactions that require a local presence for another firm that is in a remote location. A correspondent bank might perform funds transfer activities in its home market for other banks that are not members of the local clearing association. (See also "Correspondent processing or Correspondent services.")

Correspondent processing or Correspondent services   The general term for any service offered by one firm for another firm of the same type. A correspondent bank provides services for another bank, and a correspondent broker provides services for another broker. Actually, the term "correspondent" can be used to mean either of the parties in the relationship. (See also "Correspondent or Correspondent broker/dealer or Correspondent firm.")

Counterparty   The other side(s) of a trade. For the buyer, the counterparty is the seller.

Counterparty master file   A file that maintains details on static data related to another entity in the trading markets regularly doing business with the owner of it. Details—bank accounts, branch locations, and clearing accounts—may be stored in such a file.

Currencies   Deposits in banks around the world that are exchanged for corresponding deposits in other countries to facilitate international trade and investment. Trading in currencies is also known as Foreign Exchange or ForEx. ForEx is the largest trading market in the world.

Custody or Custodian   A service offered by banks to institutional investors such as mutual funds and pension funds. Custodians perform both accounting and settlement services for the funds and are responsible for holding assets in countries that do not have a central depository.

Customer accounting or Customer-side accounting   The accounting for customer holdings as well as transactions that affect customer holdings on both the buy and sell side. Broker/dealer accounting for customer holdings and accounts. Broker/dealers use this term to distinguish all accounting required to support customers.

Customer activities or Customer-side activities   All operations of a buy-side or sell-side firm oriented to support of customers and their accounts. (See also "Street-side activities.")

Customer-information systems   Information systems designed to uncover important details of customer behavior that have the potential to benefit both the customer and the firms supporting the customer. In particular, trading firms maintain information about not only the instruments bought and sold by customers, but also about interests the customer expresses that do not result in trades. Customer-information systems are an important part of a process commonly referred to as customer relationship management, or CRM.

Customer master file   One of the major master files used by entities on the Street. The customer master file includes all static information on a customer, such as name, address, account numbers, and related information. Consolidating all information on customers has been one of the major tasks required to improve efficiency of financial markets processing. (See also "Security master file.")

Customer reports or Customer statements   Statements created by entities in the trading markets explaining to customers two primary sets of information: first, the holdings in their accounts as of some defined date; and second, the activity in the account over a specified period. Month-end statements defining activity over the previous month are common but not necessary. Customer reports are frequently required by regulators but also are good business practice.

Customers   A general term for any individual or entity that is serviced by an entity in the trading markets. The buy side is a customer for the sell side, but the sell side itself can be a customer to other sell-side firms acting as correspondents and to clearing corporations and banks. The role of customer plays an important part in the design of systems as well as in regulatory responsibilities.

Daisy-chain fail   A situation that occurs when each trade must settle independently, and traders may be depending on delivery from a seller to satisfy a subsequent buyer. If one trader in the process fails to deliver, then all subsequent traders will be forced to find another source of instruments or to fail themselves. For instruments where borrowing securities is not easy or possible, these types of fails can be common. In some situations, these fails can threaten the entire market.

Dark pool   A vogue term for trading environments that employ blind negotiation or direct execution among counterparties and therefore do not result in the exposure of orders to the larger market. A portion of the larger issue of hidden liquidity described in Book 2, Part 1.

Data aggregation   The activity performed in the process of the market-data business in which data from different sources is brought together by a vendor for distribution. Data aggregation includes not only the collection of data from disparate sources, but also the contracting and administrative tasks that are required to support aggregation.

Database management systems (DBMSs)   Standardized systems that are used as the basic tools for managing data. In many cases, these basic services provide not only a structure for maintaining data, but also the tools necessary for data collection, processing, and transformation, and for data presentation as well.

Data creators   Those entities that are responsible for the generation of data that is in many cases resold. The data creator is often the data owner, but not always. For example, the data created by data contributors may be owned by the vendor that aggregates the data. Likewise, the prices that are generated by trading venues go into indexes that are owned by vendors. One of the primary areas of contention in the market-data business occurs when the data creator and the data owner are different. (See also "Content owner" and "Data owner.")

Data feed   A service usually provided by a vendor in which data from one or more sources is provided to users at a place of the user's choosing. (See also "Consolidated data feed" and "Direct data feed.")

Data governance   Established rules, generally within an organization, that control how data can be entered, altered, or deleted; who is permitted to enter, alter, or delete the data; where data is to be stored; and what tools are to be employed to store and manage it. This is part of the larger function of enterprise data management. (See also "Enterprise data management.")

Data mining   A process in which software evaluates information concerning a subject or topic using information from disparate sources. For example, data mining could evaluate customers using information from holdings files, transactions files, master files, and a customer information system to create a sophisticated understanding of the customers' behavior and needs.

Data owner   The individual or entity that holds legal title to information. (See also "Content owner" and "Data creators.")

Data state   A category defining what has been done to data from the instant it is generated. Data can be raw, normalized, or enhanced. (See also "Raw data" and "Enhanced data.")

Data visualization   A display approach in which information is presented in different formats with the intent to provide more insight than would be possible from a simple tabular display. A common technique of data visualization is in creating so-called heat maps. (See also "Heat maps.")

Dealer   A principal, making money by trading for his or her own account. In the United States, dealers are regulated as broker/dealers under the Securities Acts and therefore can be members of exchanges or the NASD. Dealers generally have special access to capital and unique margin requirements.

Dealer association   A group of dealers, usually for a specific type of instrument, that organizes to establish trading rules or promote a product. In many cases, dealer associations may become formalized and recognized by regulators in an official self-regulatory capacity.

Delivery versus payment (DVP)   A type of trade that demands cash payment upon presentation of the certificates.

Delivery instructions   Instructions on how instruments or payment should be sent to counterparties to ensure efficient receipt for the settlement of transactions. Each counterparty has unique delivery instructions, and individual departments and offices may have different instructions from other offices within the same firm. Delivery instructions are becoming reference data to simplify the amount of collection and maintenance required for settlement.

Depository   An organization that is charged with holding most or all securities within a market centrally so that deliveries of securities can be made electronically rather than physically.

Depth-of-book   A display of all limit orders from a limit-order book. Typically, orders are aggregated at each price. In almost all cases, the orders are anonymous. (See also "Top-of-book.")

Depth-of-market   A display in which order books from multiple trading venues are combined to form a view of all prices that are available for trading in a market. (See also "Depth-of-book" and "Top-of-book.")

Derivatives   Instruments (generally contracts) that are traded and derive their value based on the value of an underlying instrument, usually a security. Generally, the derivative contract obligates the writer of the contract to perform a service for the purchaser of the contract (e.g., futures and options).

Design   The process in developing systems of deciding which tasks need to be performed, in what sequence, and using which processing techniques. (See also "Functional design" and "Technical design.")

Desk unit   A unit of count in which the actual device is counted. (See also "Display device" and "Unit of count.")

Direct feed or Direct data feed   A category of market data feed provided by a vendor, exchange, or consolidator in which the feed comes directly from the source of the information to the user to eliminate latency created by a vendor's data management and distribution processes. We distinguish a direct feed from transactional feeds and/or information feeds.

Direct market access   Electronic access to the marketplace provided to a buy-side trader so that an order submitted goes directly to the point of execution, either on the floor or in an electronic matching system. Thus, direct market access bypasses brokers as human intermediaries.

Direct-access recipient or Direct recipient   A firm that takes a feed directly from an exchange or a consolidator. Typically, market data vendors and users that have a strong need for data with no latency take information directly from consolidators or exchanges.

Discount   (1) A means of providing interest on a bond or other securitized loan in which the initial amount borrowed is less than the amount owed when the bond matures. The difference between the amount borrowed and the amount repaid is the "discount" and is the lender's payment for the use of the money lent. (See also "Bond" and "Interest.") (2) The amount by which the price of a bond falls below its face amount.

Display device   The traditional unit of count for market-data services. Initial display devices from market-data vendors were "dumb" terminals that were video displays from a controller that received data from the vendor's network. Because these devices were unable to modify or retransmit the data, they made an excellent unit for counting usage. As display has migrated to computerized workstations connected to intelligent networks, the display device has become seriously out of date as a method of counting usage. Moreover, users want to be able view data on multiple devices including mobile phones. Therefore, the display device is no longer satisfactory as a unit of count. (See also "Enterprise license," "Entitlement," "Unit of count," and "Unit of pricing.")

Diversifiable risk   Risk that can be removed by diversification. For risk to be diversifiable, there must be low covariance among the assets in a portfolio.

Dividend   A payment of a portion of the profits of a company to the owner of an equity security.

Domicile   A country or jurisdiction in which an individual resides or where an event is considered to take place for legal purposes.

Duress   Extremely unfavorable conditions in which an investor, trader, or firm is forced to trade even if the conditions are unfavorable. A trader forced to liquidate a holding to meet a margin call, a short seller forced to cover the short, or a firm failing to meet its capital requirements are likely to trade under duress.

Dynamically updated   An alternative term meaning an information service that has updates streamed to the user as they occur. (See "Streaming.")

Elective action   Any action, particularly with respect to events related to instruments, that needs to be undertaken only if the owner or holder chooses.

Electronic communications network (ECN)   A special class of Alternative Trading System defined by the SEC that acts like a market center but is currently regulated as a broker/dealer.

Elemental unit   A term defined within these books to describe primary entities and other components within the trading markets that form the basis for technology-based services such as accounting and reporting.

Enhanced data   A data state in which data has been supplemented or enriched by some process or transformation. (See also "Data state" and "Raw data.")

Enterprise data management   The emerging term for the management of all data across an organization. This concept separates data from the applications that use the data and takes the management of data out of the realm of pure technology. (See "Data governance" and "Golden copy.")

Enterprise infrastructure   A class of technology that employs systems, data, and networks to support an entire firm in all its locations. Enterprise infrastructure makes all information and services available in one location available to other locations within the constraints of what is permissible by contracts and acceptable given the latency of global delivery.

Enterprise license   A pricing strategy in which a licensing entity such as an exchange or other data creator may agree with an entity that is using the services of the licensing entity that the user will pay a flat fee for each payment period. Periodically, both parties will review actual usage and adjust the price to reflect any changes. (See also "Display device," "Entitlement," "Unit of count," and "Unit of pricing.")

Entitled   The state of being permitted to view licensed information or to use licensed services and software under conditions established by the contracts governing the use of the information or service.

Entitlement   The term for granting the right to use a service and for measuring usage for invoicing purposes. The unit of count is typically the unit of entitlement. Entitlement is usually granted electronically and can be measured and reported. (See also "Display device," "Enterprise license," "Unit of count," and "Unit of pricing.")

Event   A general term used within these books to mean an occurrence that is not under the control of a user or entity that requires some action by the user or entity. (See also "Activities.")

Executable quote or Executable price   A quote that is generated by a trading venue or dealer that may be "hit" or "taken" immediately and automatically if the viewer is authorized.

Execution report   A report provided by a trading venue or dealer providing official confirmation of a trade and the details necessary to be presented at settlement.

Execution-management system (EMS)   System used by buy-side traders, often provided by broker dealers, that specifically controls the selection of trading venues and controls the release of orders to those venues.

Exercise   The process of electing to convert an option into its underlying instrument under the terms established in the options contract.

eXtensible Markup Language (XML)   A scripting language and technology designed to facilitate documents, web pages, and data presentation that enables the creator to call on defined tools and define new tools using standards for development. XML is forming the basis for standards in a wide variety of financial information, including trading messages (FIXml), business reporting (XBRL), News (NewsML), and investment research (RIXML).

Extranet   Network throughout the trading markets that brings together participants with a common area of interest such as trading or post-trade processing.

Fail or Fail to deliver or Fail to receive   A situation in which one of the parties to a transaction is unable or unwilling to provide transferable ownership (deliver) or acceptable funds (receive) as required for settlement. When a fail by a principal occurs and there is an agent representing the principal, the agent must step in and deliver or receive on the principal's behalf. If there is no agent or if the agent is unable to receive or deliver, the clearing corporation satisfies the other side of the trade and subsequently tries to recover the loss from the principal and/or the principal's agent.

Fair value   The concept of the value of an instrument that is equitable to all parties at a given moment. For actively traded or liquid securities, the market determines fair value at any instant. For illiquid instruments, the determination is more difficult.

Feedback loop   An operations concept in which successive events can serve as inputs to earlier events in a causal chain with the effect of reinforcing or damping changes in a process.

Fiber-optic cables   A connection medium that employs translucent strands to propagate light waves that are used to convey information.

Financial contract   Any contract affecting financial participants or financial instruments. This term also includes contracts that can be traded and are thus instruments as defined in this set of books.

Financial statements   A accounting or process statement presenting financial information.

FIX (Financial Information eXchange)   A message protocol that is growing rapidly as a means for institutional buy and sell sides to exchange order and trade information. The protocol defines a number of message types: orders, trades, quotes, indications of interest (IOIs), and trade reports, as well as many types of administrative messages. FIX originated with Salomon Brothers and was quickly embraced by Fidelity. Many of the largest securities firms and institutional investors are active members of the FIX community. (See *www.fixprotocol.org*.)

FIX dial tone   A term used to employ a network that has an infrastructure designed to transmit defined FIX messages among participants.

FIX engine   A piece of technology that permits FIX messages to be sent or received among participants on a network such that users operating different versions of the FIX protocol can interchange information without any bespoke programming.

Flip   A slang term meaning to turn something around or send it back to its source. Applied to indications of interest (IOIs) that are automatically returned to the source as an order.

Fragmentation   The term that has come to describe a situation in which multiple markets trade the same security at the same time with no guarantee that the prices are coordinated. This implies that a firm can get a price that is better than the best price existing among all the markets. This situation can occur if the trader is not able or entitled to get to the market with the best price or because the linkage among the markets is poor. (See also "Best execution.")

Front office   A term in common usage with respect to financial companies that generally refers to people who deal directly with customers or the markets. (See also "Backoffice" and "Middle office.")

Full broadcast   Another term for streaming or dynamic updating.

Fully connected network   A network architecture in which all nodes are connected to all other nodes.

Fully disclosed accounting   A correspondent relationship in which one firm maintains the customer accounts for another firm. The firm maintaining the customer accounts is known as a carrying broker. (See also "Carrying broker" and "Omnibus accounting.")

Function   As defined in these books, an activity represented by a job category or firm department that performs a specific need required to make the trading markets work.

Functional design   The portion of system design that focuses on the tasks and algorithms to be performed to complete the assigned purpose of an application. (See also "Design" and "Technical design.")

Fungible   The property of two or more items being completely interchangeable. Because securities are fungible, it is sufficient that someone who owns a security receive a share of the security on demand. It is not necessary that the share be exactly the same one originally purchased.

Futures   A derivative contract that promises delivery of a commodity or financial asset at a fixed future point for an established price.

Give-up   The generic term for an agreement between a sell-side firm and a customer or between two sell-side firms in which one of the sell-side firms "gives up" the name of the other sell-side firm, usually at clearing. The purpose of this action is usually to permit one firm to share in the commission for another or to permit one firm to be hidden during the trading process but to be disclosed of clearing. The term has different meanings in different markets.

Golden copy   The concept, in its strictest form, that there is a single copy of all data used within an enterprise that is certified to be the official data recognized by the firm and that should be used in any application requiring the data. This presupposes that the data is not redundant, or if it is, that only one instance is considered to be the official version. (See also "Enterprise data management.")

Good funds   A definition of what and in particular what form of funds delivery is acceptable in a market. A buyer makes "good delivery" by presenting funds in the prescribed form at the prescribed location at the prescribed time for settlement. Good delivery varies from market to market (both geographic and instrument markets), but there is a long-term trend to uniformity (generally same-day funds) across regions and shorter time frames for all instruments.

Headline   The title to a news story that summarizes the content. Headlines are often presented in scrolling format. Headlines may serve as a hyperlink to full news stories.

Heat map   The slang term for a data visualization technique in which color is used in some graphical region to provide added information about the concepts being displayed. Red or yellow are often used to suggest high interest or intense activity, and blue or green suggest less activity or interest. (See also "Data visualization.")

Held order   An order in which a broker is obligated (held) by the customer to honor the price on a limit order. A held order also obligates the broker to display the order as part of its quote. The broker acts as a market maker or transmits the order to an ECN.

Hidden liquidity   Liquidity that exists outside the market and the view of other traders. Described in Book 2, Part 1.

Hierarchical   A network structure in which nodes are arranged with successive levels connecting to fewer and fewer levels above and to increased levels below. This structure is a common method for connecting users (many) to vendors (one or a few) in a geographic distribution network.

High-frequency traders   Traders who employ automated trading algorithms to submit large numbers of orders to one or many trading venues, i.e., high-frequency trading.

High-frequency trading   A quantitative trading strategy employed by a proprietary trading firm or department, or a hedge fund, that generates orders sent to the market automatically. These strategies can result in millions of orders being sent to the markets, many of which are canceled and replaced by orders at different prices if not immediately executed.

Historical data   Data on past events, particularly sets of past instrument prices.

Holding period   Generally, a period over which an instrument is held and that is the basis for evaluation for investment returns. Most investments are not held for calendar periods, and accounting systems that are designed to report for statutory purposes are not satisfactory for measuring investment performance. A holding period is a much more attractive time frame for measuring returns.

Holdings   The instruments belonging to an account, portfolio, product, or customer. Holdings are the basis for describing ownership and reporting on investment value and activities.

Holdings report   A report describing the instruments held by an account, portfolio, product, or customer usually valued employing official prices. A holdings report can be thought of as a more general term than "customer report," which carries the implication of a report required by statute or regulations.

Hub   A node within a network where links to other nodes are connected.

Hub-and-spoke   A network architecture where a central node (the hub) is connected by direct links (spokes) to other nodes.

Identifiers   Any general identifying information, particularly about data used within the financial markets. Identifiers are required for instruments and entities, and may become quite complex when there are multiple attributes and/or locations that must be differentiated within an instrument or enterprise.

Illiquid   Not liquid, as in an instrument or market. That is, it is not easy to buy or sell the instrument (or instruments in the market) without abnormal amounts of effort and/or large price concessions. Illiquid markets are extremely problematic in periods of market stress and/or when trades are made under duress. (See also "Liquid.")

Income   Financial returns received from holding a financial asset.

Income statement   A financial statement that presents business performance for an enterprise showing the costs and profits from ongoing operations. Income statements often complement balance sheets and are the major element of most commercial business reporting to shareholders and regulators. (See also "Balance sheet.")

Independent software vendor (ISV)   A term primarily used in the futures industry for vendors that are primarily engaged in providing software to users, and not data. ISVs were given access to market data early in the introduction of automated trading in the futures industry with the goal of attracting traders who had previously used the physical markets. This strategy has caused problems as automated trading has become the norm. Exchanges would now like to collect revenues from the data the ISVs distribute, and regular market-data vendors feel ISVs have an unfair competitive advantage. (See also "Market-data vendors.")

Index   A calculated measure of the market performance of a group of securities. An index can be for an entire market or a portion of a market. Different types of indexes have different calculation methodologies that affect the characteristics of the index. The two major calculation methodologies are price weighted (such as the Dow Jones Industrial Average) and market weighted (such as the S&P 500). Indexes are typically licensed by the creator and are calculated by the vendors.

Indications of interest (IOIs)   Messages between market participants indicating that the initiating party has a position of "significant size" that is available to be traded under the right conditions and asking if the receiving party has any interest. Under the rules of decorum for this exchange, the initiating party is not supposed to send an IOI unless there really is a position. The receiving party is not supposed to take actions that would disadvantage the initiator.

Industry groups   A collection of entities or individuals within the trading markets with at least one area of common interest. This term is used to relate to both associations and working groups that unite services and users as well as competitors to achieve a common end.

Industrywide systems   They provide a service across all or a portion of the financial industry. These systems may be formed by a single entity that has developed a widely used system or by groups of systems that are interconnected to produce a common result.

Information vendor   A vendor providing market data and/or other information used by participants in the trading markets. The term is used to refer to a major participant category in the market-data business.

Informational quotes   Quotes that are provided for users' information but that are not firm. Another term is "indicative quotes."

Inquiry/response   Inquiry/response is a distribution technique in which information is only sent to a user when requested. Frequently the information is not updated unless a subsequent request is made. This technique is satisfactory for some types of information, and does not burden distribution systems with update messages that are not needed.

Instant messaging (IM)   A facility originally created by AOL to permit members to instigate chat sessions in real time. The facility was adopted by a number of buy- and sell-side firms at the instigation of the buy side to facilitate communications. Because AOL's IM service does not provide for an audit trail or archiving, the sell-side has pushed for a more secure format. Among the contenders are services offered by Bloomberg and Reuters. In addition, there is a consortium of sell-side firms operated by themarkets.com that is owned by the sell side as well a secure offering by AOL.

Institutional investors   A collective label for professional money managers. The term includes bank trust departments, hedge funds, investment advisors, insurance companies, mutual fund managers, and pension managers.

Institutional sales   The function within a broker/dealer (sell-side firm) that is responsible for the customer relationship. Institutional sales is responsible for managing the customer, providing services, delivering soft dollar services, and encouraging the customer to use the broker/dealer's products. In some firms, this function may be combined with the sales trader. (See also "Sales trader.")

Instrument identifiers   Identifiers that are used to uniquely distinguish an instrument. If the instrument is traded only in a single market or jurisdiction, the problem of identification is usually simple. When the instrument is traded by multiple markets across many jurisdictions, the problem of pinpointing the specific instrument of interest becomes more complex.

Instrument selection   The process of choosing an instrument usually for purchase or sale. Instrument selection is the primary focus of portfolio managers.

Instruments   The general term for financial assets that do not involve holding physical goods.

Intellectual property   A property right that provides an ownership interest in any value that is derived as the product of an activity or service. Intellectual property often permits the owner to lease or license a product such as data and charge for its usage.

Interdealer broker (IDB)   A broker whose customers are dealers. Prominent especially in foreign exchange and fixed-income dealing. (See also "Broker's broker.")

Interest   The payments received from a loan or from owning a fixed-income instrument.

Intermarket order routing   A system or process for routing orders among multiple trading venues when each is trading the same instruments. Usually, the goal of intermarket order routing is to transfer an order to the trading venue with the best price at the instant of transfer.

Intermediaries   Persons or firms that act as middlemen in arranging a transaction or sponsor a customer to participate in a restricted financial service. Brokers and dealers perform this function. The term "disintermediation" refers to the elimination of the broker or other middleman.

Internalized execution   An execution achieved through internalization or in an internal market.

Internal market   A trading venue that exists within a sell-side firm. The sell-side firm, acting as a dealer, permits customers to execute against the dealer's quote at prices up to the size contained in the dealer's quote. This concept was described in Book 2 as "AutoEx or AutoEx system."

International Security Identification Numbers (ISIN)   The standard for securities numbers maintained by the International Standards Organization.

Introducing broker or Introducing firm   A broker that is not a member of an exchange or clearing corporation. The introducing firm has the customer relationship, but its clearing firm provides execution services and/or clears trades.

Inventory accounting   As it relates to the market-data business, this term refers to a category of software that maintains records of the sources of information, the contractual obligations for the information's use, and which individuals and applications within an entity are entitled to see the information. Increasingly, such systems are linked to entitlement systems that permit users to turn on or off a user or application and record actual entitlements.

Investment committee   A group within an investment management company that sets firm-wide policy on what instruments can be purchased, what instruments should be held, and which instruments should be sold. The committee is often composed of senior portfolio managers and research analysts.

Investment research   Analysis of traded instruments with the intent of providing a prospective investor or trader with information that permits the market price to be compared with some notion of worth or value.

Know-your-customer obligations A term dating from the very early days of the trading markets which suggests that entities and individuals who have a direct relationship with a customer are in the best position to understand the customer's activities and needs. As regulations in the trading markets place increasing obligations on market participants to monitor customers for illegal activities, know-your-customer has come to define prescribed responsibilities to serve as agents of regulators in identifying illegal or unwanted activities.

Ladder A term we have defined in these books to describe a type of network characterized by two levels of buses, as is the case with enterprise and trading room infrastructures. One bus that we define as the acquisition bus links information sources to internal data stores and applications. A second bus that we define as the distribution bus distributes the stored data and the services performed by enterprise applications to users and supported applications.

Last sale or Last-sale price or Last-sale report or Last trade The price of the most recent trade for an instrument.

Latency The natural delays that occur in distribution systems when physical distances and computer processes slow the delivery of data. Although the delays are usually short in human terms, as more trading involves computers and models, traders and trading firms are seeking to minimize latency. Most traders accept latency as the unavoidable result of physics but are strongly opposed to "queuing." (See also "Queuing.")

Lien A security interest in an asset pledged as collateral for a loan. If a lien can be perfected, then the creditor has a preferred status with respect to others. Liens permit securities to be held by depositories because creditors who have provided financing using an instrument as collateral are not required to have physical control to prove their security interest in the instrument.

Limit A term referring to the maximal allowable position that a trader or department can have with respect to an instrument or a customer. Position limits can be long or short. Limits are a tool for risk management and control.

Liquidity or liquid Being in possession of executable buy and sell orders. A liquidity pool is a place (either physical, like an exchange floor, or virtual, like a computerized system) where executable orders come together for trading. A liquid marketplace is a set of liquidity pools that collectively provide the ability to trade reasonably sized orders at reasonable hours under all market conditions without significantly affecting the marketplace.

Listing exchange An exchange on which an instrument is registered for trading in a market. Historically, instruments were only traded on the exchange where they were listed, but with competition many different trading venues may trade the same instruments.

Local area networks A general term for small networks connecting personal computers and servers for the purpose of file and print sharing in offices. As commonly used the term implies relatively low bandwidth connections, but capacities have grown as the costs of the components have fallen.

Long or Long position A general trading term for a trader with a positive security position. Long is also used in clearing to mean the firm or individual that is obligated to deliver securities (the seller or the seller's agent). (See also "Short or Short position.")

Long-only investment or Long-only A term used to describe those investment funds that are only permitted by statute or regulation to hold instruments. These types of funds are not permitted to take short positions, even when the condition occurs inadvertently, such as when a settlement fails.

Margin financing   A financing technique in which a broker provides credit to support the trading activities or positions of a customer.

Mark to market   The process of calculating the value of a securities holding with the most current price. Traders mark to market moment to moment to calculate profit or loss. Individuals may mark to market once per day at the close, or once per month, or once per quarter, as necessary. Clearing corporations mark positions pending settlement to market to compute margin demands.

Market   A generic term used in several different ways: (1) Each issue has a market of those interested in trading that security. (2) A specific exchange or trading center is termed a market. (3) All buying and selling interests as they come together to trade are referred to as the market.

Market activities   All the operations within a firm that are directed at exchanges, market centers, utilities, and other counterparties in the trading process.

Market data   A collective term for quotes, last sales, volume statistics, and other information used by the market to evaluate trading opportunities. Market data is generally distributed by a number of firms such as Bloomberg, Thomson Reuters, and Interactive Data. Market data is sometimes imprecisely referred to as "quotes," as in "quote vendors" or as the "tape."

Market-data vendors   An entity engaged in selling data to users of data. The term is used broadly to encompass all vendors of data, but can sometimes have a narrower definition referring only to vendors that specialize in data from and about the markets, most often provided in streaming format. In the narrow definition a market-data vendor would be contrasted with a reference-data vendor.

Market identification code (MIC)   An identifier that supplements instrument identifiers by defining a market on which the instrument was traded.

Market impact   A measure of trading cost. Market impact, a major concern for institutional investors, measures the extent to which introducing a very large order into the market alters the market, causing the execution to occur at a less favorable cost than existed at the time the order was entered.

Market maker or Market making   A special class of dealer with the obligation to provide liquidity by making continuous two-sided markets (both bid and ask).

Market order   An unpriced order to a broker or dealer to execute a trade immediately at the best price available in the market at the time the broker/dealer receives the order.

Marketable limit order or Marketable limit   A priced (limit) order where the bid price is equal to or greater than the market bid or the offer price is equal to or lower than the market offer price.

Marketplace   The generic term for exchanges, dealer markets, and other trading centers.

Master files   The general term for all of the files containing static data employed in processing for the trading markets.

Matching vendors   Vendors that support the settlement process by providing services that permit investing institutions to affirm trades executed by agents on the sell side.

Mature or Maturity   The process that occurs when a bond reaches the end of its term and the face value is repaid to the lender.

Member An individual or entity that has rights to use a trading venue, clearing corporation, or depository. Historically, these support entities were mutualized membership corporations and "member" described the form of ownership. Now many support companies are independent for-profit shareholder corporations, but the term "member" is still used for a relationship that would more accurately be described by the term "customer."

Message broker A piece of middleware that links systems using different message protocols by converting the messages back and forth between the protocols.

Metadata Data that describes data. Metadata is provided as an adjunct to electronic data with the goal of making the source, ownership, and other attributes of the data clear to any users of the data.

Middle office The activities in a buy-side or sell-side firm that support primary lines of business and/or directly support customers.

Middleware The general term for software that is provided at the center of a process linking systems and providing translation and entitlement services to connected individuals and applications.

Minimum price variation (MPV) The minimum increment in which a security can be priced. For U.S. equities, this was $1/16^{th}$ prior to August 2000 and $0.01 after April of 2002. For options, the MPV was $1/16^{th}$ for options with premiums of less than $3.00 and $1/8^{th}$ for options with premiums equal to or greater than $3.00 prior to August 2000. Since April 2001, the MPV for options has been $0.05 for options with a premium of less than $3.00 and $0.10 for options with premiums equal to or greater than $3.00.

Misappropriated data A term coined to describe all forms of data usage in violation of the contractual terms for the data's usage. This can range from data that is inadvertently misused by accident or ignorance to data that is willfully stolen.

Modern Portfolio Theory The general term for the academic research, theories, and philosophy of investment management, which hold that investment in a diversified portfolio of instruments is more prudent than trying to select securities that will have superior performance or to time investments in an effort to take advantage of market movements.

Money laundering The term describing activities intended to hide the source of money such as drug profits or money supporting terrorism. Money laundering is potentially a large concern for the trading markets because it is easy to use trading and other financial transactions to mask the source of money.

Multilateral trading facility (MTF) A trading facility defined by MiFID with the intent to encourage experimentation with new methods of trading. Thus, an MTF is similar in nature to an ECN or ATS as defined by Regulation ATS in the United States. Both attempt to create two alternative types of trading venues. One is an exchange and is more highly regulated. MTFs, ECNs, and ATSs anticipate lighter regulation and depend on other entities (exchanges or other regulators) for regulatory oversight.

Multiple instances single user (MISU) or Multiple entitlements single user (MESU) The term means that a single individual is receiving information from the same source (an exchange or other data creator) through multiple entitling information-delivery channels (i.e., market-data vendors) and is paying for the same information more than once. Because each vendor entitles separately, there is no simple mechanism for resolving the problem. All exchanges have this issue, and many are happy with the added income. The NYSE began the practice of providing credits to customers who can document multiple payments, but the process requires providing vendor invoices showing the multiple entitlements. Resolution usually takes several months.

Mutual fund   A professionally managed portfolio in which shares can be purchased representing a percentage of the fund. The shares' values fluctuate based on the market value of the fund's assets. Mutual funds can be open (the number of shares can fluctuate) or closed (the number of shares are fixed). Also, funds can be "load" (a broker's commission or fee is built into the purchase price over and above the fund's proportional value) or "no load" (there is no built-in commission). Brokers or agents usually sell load funds, whereas the management company usually sells no-load funds directly.

Mutualized   The attribute of an entity or service in which the entity/service is jointly owned by a number of participants to provide the service or function performed by the entity at cost. Exchanges and clearing corporations began as mutualized entities although a number have become for-profit. In principle, mutualized entities are suited for activities where the service or function is expensive to offer but not highly valued by its beneficiary.

Mutualized activity   Any activity that can be shared by a number of participants usually with the hope of spreading the costs.

Mutualized entity   Any entity that is jointly owned and/or operated by multiple participants. Mutualized entities are often constructed to house mutualized activities. Exchanges and clearing corporations are examples of entities that may be mutualized.

Naked access   Direct market access that does not require the order to be revealed to the sell-side firm that is sponsoring the access. There is a fear that naked access permits trading positions to accumulate without sufficient risk controls. In principle, the sell-side firm is subject to risk controls by the clearing corporation, but a buy-side firm that is not a clearing member has no controls unless the order is exposed to the sell-side firm. Buy-side firms are often sensitive about exposing their trading activities for fear of market impact.

National best bid and offer (NBBO)   A term for the top-of-book quotes across a whole market or within a country. NBBO is often a regulatory mandated presentation of the best prices in a market at any instant and is usually intended to provide prospective traders with a sense of fair prices in the market. (See "Best bid and offer" and "Top-of-book")

National numbering agency (NNA)   A company or association within a country that is charged by ISO for maintaining its country's national numbering system.

Natural order   An order that arises from the activities of a trader or portfolio manager and is not solicited or stimulated by the activities of the sell side. Natural orders are believed to be untainted by short-term supply-and-demand factors and are likely to be attracted to an equilibrium price.

Net asset value   The value of shares in a mutual fund at the close of trading each day. Shares are valued by computing aggregate value of holdings (the sum of the total number of trading units times the official price for the day) divided by the total number of trading units. The net asset value is then used to redeem outstanding shares or sell new shares. (See also "Official prices.")

Network provider   A firm offering network services.

New issue   The generic term for the output from the investment banking process, including both equities and fixed-income issues.

Newsfeed   A data feed providing news information, usually in streaming format. (See also "Newswire.")

Newswire   A news information service that is presented in a feed format. (See also "Newsfeed.")

Nondiversifiable risk   Risk that cannot be removed by diversification because instruments in a portfolio move in concert with the broader market. (See also "Diversifiable risk.")

Nongovernmental organization (NGO)   An organization that performs government-like services but that is not part of any national government. Examples include the United Nations and the World Bank.

Normalization or Normalize   The activity in the market-data business distribution process in which data is put into a common format, corrections may be made for bad messages, and supporting identifiers or enhancements are added to make the data more useful.

Offer   The price at which a market maker, or any other seller, prices an instrument to be sold.

Official prices   The prices that are acceptable for valuing portfolio holdings in a market. In many markets, but not all, the last or closing price for the day in which holdings are valued is the official price. Other markets use the value-weighted average price (VWAP) as the official price. (See also "VWAP.")

Omnibus accounting   The method of correspondent processing where the processing firm does not carry the accounts of the customer firm. In many cases, the processing firm provides only the Street-side activities for the customer firm.

Omnibus clearing   One of two types of clearing relationships. The other is "fully disclosed." In an omnibus relationship, the clearing firm provides certain services for the correspondent firm, such as exchange trading staff or presence in the clearing city. The correspondent is a full member of the exchange or clearing corporation. In this relationship, the clearing firm maintains a single (omnibus) account for the correspondent. The correspondent firm, in turn, carries all the accounts for retail customers or trading accounts in the case of a market maker.

Open order   An order that has been initiated but has not yet been completed. An order pending execution.

Option   A contract to purchase (call option) or sell (put option) a specified quantity of a financial asset at a specified price at a specified future date or during a specified time period. Options differ from futures in that an option is an opportunity to buy, but there is no obligation as there is with a future. If no action is taken at the end of the option period, the option expires without value. (See also "Call option," "Exercise," and "Put option.")

Options Price Reporting Authority (OPRA)   A jointly owned facility of the options exchanges (plus the NYSE for historical reasons) that manages the collection, distribution, pricing, and revenue allocations for market data for options. OPRA also sets the conditions for usage of market data. OPRA is analogous to CTA/CQOC and, like CTA/CQOC, has its facilities managed by the Securities Industry Automation Corporation (SIAC). (See also "CTA/CQOC.")

Order   An instruction to buy or sell an instrument.

Order-input network   A network that is primarily designed to route orders from a source to a trading venue or dealer for execution. The same network may also provide a medium for transmitting execution confirmations and to handle order cancellation.

Order management algorithm   An algorithm that defines how an order is to be maintained prior to release to the markets. (See also "Order-management system.")

Order-management system (OMS)   Information systems and networks that enable traders to enter and transmit orders to multiple execution points through electronic linkages, and to keep track of the results. Functionality includes the ability to handle various order types (e.g., market orders, limit orders, baskets). (See also "Buy-side order-management system" and "Sell-side order-management system.")

Order release algorithm   An algorithm that defines how orders are to be released to the trading venue(s) for execution. (See also "TWAP" and "VWAP.")

Order routing   The process of sending orders to an intermediary or to a trading venue. Often used in reference to automated routing or systems for routing orders.

Order routing algorithm   A set of rules for determining where an order to buy or sell an instrument(s) should be sent. The rules are usually programed as calculations employing input prices or quotes from alternate destination markets.

Other side   The other party to a situation for any trade or counterparty situation. In a simple trade, the buyer is the other side to the seller. In a situation where there is a central counterparty, the counterparty (usually a clearing corporation) is the other side to both the buyer and seller.

Packaged instruments   An aggregate term for instruments available for investment that represent participation units in an investment portfolio. (See also "Mutual fund.")

Participant   Any firm or individual that is a member or competitor in a system or process.

Paying agent   An entity, most often a bank, that serves to pay dividends to stockholders or interest payments to bond holders. The paying agent is one function in the general banking line of business referred to as a corporate trust.

Payment   The process for exchanging funds, usually involving the banking system as agent.

Pension or Pension plan   Money set aside to be professionally managed on behalf of workers who will use the money for their retirement.

Physical execution   Execution that occurs between individuals either in person or through a direct connection such as a telephone conversation.

Physical trading floor   A physical location where trading occurs. Usually, a specific location provided by an exchange, but also in taverns and in informal locations agreed among participants formally or informally.

Point-of-presence (POP)   A location where a user can connect to a network.

Point-to-point   A form of network architecture where nodes are connected directly to all other nodes with which they interact.

Portfolio management   The role of the individual charged with making investment decisions such as in which securities to invest and how to allocate the assets of an institutional portfolio among different classes of assets.

Portfolio management systems   Systems designed to help a portfolio manager evaluate and manage investment decisions. Portfolio management is related to, but distinct from, statutory reporting and accounting and also trade/order-management systems. (See also "Statutory reporting.")

Portfolio manager   The role of the individual charged with making investment decisions such as in which securities to invest and how to allocate the assets of an institutional portfolio among different classes of assets.

Portfolio reports   Reports provided on portfolios. These reports focus on the portfolio and the way it is managed even though the portfolio may support a product or represent holdings for multiple customers. Portfolio reports are usually provided for portfolio managers to support investment decision making.

Position   A holding in a security. Also, all or a portion of a dealer's inventory of securities.

Position management   The process of managing instrument positions acquired in the trading or market-making process. Usually applied to short-term positions most often by a sell-side firm engaged in dealing.

Position reports   Reports designed to support dealers and other principals. The positions managed by principals often include short positions and usually require the production of profit and loss (P&L) statements.

Position trader or Position manager   An individual within the trading operation of a broker/dealer who is responsible for managing the firm's inventory position in a specific security. This individual would typically set the firm's quote (if firm is a market maker) and determine the quantity and price to bid or offer as a participant in a block trade.

Postal, telephone, and telegraph (PTT)   The common term for governmental agencies that provide communications services, often combined with postal services.

Posted or Posting   A data or software term meaning to update a position or computer record. The term is also used in accounting to mean updating accounting records.

Price improvement   The concept that a dealer or trading venue could provide a better price than the posted best bid or offer in a market and would then use some different trading rules to cause the improvement to occur. In some situations, the promise of price improvement has been used as an excuse to deviate from expected or standard trading practices.

Prices   The general term for data on instruments related to last-sold prices and quotes. The term is also sometimes used loosely to apply to market-data information surrounding instruments that center on the prices and quotes but also including incidental information.

Primary market   (1) The initial issuance of securities. Securities are underwritten in the primary market to raise capital. (See also "Secondary market.") (2) When an instrument is traded on multiple markets, the market of original listing is sometimes designated as the primary market. The primary market may set the official trading hours for the instrument and determine other conditions for trading.

Prime broker or Prime brokerage   A broker that services hedge funds. The prime broker can consolidate trades from multiple broker/dealers, provide financing for trading, clear trades, and provide technical infrastructure for the hedge funds.

Principal   Any person who buys or sells a security for his or her own account. Also refers to an executive of a firm that actively engages in that firm's trading business.

Process data   Data that is created "on-the-fly" and/or is internal to a given entity. At the beginning of the automation of market processes, substantially all data was process data. Even prices had to be input manually to applications. In time, vendors began to offer increasing amounts of process data as either market data or reference data. The migration of data from process data that is, by its nature, bespoke means that smaller portions of firms' technology budgets are consumed by creating and maintaining data. (See also "Market data" and "Reference data.")

Processor symbols   This book uses the term "processor symbols" to distinguish instrument identifiers that are used by computers from identifiers used by people. The identifiers used by people are commonly referred to as "ticker symbols." (See also "Instrument identifiers" and "Ticker symbol.")

Process units   A term we coined to describe the major types of messages or transactions serving as the focus of the activities taking place in the processes that are the major purpose of the trading markets. Process units include IOIs, orders, trade reports, and the like.

Profit and loss (P&L) statement   A statement providing information on the profits earned on principal positions. One characteristic of P&L statements is that profitability is usually measured after assigning some cost for the capital employed in trading.

Propagation delay   The delay or latency created because of the time required for a message to travel the distance from its source to its destination.

Proprietary trading (Prop trading)   A department or function within a sell-side firm that invests the firm's capital to profit based on market knowledge gained in the process of the firm's other market operations. (See also "Treasury.")

Proprietary trading (prop trading) unit   A group or department engaged in proprietary trading.

Protocol   A definition for communications messages that usually includes the structure for messages (the syntax) and a description of the procedural methods for the implementation of the protocol by users, such as how errors are handled.

Public information   Information that is considered to be in the public domain and is therefore free except for possible charges for the cost of providing the information. Public information cannot be licensed for use.

Publish/subscribe (Pub/Sub)   A method of distributing market data in which the recipient registers (subscribes) with the producer (publisher) of the information to receive only the information that is of interest. In the case of market data, this can substantially reduce the broadcast of information that is not of specific interest to the user. This substantially reduces communications capacity requirements.

Publish   The process of making data available in a publish/subscribe environment.

Purchases and sales (P&S)   The department in a securities firm responsible for resolving problems with execution details prior to settlement, and managing the broker/dealer's input to the affirmation process.

Put or Put option   An option contract in which the writer promises to purchase a fixed quantity of the underlying at a set strike price if the holder elects to exercise the option. (See "Call option," "Exercise," and "Option.")

Quantitative investors Investors that deploy algorithms to manage the investment process.

Queuing The phenomenon that occurs when the volume of data put through a network or process exceeds the capacity of that network or process. Typically, data begins to build up in system buffers or is completely lost. Queuing is particularly troublesome to a user of market data because the system appears to the user, or using application, to be functioning normally, but the data used is either delayed or is missing elements. (See also "Latency.")

Quote The price at which a firm or an individual will buy or sell a security, also referred to as "bid" and "offer" (sometimes called "ask"). A two-sided quote consists of a bid and an offer for the security. A one-sided quote is only the bid or the ask. (See also "Bid," "Best bid and Offer," and "Ask.")

Ratings The assessments employed by ratings agencies to help investors appraise the quality of instruments.

Raw data One of the data states that describes data as it is produced with no effort to check for errors or add supporting information or enhancement. (See also "Data state" and "Enhanced data.")

Realized Changes in the market value (gain or loss) of a portfolio that have been converted to cash through a sale in the market. (In the case of a short sale, the profit or loss is realized when the instrument that has been shorted is purchased to close the position.)

Real time An activity, particularly a computer process, which takes place as events unfold. Real-time data is processed and usually transmitted as events generate the content.

Reconciling The process of resolving problems among accounts or in computer processes.

Recursive A situation in which an item or process repeats. For example, an account can own another account and can be owned by a third account.

Redistribution The situation that occurs in the data business in which a user of data distributes that data to others either in its original form or with enhancements. Usually, data contracts define the conditions under which data can be redistributed.

Redundancy A situation in which a data or a process is repeated either needlessly because the repetition is not intended, or intentionally because there is a need to have a backup for the original.

Reference data A general term for data generally provided by vendors (and thus originating outside the purchasing firm) that is used primarily for post-trade processing. Historically, reference data was considered materially different from "market data" because the latter tended to be delivered in real time, and the former was delivered periodically and in bulk. Also, a good portion of reference data comes from the market, and thus the distinction between market data and reference data fails to be aptly named. Perhaps the best distinction between what is commonly referred to as market data and reference data is that market data is generally input into trading decisions. Pricing and news helps in the evaluation of potential and actual trading decisions, including indications of interest, instant messaging and tweets, last sale prices (dynamically updated), quotes, news, research, and commentary. In contrast, most reference data, historical data, capital changes, counterparty data, issue identifiers, and data linking issues and the entities to which they belong all support post-trade applications. Even this distinction breaks down as historical prices can, in turn, be input to future trading decisions. (See also "Market data" and "Process data.")

Reference market A market used to determine the price of transactions in a passive market.

Replay information The general term for taking information after it is generated and playing it again as if it were new, including any gaps, delays, or asynchronous patterns found in the original data stream. Also a service in which data can be accessed for playback after it is generated.

Report (1) Verb: An official response to a requirement to make information available either to a regulator or to the public. (2) Noun: Any formal presentation of information; often required by regulators.

Reporting exchanges An exchange that collects information from other trading venues for some defined purpose such as creating an NBBO or producing a consolidated data feed.

Repurchase agreement or Repo A financing technique in which liquid instruments are sold to a bank or other entity providing financing by a dealer at the end of a trading day and repurchased at the beginning of the next day. The transaction has the effect of taking the instrument position off the books of the dealer, thus freeing capital. The financing entity assumes ownership of an asset and provides a de facto loan. Interest is paid for the service based on the size of the loan and current interest rates. The interest is paid as an increment to the repurchase price.

Required minimum capital The amount of capital, usually specified as a combination of equity and subordinated debt, which a firm must maintain given the size of the positions it takes as a principal and other factors. Either regulators, markets, or both require minimum capital to protect against a firm taking too many risks as a threat against itself, other firms, and the market.

Research or Investment research The activity undertaken by buy-side firms, sell-side firms, and third-party research firms to assess the value and possibly the market price of investment assets.

Retail brokerage or Retail brokers The agency activities or sales personnel of sell-side firms directed to or on behalf of individuals as customers.

Retail investors Individuals who are managing money for their own benefit or that of their family.

Retail sales That portion of the sales activities of both buy- and sell-side firms that is directed at individuals.

Retransmit A service provided by some data creators in which they repeat the transmission of information that may have been garbled or lost by downstream vendors or users. Typically messages are transmitted with an associated sequence number. If the sequence is broken the recipient knows that messages have been lost and can ask for a retransmission.

Reverse stock split A corporate event in which multiple units of an instrument (usually shares of an equity) are exchanged for fewer units after the event. In principle, the process should result in fewer units after the exchange, but with each unit being worth more so that the aggregate value just before and just after the exchange becomes effective is unchanged.

Risk A generalized term for uncertainty that can affect the profitability, and in some cases survival, of a financial organization. As many as 20 unique types of risk have been identified.

Risk management A name given to both the process and support systems used to measure and ameliorate risk. Because there are many different definitions of risk, any discussion of risk management must begin with an agreement regarding what types of risk are being discussed and what management means to the participants.

Risking capital   The process in which a dealer or a firm is willing to commit its capital in the dealing process. This can include purchasing instruments into inventory or assuming a short position. Firms risk capital both to profit from the exposure and to assist customers.

Roll up or Rolled up   An action taken to combine accounts or positions to create a broader picture of the account or position. Frequently, the positions of several dealers are combined to better understand the cumulative effect of their independent positions on risk.

Rules-based order routing or Rules-based routing   An order routing process in which all of an order is routed to various execution facilities based on fixed, predetermined rules for how to handle the order.

Sales   The activities within a securities firm that are directed at generating more customers or more revenue-generating activities from existing customers.

Sales trader   An individual in a trading room of a broker/dealer that has customer responsibility. The sales trader can typically execute orders from customers that are below limits established by a position trader at the firm's established quote. May also be referred to as an "institutional salesperson."

Sales trading   The activities associated with the function of sales trader. (See also "Sales trader.")

Scripting languages   A means of controlling a system or process using commands or instructions often written as text files. The scripts are often interpreted by the system/process "on the fly." Scripts are often more accessible to non-programmers because they do not require compiling in the way computer languages frequently do.

Scrolling formats   A presentation method that employs streaming information as a succession of lines of information presented as it is received in a dedicated part of a display. New lines usually build from left to right, and when the line is complete it is pushed up or down and is replaced by a new line. Displays often have a fixed number of displayed lines with the oldest line pushed off as the line limit is reached.

Scrolling headlines   An electronic method for presenting headlines from news stories using the scrolling format. (See "Scrolling format")

Secondary market   The term used to describe trading in a security or instrument after it is issued initially. Securities are issued in the primary market. Once issued, trading occurs in the secondary market. (See also "Primary market.")

Sectors   A grouping of industries with common characteristics. For example, the energy sector might be made up of oil and gas, wind, solar, coal, and geothermal industries.

Securities   Instruments that raise capital, including debt and equity instruments.

Securities markets   The imprecise term often used to mean the "trading markets." We define trading markets because we believe trading occurs in instruments that are not technically defined as securities.

Securities movement and control   The functions required to monitor and, in some cases, manage the post-trade processes for a buy-side firm.

Security master file   A file that is common to substantially all entities in the trading markets; it carries general information on all instruments held in or commonly held in the entity. The file includes data such as the official name of each instrument, the current official price, and other data that is common to all holdings. (See also "Customer master file.")

SEDOL   The ISIN number for U.K. securities that is maintained by the London Stock Exchange.

Segregation   The activity within broker/dealers in which securities held by the firm or its custodians must be classified in accordance with regulations. Some securities are eligible to be counted as part of the firm's capital; other securities may be available for lending; and yet other securities may not be used for some purposes. The classes of segregation are determined by local regulation, particularly the rules of clearing corporations.

Sell side   Organizations such as brokers, dealers, banks, and exchanges that provide services required to trade securities and currencies. Also known as the "wholesale marketplace."

Sell-side order-management systems   Order-management systems (OMS) designed for use by dealers and other sell-side firms. In addition to managing orders during execution, these systems also have facilities to support dealing. They may include dealer AutoEx services and may also include internal markets where customers' orders can interact with each other and with the firms' dealer market. Sell-side order management systems may also provide or connect to execution-management systems. (See also "Buy-side order-management system" and "Order-management system.")

Short or Short position or Shorting   (1) A trader who has a negative (borrowed) security position. The term can also mean the firm or individual that must deliver money (buyer or the buyer's agent) in clearing. (See also "Long or Long position.") (2) In futures, the party that sells the contract and is obligated to deliver to satisfy the contract.

Single point of failure   The idea of a chokepoint wherein a failure by a system or component can cause the entire process or system to fail. Technology design often focuses on there being no single point of failure in a system or process.

Single update   A data network design in which information is distributed as individual updates rather than streaming all new updates.

Smart order routing or Smart-routing system   An automated form of routing that allows traders to submit orders (perhaps large in size) to a sophisticated computerized algorithm that determines where to send the order based on real-time price information available from exchanges, ECNs, and dealers. Other information incorporated into the decision may include computer-generated estimates of the probability of execution at the various alternative execution points and the cost of execution at each point. Different strategies may be implemented. For instance, in some systems, large orders are split into smaller sub-orders that are sent to multiple market centers simultaneously. A large order may also be split and issued in waves so that the market is not overwhelmed at any single time. This type of routing technology is also sometimes called "dynamic order routing."

Soft dollars (U.S.) or Soft commissions (UK) or Softing (UK)   Soft dollars refers to commissions paid to brokers by institutions with an agreement that the broker will pay for certain research services on behalf of the institution. In the United States, soft dollars are regulated by the U.S. Department of Labor (ERISA) and the SEC under section 28e of the Securities Acts. In the United Kingdom, soft dollars are referred to as "soft commissions" (the process is known as "softing" and is regulated by the FSA).

Span   A term we coin to mean the coverage of a network. Span is usually a geographic concept but can also be used to imply organizational coverage.

Spread   The difference between the lowest offer and the highest bid. When a dealer or market maker provides the bid and offer, the spread represents the dealer's potential profit at any moment.

Standards   The use of mutually agreed definitions or procedures to reduce the cost of processes and processing. Standards are frequently used for message protocols but have wider applications as well. When standards are employed, the amount of bespoke development can be significantly reduced.

Standards organizations   An organization, corporation, or association that manages the ongoing support for a standard.

Static information   Information that does not change or does not change frequently.

Statutory data   Data that is required to be produced or distributed as the result of governmental statutes or regulations.

Statutory reporting   Any reporting required by law or statute or by regulators. Statutory reports may be made to the regulator but may also be for customers as required by a rule or statute.

Stock dividend   Income paid to shareholders and others in the form of additional shares in a fixed relationship to their current holdings. Although the shares go to all holders in a fixed proportion, leaving percentage holdings unchanged, stock dividends represent new shares that the holder can choose to sell. Stock dividends do not require cash and are often favored by fast-growing companies. As a result, they are often seen as an indication that a company has good prospects.

Stock loan or Stock loan and borrow or Securities lending   A function or department within an entity (usually on the sell side) that is responsible for borrowing securities either for short sales, or to satisfy the need to deliver instruments that are temporarily unavailable. Any instrument that can be sold short or that may not be available when it must be delivered may be borrowed, but common usage often refers to "stock" lending.

Stock repurchase   An instrument event, particularly for equities, wherein a company decides to repurchase its own shares either by a formal offer to stockholders or through purchases in the open market. When there is a tender for the shares, then firms owning the shares must decide whether to accept the tender and, if so, how much.

Stock split   A capital change that occurs when an issuing company chooses to divide (or, in some cases, combine) stocks in a fixed proportion. The transaction leaves all stockholders unchanged in terms of their proportion of ownership, but often by splitting stock shares become more affordable to smaller investors. This transaction is particularly used when an equity security experiences a strong run-up in price.

Stocks   The familiar name for equity securities that convey ownership rights in a company or other organization. In addition to common shares, there are variations such as preferred stocks that promise a dividend if there are sufficient revenues. Other variations may have different amounts of voting rights.

Straight-through processing (STP)   End-to-end automation of the trading cycle so that order and trade details, once entered, are never subsequently re-entered or processed manually.

Strategic data stores   Data stores that, both in the kind of data stored and the location of the storage facilities, enhance the strategic goals of the firm.

Streaming   The process of sending data to users without a triggering request. Streaming data is sent to all those interested in seeing the data as it is generated. Users receiving a streaming data feed see the data change on the screen (or in their applications) in real time as new updates occur. (See also "Dynamically updated.")

Street name   The term referring to customer-owned securities registered in the name of the securities firm where the customer has an account. The use of a street name significantly facilitates the clearing and settlement of securities transactions.

Street-side activities or Street-side functions   All activities related to trading and settling securities transactions.

Subscribe   The act of an investor that pledges the intent to purchase a new issue before all the underwriting details are complete. The pledge comes with the understanding that the number of shares and price are yet to be determined.

Sweep the market or Sweeping the Street   Buy (or sell) all the stock available up to a certain price in the entire market by sending simultaneous orders to multiple limit-order books

SWIFT   Society for Worldwide Interbank Financial Telecommunication; the organization that banks use to move money among countries as opposed to CHAPS, CHIPS, and the FED Wire that move money within countries. In addition to funds transfers, SWIFT also performs international settlement processes for securities.

System   One of the three major categories of technology supporting the financial markets. In this book we define systems as the combination of computer hardware and software, usually organized for a specific purpose or to perform one or more tasks.

System's purpose   The function or role that a system is intended to perform or the need that it is to satisfy.

Systematic internalizer   A term created by MiFID that describes a sell-side firm that sets up an internal market and holds itself out as an official trading venue. MiFID legalizes the practice and demands that internalizers operate under the same rules as registered exchanges.

Tabular market data   A presentation method in which text and numerical data are presented in spreadsheet-like tables.

Tax lots   For investments such as trusts where the investment itself is taxable, every different execution price for the holdings in the account must be recorded so that capital gains can be accounted for tax purposes. Also, the tax cost or basis enters into decisions about what holdings should be sold to minimize the tax effects of partial liquidations of holdings.

Technical design   The system development task of converting the functional design into specific instructions that can be used to program an application. (See also "Design" and "Functional design.")

Technical traders   Traders that employ technical strategies such as historical price patterns to guide trading decisions.

Terms-and-conditions   The common term for an information service that provides access to details usually found in registration documents when an issue is created. This information is critical to understanding how to price instruments with unique attributes, such as the ability for a bond to be called before maturity.

Ticker or Ticker displays   Dynamically updated instrument prices. A typical ticker display either presents moving prices, usually across the top or bottom of a display screen, or as a cascade in which a line fills with prices and is then pushed up or down as a new line is formed. The term stems from the noise made by telegraph-based pricing devices that made ticking noises as they printed to paper tape.

Ticker machines or Ticker-tape machines   A telegraph-based market information device developed in the mid-1800s to transmit instrument prices from exchanges. The earliest displays were cylindrical machines capped by a glass dome. Prices were printed on paper tape that came from a roll in the device and emerged from the side of the device. (The icon we use for an information vendor is a representation of a ticker machine.)

Ticker symbol   The commonly used symbol for a security, such as "IBM" for International Business Machines, Inc., or "T" for AT&T. The route symbol for the security is often granted by the listing exchange, but the full ticker symbol (e.g., "IBM.N" to indicate IBM traded on the NYSE) is developed by the quote vendor and is not standardized.

Time-and-sales   A price display from vendors that shows prices from a market in time sequence often with contemporaneous quotes interspersed. The display is useful for compliance officers and those tasked with responding to customer questions and complaints about the prices received for executions.

Time-weighted average price (or TWAP) or Wave trades   An algorithmic trading technique that involves trading equal portions of a large order at specified time periods over the course of a trading day. (See also "VWAP.")

To work (an order)   A term that implies a trader is aggressively trying to execute an order.

Top-of-book   A market data display in which only the best prices (highest bid and lowest offer) are displayed. (See "Best bid and offer" and "National best bid and offer")

Trade break   A trade for which some details are in dispute, preventing it from settling.

Trading   (1) Noun: The term for the division or department within a financial markets firm that is charged with executing customer orders, proprietary trades, and market making. (2) Verb: The process of executing all orders.

Trading-floor platform   Another term for a trading-room infrastructure.

Trading markets   The term used throughout this set of books to mean the markets for all instruments that trade with reasonable liquidity. It is a broader term than the securities markets and includes commodities, currencies, and actively traded derivatives.

Trading-room infrastructure   A specialized form of an enterprise infrastructure designed primarily to support trading, whether human traders or computer-based trading models. These systems have many of the same features as an enterprise infrastructure but are optimized to keep latency low and provide specialized tools that support traders and assist in developing and testing models.

Trading venue   Our most general term for any type of facility that permits participants to execute orders in instruments. A trading venue includes exchanges and trading facilities registered as brokers. The trading mechanism may involve physical or electronic executions, and any type of instrument may be traded.

Transaction   A general term for an interaction between two parties or two things. Within the trading markets, we typically mean a trade, a payment, or some other trading-related interaction. In technology, a transaction can mean the interaction of two systems or an activity within a process.

Transactional networks   Networks that support transaction processing as opposed to information distribution for display and processing. Transactional networks include trading networks, post-trade networks, and payments networks.

Transfer agent   The banking function that records beneficial ownership of securities to track recipients of dividends and proxy statements, and to satisfy other needs for companies to know their shareholders.

Transition management   An investment service that helps funds (particularly pensions) transfer assets from one manager to another. Typically, the transition manager effects a series of sales from the custody account of the old manager followed by purchases that are put in the custodian for the new manager. Trades take place at a single instant using the closing price of the effective date for both sides of the transaction. There is no trading gain or loss, but there is a fee for the manager.

Treasury or Treasury department or Treasury function   The department, particularly within a sell-side firm or bank, that is responsible for managing the capital of the firm.

Trust   An account set up with an entity having trust powers (usually a bank) that requires the assets managed be handled with greater care than normal business obligations would suggest. A trust must be managed by the trustee "…with the same care with which a prudent man would manage his own affairs." Trusts originated in English Common Law, and have many variations. They are often used to protect the assets of very young or incompetent beneficiaries.

Twitter   A commercial product embraced by the trading markets to distribute brief messages, particularly trading ideas.

Ultra-low latency   A marketing term meant to imply that a service has lower latency than competitive products. We know of no measure that represents the threshold of what is "ultra-low."

Unidirectional   A term applied to networks wherein a channel carries information in only one direction, as in the case of market data from a trading venue to a user or orders from a user back to the trading venue.

Unit aggregation   Our coined term intended to be more comprehensive than the term "report" that usually represents fixed printouts and displays. As more and more systems operate in real time, there is less need for fixed reports except as required by regulations.

Unit of count   A measurable unit such as a display device, an individual, or a message that is employed by a pricing strategy to establish usage. The unit of count should be easy to entitle and must be reported periodically to facilitate invoicing. In many cases, the unit of count is also the unit of pricing. (See also "Display device," "Enterprise license," "Entitlement," and "Unit of pricing.")

Unit of pricing   The method or feature that produces invoices. The unit of pricing is a number that is multiplied by the price to get the invoice line item. As a complex example, in an enterprise license, the enterprise is the unit of pricing, the individual may be the unit of count, and an IP address may be the unit of entitlement. (See "Display device," "Enterprise license," "Entitlement," and "Unit of count")

Universes A group of similar entities, portfolios, funds, or the like that are grouped for measurement purposes. Vendors publish periodic attributes for the universes the vendor monitors and members of those universes are then able to compare their own attributes against statistics for the universe.

Users The term in the market data business for consumers of data. The term is general, applying to all consumers whatever their job functions.

Value-based pricing A pricing scheme that uses units of count and a pricing structure that both reflects how the service is used and employs prices that are consistent with a user's ability to pay. Properly designed, a value-based pricing system benefits both the user and the data owner or vendor.

Variable interest rate or Variable rate Interest on an instrument that changes as general rates in the market change. The rate is not fixed for the life of the instrument. Although the rate can fluctuate in any manner defined by the instrument definition, the rate most often changes periodically.

Vendor account reporting system (VARS) A reporting system using a fixed format in which vendors report usage of exchange information back to the exchanges periodically.

Vendor A company that supplies information, technology, and services to the financial markets. In particular, firms such as Bloomberg and Thomson Reuters that provide market data.

Video switch An antiquated technology that permitted controllers to distribute video signals to user displays through a switch that permitted the user to view different sources on the same display device. The technology grew out of television production and editing suites. The user was effectively changing channels on the display device.

Voice over Internet Protocol (VoIP) An emerging technology that permits voice messages to employ the public Internet rather than dedicated telephone networks. Video messages also use this distribution method.

Volume data Information on the quantities of instruments involved in trading.

Volume-weighted average price (VWAP) The share volume-weighted average price for a defined period of time. On some exchanges, the closing price is defined by the VWAP of the last five minutes of trading, for example. In the United States, buy-side traders often measure the quality of their trading by whether they equal or better the VWAP on their trades for the entire trading day. Some investment management firms construct incentive schemes for their brokers by rewarding a broker if it exceeds VWAP and punishing if it does worse. Alternatively, some brokers will take orders from institutions and guarantee VWAP.

VRXML An XML-based reporting standard aimed at replacing the VARS format developed by the NYSE.

Warrants Financial instruments issued by a company that the holder can exercise like a call option to buy company shares at a predetermined price. Although a warrant works like an option, the warrant is issued by the company often as an alternative to paying a dividend if the company wishes to retain its earnings. In contrast, an option is created in the secondary market and does not affect the company directly. (See also "Option.")

Wealth management A term for traditional retail brokerage, particularly where the customer is considered "upscale" and where the method of pricing is assets-under-management rather than commissions.

Web applications   A concept that is part of what has been called "cloud computing" in which applications are available for use over the Internet.

What-if analysis   A means of evaluating alternatives by simulating events and attempting to assess how a system or a strategy would respond to the events.

Wire houses   An antiquated term for retail investment companies that linked their branches to the head office and the markets by a teletype network initially. The teletype networks were replaced in time by computer networks. Now enterprise infrastructure provides the linkages. However, the term has faded from use.

Workflow management   A class of software designed to facilitate an ongoing process such as trading. The purpose of the software is to ensure that all important steps in the process are executed and to provide reminders of important events. These systems are frequently fed by and, in turn, feed accounting systems.

Writer   The individual that creates an open interest by writing an option to sell (put) or buy (call) an underlying instrument at a future date. Note that the writer is taking the opposite side of the contract. A purchaser of a put contract has the right to sell to the writer. The writer receives a premium when the contract is first sold.

Y2K (or YK)   A term derived from "year 2000" that came to represent the problems and fears that date algorithms designed into early computer systems employing a two-digit date to save space would cause massive problems when they were forced to process dates on and after January 1, 2000.

References

Alvarez, M. (2007). *Market Data Explained*. Boston: Butterworth-Heinemann.

Ascher, K. (2005). *The Works: Anatomy of a City*. New York: Penguin Books.

Bernstein, P. L. (1998). *Against the Gods: The Remarkable Story of Risk*. Hoboken, NJ: John Wiley & Sons, Inc.

Bernstein, P. L. (2005). *Capital Ideas: The Improbable Origins of Modern Wall Street*. Hoboken, NJ: John Wiley & Sons, Inc.

Bernstein, P. L. (2007). *Capital Ideas Evolving* (1st ed.). Hoboken, NJ: John Wiley & Sons, Inc.

Boumphrey, F., & Tittel, E. (2000). *XML for Dummies* (2nd ed.). Foster City, CA: IDG Books Worldwide, Inc.

Brooks, J. (1997). *Once in Golconda: A True Story of Wall Street 1920–1938* (2nd ed.). New York: John Wiley & Sons, Inc.

Brooks, J. (1999). *The Go-Go Years: The Drama and Crashing Finale of Wall Street's Bullish 60s* (2nd ed.). New York: John Wiley & Sons, Inc.

Bruck, C. (1989). *The Predators' Ball: The Inside Story of Drexel Burnham and the Rise of the Junk Bond Raiders* (2nd ed.). New York: Penguin Books.

Choudhry, M. (2004a). *Advanced Fixed Income Analysis*. Oxford: Butterworth-Heinemann.

Choudhry, M. (2004b). *Corporate Bonds and Structured Financial Products*. Oxford: Butterworth-Heinemann.

Choudhry, M. (2004c). *An Introduction to Credit Derivatives*. Oxford: Butterworth-Heinemann.

Choudhry, M. (2006). *The Bond & Money Markets: Strategy, Trading, Analysis*. Oxford: Butterworth-Heinemann.

Eales, B. A., & Choudhry, M. (2003). *Derivative Instruments: A Guide to Theory and Practice*. Oxford: Butterworth-Heinemann.

Farwell, L. C., Gane, F. H., Jacobs, D. P., Jones, S. L., & Robinson, R. L. (1966). *Financial Institutions* (4th ed.). Homewood, IL: Dow Jones-Irwin.

Fink, R. E., & Feduniak, R. B. (1988). *Futures Trading: Concepts and Strategies*. New York: Institute of Finance.

Friend, I., Longstreet, J. R., Mendelson, M., Miller, E., & Hess, A. P. Jr. (1967). *Investment Banking and the New Issues Market*. Cleveland and New York: The World Publishing Company.

Garbade, K. D. (1982). *The Securities Markets*. New York: McGraw-Hill.

Gastineau, G. L. (1975). *The Stock Options Manual*. New York: McGraw-Hill.

Giles, T. G., & Apilado, V. P. (Eds.), (1971). *Banking Markets and Financial Institutions*. Homewood, IL: Richard D. Irwin, Inc.

Goetzmann, W. N., & Rouwenhorst, K. G. (2005). *The Origins of Value: The Financial Innovations That Created Modern Capital Markets*. New York: Oxford University Press.

Graham, B. 1949. *The Intelligent Investor*. New York: HarperCollins.

Graham, B., & Dodd, D. L. (2009). *Security Analysis* (6th ed.). New York: McGraw-Hill.

Groot, M. (2008). *Managing Financial Information in the Trade Lifecycle: A Concise Atlas of Financial Instruments and Processes*. Boston: Academic Press.

Hieronymus, T. A. (1977). *Economics of Futures Trading: For Commercial and Personal Profit* (2nd ed.). New York: Commodity Research Bureau, Inc.

Lee, R. (1998). *What Is an Exchange? The Automation, Management, and Regulation of Financial Markets*. Oxford: Oxford University Press.

Lewis, M. (1990). *Liar's Poker* (2nd ed.). New York: Penguin Books.

Loader, D. (2008). *Clearing, Settlement and Custody: A Guide*. Boston: Butterworth-Heinemann.

Loader, D. (2005). *Clearing and Settlement of Derivatives*. Boston: Butterworth-Heinemann.

Loader, D. (2007). *Fundamentals of Fund Administration: A Guide*. Oxford: Butterworth-Heinemann.

Malkiel, B. G. (2003). *A Random Walk Down Wall Street* (8th ed.). New York: W.W. Norton.

Mayle, J. (1997). *Standard Securities Calculation Methods: Fixed Income Securities Formulas, Volumes 1 and 2*. New York: The Securities Industry Association (SIA). (Note the SIA is now the Securities Industry and Financial Markets Association, SIFMA.)

Melamed, L. (2009). *For Crying Out Loud: From Open Outcry to the Electronic Screen*. Hoboken, NJ: John Wiley & Sons, Inc.

Neftci, S. N. (2008). *Principles of Financial Engineering* (2nd ed.). Boston: Academic Press.

Parks, T. (2005). *Medici Money: Banking, Metaphysics, and Art in Fifteenth-Century Florence*. New York: W.W. Norton.

The Staff of the House Committee on Interstate and Foreign Commerce (1975). *Legislative History of Securities Acts Amendments of 1975*. Washington, DC: U.S. Government Printing Office.

U.S. Securities and Exchange Commission. (1998). *Interpretation: Confirmation and Affirmation of Securities Trades—Matching*, 17 CFR Part 241 (Release No. 34-39829; File No. S7-10-98), Washington, DC.

Williams, W. Tee (ed.) (1985). *The Creation and Distribution of Securities-Related Information in North America*. Washington, DC: Financial Information Services Division, Information Industry Association (now known as the Software & Information Industry Association, SIIA).

Index

Note: Page numbers followed by *b* indicates boxes, *f* indicates figures, and *t* indicates tables.